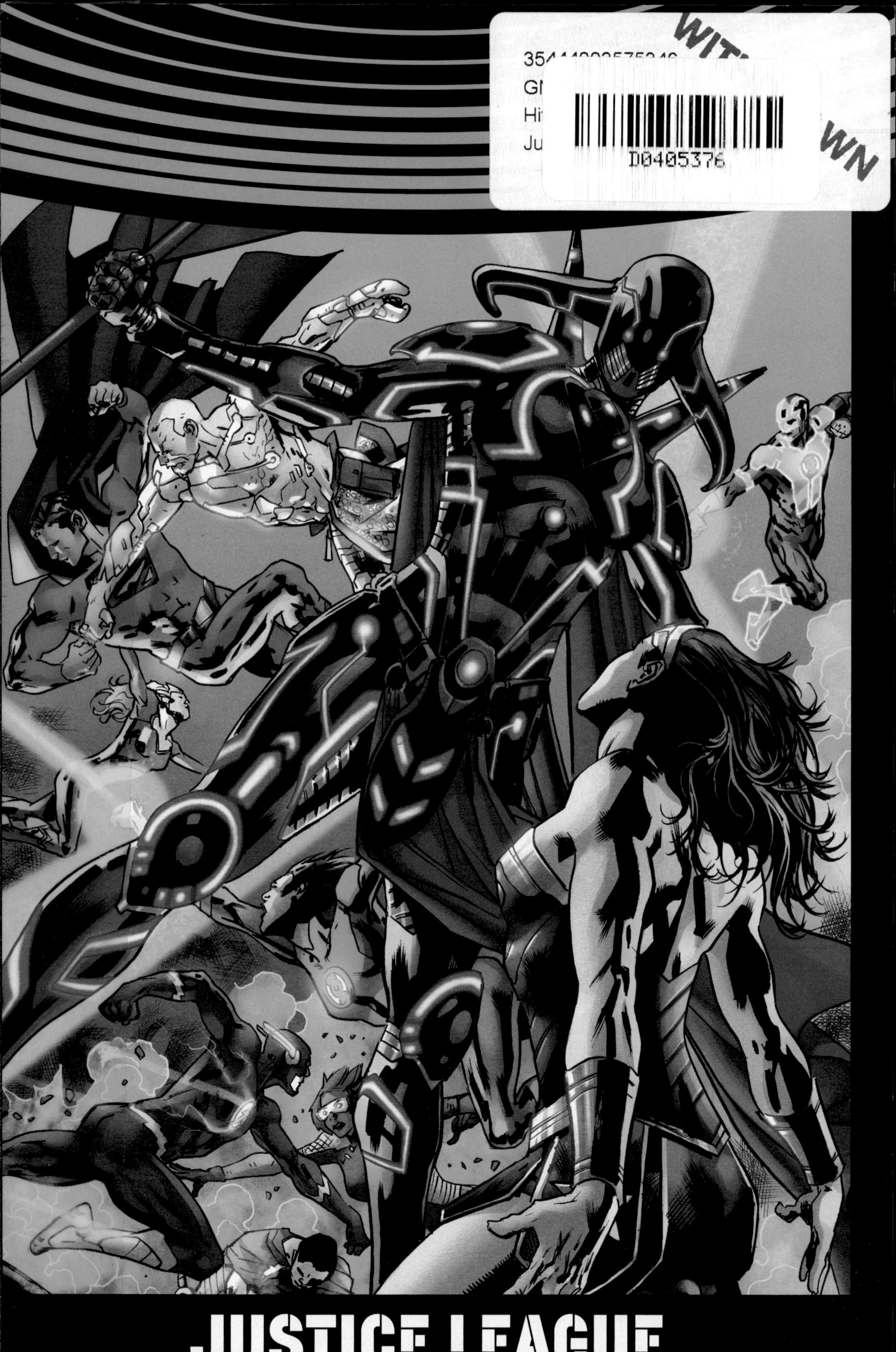

JUSTICE LEAGUE

VOL.5 LEGACY

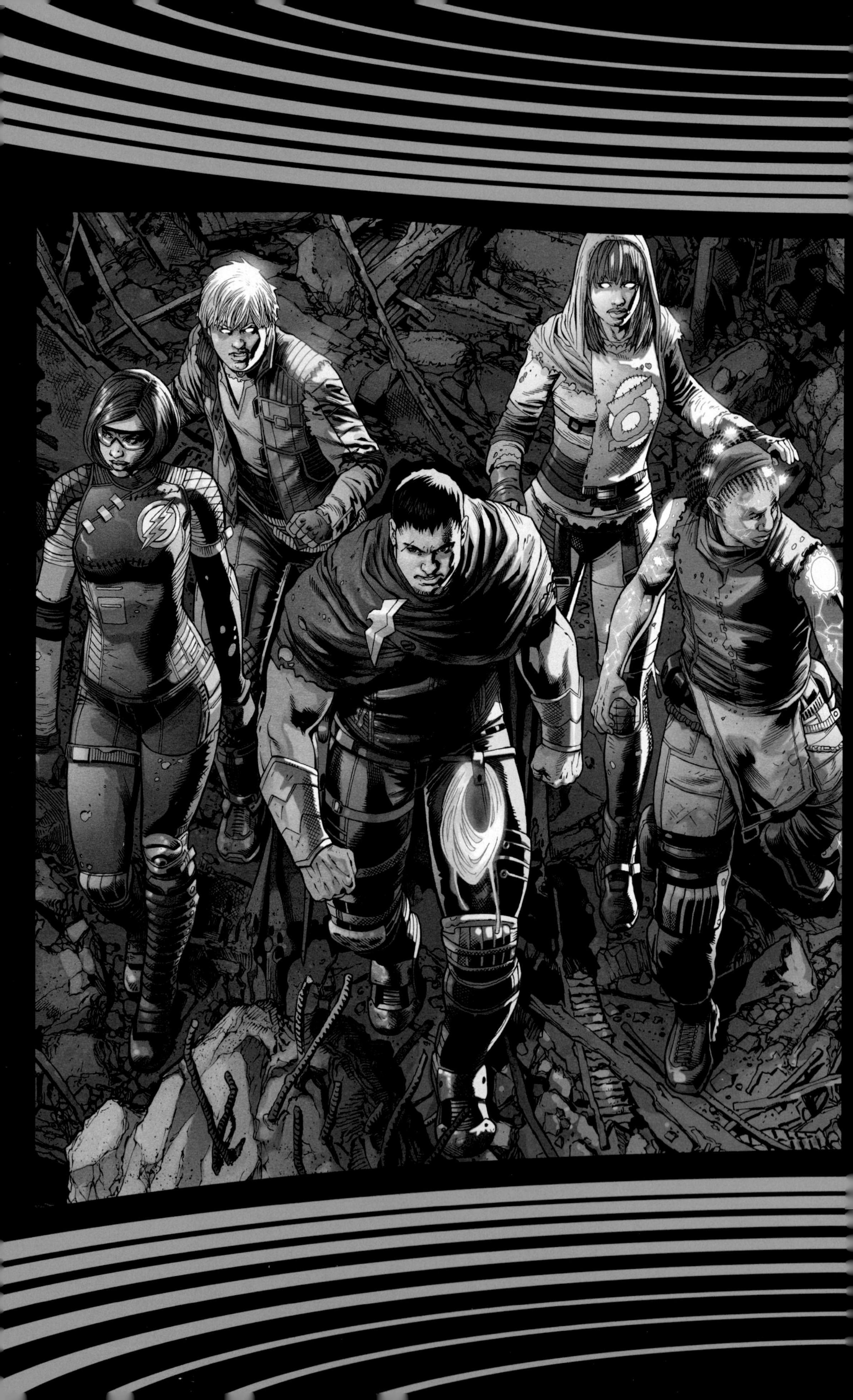

3 5444 00357534 6

JUSTICE LEAGUE
VOL.5 LEGACY

BRYAN HITCH
writer

FERNANDO PASARIN
penciller

OCLAIR ALBERT * **ANDY OWENS** * **BATT**
MICK GRAY * **SCOTT HANNA**
inkers

BRAD ANDERSON
colorist

RICHARD STARKINGS & COMICRAFT'S JIMMY
letterers

BRYAN HITCH & ALEX SINCLAIR
collection cover artists

SUPERMAN created by **JERRY SIEGEL** and **JOE SHUSTER**
By special arrangement with the Jerry Siegel family
AQUAMAN created by **PAUL NORRIS**

BRIAN CUNNINGHAM Editor – Original Series ✻ AMEDEO TURTURRO Associate Editor – Original Series
JEB WOODARD Group Editor – Collected Editions ✻ ROBIN WILDMAN Editor – Collected Edition
STEVE COOK Design Director – Books ✻ MONIQUE NARBONETA Publication Design

BOB HARRAS Senior VP - Editor-in-Chief, DC Comics
PAT McCALLUM Executive Editor, DC Comics

DIANE NELSON President ✻ DAN DiDIO Publisher ✻ JIM LEE Publisher ✻ GEOFF JOHNS President & Chief Creative Officer
AMIT DESAI Executive VP - Business & Marketing Strategy, Direct to Consumer & Global Franchise Management
SAM ADES Senior VP & General Manager, Digital Services ✻ BOBBIE CHASE VP & Executive Editor, Young Reader & Talent Development
MARK CHIARELLO Senior VP - Art, Design & Collected Editions ✻ JOHN CUNNINGHAM Senior VP - Sales & Trade Marketing
ANNE DePIES Senior VP - Business Strategy, Finance & Administration ✻ DON FALLETTI VP - Manufacturing Operations
LAWRENCE GANEM VP - Editorial Administration & Talent Relations ✻ ALISON GILL Senior VP - Manufacturing & Operations
HANK KANALZ Senior VP - Editorial Strategy & Administration ✻ JAY KOGAN VP - Legal Affairs ✻ JACK MAHAN VP - Business Affairs
NICK J. NAPOLITANO VP - Manufacturing Administration ✻ EDDIE SCANNELL VP - Consumer Marketing
COURTNEY SIMMONS Senior VP - Publicity & Communications ✻ JIM (SKI) SOKOLOWSKI VP - Comic Book Specialty Sales & Trade Marketing
NANCY SPEARS VP - Mass, Book, Digital Sales & Trade Marketing ✻ MICHELE R. WELLS VP - Content Strategy

JUSTICE LEAGUE VOL. 5: LEGACY

Published by DC Comics. Compilation and all new material Copyright © 2018 DC Comics. All Rights Reserved.
Originally published in single magazine form in JUSTICE LEAGUE 26-31. Copyright © 2017 DC Comics. All Rights Reserved.
All characters, their distinctive likenesses and related elements featured in this publication are trademarks of DC Comics.
The stories, characters and incidents featured in this publication are entirely fictional.
DC Comics does not read or accept unsolicited submissions of ideas, stories or artwork.

DC Comics, 2900 West Alameda Ave., Burbank, CA 91505
Printed by LSC Communications, Kendallville, IN, USA. 1/26/18. First Printing.
ISBN: 978-1-4012-7725-3

Library of Congress Cataloging-in-Publication Data is available.

PEFC Certified

Printed on paper from
sustainably managed
forests, controlled
sources

PEFC/29-31-337   www.pefc.org

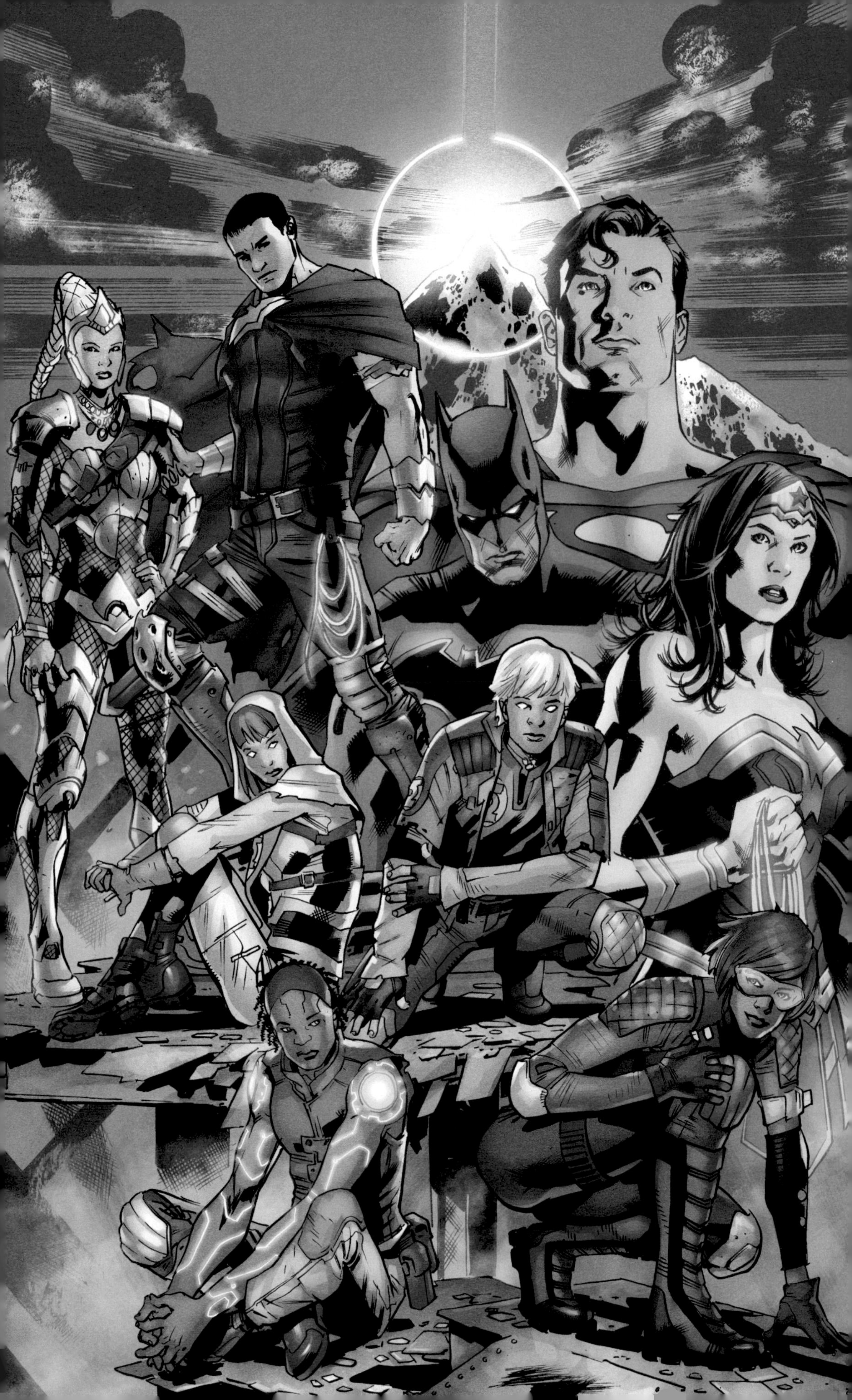

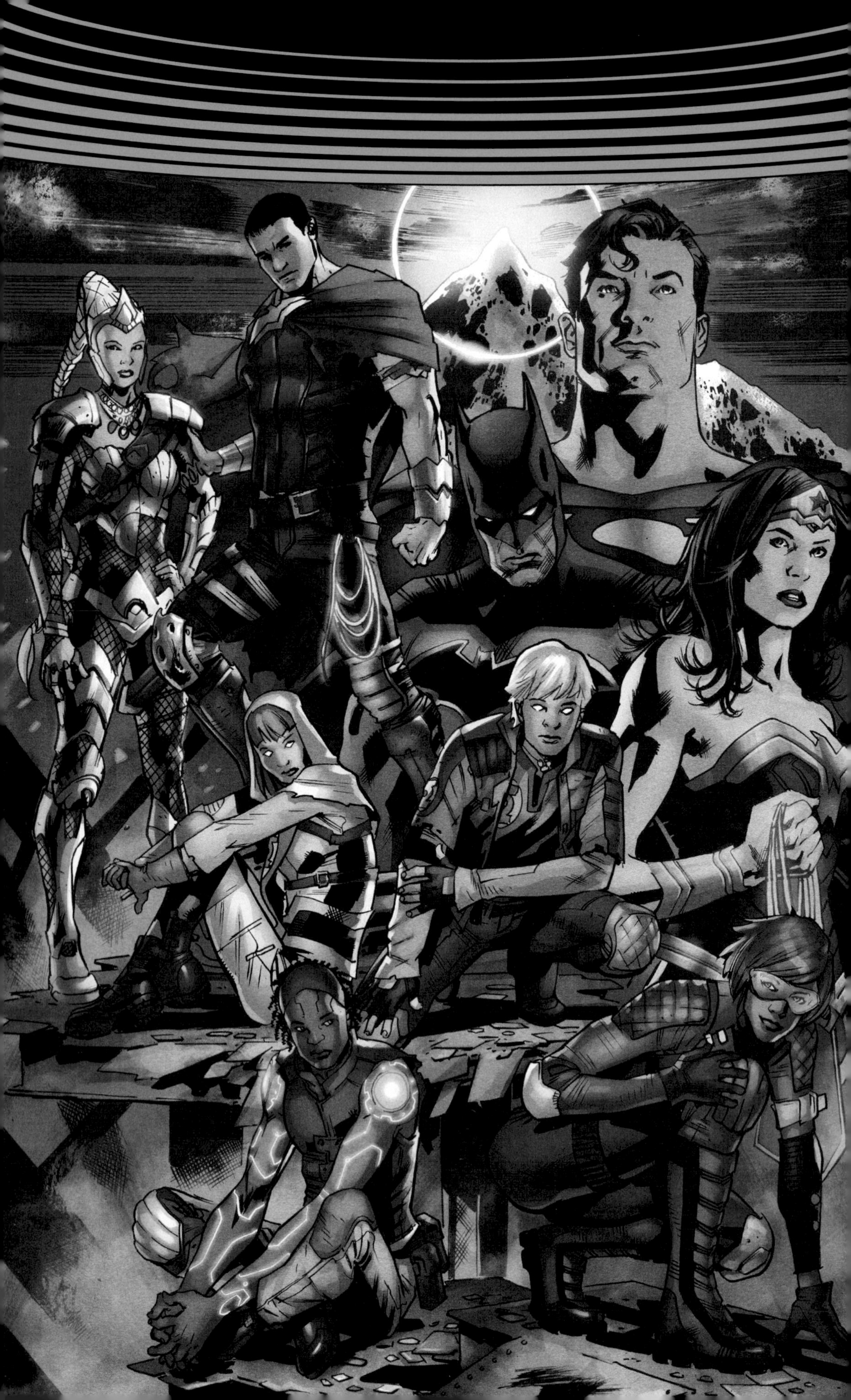

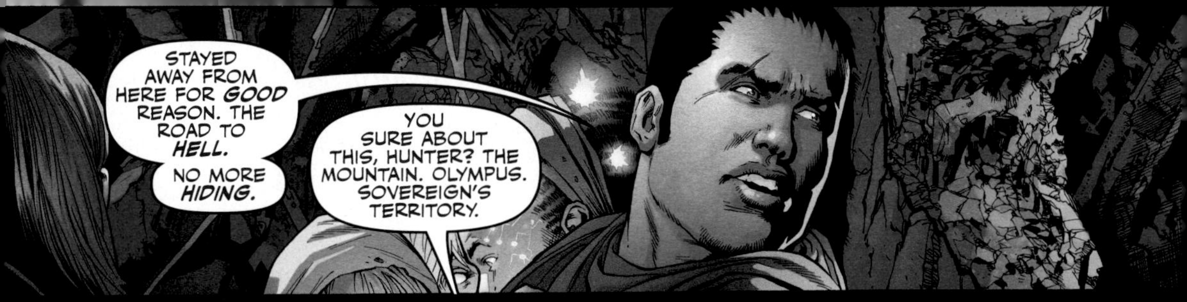
STAYED AWAY FROM HERE FOR *GOOD* REASON. THE ROAD TO *HELL.*
NO MORE *HIDING.*
YOU SURE ABOUT THIS, HUNTER? THE MOUNTAIN. OLYMPUS. SOVEREIGN'S TERRITORY.

LEGACY PART ONE

BRYAN HITCH writer FERNANDO PASARIN penciller OCLAIR ALBERT inker

COLORED by BRAD ANDERSON | LETTERED by RICHARD STARKINGS & COMICRAFT'S JIMMY | COVER by BRYAN HITCH & ALEX SINCLAIR | VARIANT COVER by YANICK PAQUETTE | ASSOCIATE ED. AMEDEO TURTURRO | EDITOR BRIAN CUNNINGHAM

SUPERMAN CREATED by JERRY SIEGEL and JOE SHUSTER. By special arrangement with the JERRY SIEGEL FAMILY.

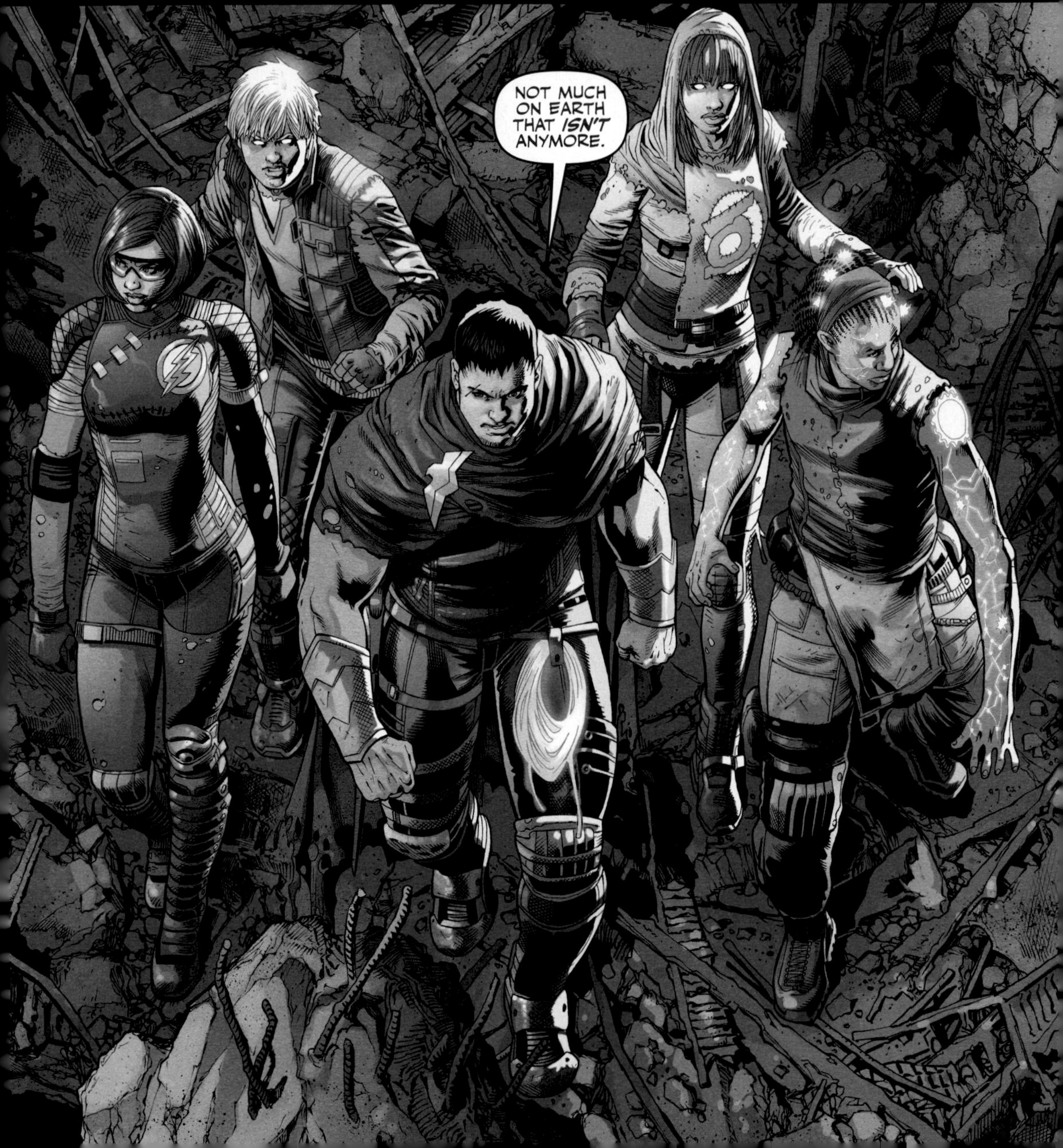
NOT MUCH ON EARTH THAT *ISN'T* ANYMORE.

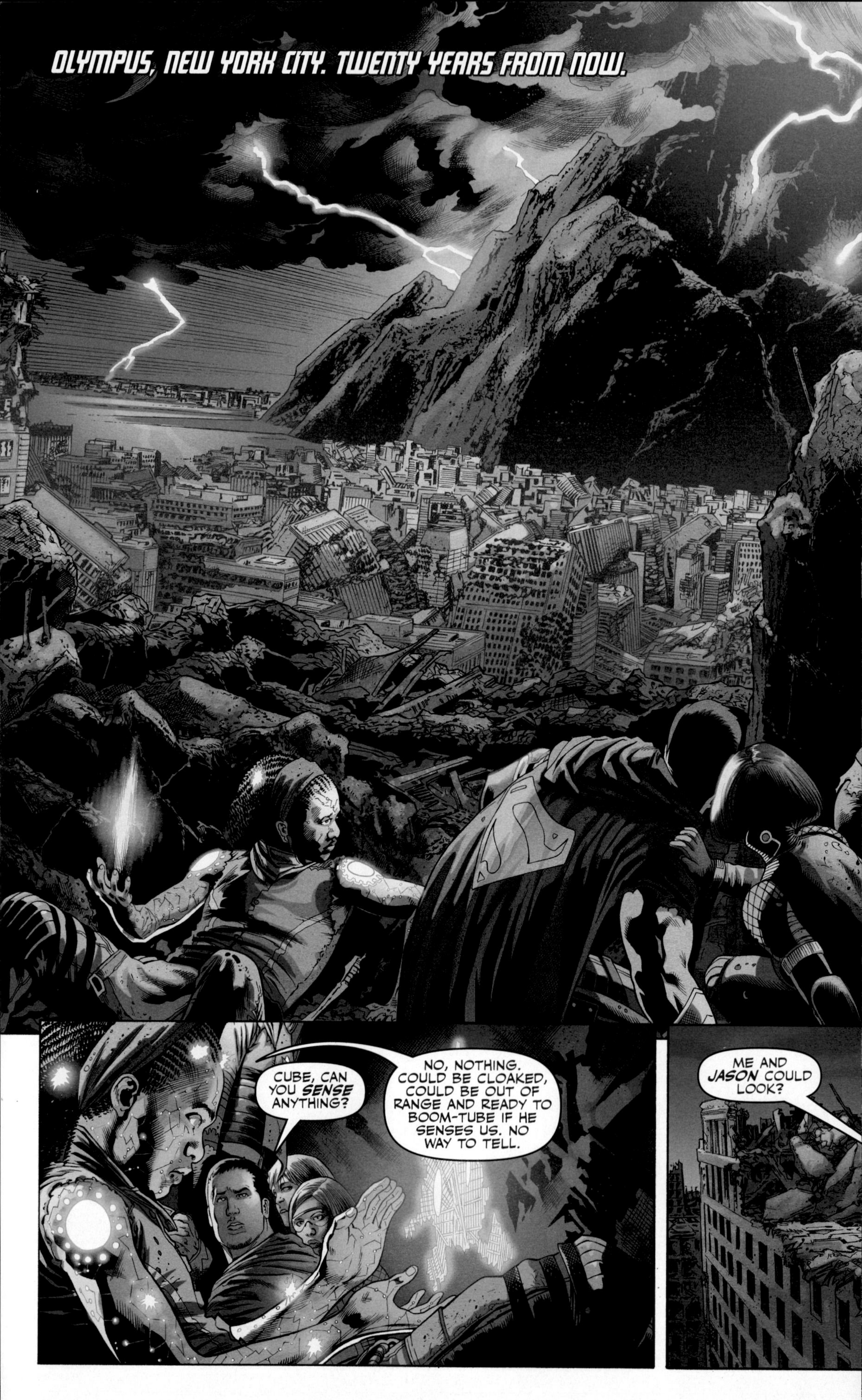
OLYMPUS, NEW YORK CITY. TWENTY YEARS FROM NOW.
CUBE, CAN YOU SENSE ANYTHING?
NO, NOTHING. COULD BE CLOAKED, COULD BE OUT OF RANGE AND READY TO BOOM-TUBE IF HE SENSES US. NO WAY TO TELL.
ME AND JASON COULD LOOK?

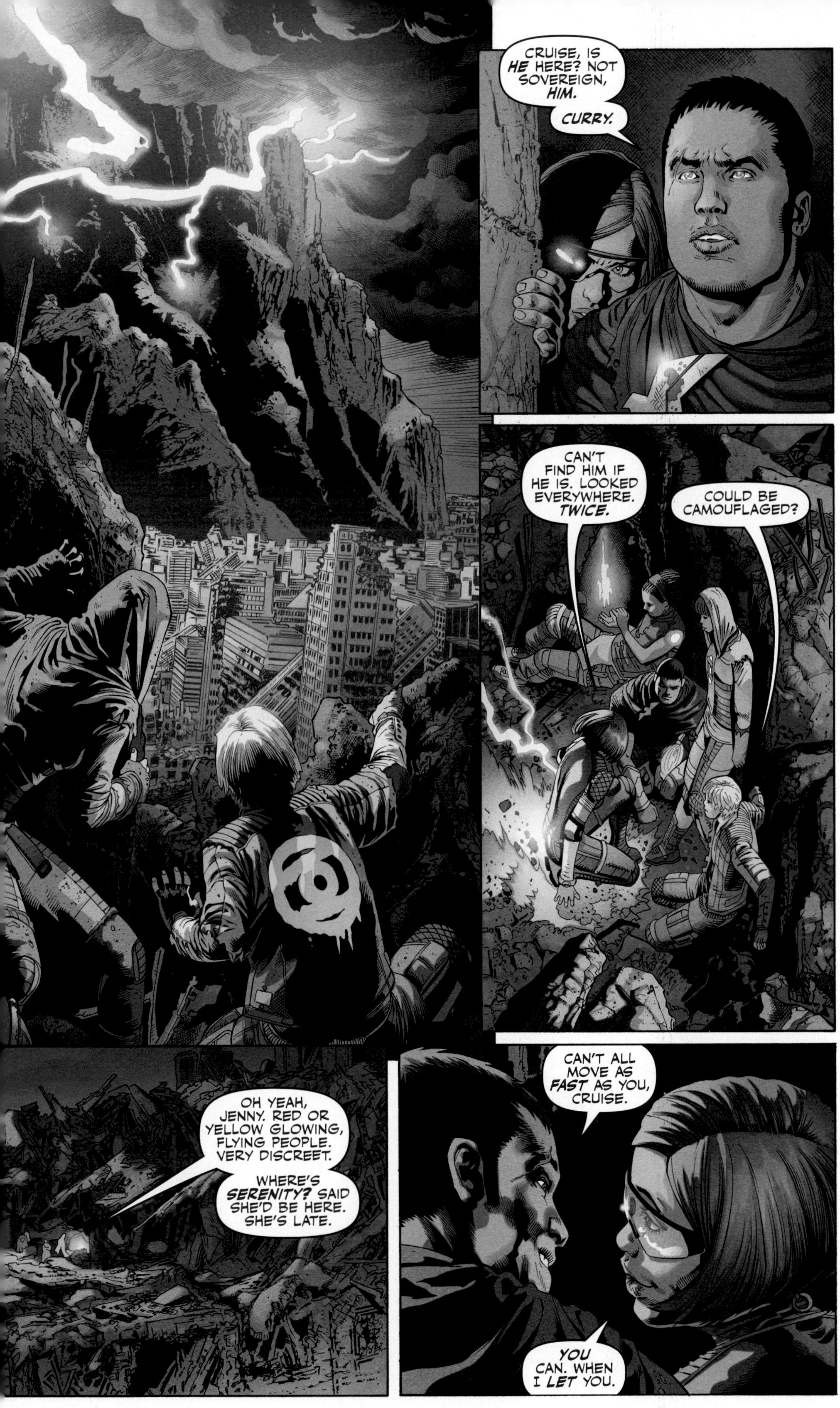
CRUISE, IS HE HERE? NOT SOVEREIGN, HIM.
CURRY.
CAN'T FIND HIM IF HE IS. LOOKED EVERYWHERE. TWICE.
COULD BE CAMOUFLAGED?
OH YEAH, JENNY. RED OR YELLOW GLOWING, FLYING PEOPLE. VERY DISCREET.
WHERE'S SERENITY? SAID SHE'D BE HERE. SHE'S LATE.
CAN'T ALL MOVE AS FAST AS YOU, CRUISE.
YOU CAN. WHEN I LET YOU.

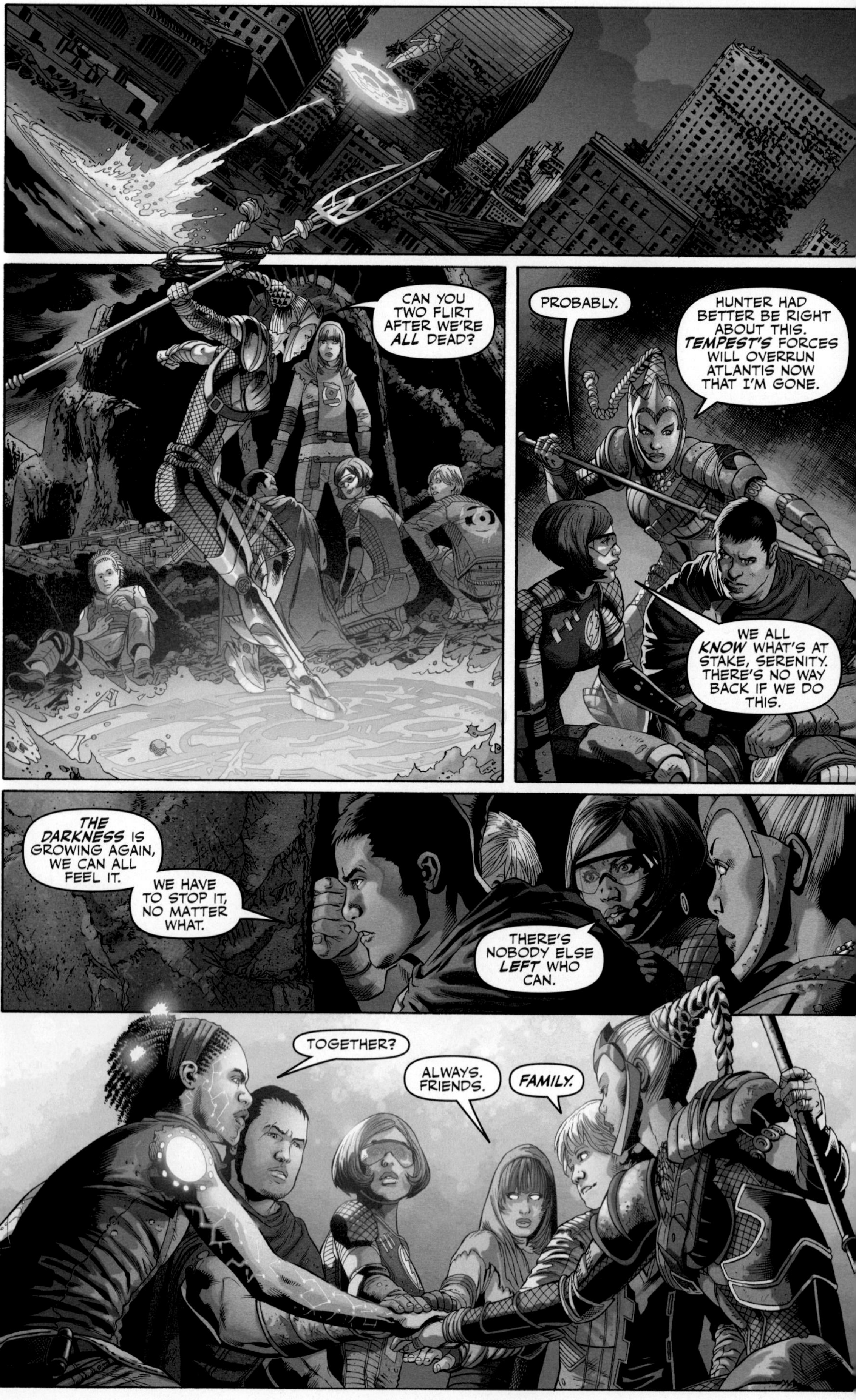
CAN YOU TWO FLIRT AFTER WE'RE *ALL* DEAD?
PROBABLY.
HUNTER HAD BETTER BE RIGHT ABOUT THIS. *TEMPEST'S* FORCES WILL OVERRUN ATLANTIS NOW THAT I'M GONE.
WE ALL *KNOW* WHAT'S AT STAKE, SERENITY. THERE'S NO WAY BACK IF WE DO THIS.
THE DARKNESS IS GROWING AGAIN, WE CAN ALL FEEL IT.
WE HAVE TO STOP IT, NO MATTER WHAT.
THERE'S NOBODY ELSE *LEFT* WHO CAN.
TOGETHER?
ALWAYS. FRIENDS.
FAMILY.

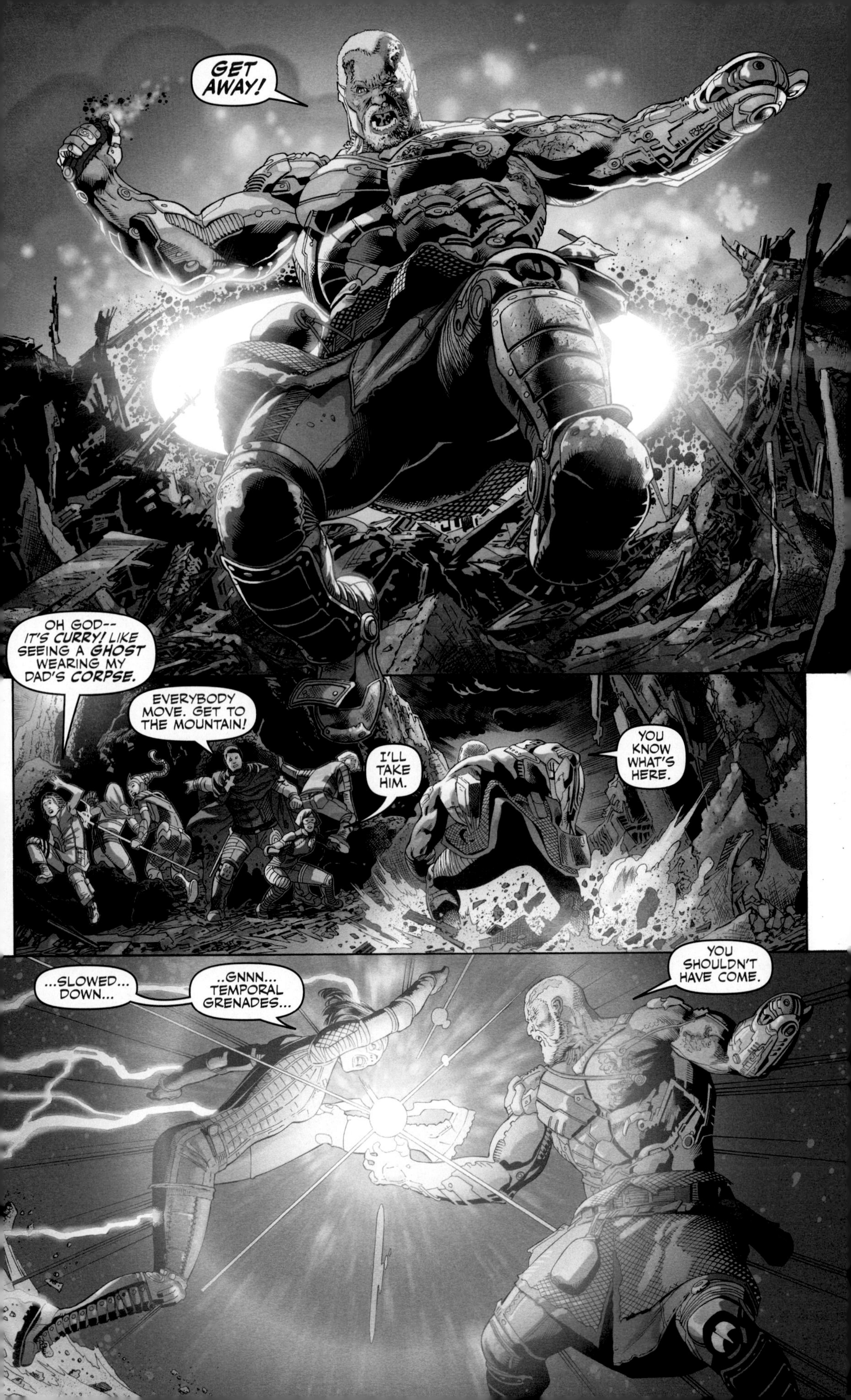
GET AWAY!
OH GOD-- IT'S CURRY! LIKE SEEING A GHOST WEARING MY DAD'S CORPSE.
EVERYBODY MOVE. GET TO THE MOUNTAIN!
I'LL TAKE HIM.
YOU KNOW WHAT'S HERE.
...SLOWED... DOWN...
..GNNN... TEMPORAL GRENADES...
YOU SHOULDN'T HAVE COME.

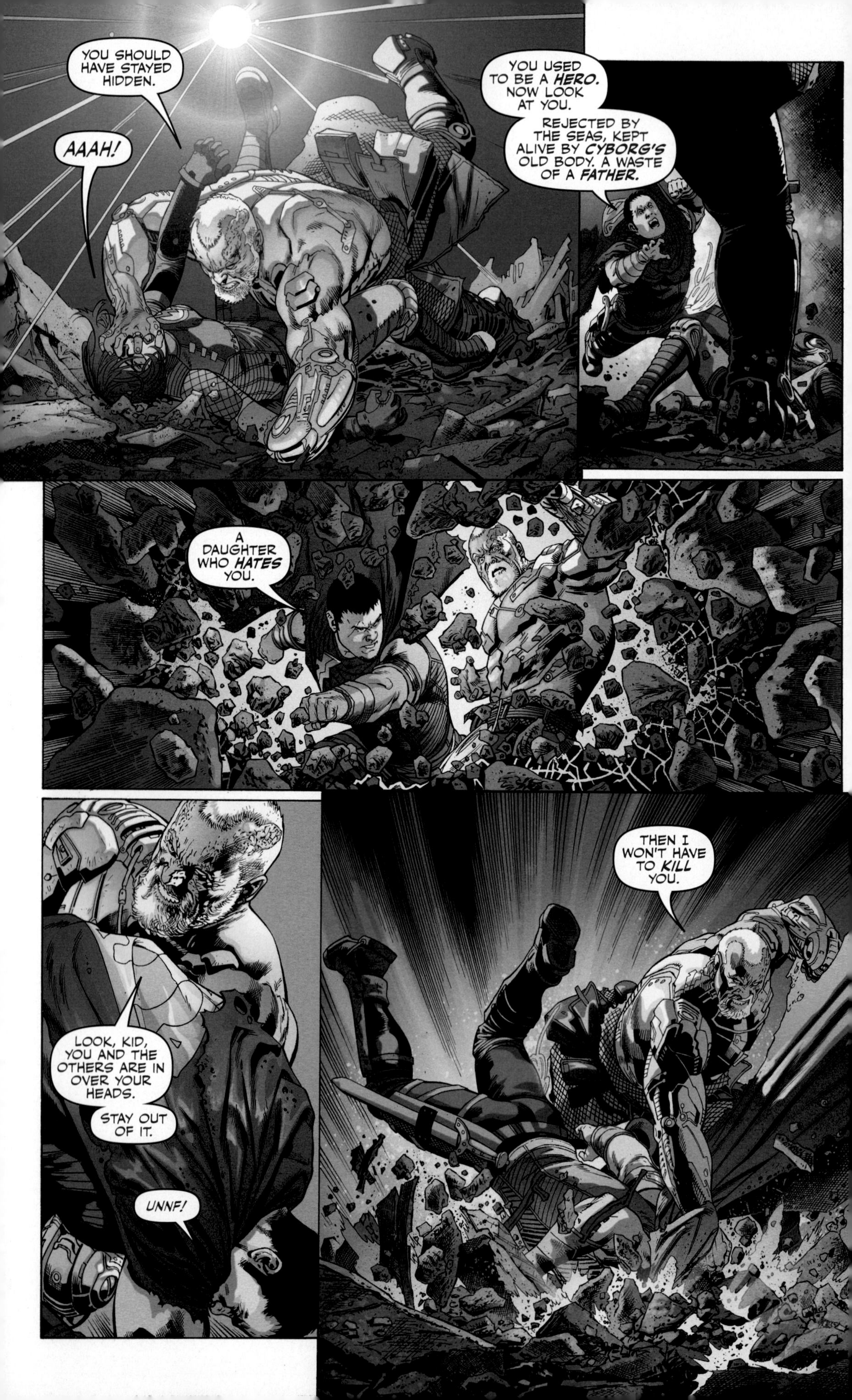

YOU SHOULD HAVE STAYED HIDDEN.
AAAH!
YOU USED TO BE A HERO. NOW LOOK AT YOU.
REJECTED BY THE SEAS, KEPT ALIVE BY CYBORG'S OLD BODY. A WASTE OF A FATHER.
A DAUGHTER WHO HATES YOU.
LOOK, KID, YOU AND THE OTHERS ARE IN OVER YOUR HEADS.
STAY OUT OF IT.
UNNF!
THEN I WON'T HAVE TO KILL YOU.

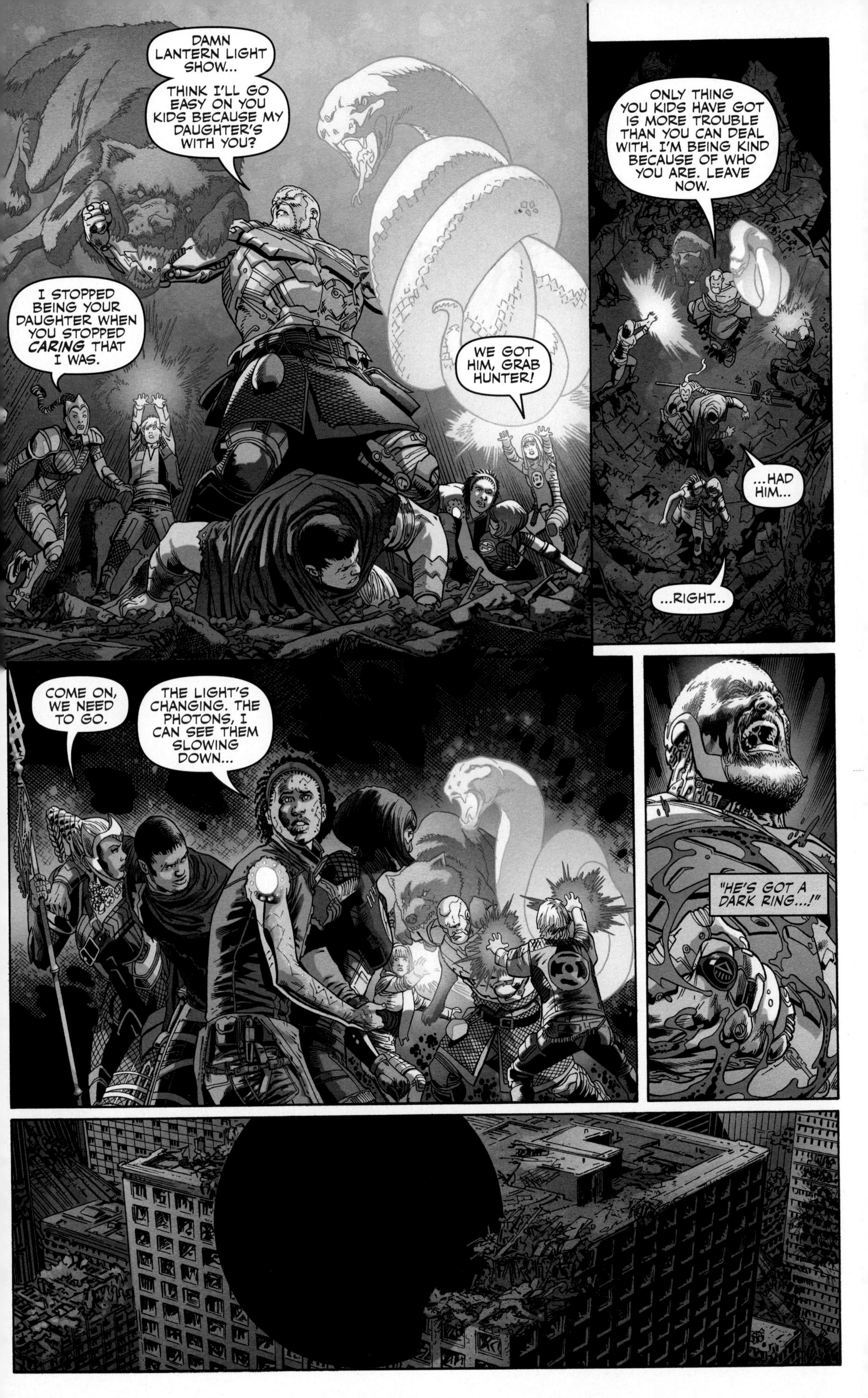
DAMN LANTERN LIGHT SHOW...
THINK I'LL GO EASY ON YOU KIDS BECAUSE MY DAUGHTER'S WITH YOU?
I STOPPED BEING YOUR DAUGHTER WHEN YOU STOPPED CARING THAT I WAS.
WE GOT HIM, GRAB HUNTER!
ONLY THING YOU KIDS HAVE GOT IS MORE TROUBLE THAN YOU CAN DEAL WITH. I'M BEING KIND BECAUSE OF WHO YOU ARE. LEAVE NOW.
...HAD HIM...
...RIGHT...
COME ON, WE NEED TO GO.
THE LIGHT'S CHANGING. THE PHOTONS, I CAN SEE THEM SLOWING DOWN...
"HE'S GOT A DARK RING...!"

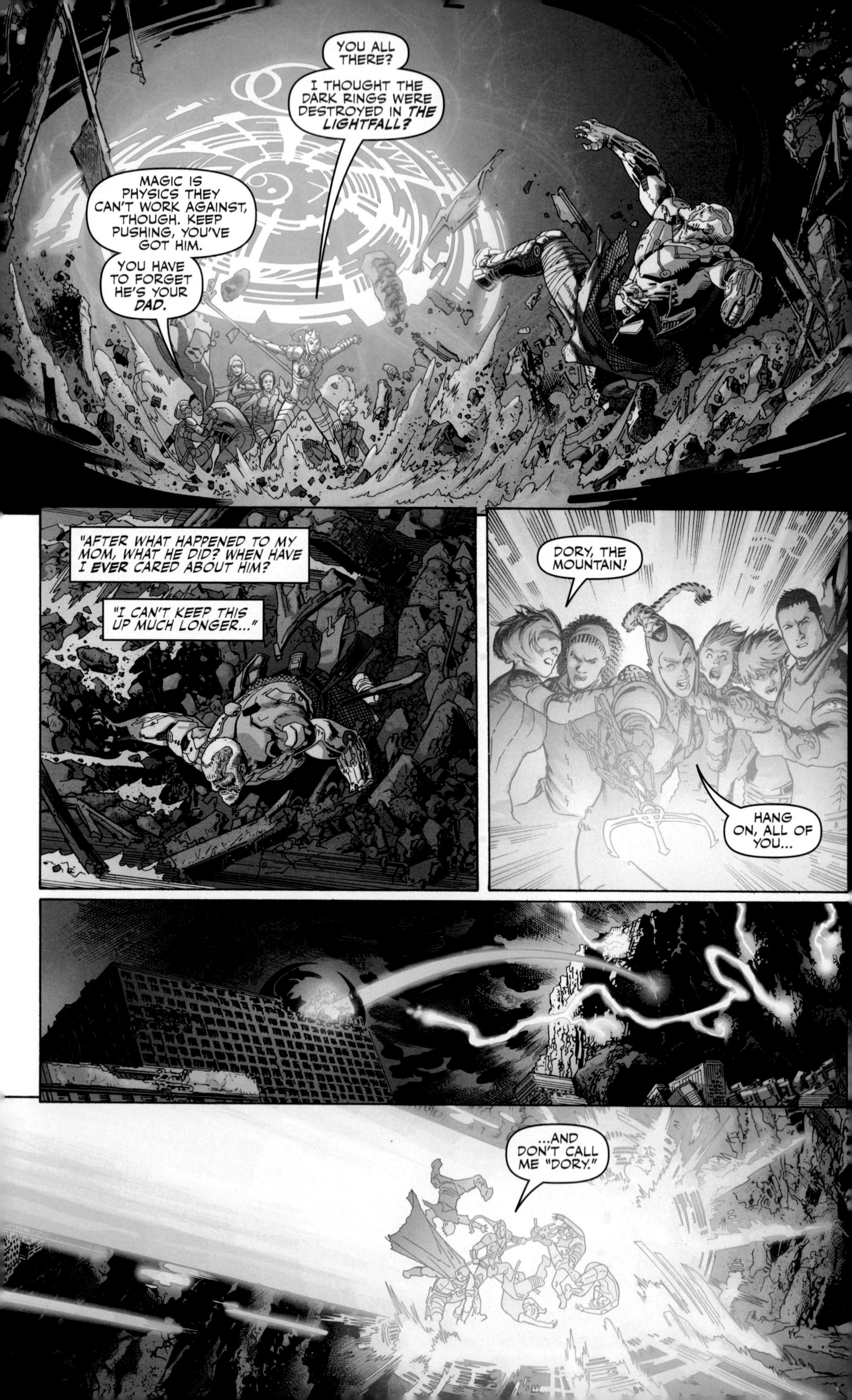
YOU ALL THERE?
I THOUGHT THE DARK RINGS WERE DESTROYED IN THE LIGHTFALL?
MAGIC IS PHYSICS THEY CAN'T WORK AGAINST, THOUGH. KEEP PUSHING, YOU'VE GOT HIM.
YOU HAVE TO FORGET HE'S YOUR DAD.
"AFTER WHAT HAPPENED TO MY MOM, WHAT HE DID? WHEN HAVE I EVER CARED ABOUT HIM?
"I CAN'T KEEP THIS UP MUCH LONGER..."
DORY, THE MOUNTAIN!
HANG ON, ALL OF YOU...
...AND DON'T CALL ME "DORY."

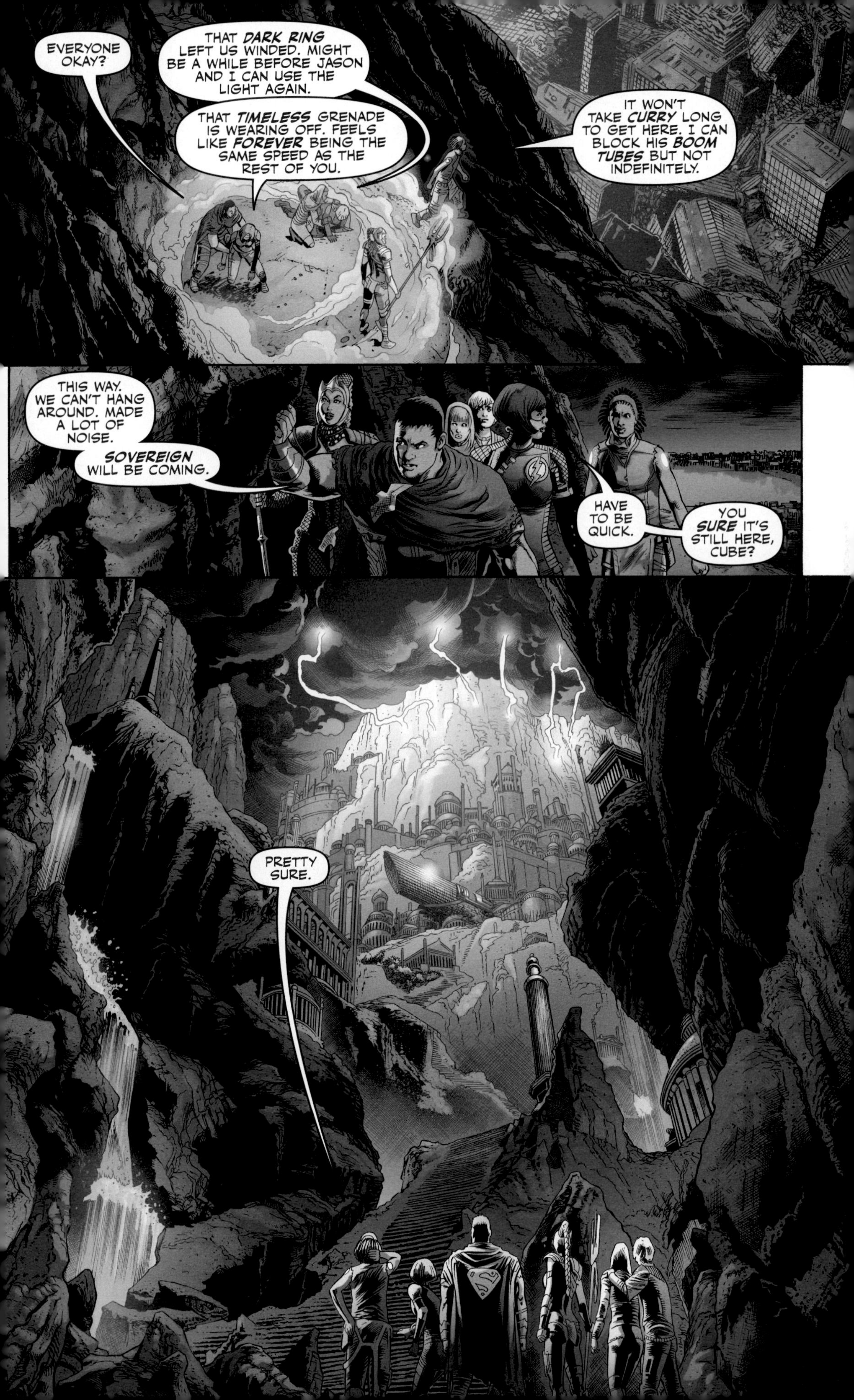
EVERYONE OKAY?
THAT DARK RING LEFT US WINDED. MIGHT BE A WHILE BEFORE JASON AND I CAN USE THE LIGHT AGAIN.
THAT TIMELESS GRENADE IS WEARING OFF. FEELS LIKE FOREVER BEING THE SAME SPEED AS THE REST OF YOU.
IT WON'T TAKE CURRY LONG TO GET HERE. I CAN BLOCK HIS BOOM TUBES BUT NOT INDEFINITELY.
THIS WAY. WE CAN'T HANG AROUND. MADE A LOT OF NOISE.
SOVEREIGN WILL BE COMING.
HAVE TO BE QUICK.
YOU SURE IT'S STILL HERE, CUBE?
PRETTY SURE.

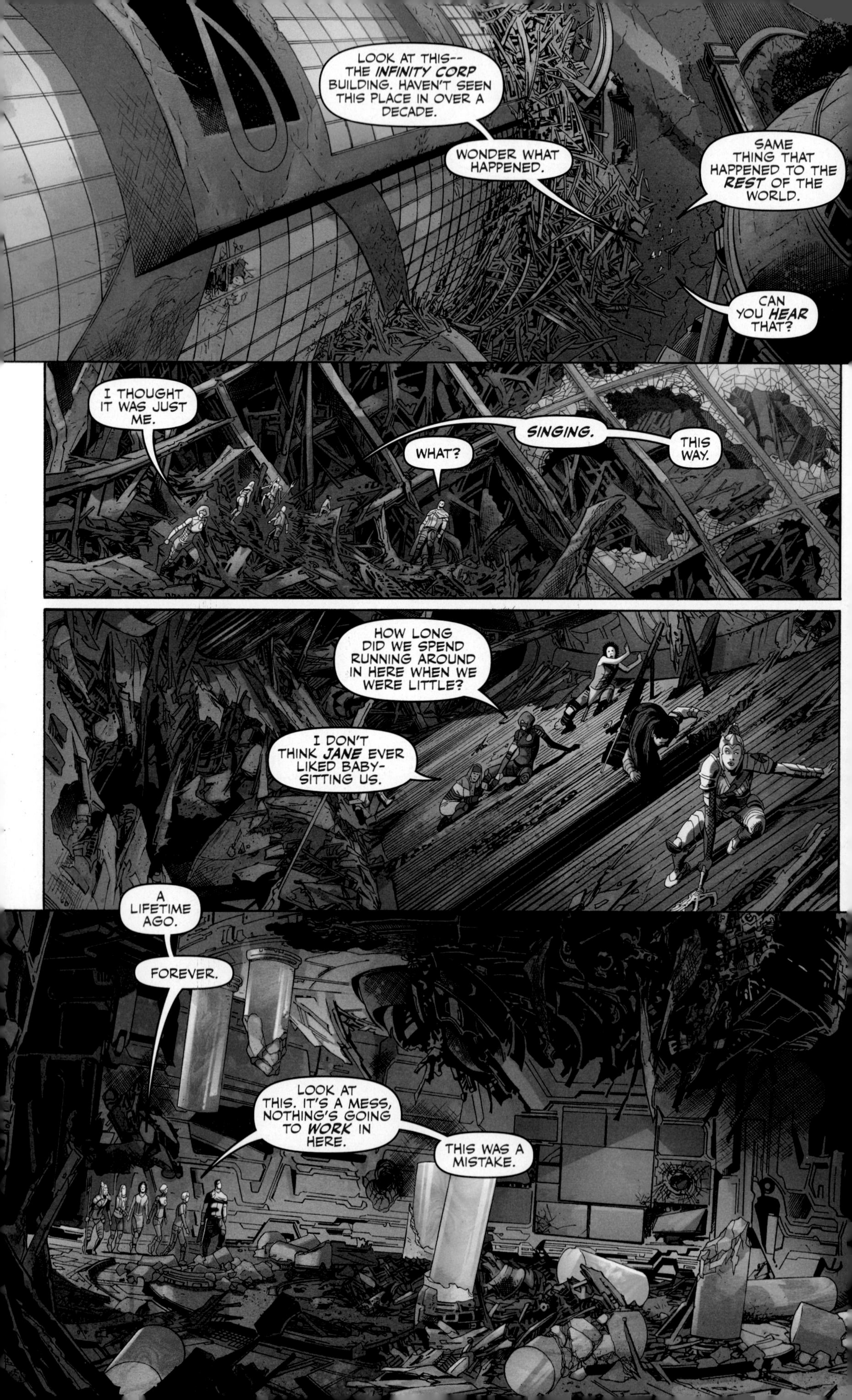
LOOK AT THIS-- THE INFINITY CORP BUILDING. HAVEN'T SEEN THIS PLACE IN OVER A DECADE.
WONDER WHAT HAPPENED.
SAME THING THAT HAPPENED TO THE REST OF THE WORLD.
CAN YOU HEAR THAT?
I THOUGHT IT WAS JUST ME.
WHAT?
SINGING.
THIS WAY.
HOW LONG DID WE SPEND RUNNING AROUND IN HERE WHEN WE WERE LITTLE?
I DON'T THINK JANE EVER LIKED BABY-SITTING US.
A LIFETIME AGO.
FOREVER.
LOOK AT THIS. IT'S A MESS, NOTHING'S GOING TO WORK IN HERE.
THIS WAS A MISTAKE.

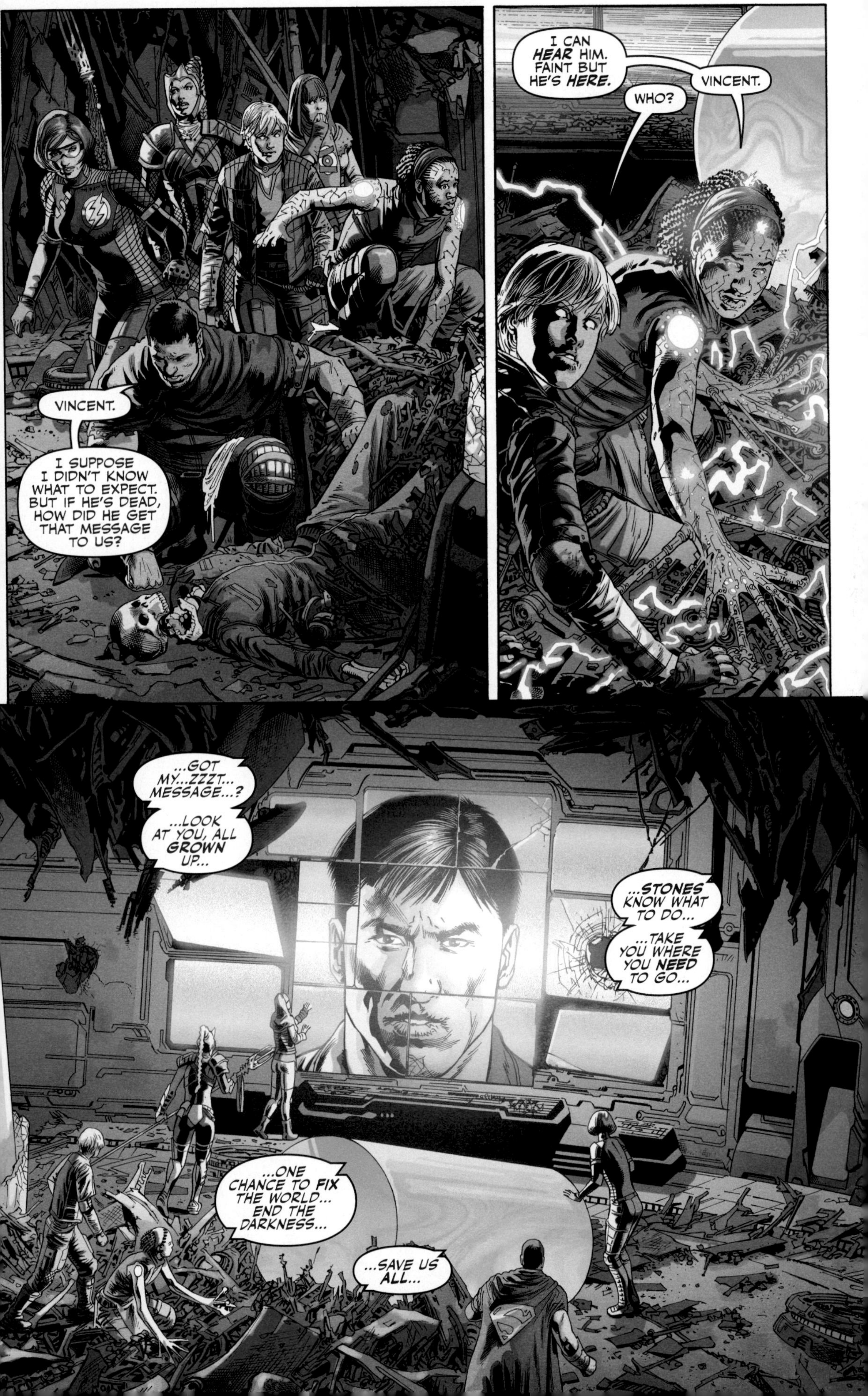
VINCENT.
I SUPPOSE I DIDN'T KNOW WHAT TO EXPECT. BUT IF HE'S DEAD, HOW DID HE GET THAT MESSAGE TO US?
I CAN HEAR HIM. FAINT BUT HE'S HERE.
WHO?
VINCENT.
...GOT MY...ZZZT... MESSAGE...?
...LOOK AT YOU, ALL GROWN UP...
...STONES KNOW WHAT TO DO...
...TAKE YOU WHERE YOU NEED TO GO...
...ONE CHANCE TO FIX THE WORLD... END THE DARKNESS...
...SAVE US ALL...

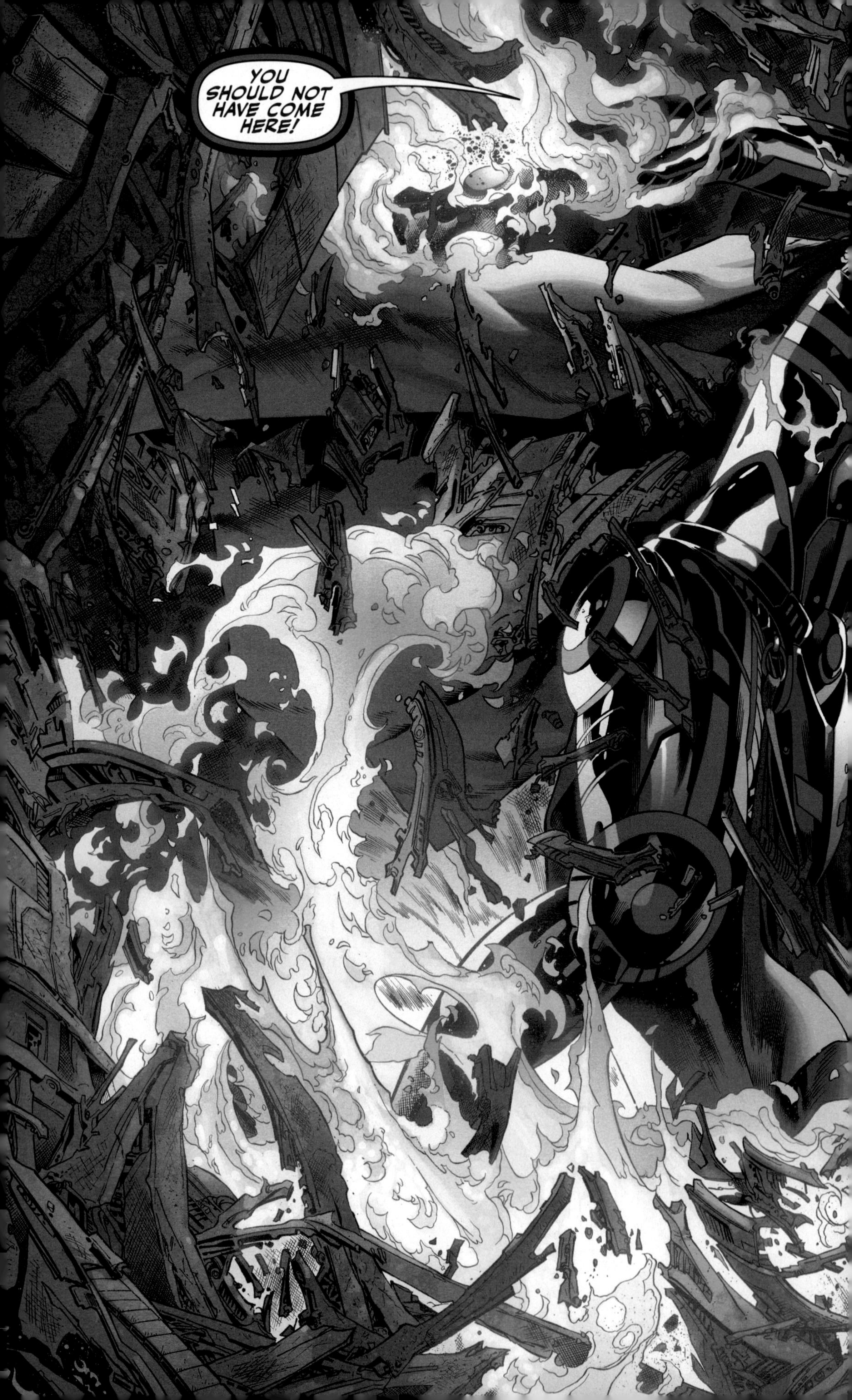
YOU SHOULD NOT HAVE COME HERE!

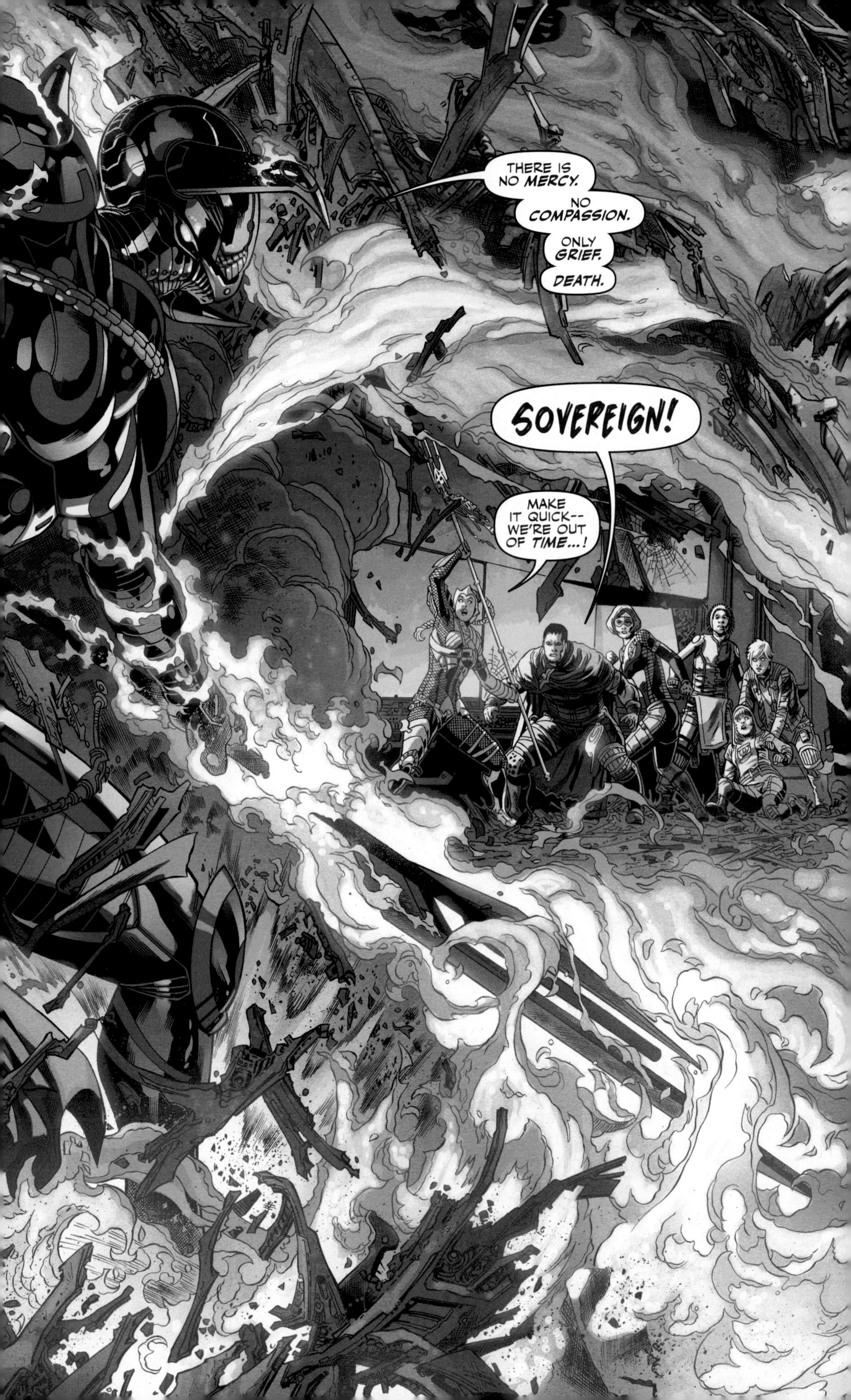
THERE IS NO *MERCY.*
NO *COMPASSION.*
ONLY *GRIEF.*
DEATH.
SOVEREIGN!
MAKE IT QUICK-- WE'RE OUT OF *TIME*...!

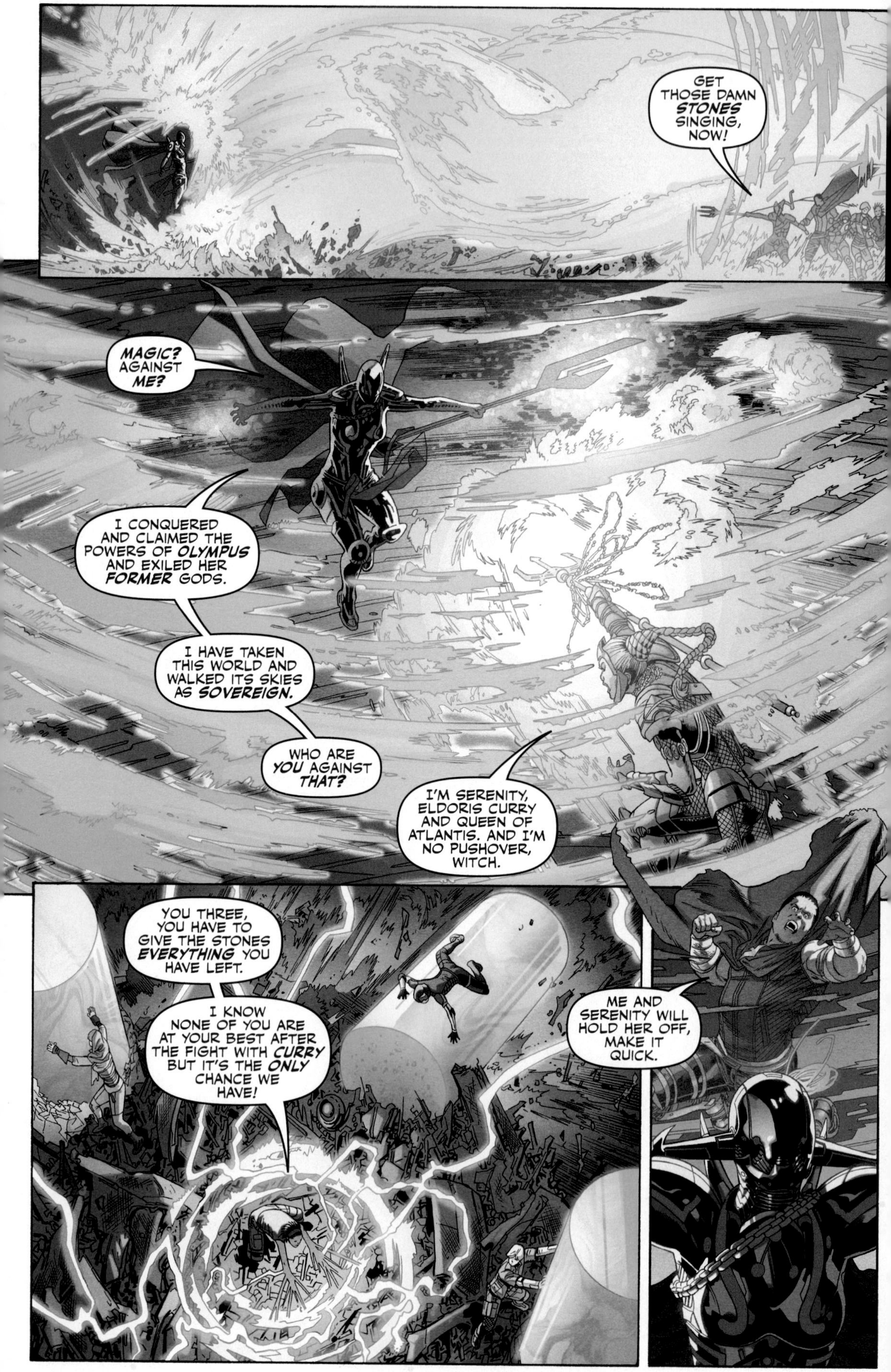

GET THOSE DAMN STONES SINGING, NOW!
MAGIC? AGAINST ME?
I CONQUERED AND CLAIMED THE POWERS OF OLYMPUS AND EXILED HER FORMER GODS.
I HAVE TAKEN THIS WORLD AND WALKED ITS SKIES AS SOVEREIGN.
WHO ARE YOU AGAINST THAT?
I'M SERENITY, ELDORIS CURRY AND QUEEN OF ATLANTIS. AND I'M NO PUSHOVER, WITCH.
YOU THREE, YOU HAVE TO GIVE THE STONES EVERYTHING YOU HAVE LEFT.
I KNOW NONE OF YOU ARE AT YOUR BEST AFTER THE FIGHT WITH CURRY BUT IT'S THE ONLY CHANCE WE HAVE!
ME AND SERENITY WILL HOLD HER OFF, MAKE IT QUICK.

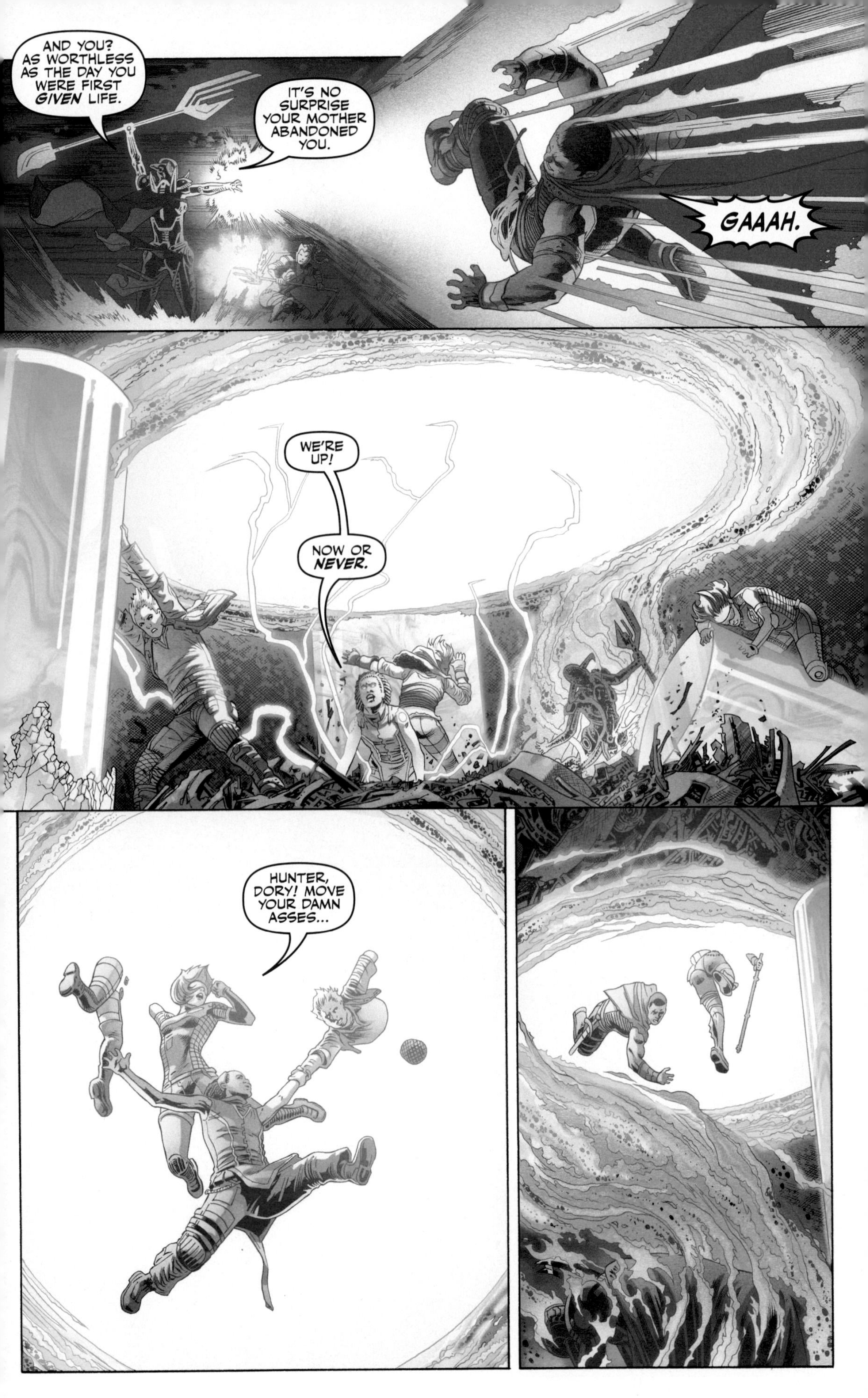
AND YOU? AS WORTHLESS AS THE DAY YOU WERE FIRST *GIVEN* LIFE.
IT'S NO SURPRISE YOUR MOTHER ABANDONED YOU.
GAAAH.
WE'RE UP!
NOW OR *NEVER*.
HUNTER, DORY! MOVE YOUR DAMN ASSES...

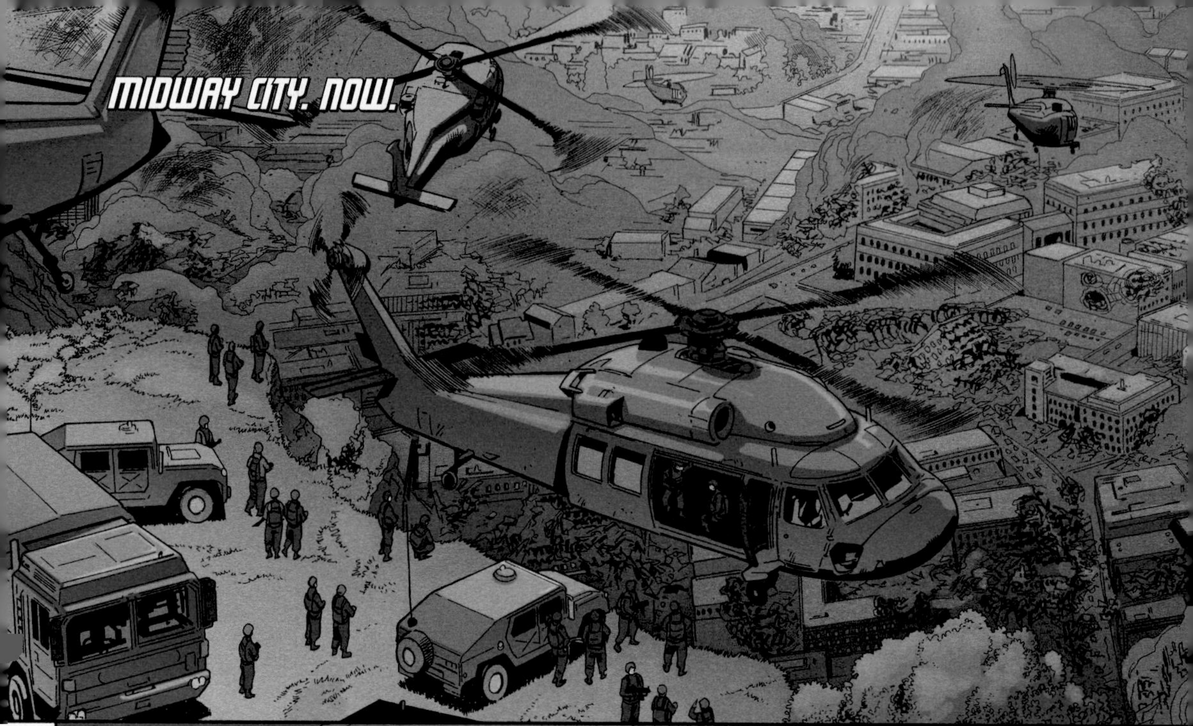
MIDWAY CITY. NOW.

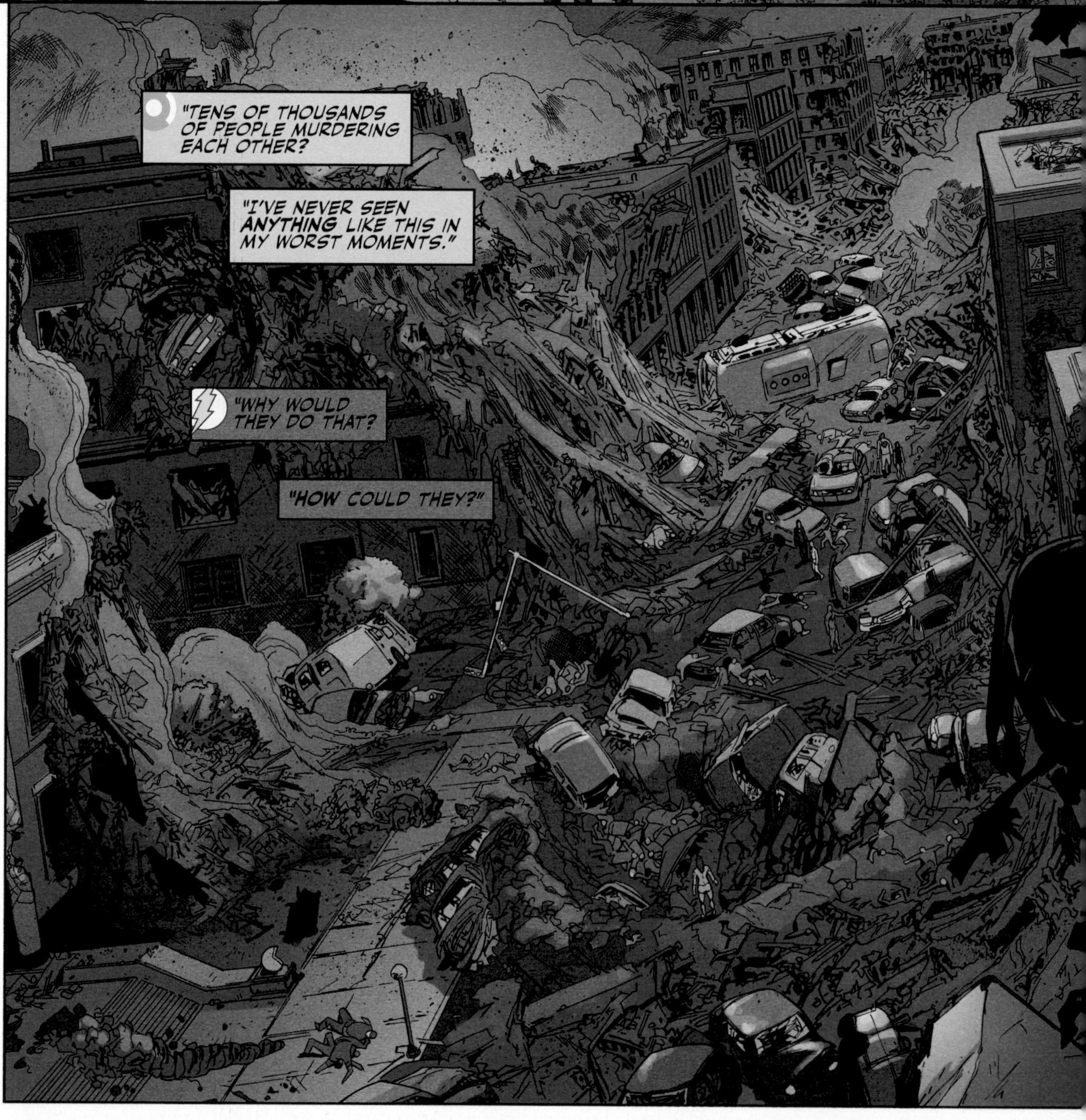
"TENS OF THOUSANDS OF PEOPLE MURDERING EACH OTHER?
"I'VE NEVER SEEN ANYTHING LIKE THIS IN MY WORST MOMENTS."
"WHY WOULD THEY DO THAT?
"HOW COULD THEY?"

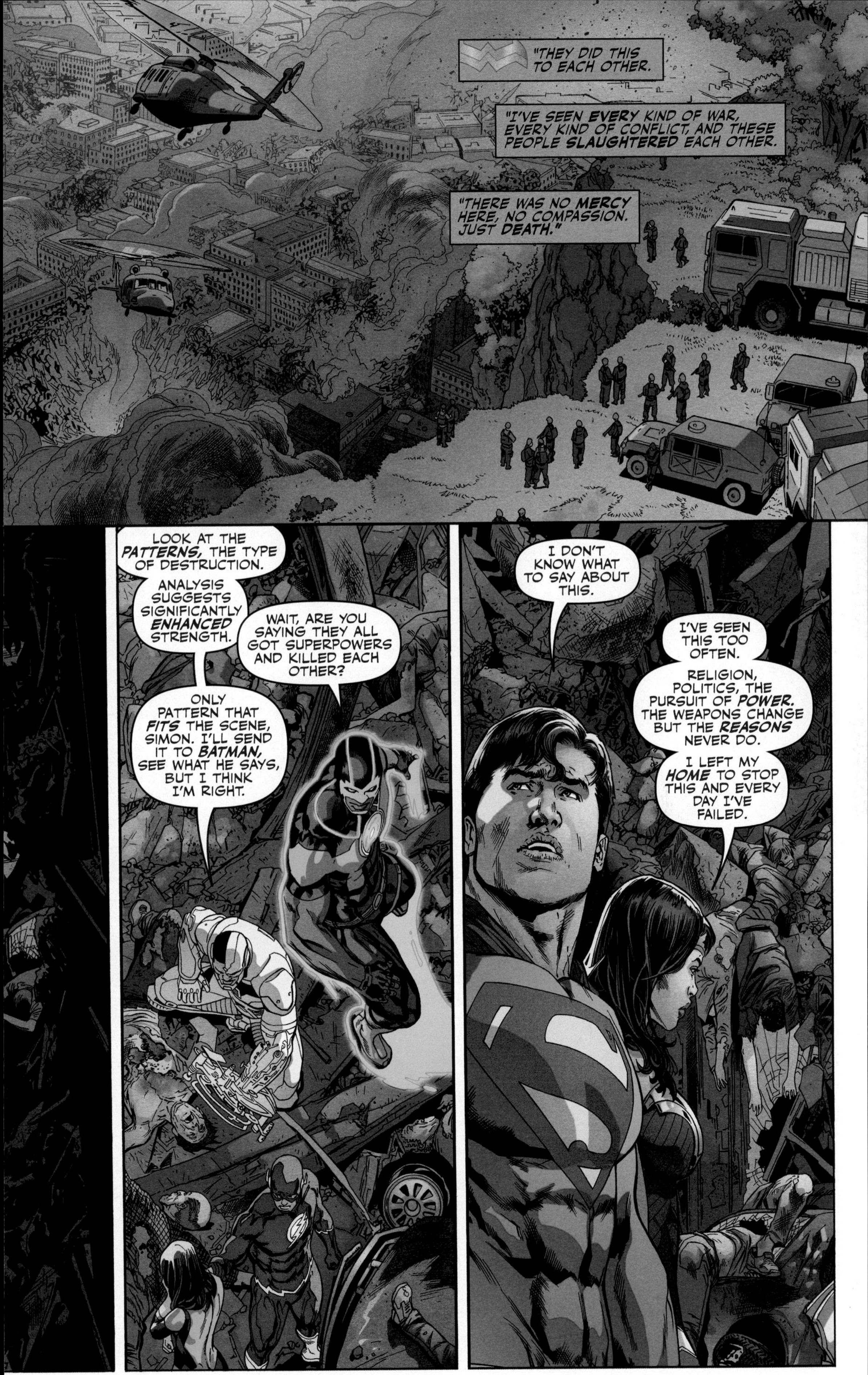
"THEY DID THIS TO EACH OTHER.
"I'VE SEEN EVERY KIND OF WAR, EVERY KIND OF CONFLICT, AND THESE PEOPLE SLAUGHTERED EACH OTHER.
"THERE WAS NO MERCY HERE, NO COMPASSION. JUST DEATH."
LOOK AT THE PATTERNS, THE TYPE OF DESTRUCTION.
ANALYSIS SUGGESTS SIGNIFICANTLY ENHANCED STRENGTH.
WAIT, ARE YOU SAYING THEY ALL GOT SUPERPOWERS AND KILLED EACH OTHER?
ONLY PATTERN THAT FITS THE SCENE, SIMON. I'LL SEND IT TO BATMAN, SEE WHAT HE SAYS, BUT I THINK I'M RIGHT.
I DON'T KNOW WHAT TO SAY ABOUT THIS.
I'VE SEEN THIS TOO OFTEN.
RELIGION, POLITICS, THE PURSUIT OF POWER. THE WEAPONS CHANGE BUT THE REASONS NEVER DO.
I LEFT MY HOME TO STOP THIS AND EVERY DAY I'VE FAILED.

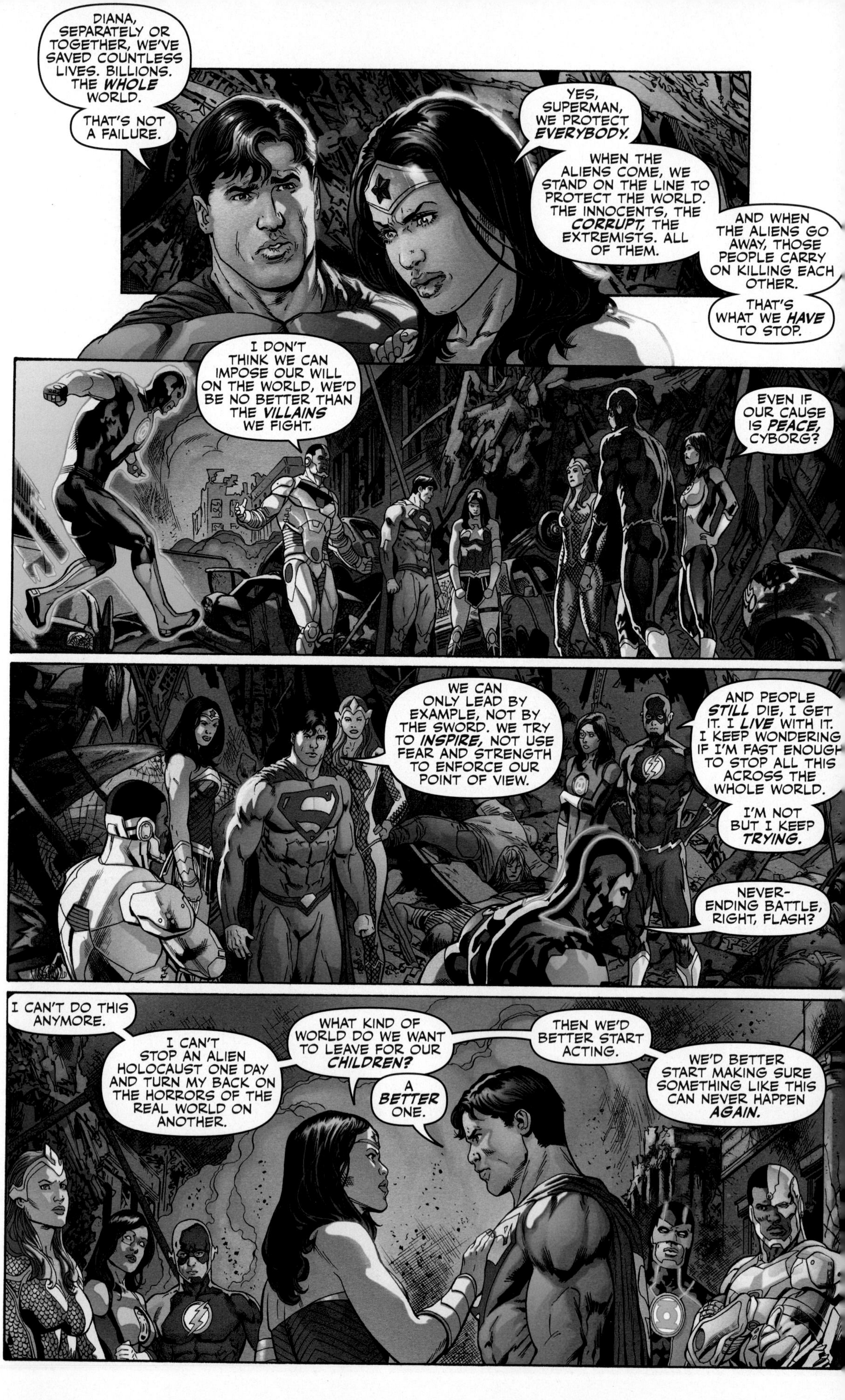
DIANA, SEPARATELY OR TOGETHER, WE'VE SAVED COUNTLESS LIVES. BILLIONS. THE WHOLE WORLD.
THAT'S NOT A FAILURE.
YES, SUPERMAN, WE PROTECT EVERYBODY.
WHEN THE ALIENS COME, WE STAND ON THE LINE TO PROTECT THE WORLD. THE INNOCENTS, THE CORRUPT, THE EXTREMISTS. ALL OF THEM.
AND WHEN THE ALIENS GO AWAY, THOSE PEOPLE CARRY ON KILLING EACH OTHER.
THAT'S WHAT WE HAVE TO STOP.
I DON'T THINK WE CAN IMPOSE OUR WILL ON THE WORLD, WE'D BE NO BETTER THAN THE VILLAINS WE FIGHT.
EVEN IF OUR CAUSE IS PEACE, CYBORG?
WE CAN ONLY LEAD BY EXAMPLE, NOT BY THE SWORD. WE TRY TO INSPIRE, NOT USE FEAR AND STRENGTH TO ENFORCE OUR POINT OF VIEW.
AND PEOPLE STILL DIE, I GET IT. I LIVE WITH IT. I KEEP WONDERING IF I'M FAST ENOUGH TO STOP ALL THIS ACROSS THE WHOLE WORLD.
I'M NOT BUT I KEEP TRYING.
NEVER-ENDING BATTLE, RIGHT, FLASH?
I CAN'T DO THIS ANYMORE.
I CAN'T STOP AN ALIEN HOLOCAUST ONE DAY AND TURN MY BACK ON THE HORRORS OF THE REAL WORLD ON ANOTHER.
WHAT KIND OF WORLD DO WE WANT TO LEAVE FOR OUR CHILDREN?
A BETTER ONE.
THEN WE'D BETTER START ACTING.
WE'D BETTER START MAKING SURE SOMETHING LIKE THIS CAN NEVER HAPPEN AGAIN.

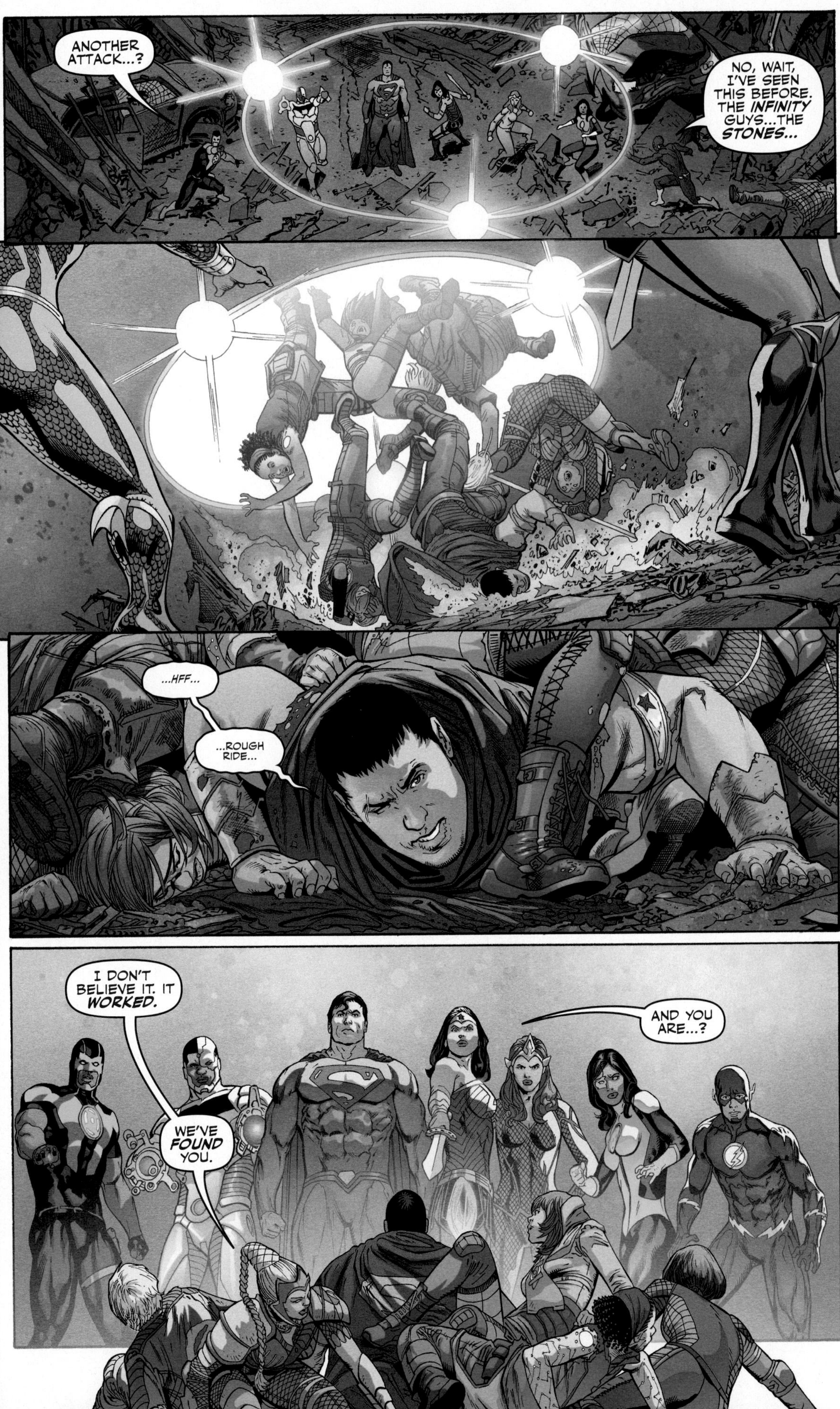
ANOTHER ATTACK...?
NO, WAIT, I'VE SEEN THIS BEFORE. THE *INFINITY* GUYS...THE *STONES*...
...HFF...
...ROUGH RIDE...
I DON'T BELIEVE IT. IT *WORKED.*
WE'VE *FOUND* YOU.
AND YOU ARE...?

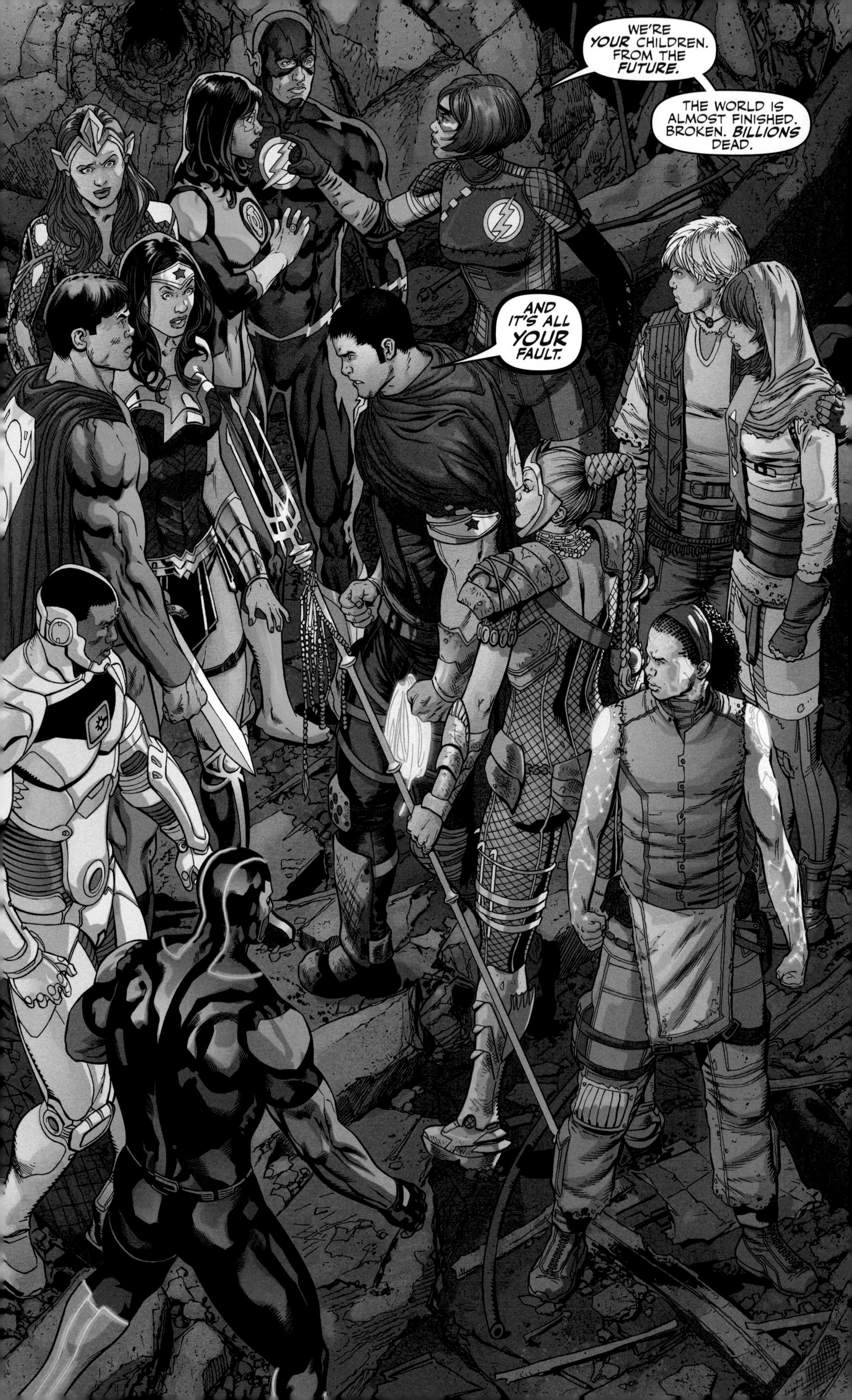
WE'RE *YOUR* CHILDREN. FROM THE *FUTURE.*
THE WORLD IS ALMOST FINISHED. BROKEN. *BILLIONS* DEAD.
AND IT'S ALL *YOUR* FAULT.

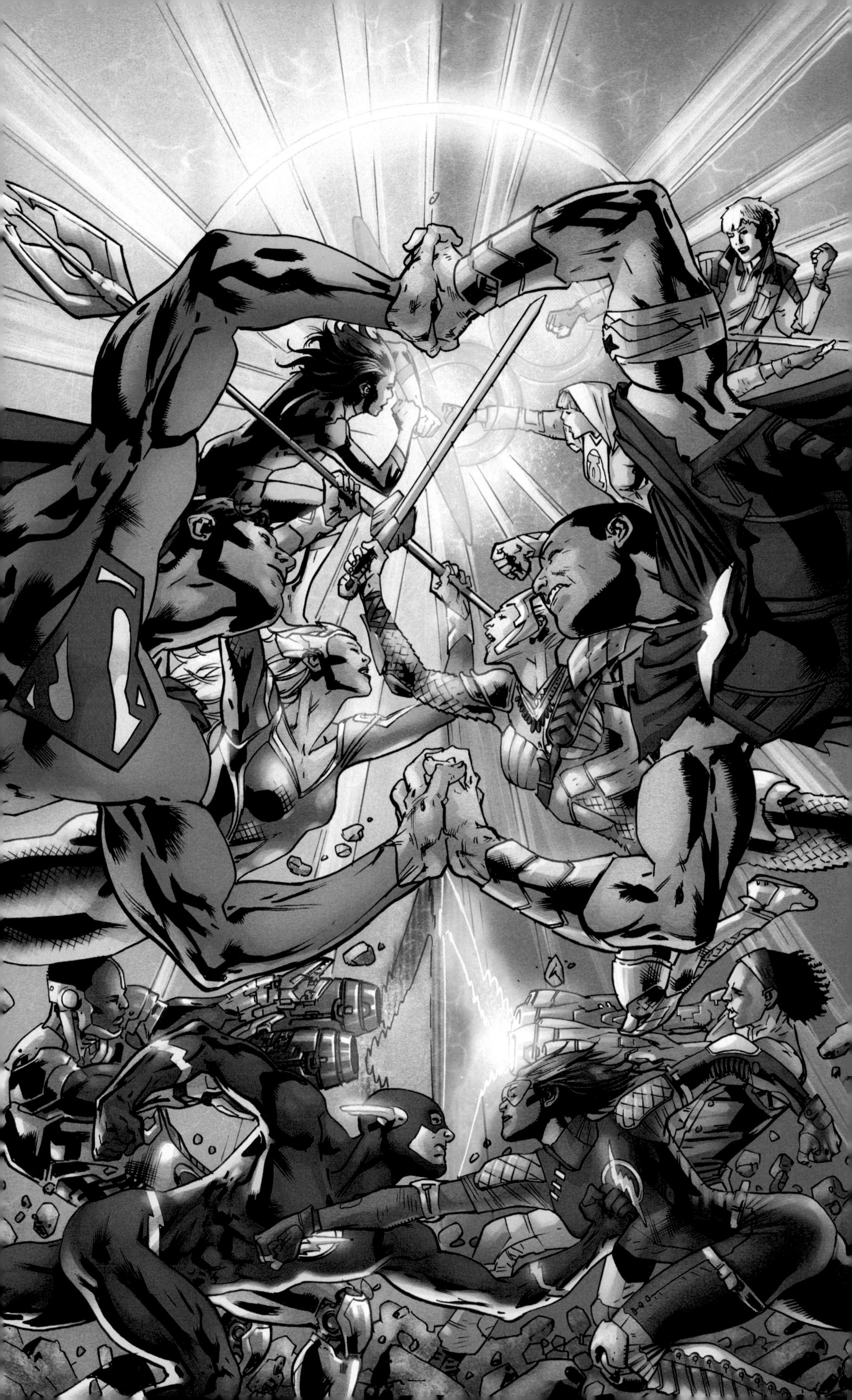

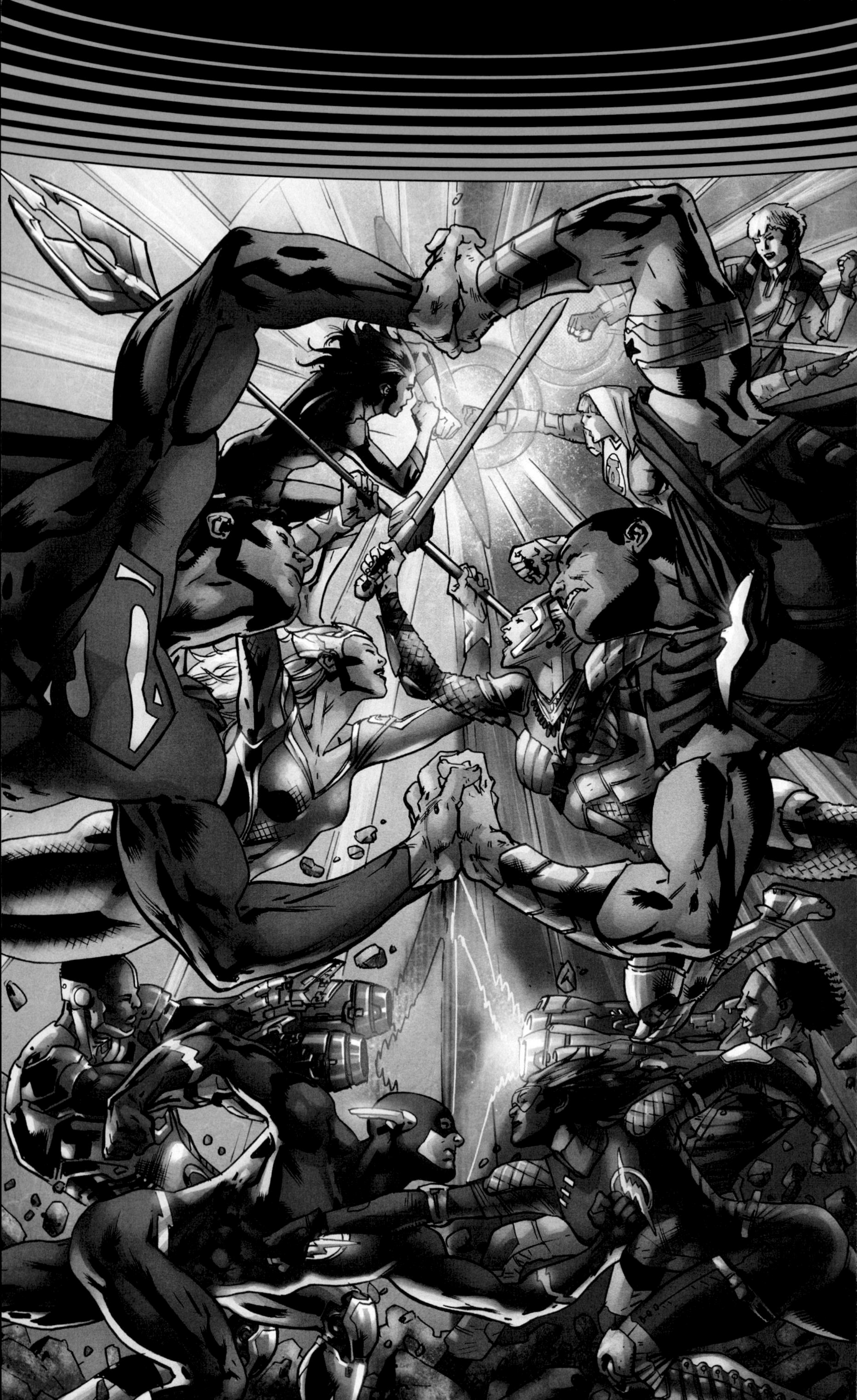

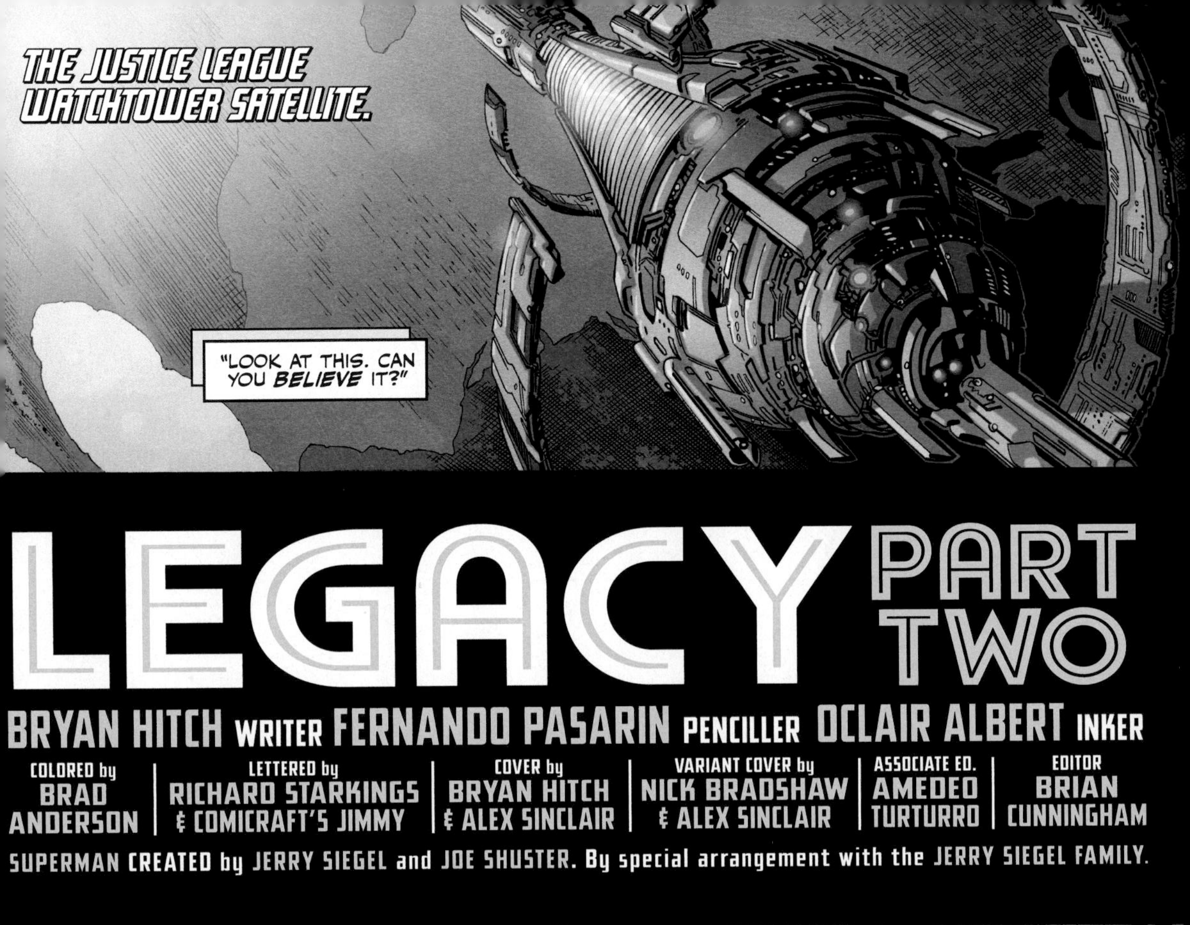
THE JUSTICE LEAGUE WATCHTOWER SATELLITE.
"LOOK AT THIS. CAN YOU BELIEVE IT?"

LEGACY PART TWO

BRYAN HITCH writer FERNANDO PASARIN penciller OCLAIR ALBERT inker

COLORED by BRAD ANDERSON | LETTERED by RICHARD STARKINGS & COMICRAFT'S JIMMY | COVER by BRYAN HITCH & ALEX SINCLAIR | VARIANT COVER by NICK BRADSHAW & ALEX SINCLAIR | ASSOCIATE ED. AMEDEO TURTURRO | EDITOR BRIAN CUNNINGHAM

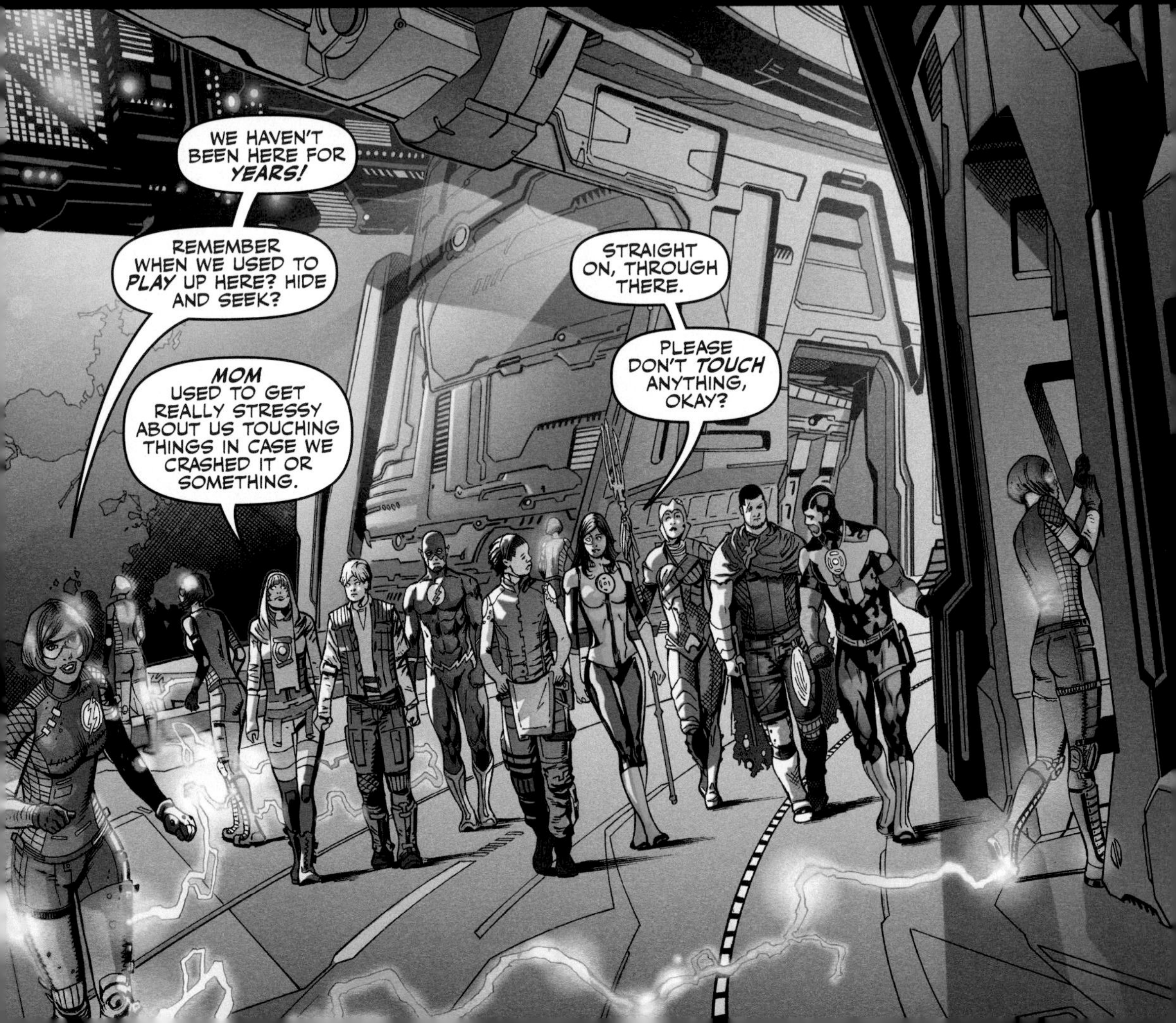
WE HAVEN'T BEEN HERE FOR YEARS!
REMEMBER WHEN WE USED TO PLAY UP HERE? HIDE AND SEEK?
MOM USED TO GET REALLY STRESSY ABOUT US TOUCHING THINGS IN CASE WE CRASHED IT OR SOMETHING.
STRAIGHT ON, THROUGH THERE.
PLEASE DON'T TOUCH ANYTHING, OKAY?

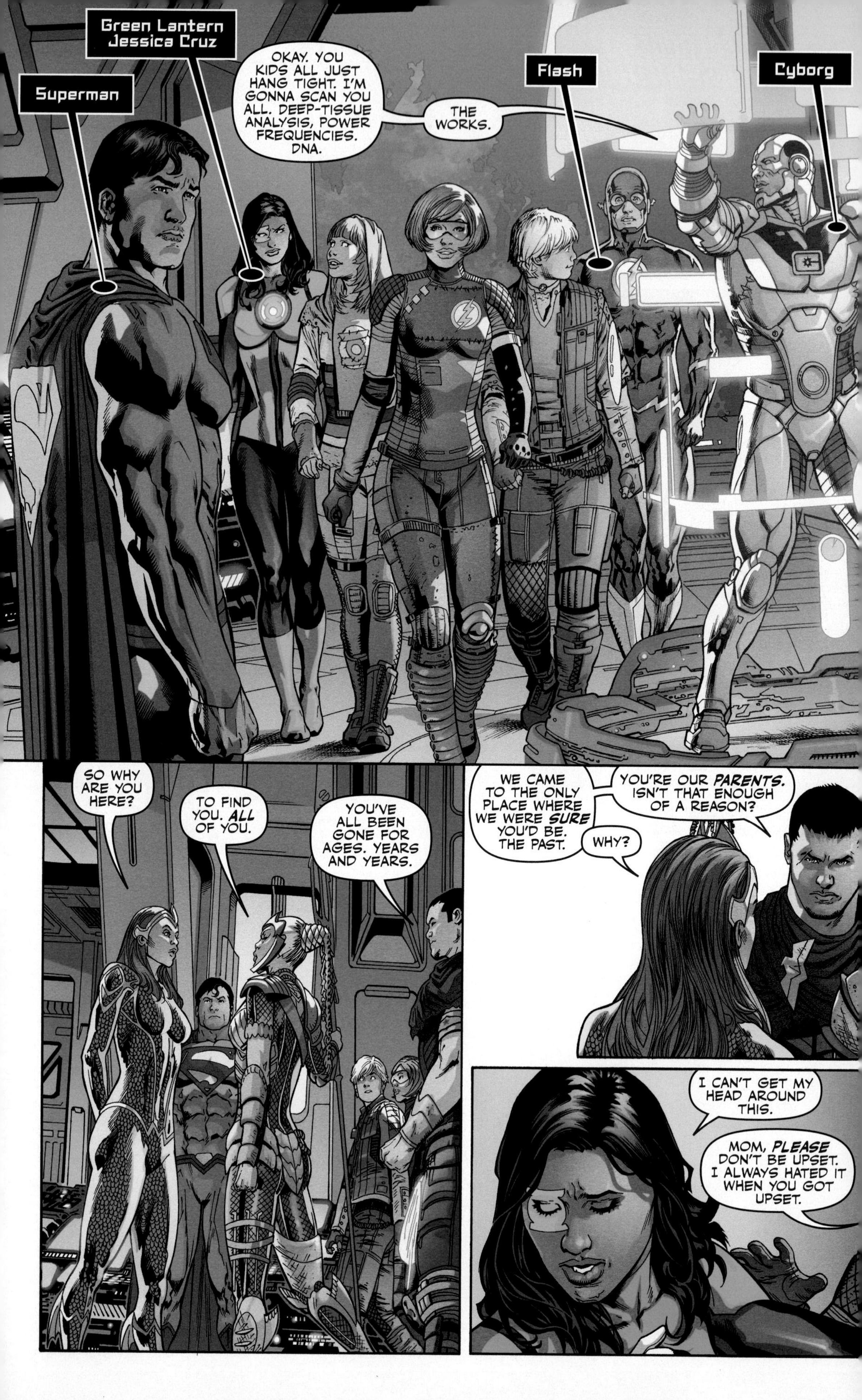
Green Lantern Jessica Cruz
Superman
OKAY. YOU KIDS ALL JUST HANG TIGHT. I'M GONNA SCAN YOU ALL. DEEP-TISSUE ANALYSIS, POWER FREQUENCIES. DNA.
THE WORKS.
Flash
Cyborg
SO WHY ARE YOU HERE?
TO FIND YOU. ALL OF YOU.
YOU'VE ALL BEEN GONE FOR AGES. YEARS AND YEARS.
WE CAME TO THE ONLY PLACE WHERE WE WERE SURE YOU'D BE. THE PAST.
YOU'RE OUR PARENTS. ISN'T THAT ENOUGH OF A REASON?
WHY?
I CAN'T GET MY HEAD AROUND THIS.
MOM, PLEASE DON'T BE UPSET. I ALWAYS HATED IT WHEN YOU GOT UPSET.

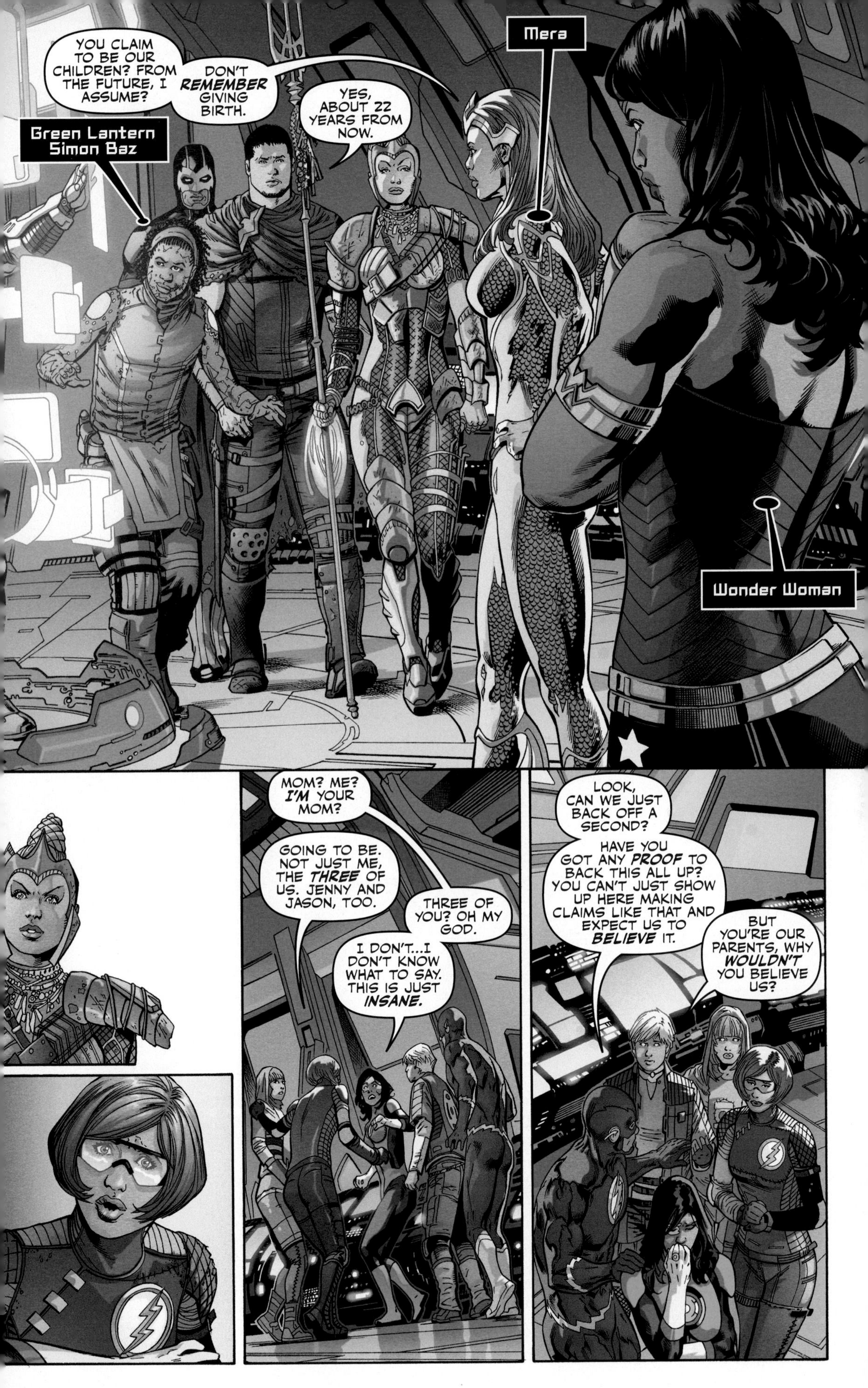
YOU CLAIM TO BE OUR CHILDREN? FROM THE FUTURE, I ASSUME?
DON'T *REMEMBER* GIVING BIRTH.
YES, ABOUT 22 YEARS FROM NOW.
Mera
Green Lantern Simon Baz
Wonder Woman
MOM? ME? *I'M* YOUR MOM?
GOING TO BE. NOT JUST ME, THE *THREE* OF US. JENNY AND JASON, TOO.
THREE OF YOU? OH MY GOD.
I DON'T...I DON'T KNOW WHAT TO SAY. THIS IS JUST *INSANE.*
LOOK, CAN WE JUST BACK OFF A SECOND?
HAVE YOU GOT ANY *PROOF* TO BACK THIS ALL UP? YOU CAN'T JUST SHOW UP HERE MAKING CLAIMS LIKE THAT AND EXPECT US TO *BELIEVE* IT.
BUT YOU'RE OUR PARENTS, WHY *WOULDN'T* YOU BELIEVE US?

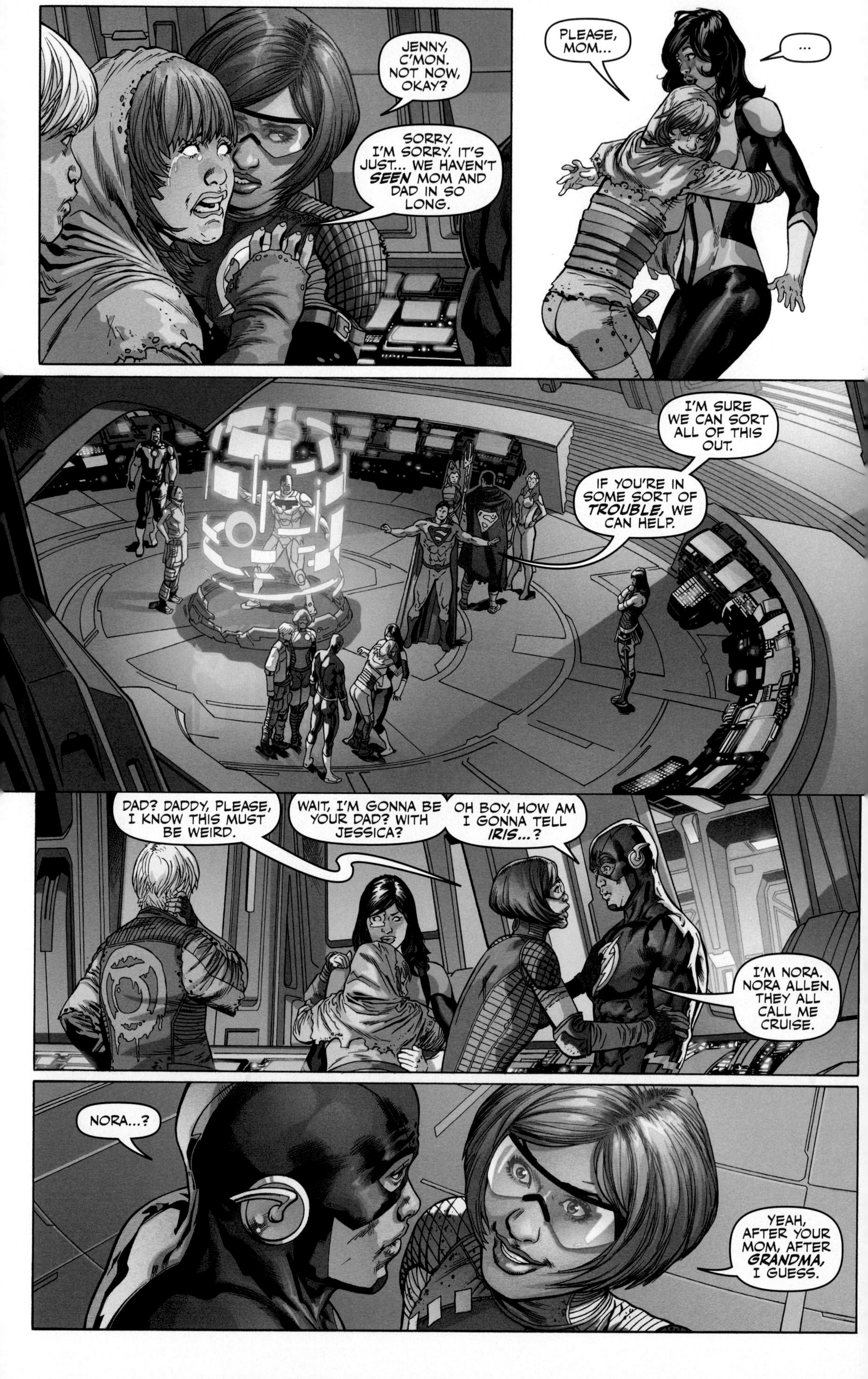
JENNY, C'MON. NOT NOW, OKAY?
SORRY. I'M SORRY. IT'S JUST... WE HAVEN'T SEEN MOM AND DAD IN SO LONG.
PLEASE, MOM...
...
I'M SURE WE CAN SORT ALL OF THIS OUT.
IF YOU'RE IN SOME SORT OF TROUBLE, WE CAN HELP.
DAD? DADDY, PLEASE, I KNOW THIS MUST BE WEIRD.
WAIT, I'M GONNA BE YOUR DAD? WITH JESSICA?
OH BOY, HOW AM I GONNA TELL IRIS...?
I'M NORA. NORA ALLEN. THEY ALL CALL ME CRUISE.
NORA...?
YEAH, AFTER YOUR MOM, AFTER GRANDMA, I GUESS.

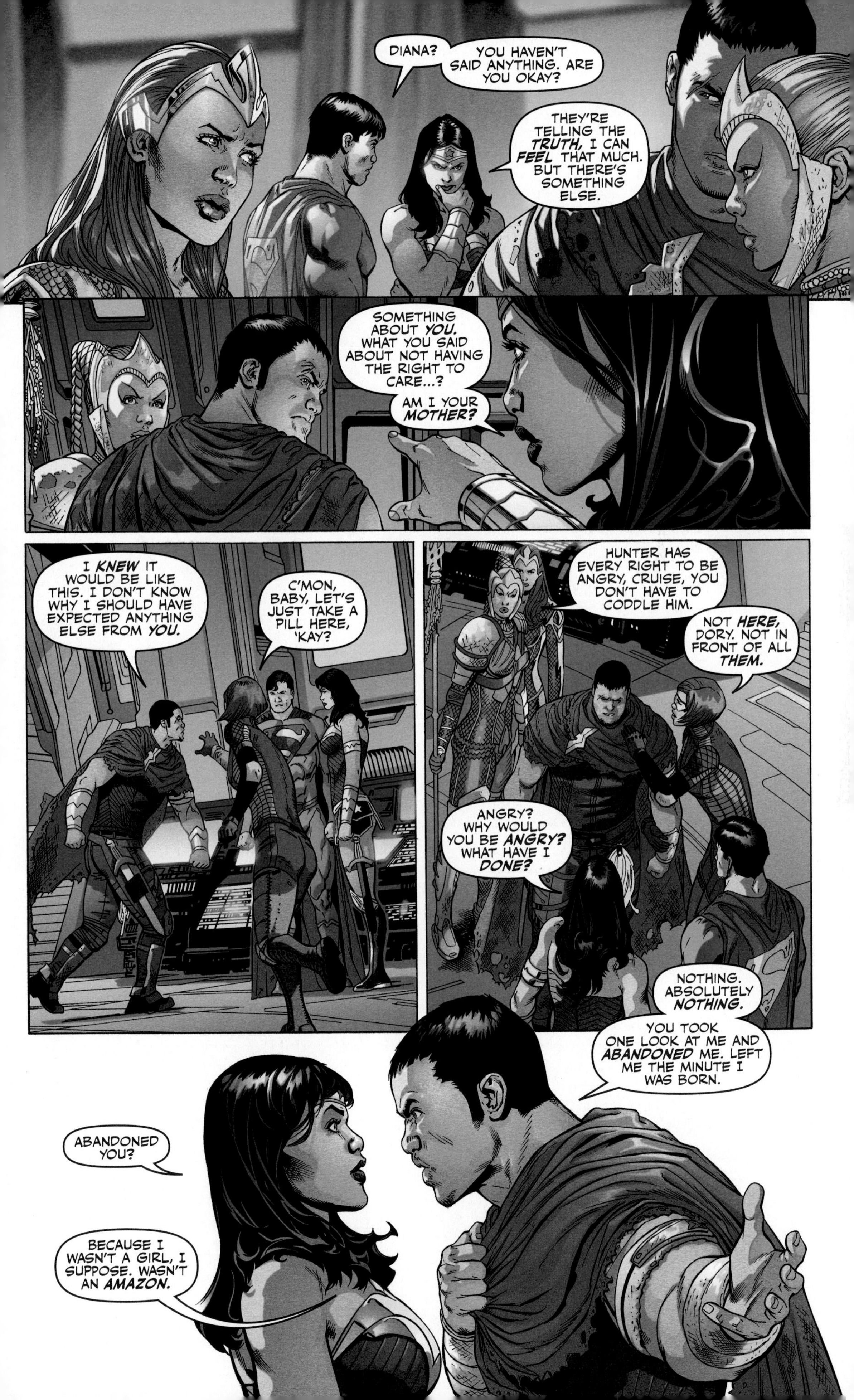
DIANA?
YOU HAVEN'T SAID ANYTHING. ARE YOU OKAY?
THEY'RE TELLING THE TRUTH, I CAN FEEL THAT MUCH. BUT THERE'S SOMETHING ELSE.
SOMETHING ABOUT YOU. WHAT YOU SAID ABOUT NOT HAVING THE RIGHT TO CARE...?
AM I YOUR MOTHER?
I KNEW IT WOULD BE LIKE THIS. I DON'T KNOW WHY I SHOULD HAVE EXPECTED ANYTHING ELSE FROM YOU.
C'MON, BABY, LET'S JUST TAKE A PILL HERE, 'KAY?
HUNTER HAS EVERY RIGHT TO BE ANGRY, CRUISE, YOU DON'T HAVE TO CODDLE HIM.
NOT HERE, DORY. NOT IN FRONT OF ALL THEM.
ANGRY? WHY WOULD YOU BE ANGRY? WHAT HAVE I DONE?
NOTHING. ABSOLUTELY NOTHING.
YOU TOOK ONE LOOK AT ME AND ABANDONED ME. LEFT ME THE MINUTE I WAS BORN.
ABANDONED YOU?
BECAUSE I WASN'T A GIRL, I SUPPOSE. WASN'T AN AMAZON.

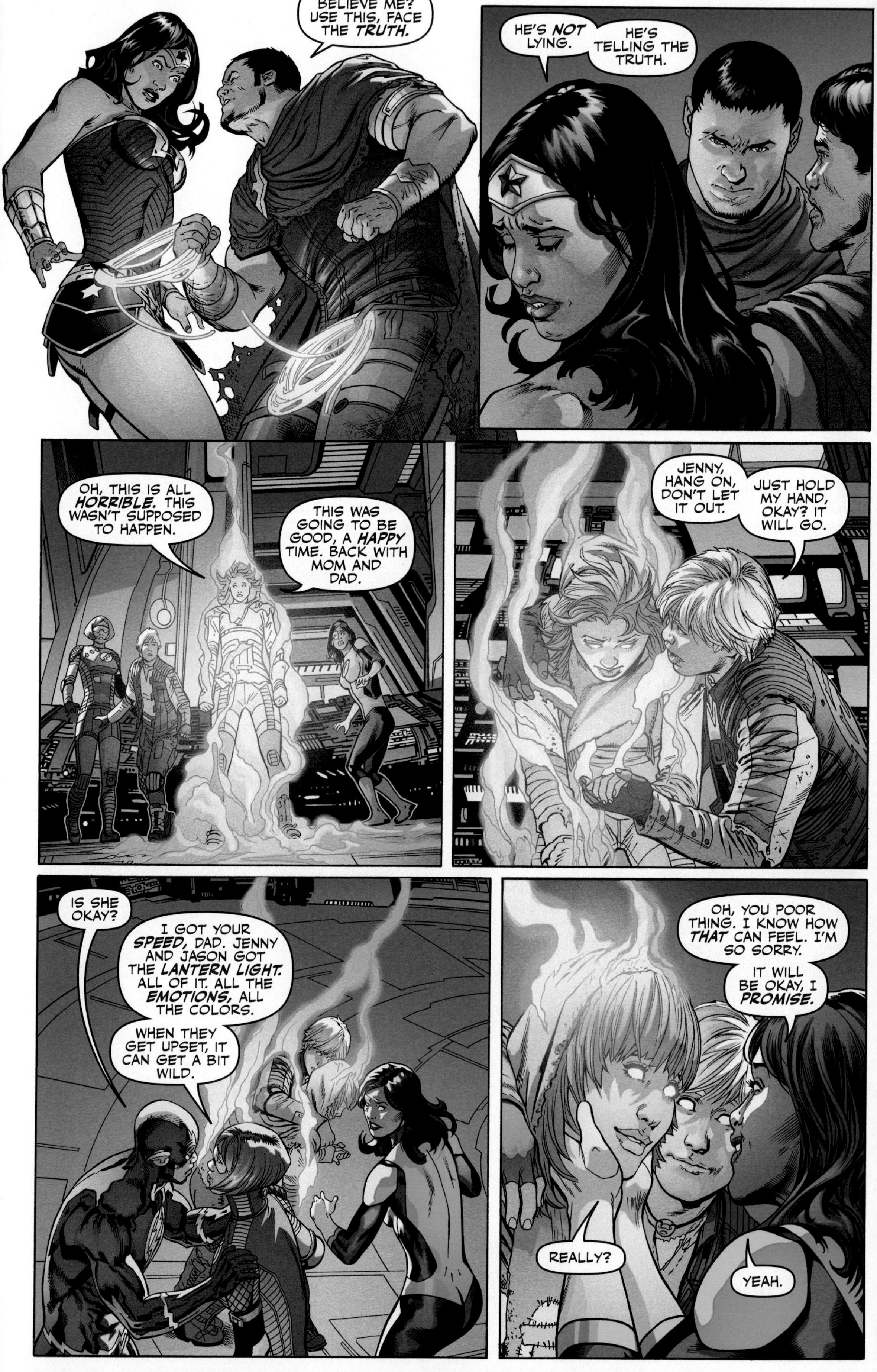
DON'T BELIEVE ME? USE THIS, FACE THE TRUTH.
HE'S NOT LYING.
HE'S TELLING THE TRUTH.
OH, THIS IS ALL HORRIBLE. THIS WASN'T SUPPOSED TO HAPPEN.
THIS WAS GOING TO BE GOOD, A HAPPY TIME. BACK WITH MOM AND DAD.
JENNY, HANG ON, DON'T LET IT OUT.
JUST HOLD MY HAND, OKAY? IT WILL GO.
IS SHE OKAY?
I GOT YOUR SPEED, DAD. JENNY AND JASON GOT THE LANTERN LIGHT. ALL OF IT. ALL THE EMOTIONS, ALL THE COLORS.
WHEN THEY GET UPSET, IT CAN GET A BIT WILD.
OH, YOU POOR THING. I KNOW HOW THAT CAN FEEL. I'M SO SORRY.
IT WILL BE OKAY, I PROMISE.
REALLY?
YEAH.

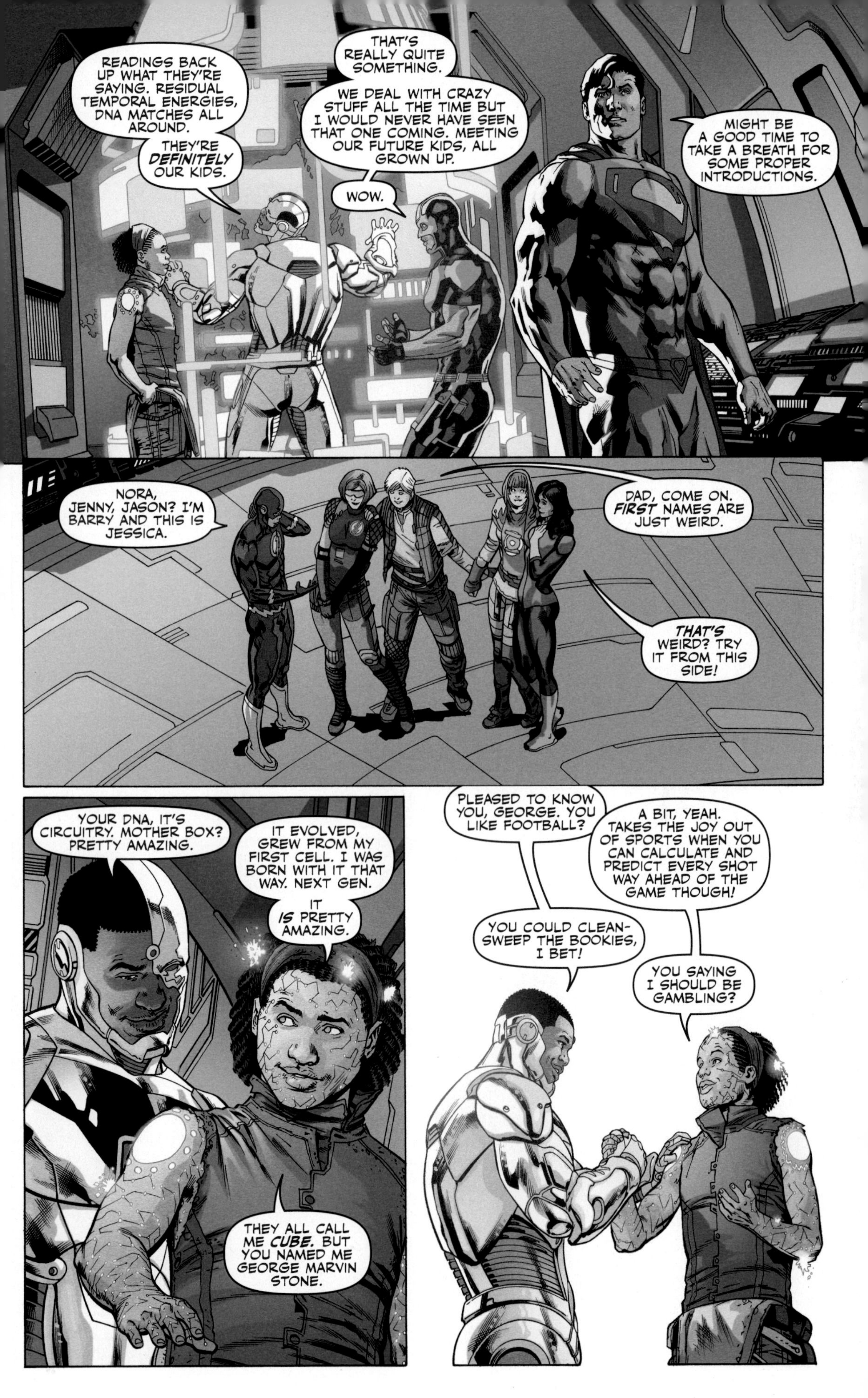

READINGS BACK UP WHAT THEY'RE SAYING. RESIDUAL TEMPORAL ENERGIES, DNA MATCHES ALL AROUND.
THEY'RE *DEFINITELY* OUR KIDS.
THAT'S REALLY QUITE SOMETHING.
WE DEAL WITH CRAZY STUFF ALL THE TIME BUT I WOULD NEVER HAVE SEEN THAT ONE COMING. MEETING OUR FUTURE KIDS, ALL GROWN UP.
WOW.
MIGHT BE A GOOD TIME TO TAKE A BREATH FOR SOME PROPER INTRODUCTIONS.
NORA, JENNY, JASON? I'M BARRY AND THIS IS JESSICA.
DAD, COME ON. *FIRST* NAMES ARE JUST WEIRD.
THAT'S WEIRD? TRY IT FROM THIS SIDE!
YOUR DNA, IT'S CIRCUITRY. MOTHER BOX? PRETTY AMAZING.
IT EVOLVED, GREW FROM MY FIRST CELL. I WAS BORN WITH IT THAT WAY. NEXT GEN.
IT *IS* PRETTY AMAZING.
THEY ALL CALL ME *CUBE*. BUT YOU NAMED ME GEORGE MARVIN STONE.
PLEASED TO KNOW YOU, GEORGE. YOU LIKE FOOTBALL?
A BIT, YEAH. TAKES THE JOY OUT OF SPORTS WHEN YOU CAN CALCULATE AND PREDICT EVERY SHOT WAY AHEAD OF THE GAME THOUGH!
YOU COULD CLEAN-SWEEP THE BOOKIES, I BET!
YOU SAYING I SHOULD BE GAMBLING?

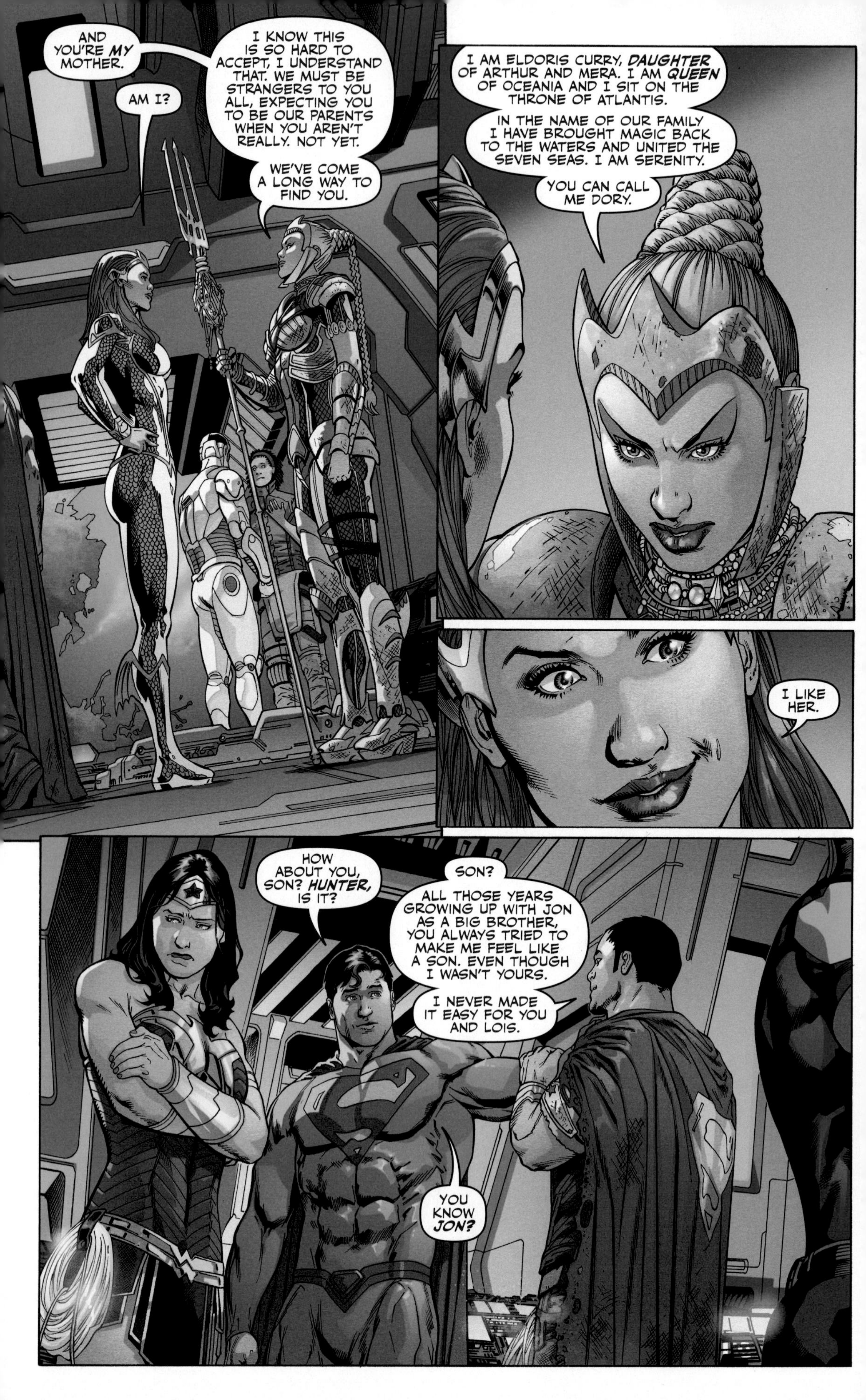

AND YOU'RE *MY* MOTHER.
I KNOW THIS IS SO HARD TO ACCEPT, I UNDERSTAND THAT. WE MUST BE STRANGERS TO YOU ALL, EXPECTING YOU TO BE OUR PARENTS WHEN YOU AREN'T REALLY. NOT YET.
AM I?
WE'VE COME A LONG WAY TO FIND YOU.
I AM ELDORIS CURRY, *DAUGHTER* OF ARTHUR AND MERA. I AM *QUEEN* OF OCEANIA AND I SIT ON THE THRONE OF ATLANTIS.
IN THE NAME OF OUR FAMILY I HAVE BROUGHT MAGIC BACK TO THE WATERS AND UNITED THE SEVEN SEAS. I AM SERENITY.
YOU CAN CALL ME DORY.
I LIKE HER.
HOW ABOUT YOU, SON? *HUNTER,* IS IT?
SON?
ALL THOSE YEARS GROWING UP WITH JON AS A BIG BROTHER, YOU ALWAYS TRIED TO MAKE ME FEEL LIKE A SON. EVEN THOUGH I WASN'T YOURS.
I NEVER MADE IT EASY FOR YOU AND LOIS.
YOU KNOW *JON?*

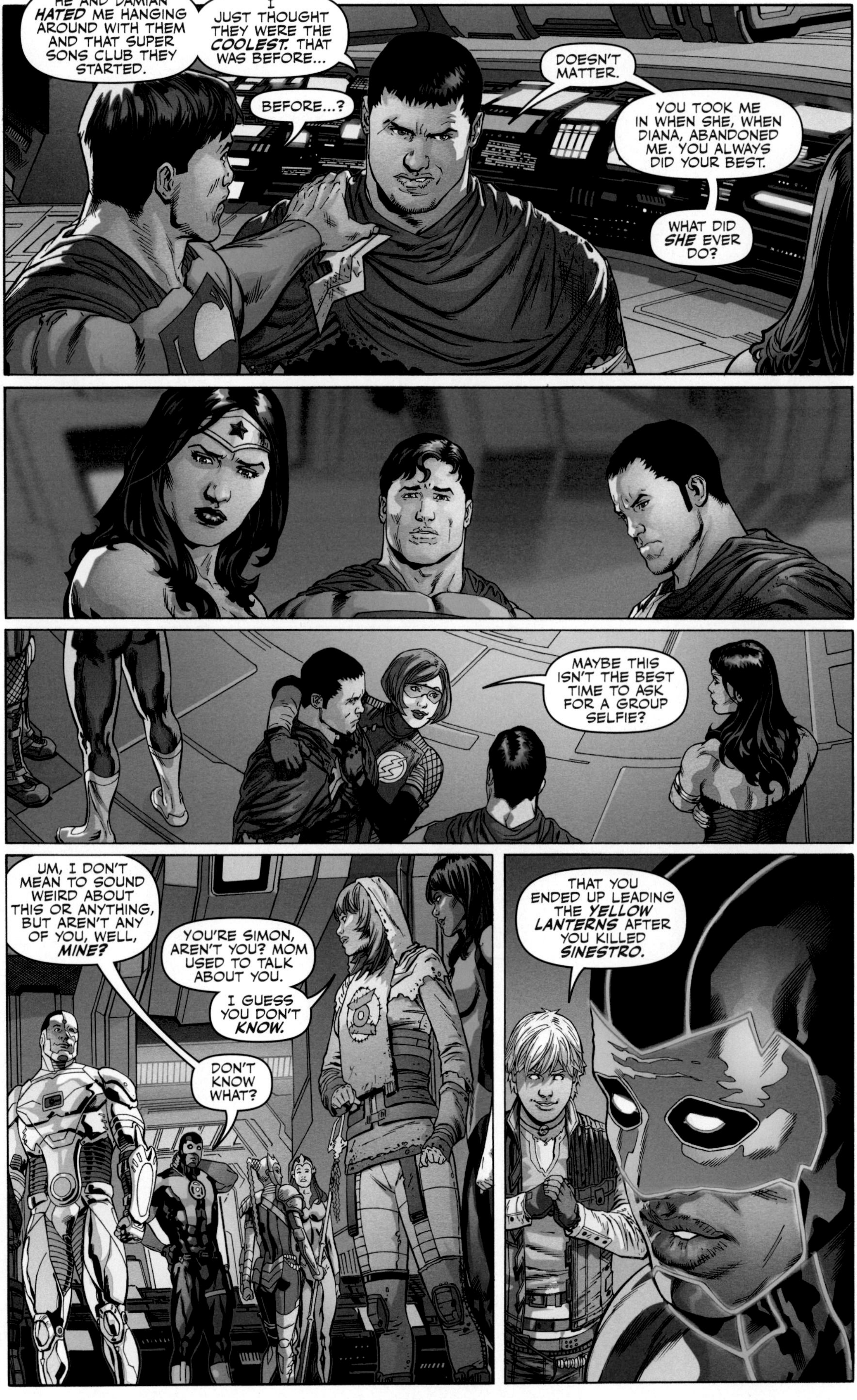

HE AND DAMIAN *HATED* ME HANGING AROUND WITH THEM AND THAT SUPER SONS CLUB THEY STARTED.
I JUST THOUGHT THEY WERE THE *COOLEST.* THAT WAS BEFORE...
BEFORE...?
DOESN'T MATTER.
YOU TOOK ME IN WHEN SHE, WHEN DIANA, ABANDONED ME. YOU ALWAYS DID YOUR BEST.
WHAT DID *SHE* EVER DO?
MAYBE THIS ISN'T THE BEST TIME TO ASK FOR A GROUP SELFIE?
UM, I DON'T MEAN TO SOUND WEIRD ABOUT THIS OR ANYTHING, BUT AREN'T ANY OF YOU, WELL, *MINE?*
YOU'RE SIMON, AREN'T YOU? MOM USED TO TALK ABOUT YOU.
I GUESS YOU DON'T *KNOW.*
DON'T KNOW WHAT?
THAT YOU ENDED UP LEADING THE *YELLOW LANTERNS* AFTER YOU KILLED *SINESTRO.*

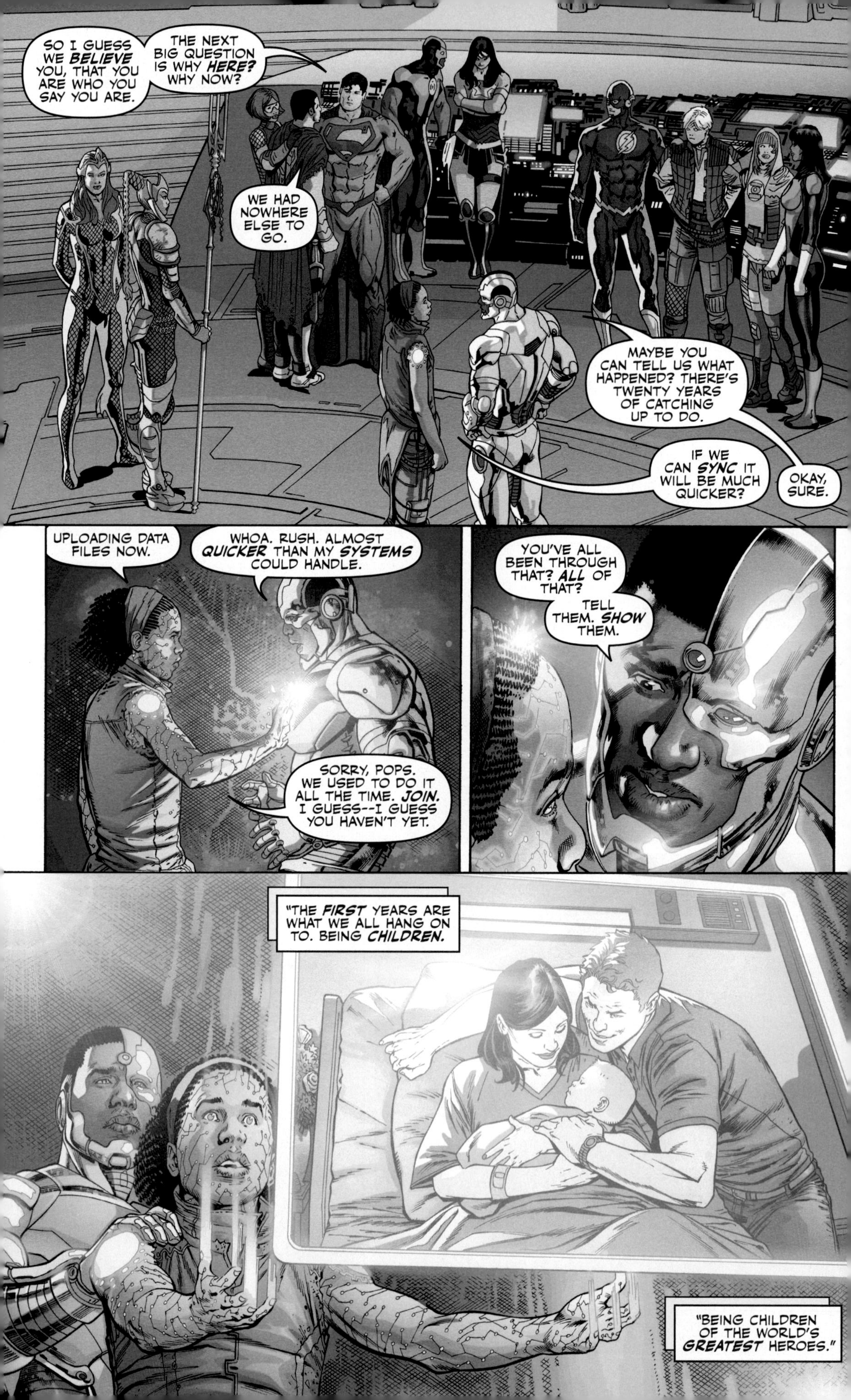

SO I GUESS WE BELIEVE YOU, THAT YOU ARE WHO YOU SAY YOU ARE.
THE NEXT BIG QUESTION IS WHY HERE? WHY NOW?
WE HAD NOWHERE ELSE TO GO.
MAYBE YOU CAN TELL US WHAT HAPPENED? THERE'S TWENTY YEARS OF CATCHING UP TO DO.
IF WE CAN SYNC IT WILL BE MUCH QUICKER?
OKAY, SURE.
UPLOADING DATA FILES NOW.
WHOA. RUSH. ALMOST QUICKER THAN MY SYSTEMS COULD HANDLE.
SORRY, POPS. WE USED TO DO IT ALL THE TIME. JOIN. I GUESS--I GUESS YOU HAVEN'T YET.
YOU'VE ALL BEEN THROUGH THAT? ALL OF THAT?
TELL THEM. SHOW THEM.
"THE FIRST YEARS ARE WHAT WE ALL HANG ON TO. BEING CHILDREN.
"BEING CHILDREN OF THE WORLD'S GREATEST HEROES."

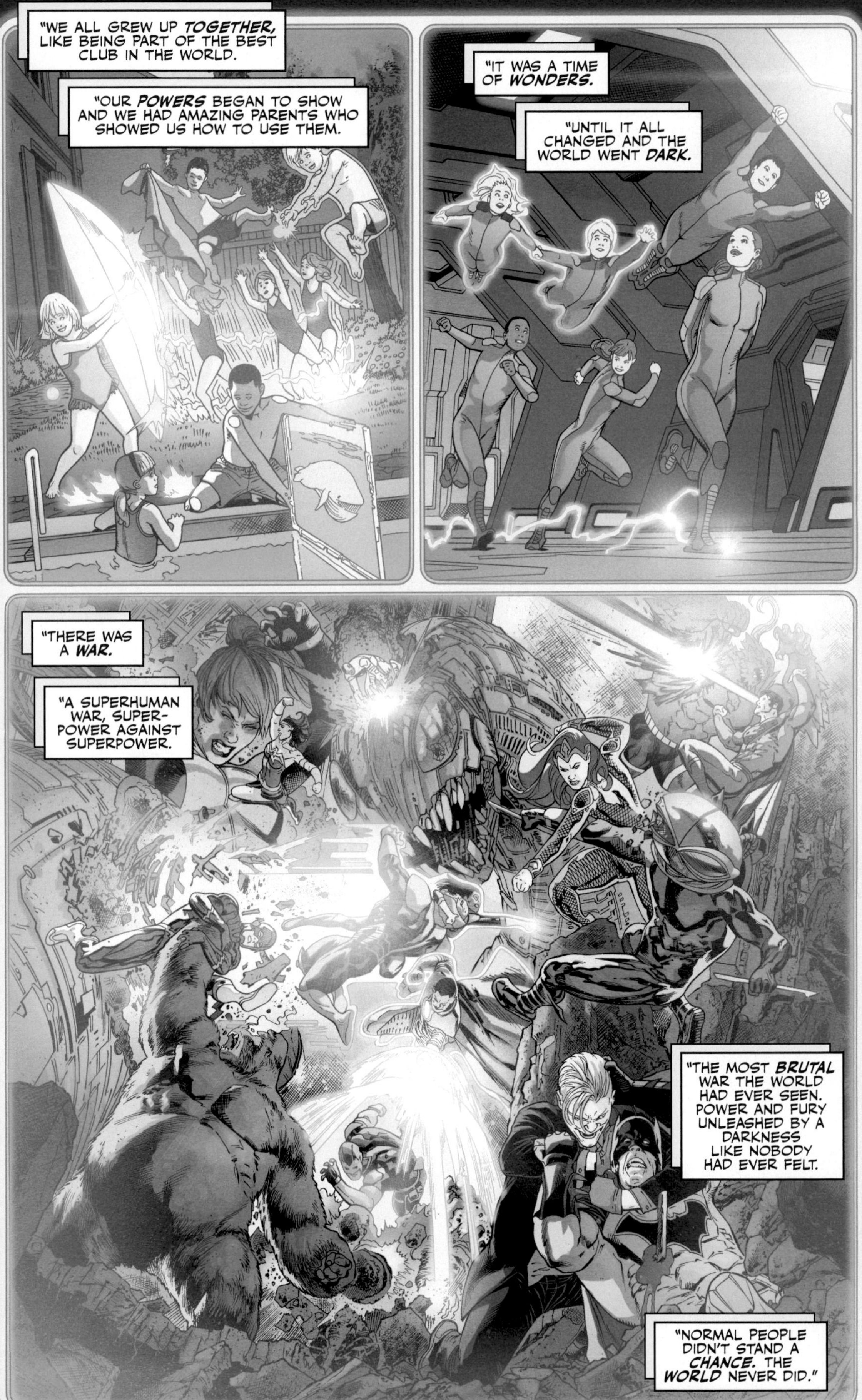
"WE ALL GREW UP TOGETHER, LIKE BEING PART OF THE BEST CLUB IN THE WORLD.
"OUR POWERS BEGAN TO SHOW AND WE HAD AMAZING PARENTS WHO SHOWED US HOW TO USE THEM.
"IT WAS A TIME OF WONDERS.
"UNTIL IT ALL CHANGED AND THE WORLD WENT DARK.
"THERE WAS A WAR.
"A SUPERHUMAN WAR, SUPER-POWER AGAINST SUPERPOWER.
"THE MOST BRUTAL WAR THE WORLD HAD EVER SEEN. POWER AND FURY UNLEASHED BY A DARKNESS LIKE NOBODY HAD EVER FELT.
"NORMAL PEOPLE DIDN'T STAND A CHANCE. THE WORLD NEVER DID."

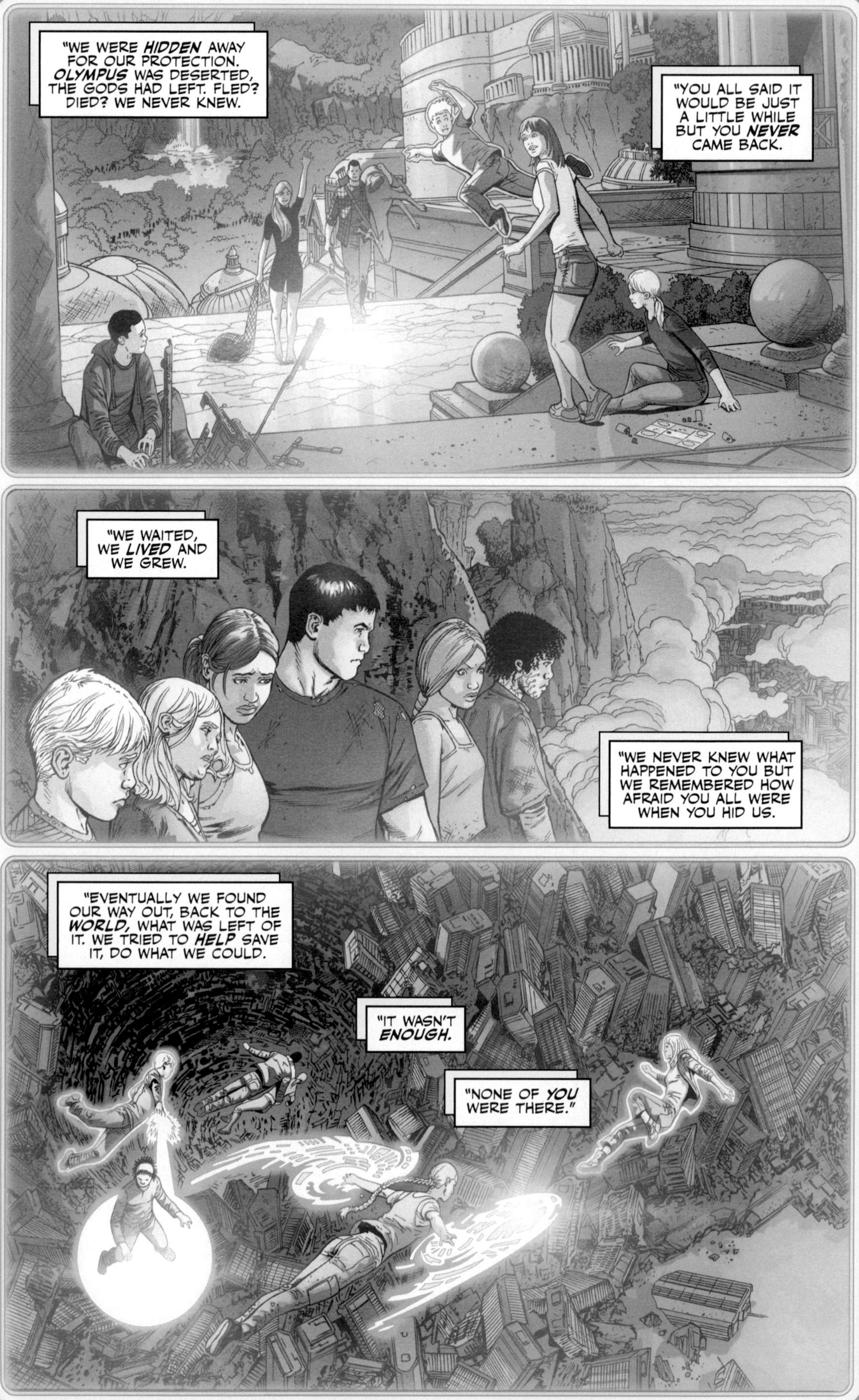
"WE WERE *HIDDEN* AWAY FOR OUR PROTECTION. *OLYMPUS* WAS DESERTED, THE GODS HAD LEFT. FLED? DIED? WE NEVER KNEW.
"YOU ALL SAID IT WOULD BE JUST A LITTLE WHILE BUT YOU *NEVER* CAME BACK.
"WE WAITED, WE *LIVED* AND WE GREW.
"WE NEVER KNEW WHAT HAPPENED TO YOU BUT WE REMEMBERED HOW AFRAID YOU ALL WERE WHEN YOU HID US.
"EVENTUALLY WE FOUND OUR WAY OUT, BACK TO THE *WORLD,* WHAT WAS LEFT OF IT. WE TRIED TO *HELP* SAVE IT, DO WHAT WE COULD.
"IT WASN'T *ENOUGH.*
"NONE OF *YOU* WERE THERE."

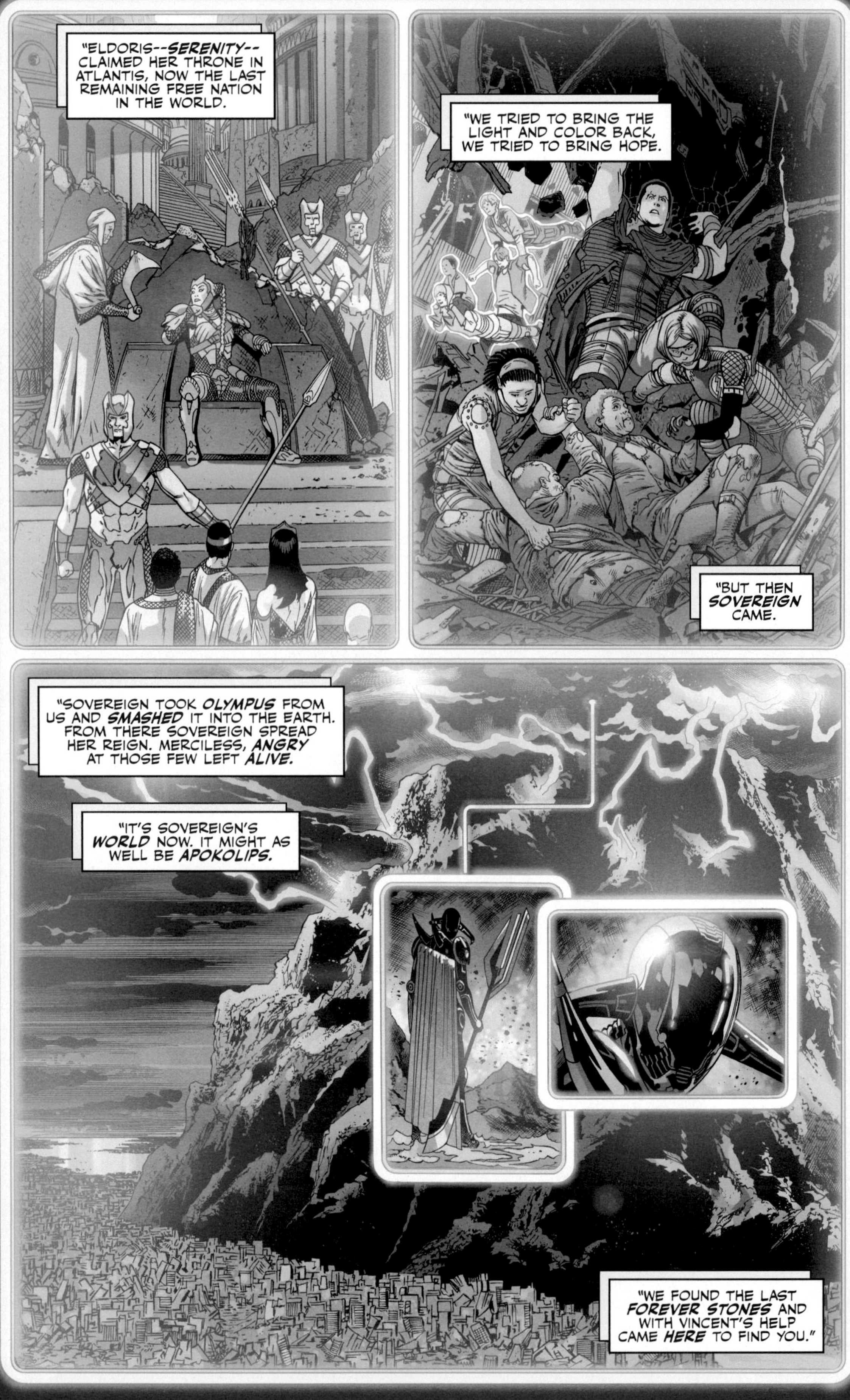
"ELDORIS--SERENITY--CLAIMED HER THRONE IN ATLANTIS, NOW THE LAST REMAINING FREE NATION IN THE WORLD.
"WE TRIED TO BRING THE LIGHT AND COLOR BACK, WE TRIED TO BRING HOPE.
"BUT THEN SOVEREIGN CAME.
"SOVEREIGN TOOK OLYMPUS FROM US AND SMASHED IT INTO THE EARTH. FROM THERE SOVEREIGN SPREAD HER REIGN. MERCILESS, ANGRY AT THOSE FEW LEFT ALIVE.
"IT'S SOVEREIGN'S WORLD NOW. IT MIGHT AS WELL BE APOKOLIPS.
"WE FOUND THE LAST FOREVER STONES AND WITH VINCENT'S HELP CAME HERE TO FIND YOU."

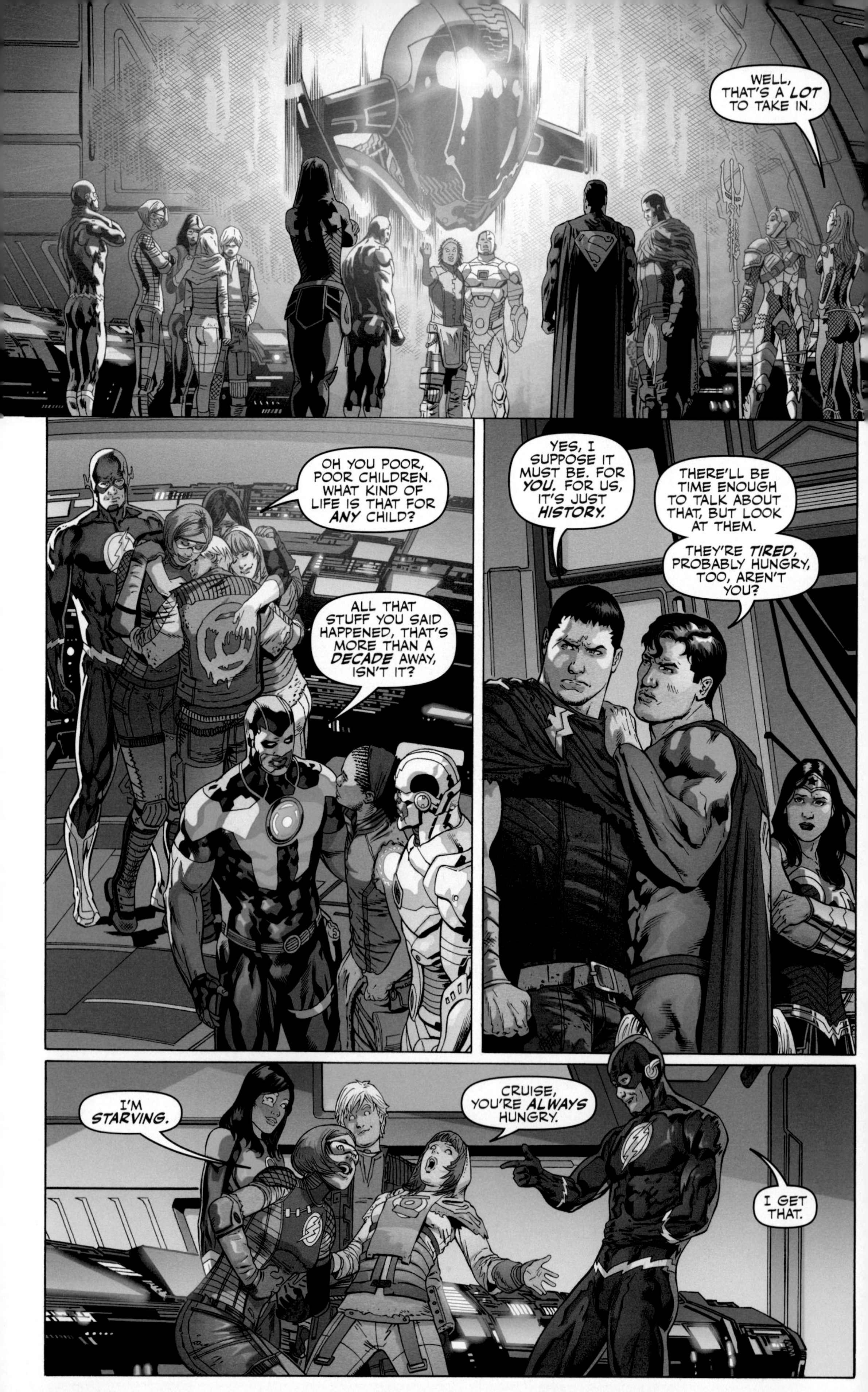
WELL, THAT'S A LOT TO TAKE IN.
OH YOU POOR, POOR CHILDREN. WHAT KIND OF LIFE IS THAT FOR ANY CHILD?
ALL THAT STUFF YOU SAID HAPPENED, THAT'S MORE THAN A DECADE AWAY, ISN'T IT?
YES, I SUPPOSE IT MUST BE. FOR YOU. FOR US, IT'S JUST HISTORY.
THERE'LL BE TIME ENOUGH TO TALK ABOUT THAT, BUT LOOK AT THEM.
THEY'RE TIRED, PROBABLY HUNGRY, TOO, AREN'T YOU?
I'M STARVING.
CRUISE, YOU'RE ALWAYS HUNGRY.
I GET THAT.

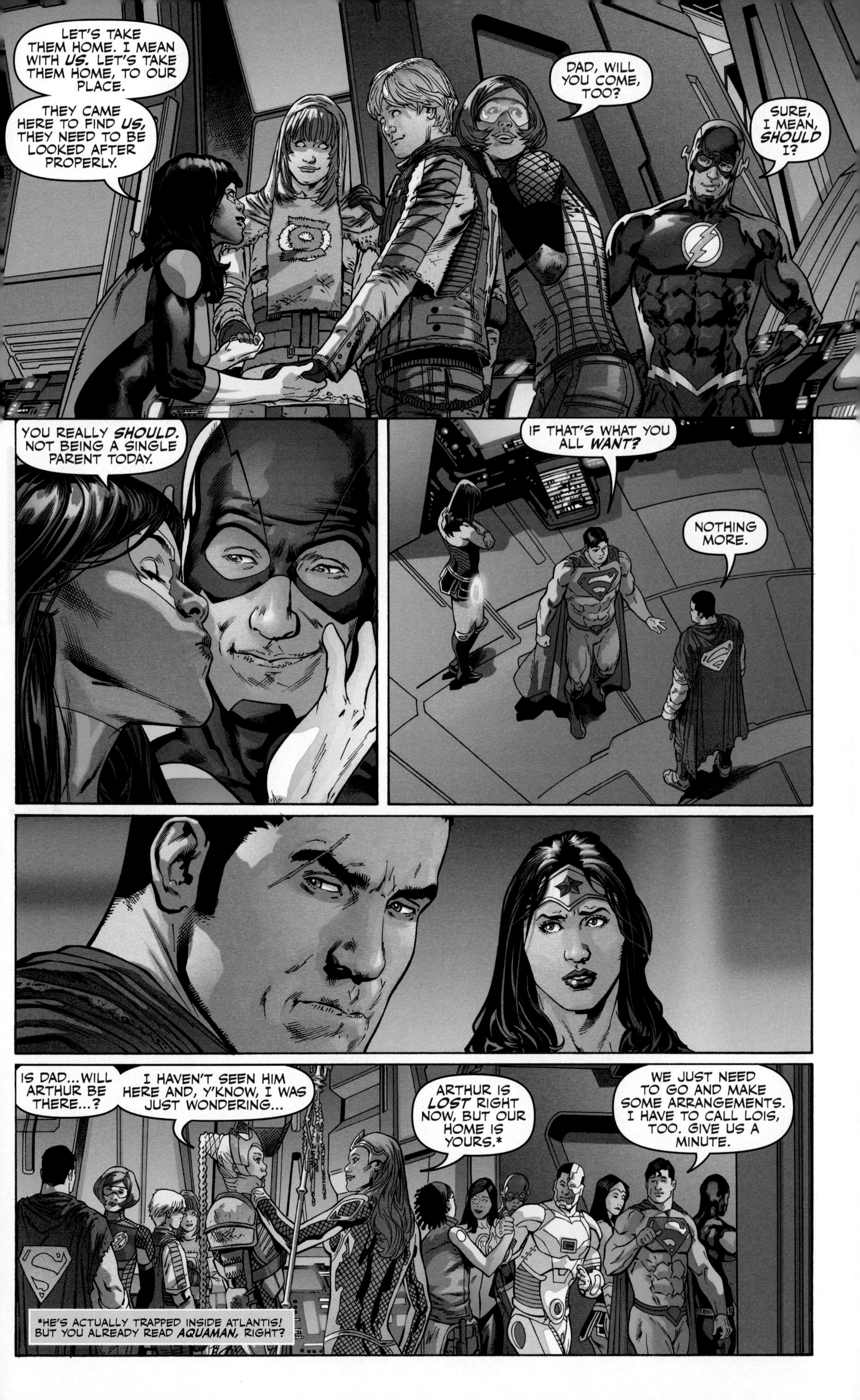

LET'S TAKE THEM HOME. I MEAN WITH US. LET'S TAKE THEM HOME, TO OUR PLACE.
THEY CAME HERE TO FIND US, THEY NEED TO BE LOOKED AFTER PROPERLY.
DAD, WILL YOU COME, TOO?
SURE, I MEAN, SHOULD I?
YOU REALLY SHOULD. NOT BEING A SINGLE PARENT TODAY.
IF THAT'S WHAT YOU ALL WANT?
NOTHING MORE.
IS DAD...WILL ARTHUR BE THERE...?
I HAVEN'T SEEN HIM HERE AND, Y'KNOW, I WAS JUST WONDERING...
ARTHUR IS LOST RIGHT NOW, BUT OUR HOME IS YOURS.*
WE JUST NEED TO GO AND MAKE SOME ARRANGEMENTS. I HAVE TO CALL LOIS, TOO. GIVE US A MINUTE.
*HE'S ACTUALLY TRAPPED INSIDE ATLANTIS! BUT YOU ALREADY READ AQUAMAN, RIGHT?

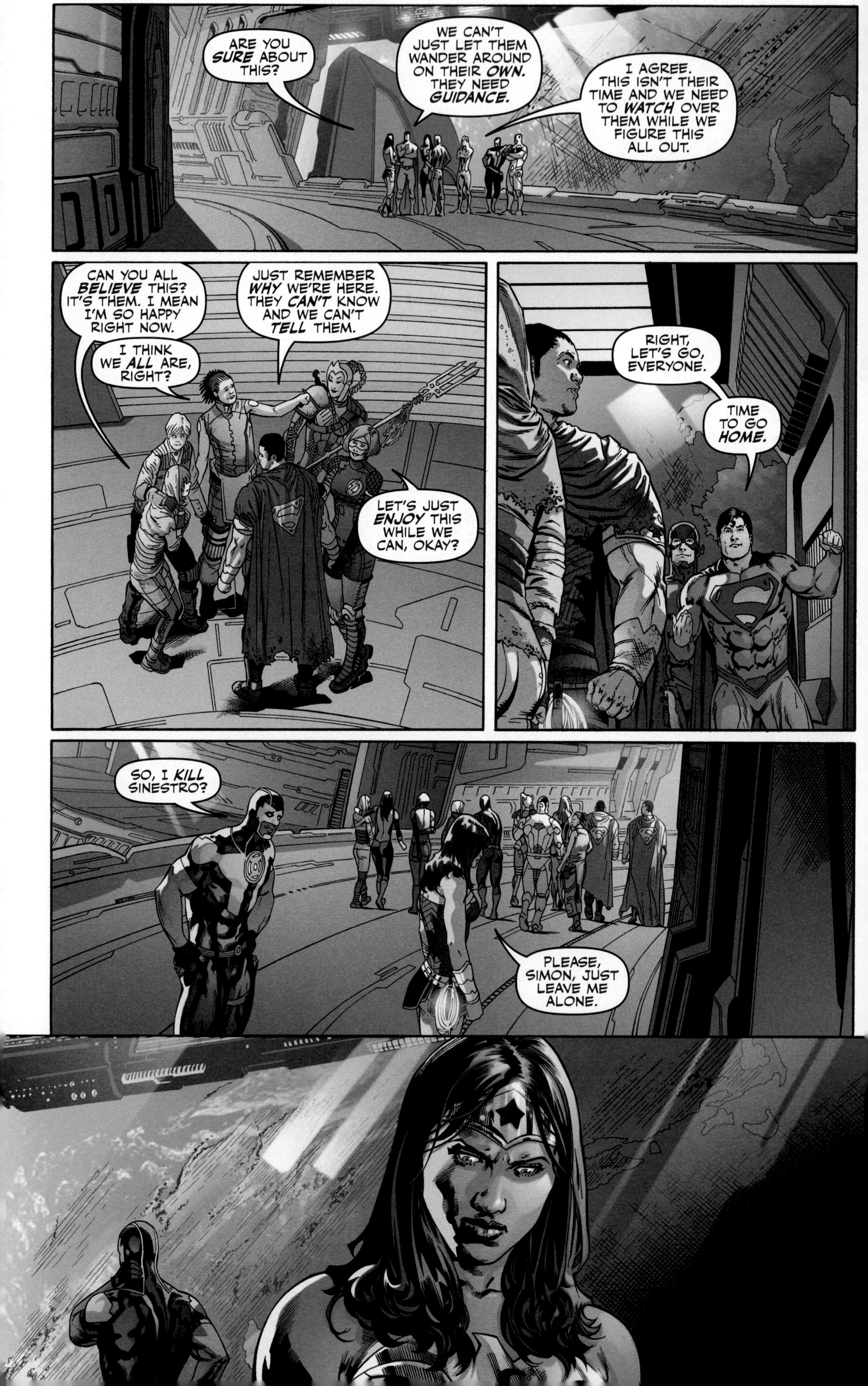
ARE YOU SURE ABOUT THIS?
WE CAN'T JUST LET THEM WANDER AROUND ON THEIR OWN. THEY NEED GUIDANCE.
I AGREE. THIS ISN'T THEIR TIME AND WE NEED TO WATCH OVER THEM WHILE WE FIGURE THIS ALL OUT.
CAN YOU ALL BELIEVE THIS? IT'S THEM. I MEAN I'M SO HAPPY RIGHT NOW.
I THINK WE ALL ARE, RIGHT?
JUST REMEMBER WHY WE'RE HERE. THEY CAN'T KNOW AND WE CAN'T TELL THEM.
LET'S JUST ENJOY THIS WHILE WE CAN, OKAY?
RIGHT, LET'S GO, EVERYONE.
TIME TO GO HOME.
SO, I KILL SINESTRO?
PLEASE, SIMON, JUST LEAVE ME ALONE.

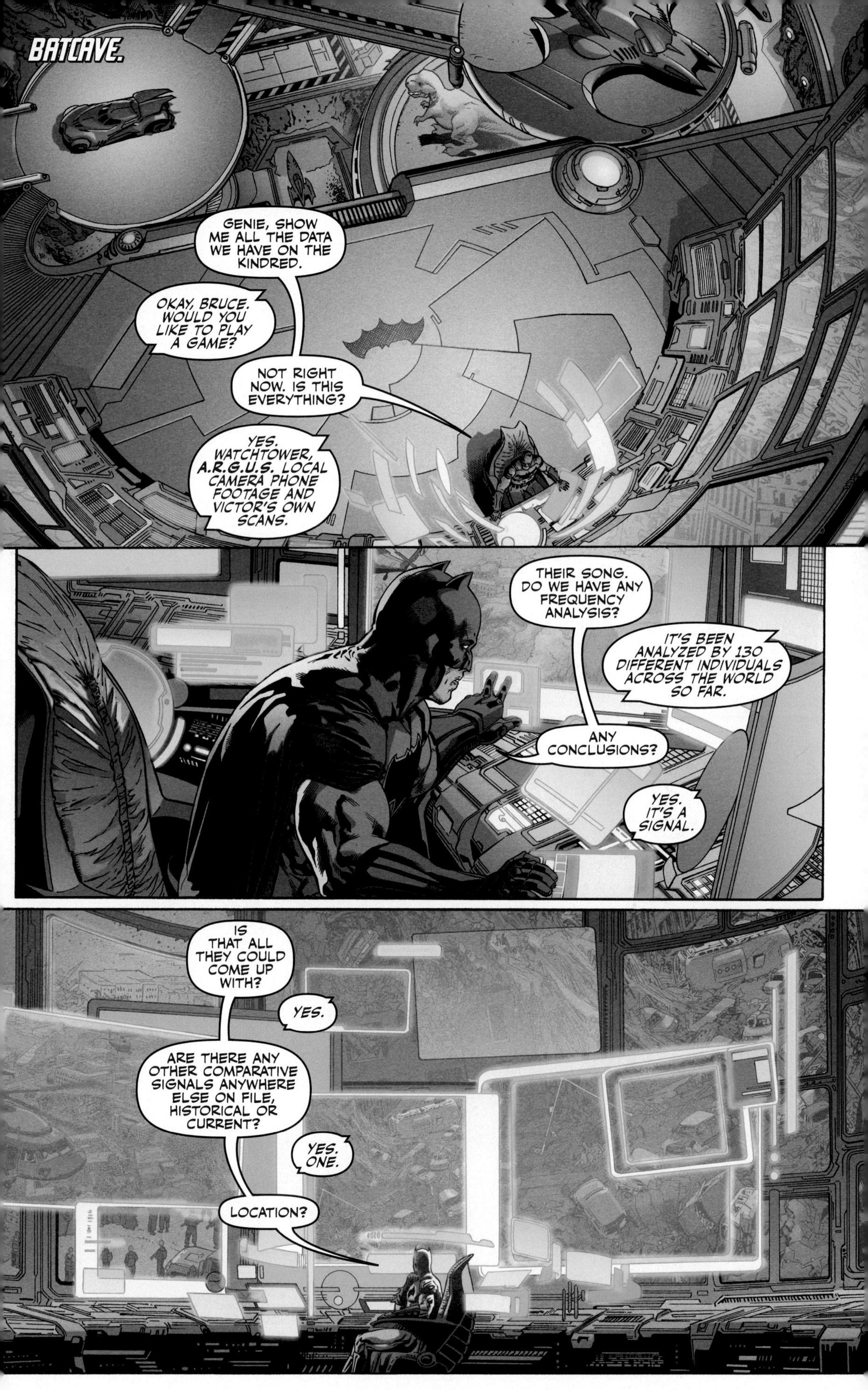
BATCAVE.
GENIE, SHOW ME ALL THE DATA WE HAVE ON THE KINDRED.
OKAY, BRUCE. WOULD YOU LIKE TO PLAY A GAME?
NOT RIGHT NOW. IS THIS EVERYTHING?
YES. WATCHTOWER, A.R.G.U.S. LOCAL CAMERA PHONE FOOTAGE AND VICTOR'S OWN SCANS.
THEIR SONG. DO WE HAVE ANY FREQUENCY ANALYSIS?
IT'S BEEN ANALYZED BY 130 DIFFERENT INDIVIDUALS ACROSS THE WORLD SO FAR.
ANY CONCLUSIONS?
YES. IT'S A SIGNAL.
IS THAT ALL THEY COULD COME UP WITH?
YES.
ARE THERE ANY OTHER COMPARATIVE SIGNALS ANYWHERE ELSE ON FILE, HISTORICAL OR CURRENT?
YES. ONE.
LOCATION?

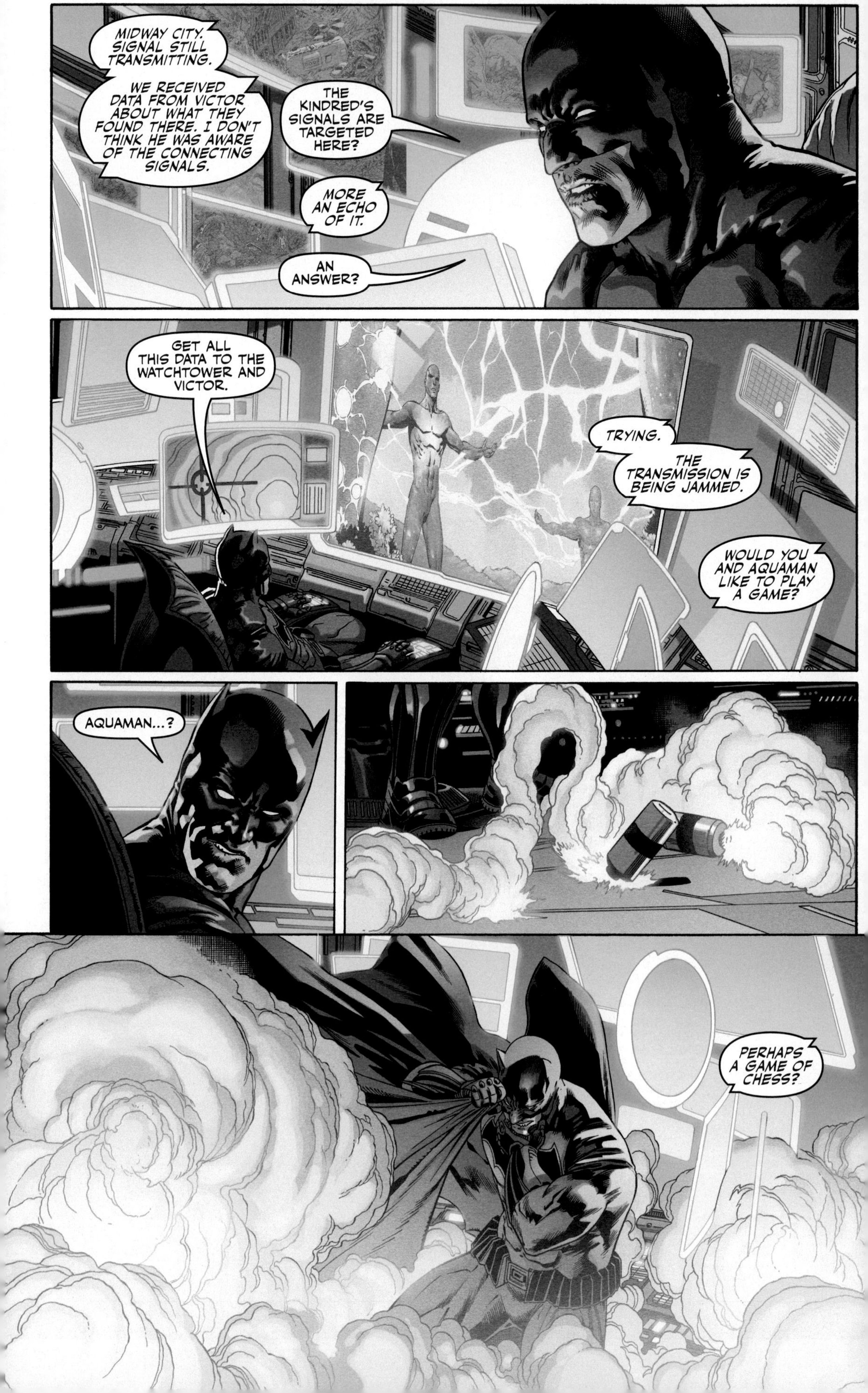
MIDWAY CITY. SIGNAL STILL TRANSMITTING.
WE RECEIVED DATA FROM VICTOR ABOUT WHAT THEY FOUND THERE. I DON'T THINK HE WAS AWARE OF THE CONNECTING SIGNALS.
THE KINDRED'S SIGNALS ARE TARGETED HERE?
MORE AN ECHO OF IT.
AN ANSWER?
GET ALL THIS DATA TO THE WATCHTOWER AND VICTOR.
TRYING.
THE TRANSMISSION IS BEING JAMMED.
WOULD YOU AND AQUAMAN LIKE TO PLAY A GAME?
AQUAMAN...?
PERHAPS A GAME OF CHESS?

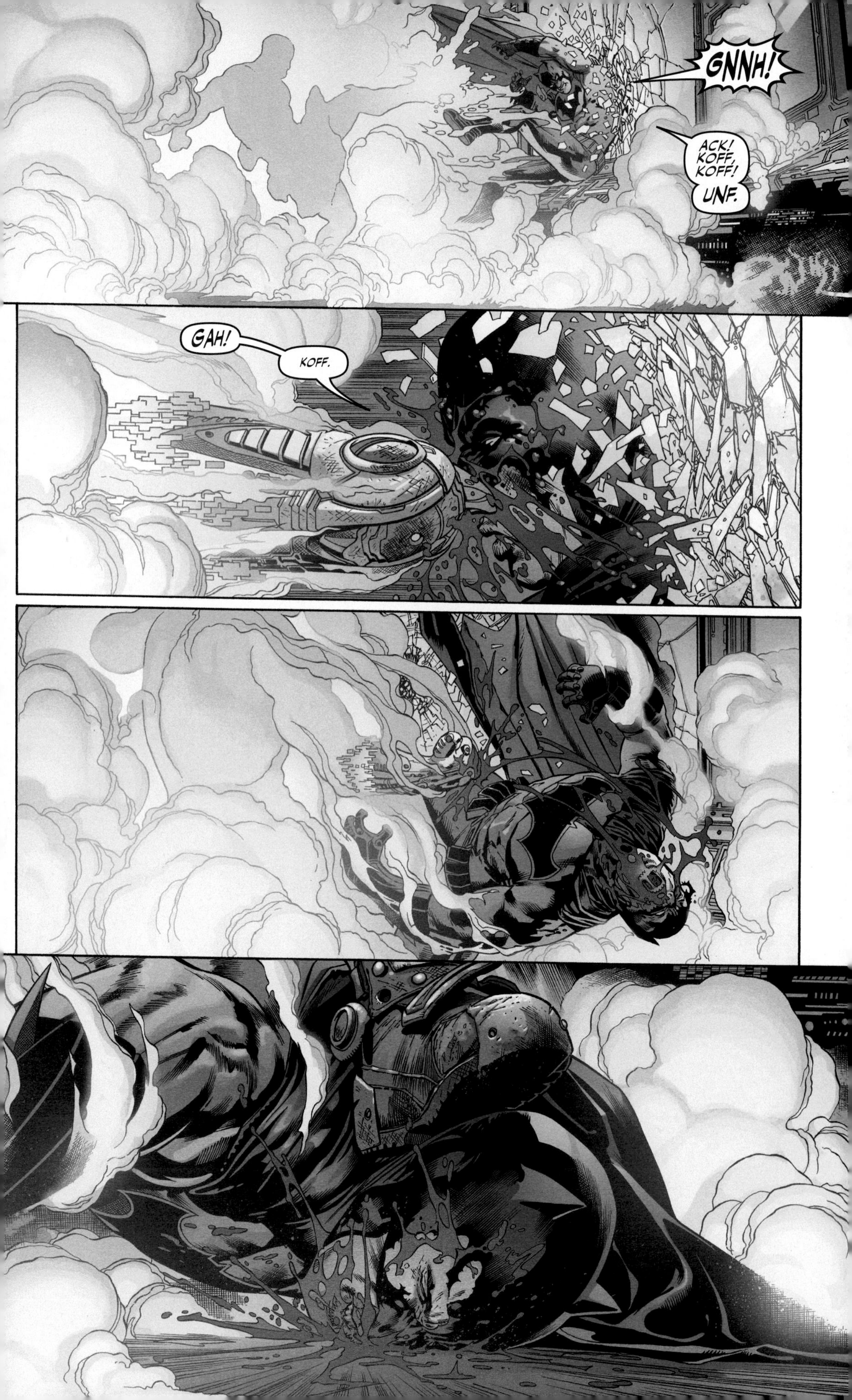
GNNH!
ACK! KOFF, KOFF!
UNF.
GAH!
KOFF.

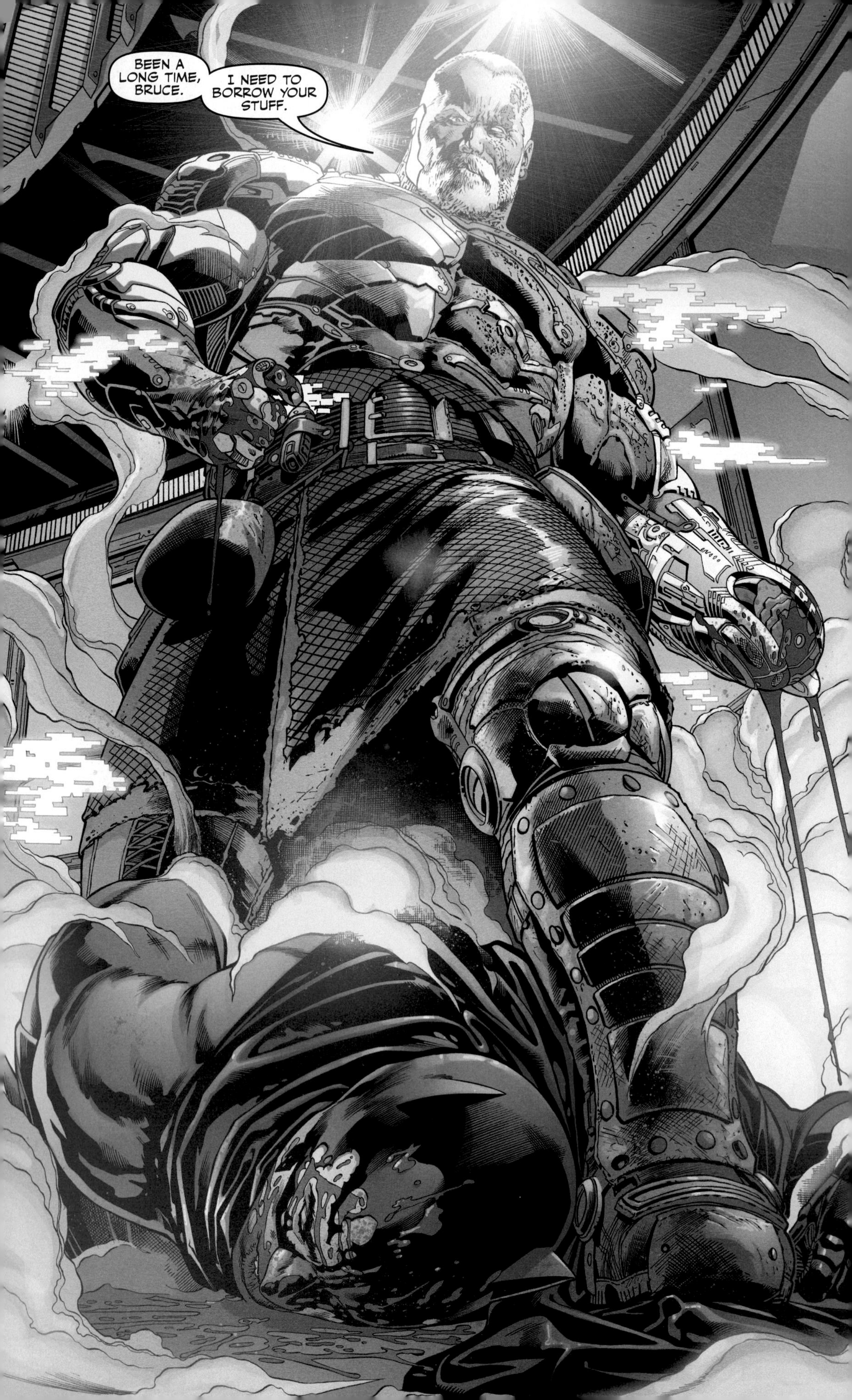
BEEN A LONG TIME, BRUCE.
I NEED TO BORROW YOUR STUFF.

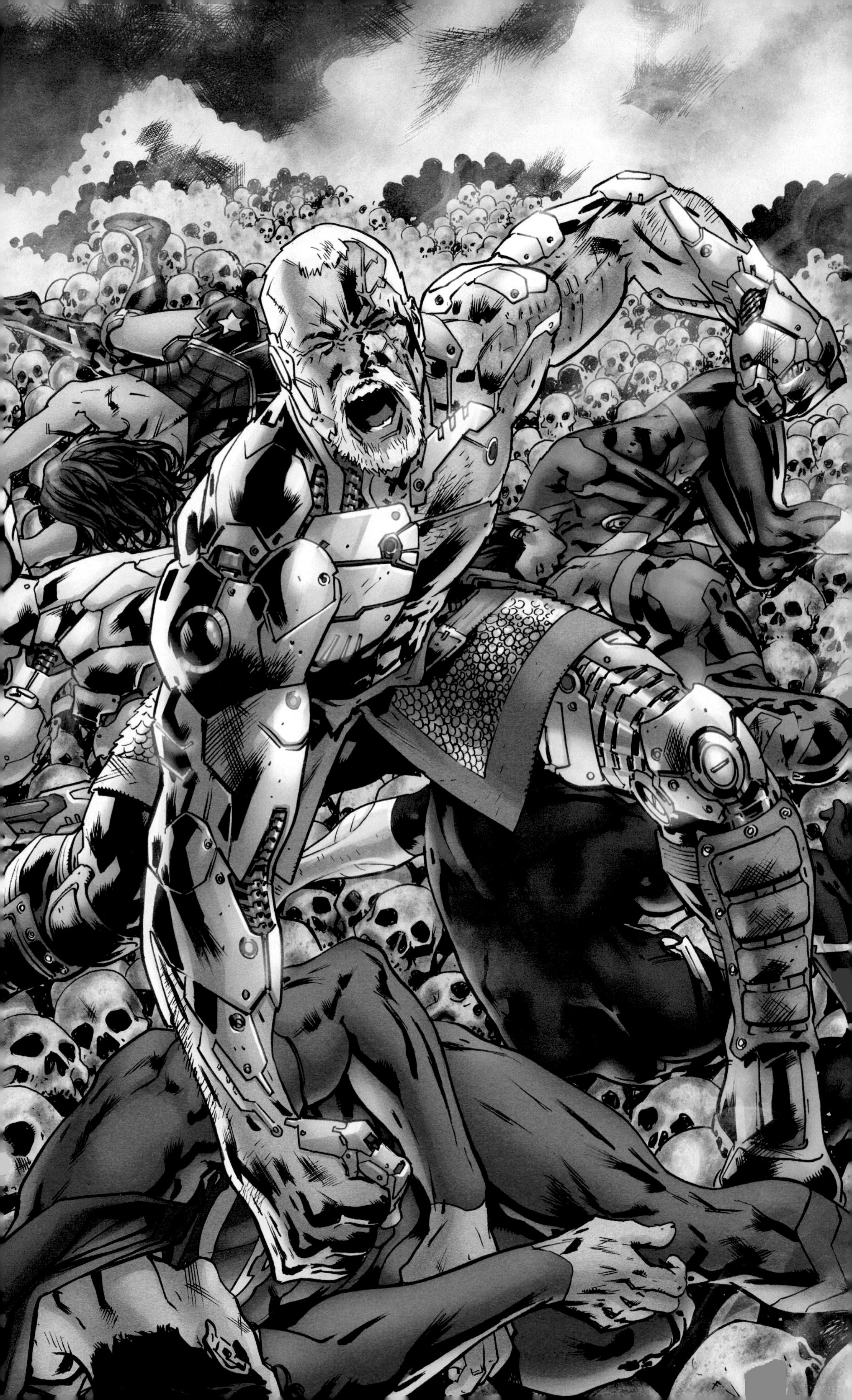

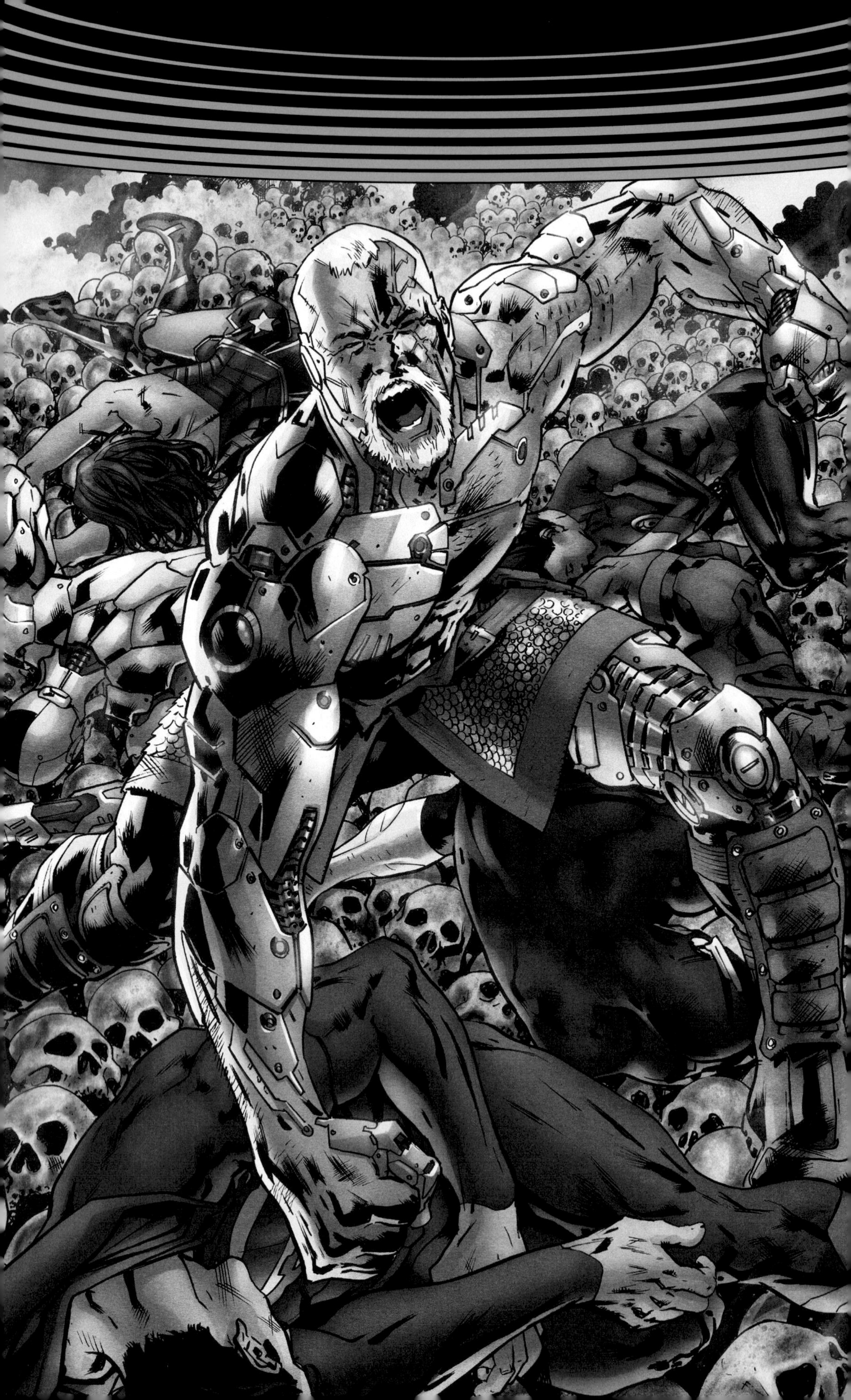

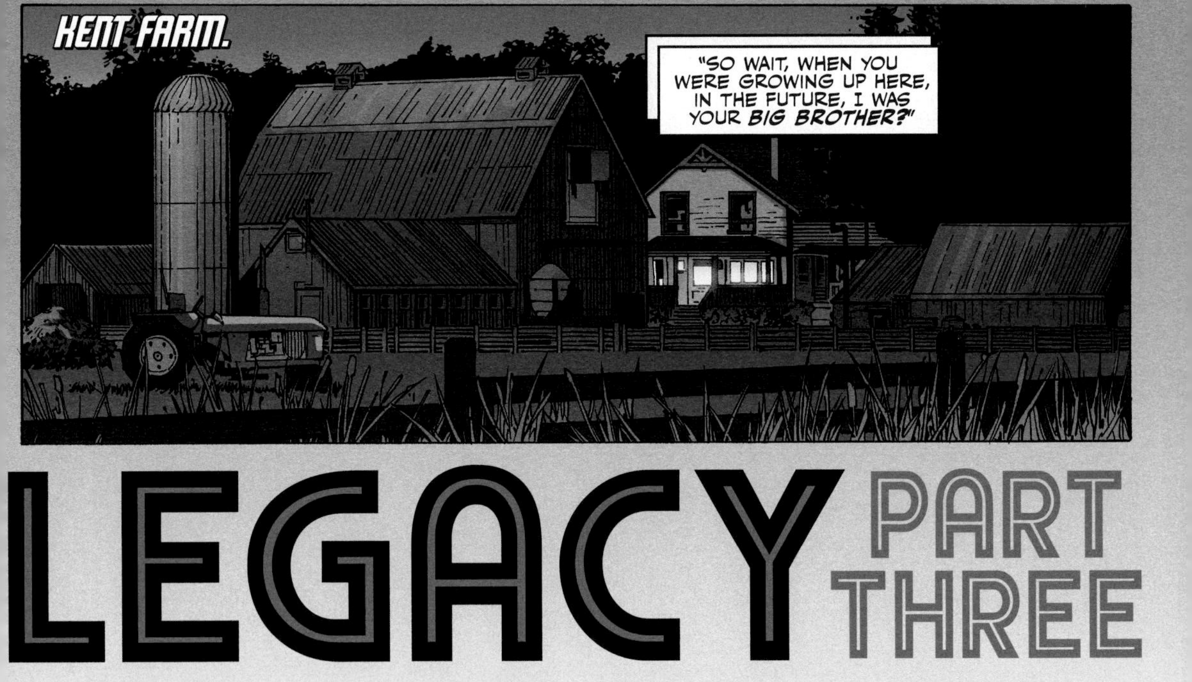
KENT FARM.
"SO WAIT, WHEN YOU WERE GROWING UP HERE, IN THE FUTURE, I WAS YOUR BIG BROTHER?"

LEGACY PART THREE

BRYAN HITCH WRITER **FERNANDO PASARIN** PENCILLER **BATT** INKER

COLORED by BRAD ANDERSON | LETTERED by RICHARD STARKINGS & COMICRAFT'S JIMMY | COVER by BRYAN HITCH & ALEX SINCLAIR | VARIANT COVER by NICK BRADSHAW & ALEX SINCLAIR | ASSOCIATE ED. AMEDEO TURTURRO | EDITOR BRIAN CUNNINGHAM

SUPERMAN created by JERRY SIEGEL and JOE SHUSTER. By special arrangement with the JERRY SIEGEL FAMILY. AQUAMAN created by PAUL NORRIS.

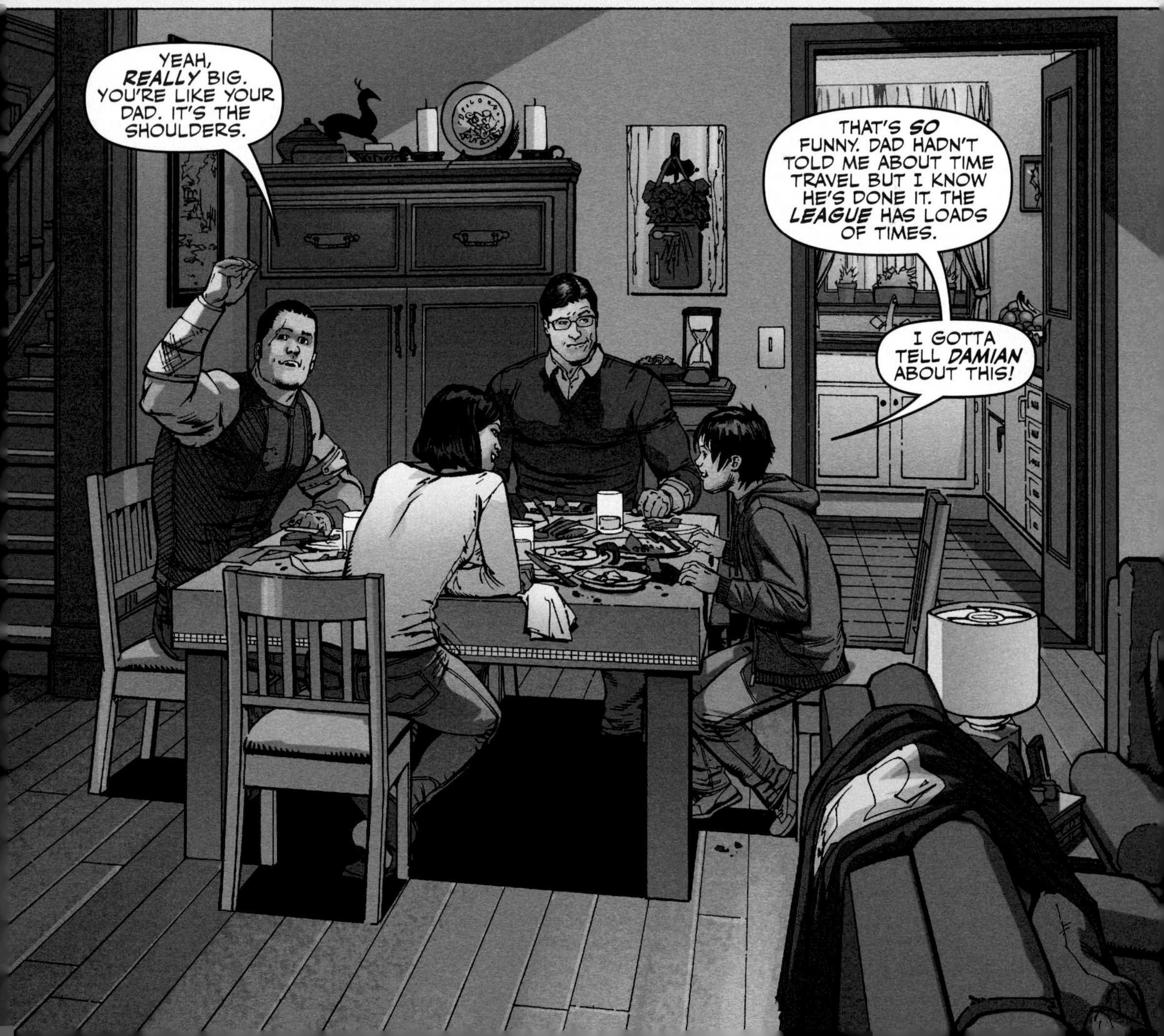
YEAH, REALLY BIG. YOU'RE LIKE YOUR DAD. IT'S THE SHOULDERS.
THAT'S SO FUNNY. DAD HADN'T TOLD ME ABOUT TIME TRAVEL BUT I KNOW HE'S DONE IT. THE LEAGUE HAS LOADS OF TIMES.
I GOTTA TELL DAMIAN ABOUT THIS!

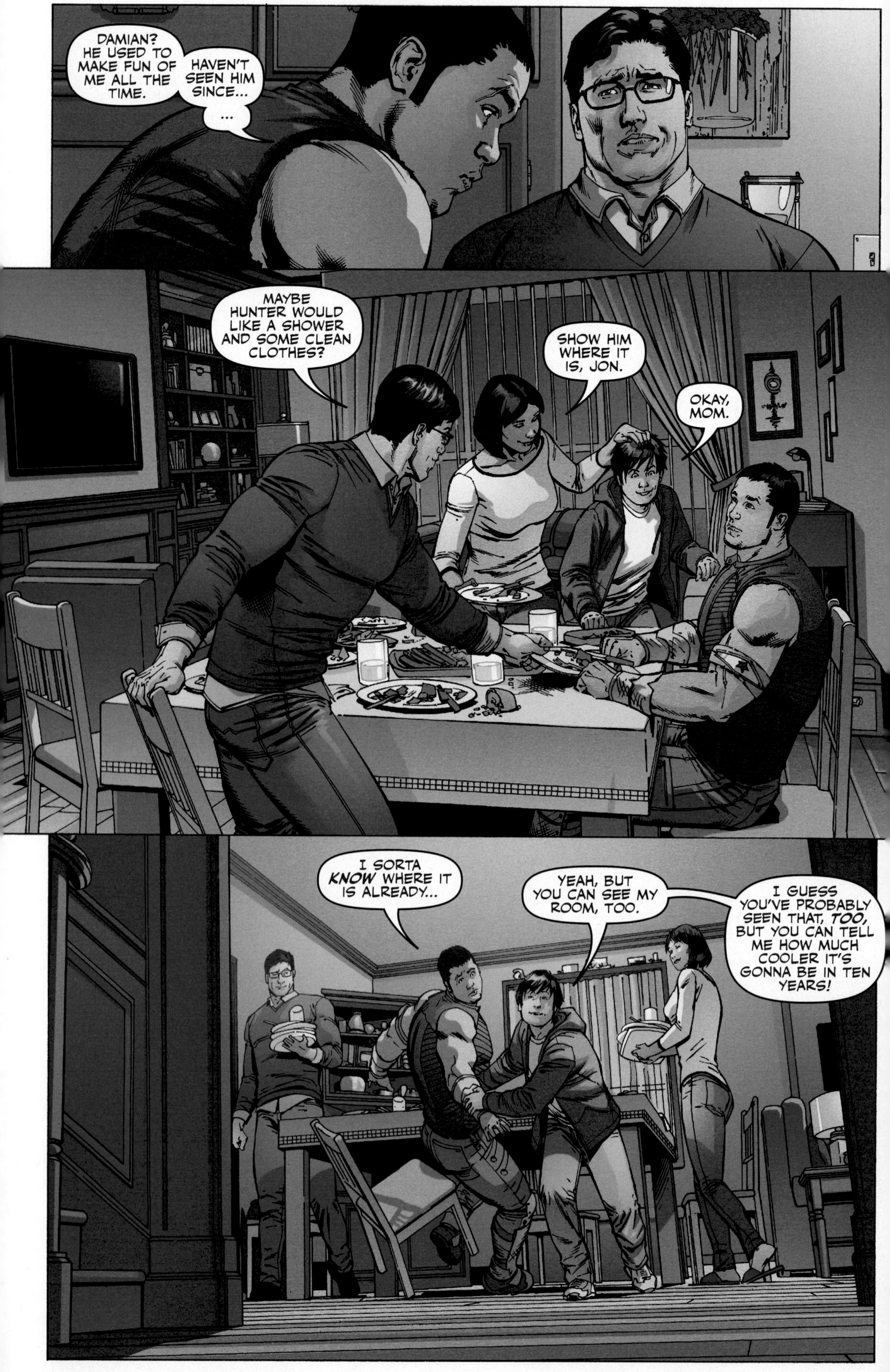
DAMIAN? HE USED TO MAKE FUN OF ME ALL THE TIME.
HAVEN'T SEEN HIM SINCE...
...
MAYBE HUNTER WOULD LIKE A SHOWER AND SOME CLEAN CLOTHES?
SHOW HIM WHERE IT IS, JON.
OKAY, MOM.
I SORTA KNOW WHERE IT IS ALREADY...
YEAH, BUT YOU CAN SEE MY ROOM, TOO.
I GUESS YOU'VE PROBABLY SEEN THAT, TOO, BUT YOU CAN TELL ME HOW MUCH COOLER IT'S GONNA BE IN TEN YEARS!

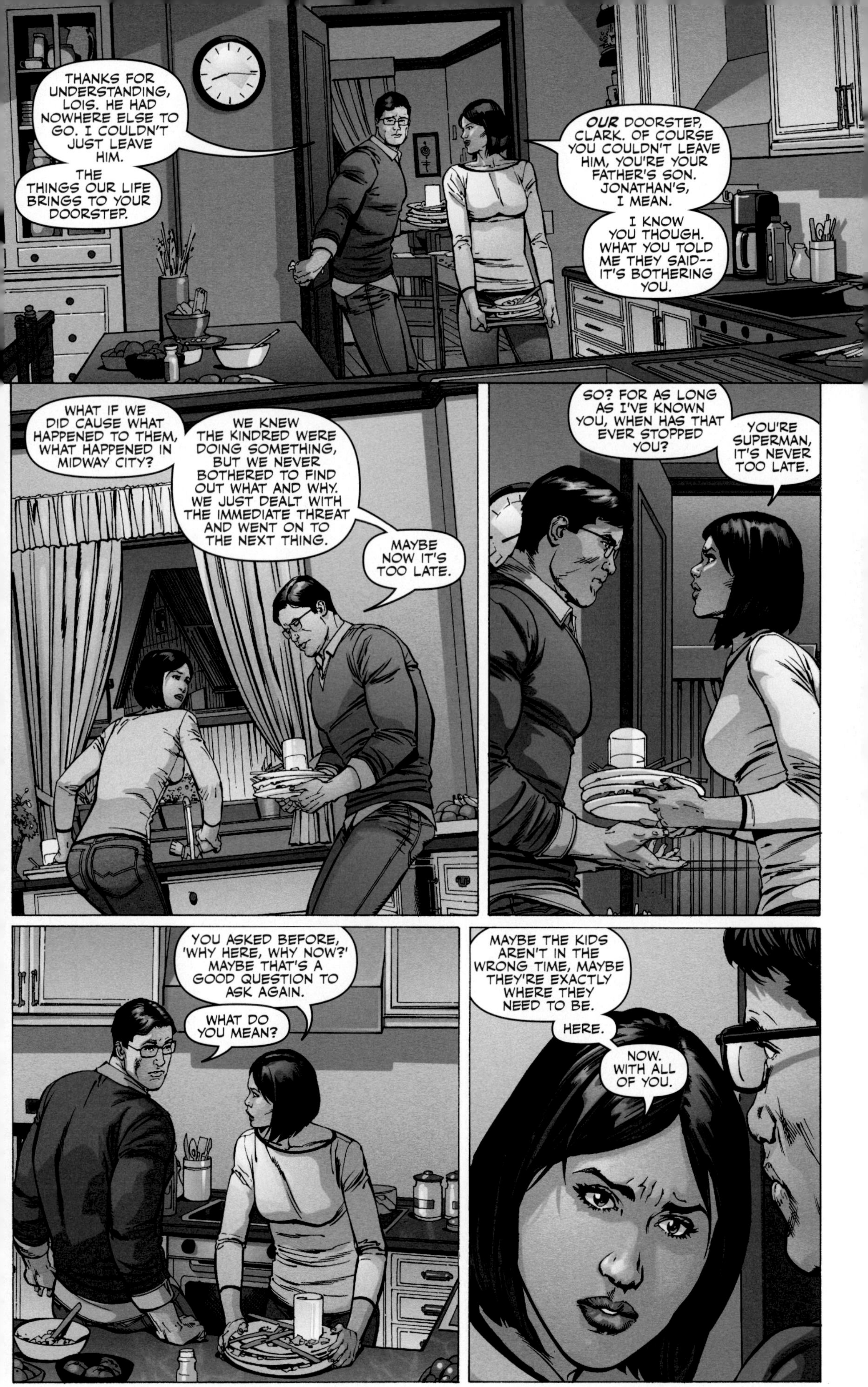
THANKS FOR UNDERSTANDING, LOIS. HE HAD NOWHERE ELSE TO GO. I COULDN'T JUST LEAVE HIM.
THE THINGS OUR LIFE BRINGS TO YOUR DOORSTEP.
OUR DOORSTEP, CLARK. OF COURSE YOU COULDN'T LEAVE HIM, YOU'RE YOUR FATHER'S SON. JONATHAN'S, I MEAN.
I KNOW YOU THOUGH. WHAT YOU TOLD ME THEY SAID-- IT'S BOTHERING YOU.
WHAT IF WE DID CAUSE WHAT HAPPENED TO THEM, WHAT HAPPENED IN MIDWAY CITY?
WE KNEW THE KINDRED WERE DOING SOMETHING, BUT WE NEVER BOTHERED TO FIND OUT WHAT AND WHY. WE JUST DEALT WITH THE IMMEDIATE THREAT AND WENT ON TO THE NEXT THING.
MAYBE NOW IT'S TOO LATE.
SO? FOR AS LONG AS I'VE KNOWN YOU, WHEN HAS THAT EVER STOPPED YOU?
YOU'RE SUPERMAN, IT'S NEVER TOO LATE.
YOU ASKED BEFORE, 'WHY HERE, WHY NOW?' MAYBE THAT'S A GOOD QUESTION TO ASK AGAIN.
WHAT DO YOU MEAN?
MAYBE THE KIDS AREN'T IN THE WRONG TIME, MAYBE THEY'RE EXACTLY WHERE THEY NEED TO BE.
HERE.
NOW. WITH ALL OF YOU.

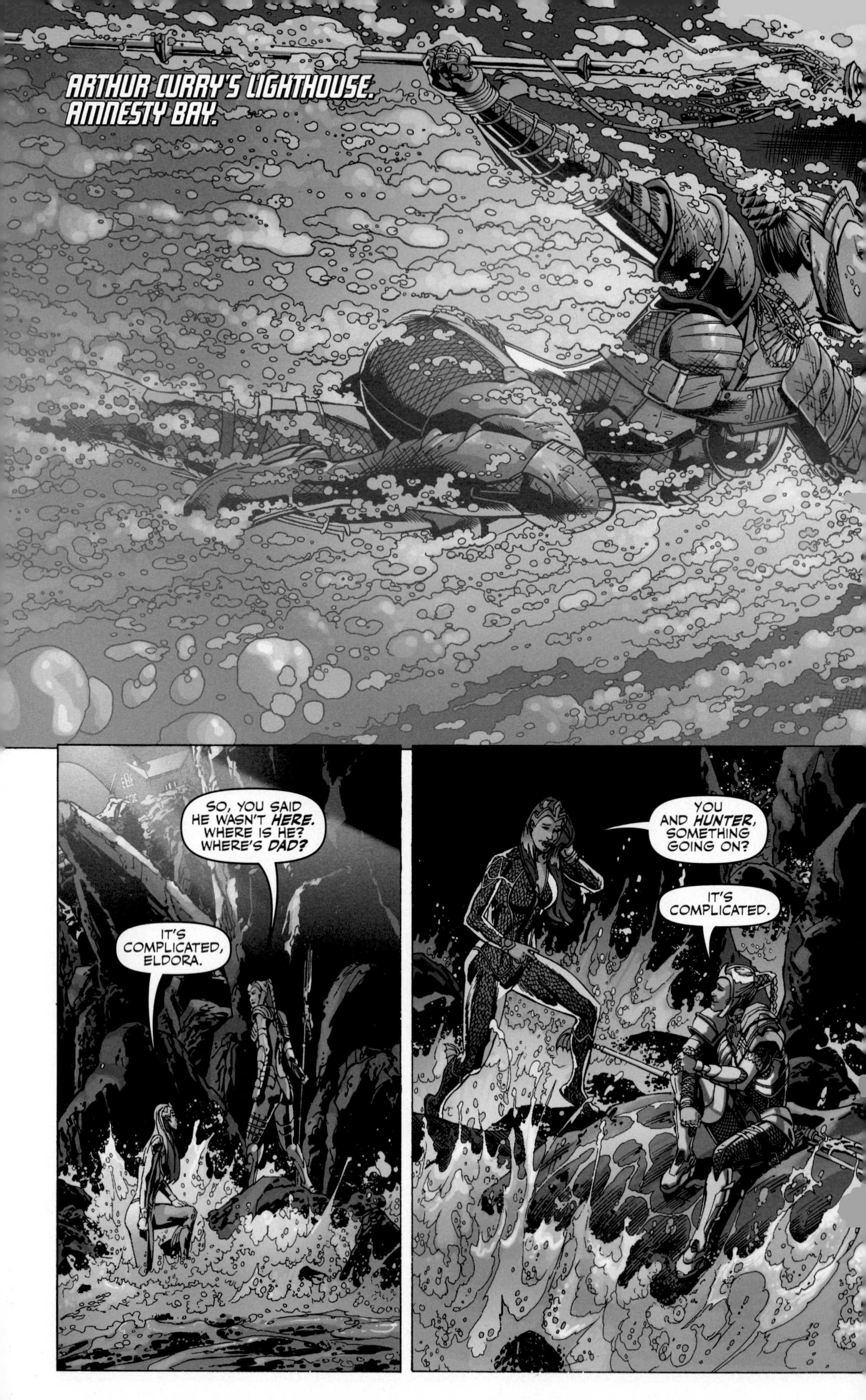
ARTHUR CURRY'S LIGHTHOUSE. AMNESTY BAY.
SO, YOU SAID HE WASN'T HERE. WHERE IS HE? WHERE'S DAD?
IT'S COMPLICATED, ELDORA.
YOU AND HUNTER, SOMETHING GOING ON?
IT'S COMPLICATED.

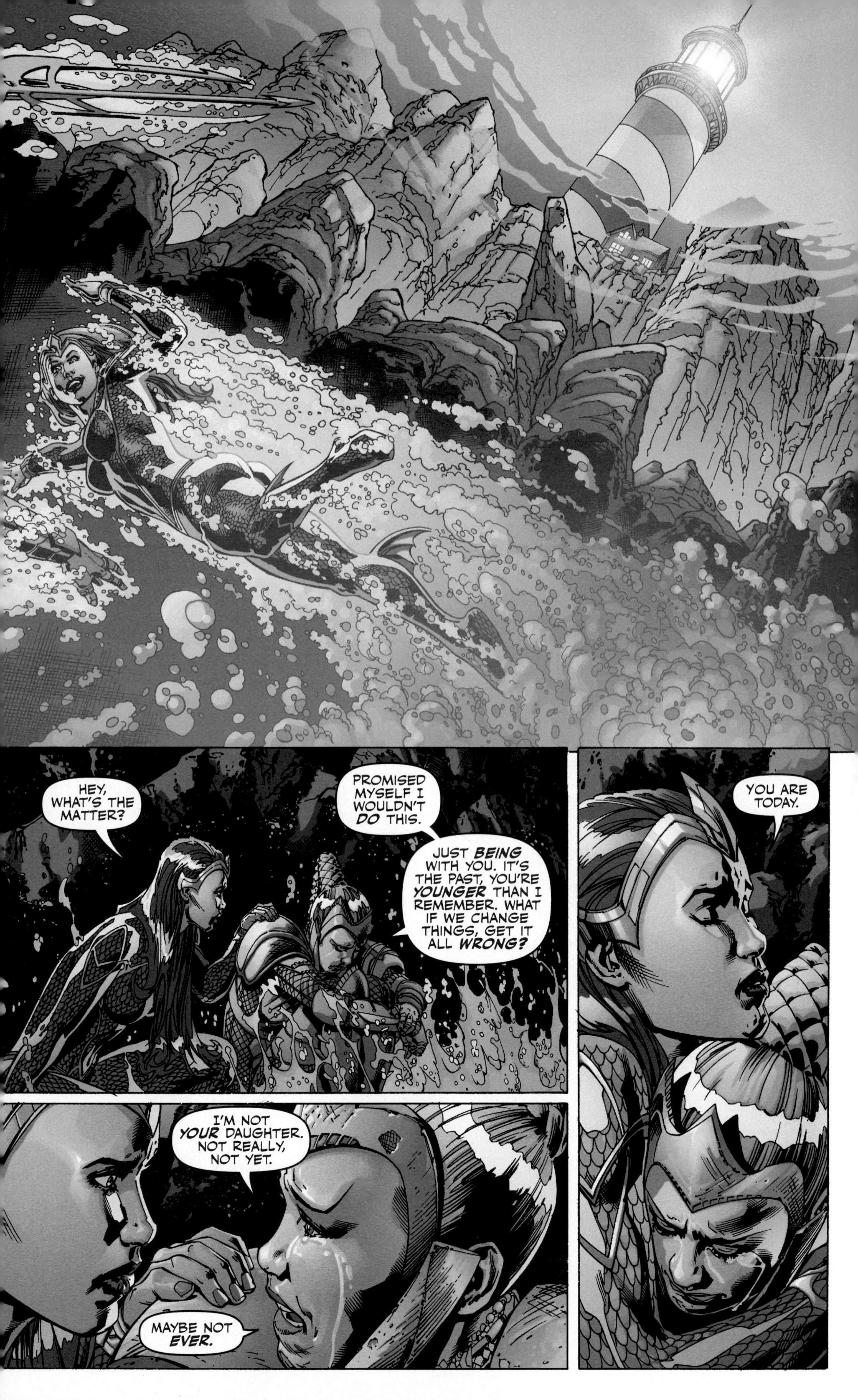
HEY, WHAT'S THE MATTER?
PROMISED MYSELF I WOULDN'T DO THIS.
JUST BEING WITH YOU. IT'S THE PAST, YOU'RE YOUNGER THAN I REMEMBER. WHAT IF WE CHANGE THINGS, GET IT ALL WRONG?
YOU ARE TODAY.
I'M NOT YOUR DAUGHTER. NOT REALLY, NOT YET.
MAYBE NOT EVER.

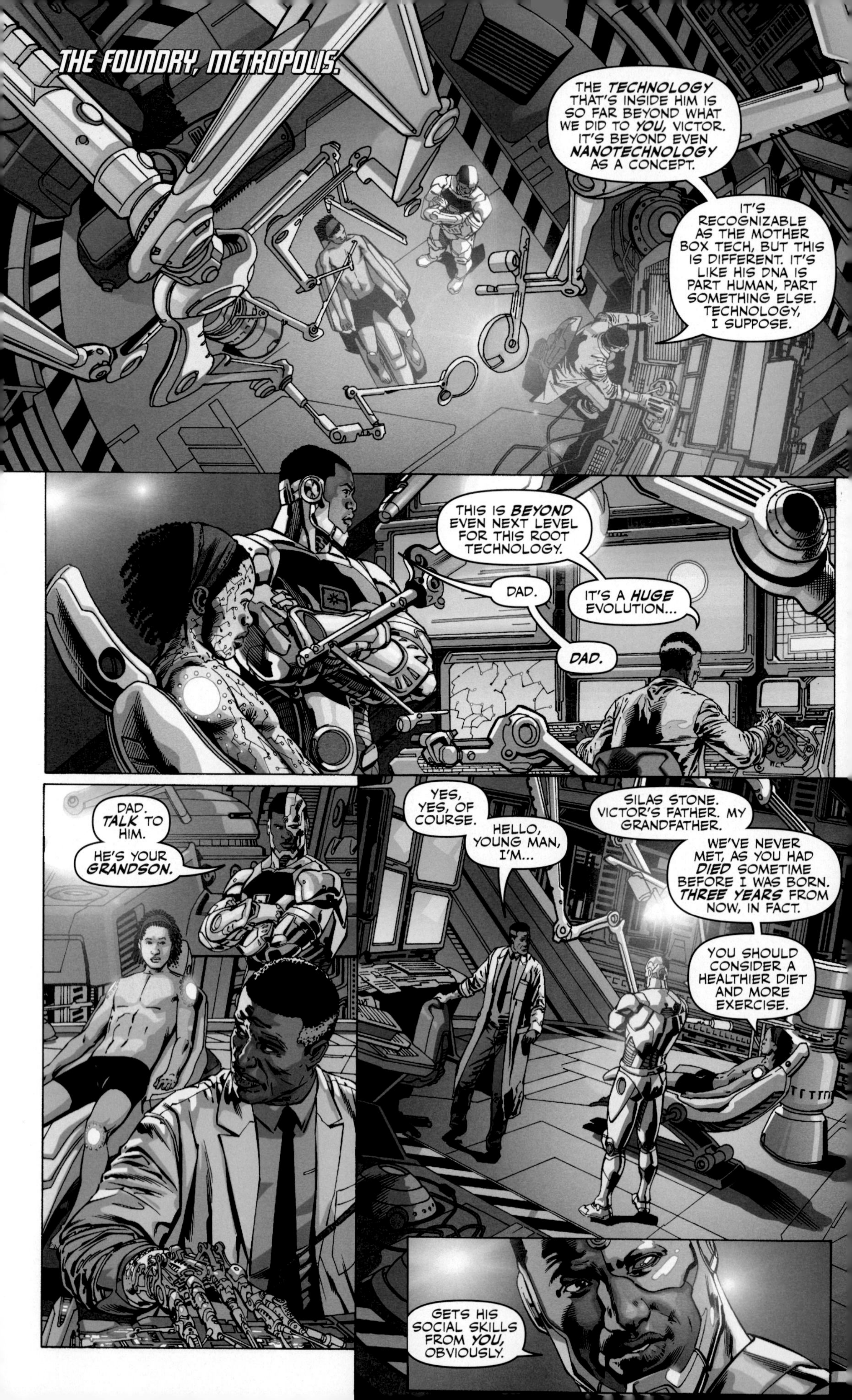
THE FOUNDRY, METROPOLIS.
THE TECHNOLOGY THAT'S INSIDE HIM IS SO FAR BEYOND WHAT WE DID TO YOU, VICTOR. IT'S BEYOND EVEN NANOTECHNOLOGY AS A CONCEPT.
IT'S RECOGNIZABLE AS THE MOTHER BOX TECH, BUT THIS IS DIFFERENT. IT'S LIKE HIS DNA IS PART HUMAN, PART SOMETHING ELSE. TECHNOLOGY, I SUPPOSE.
THIS IS BEYOND EVEN NEXT LEVEL FOR THIS ROOT TECHNOLOGY.
DAD.
IT'S A HUGE EVOLUTION...
DAD.
DAD. TALK TO HIM.
HE'S YOUR GRANDSON.
YES, YES, OF COURSE.
HELLO, YOUNG MAN, I'M...
SILAS STONE. VICTOR'S FATHER. MY GRANDFATHER.
WE'VE NEVER MET, AS YOU HAD DIED SOMETIME BEFORE I WAS BORN. THREE YEARS FROM NOW, IN FACT.
YOU SHOULD CONSIDER A HEALTHIER DIET AND MORE EXERCISE.
GETS HIS SOCIAL SKILLS FROM YOU, OBVIOUSLY.

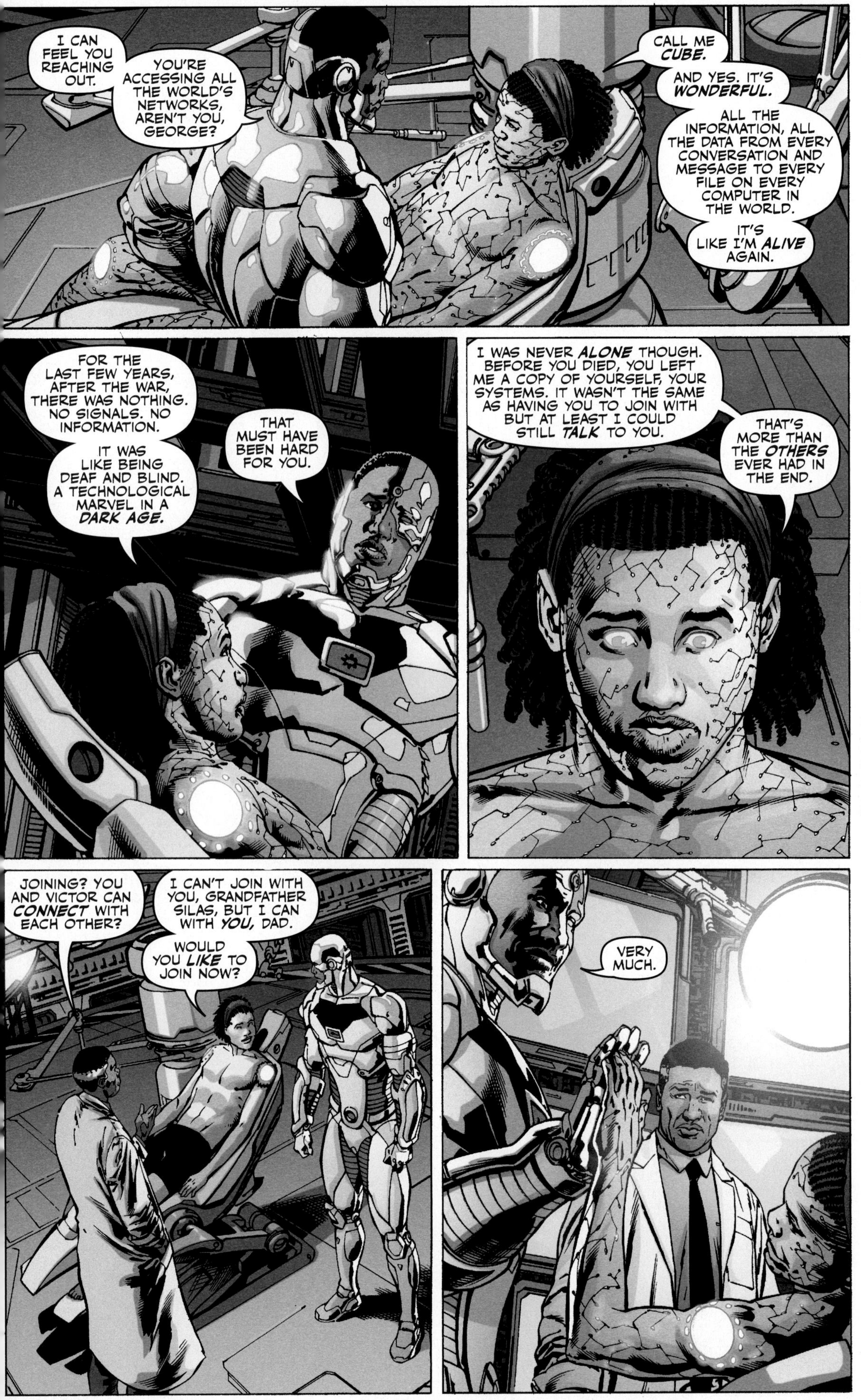
I CAN FEEL YOU REACHING OUT.
YOU'RE ACCESSING ALL THE WORLD'S NETWORKS, AREN'T YOU, GEORGE?
CALL ME CUBE.
AND YES. IT'S WONDERFUL.
ALL THE INFORMATION, ALL THE DATA FROM EVERY CONVERSATION AND MESSAGE TO EVERY FILE ON EVERY COMPUTER IN THE WORLD.
IT'S LIKE I'M ALIVE AGAIN.
FOR THE LAST FEW YEARS, AFTER THE WAR, THERE WAS NOTHING. NO SIGNALS. NO INFORMATION.
IT WAS LIKE BEING DEAF AND BLIND. A TECHNOLOGICAL MARVEL IN A DARK AGE.
THAT MUST HAVE BEEN HARD FOR YOU.
I WAS NEVER ALONE THOUGH. BEFORE YOU DIED, YOU LEFT ME A COPY OF YOURSELF, YOUR SYSTEMS. IT WASN'T THE SAME AS HAVING YOU TO JOIN WITH BUT AT LEAST I COULD STILL TALK TO YOU.
THAT'S MORE THAN THE OTHERS EVER HAD IN THE END.
JOINING? YOU AND VICTOR CAN CONNECT WITH EACH OTHER?
I CAN'T JOIN WITH YOU, GRANDFATHER SILAS, BUT I CAN WITH YOU, DAD.
WOULD YOU LIKE TO JOIN NOW?
VERY MUCH.

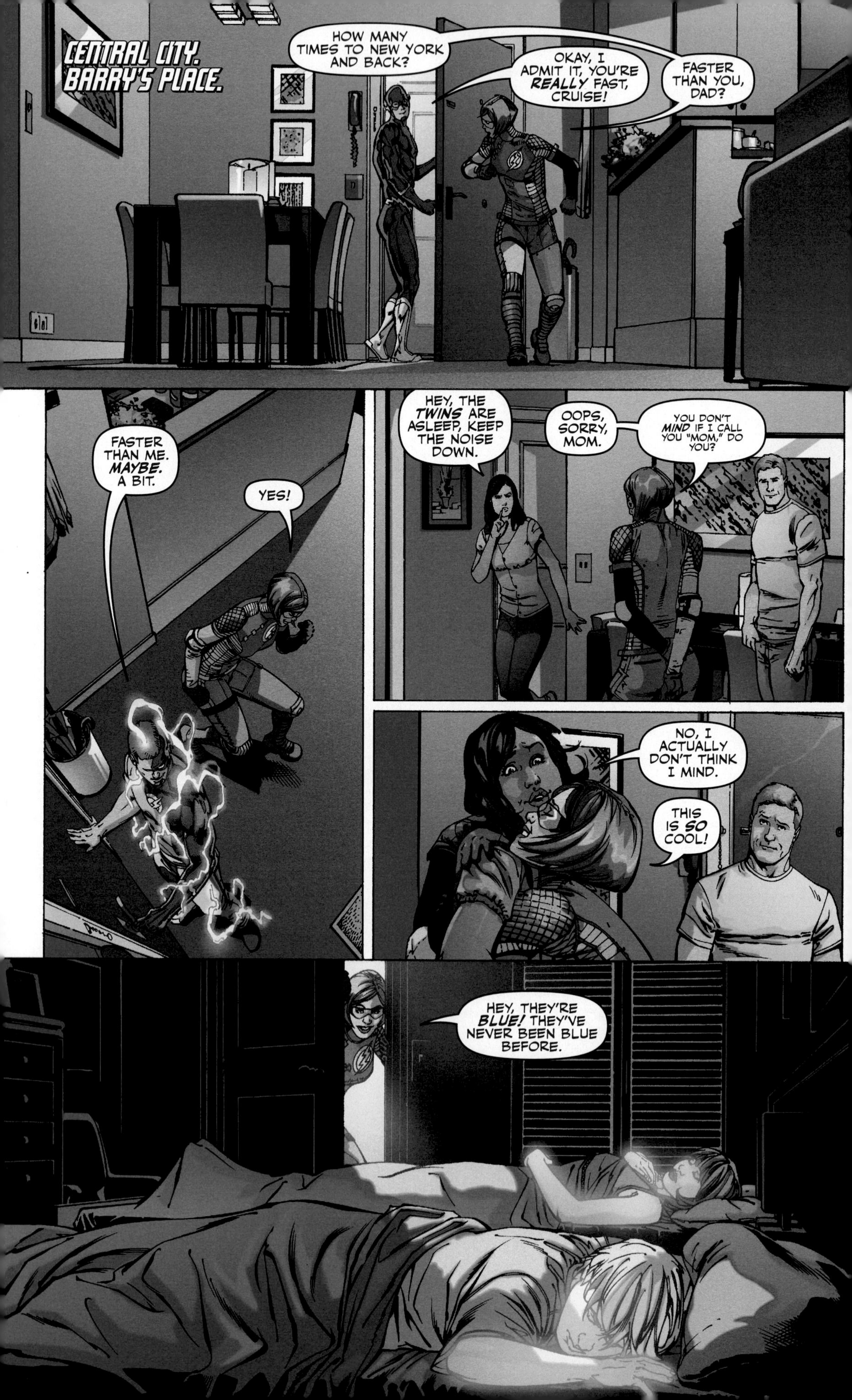
CENTRAL CITY. BARRY'S PLACE.
HOW MANY TIMES TO NEW YORK AND BACK?
OKAY, I ADMIT IT, YOU'RE REALLY FAST, CRUISE!
FASTER THAN YOU, DAD?
FASTER THAN ME. MAYBE. A BIT.
YES!
HEY, THE TWINS ARE ASLEEP, KEEP THE NOISE DOWN.
OOPS, SORRY, MOM.
YOU DON'T MIND IF I CALL YOU "MOM," DO YOU?
NO, I ACTUALLY DON'T THINK I MIND.
THIS IS SO COOL!
HEY, THEY'RE BLUE! THEY'VE NEVER BEEN BLUE BEFORE.

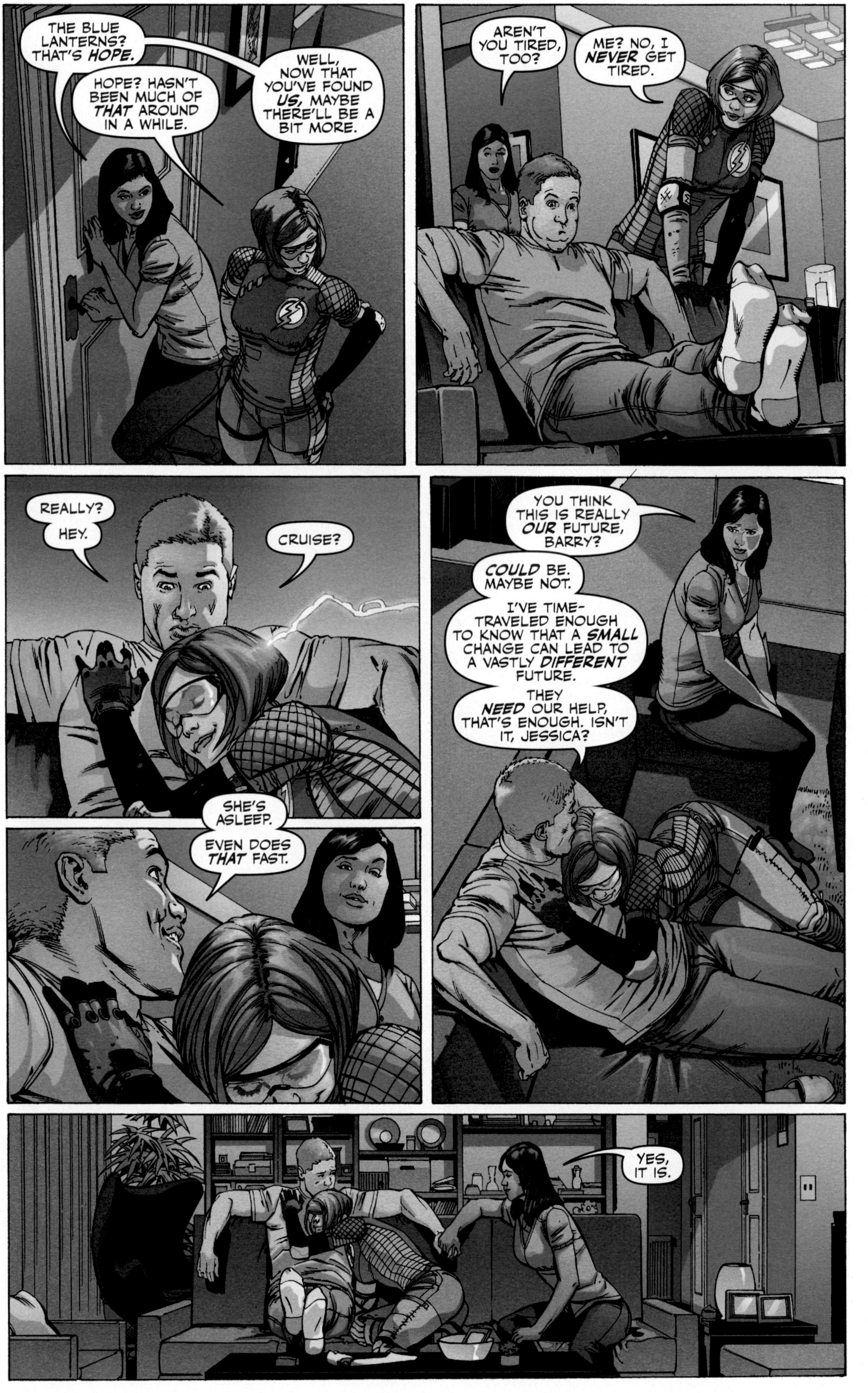
THE BLUE LANTERNS? THAT'S HOPE.
HOPE? HASN'T BEEN MUCH OF THAT AROUND IN A WHILE.
WELL, NOW THAT YOU'VE FOUND US, MAYBE THERE'LL BE A BIT MORE.
AREN'T YOU TIRED, TOO?
ME? NO, I NEVER GET TIRED.
REALLY?
HEY.
CRUISE?
SHE'S ASLEEP.
EVEN DOES THAT FAST.
YOU THINK THIS IS REALLY OUR FUTURE, BARRY?
COULD BE. MAYBE NOT.
I'VE TIME-TRAVELED ENOUGH TO KNOW THAT A SMALL CHANGE CAN LEAD TO A VASTLY DIFFERENT FUTURE.
THEY NEED OUR HELP, THAT'S ENOUGH. ISN'T IT, JESSICA?
YES, IT IS.

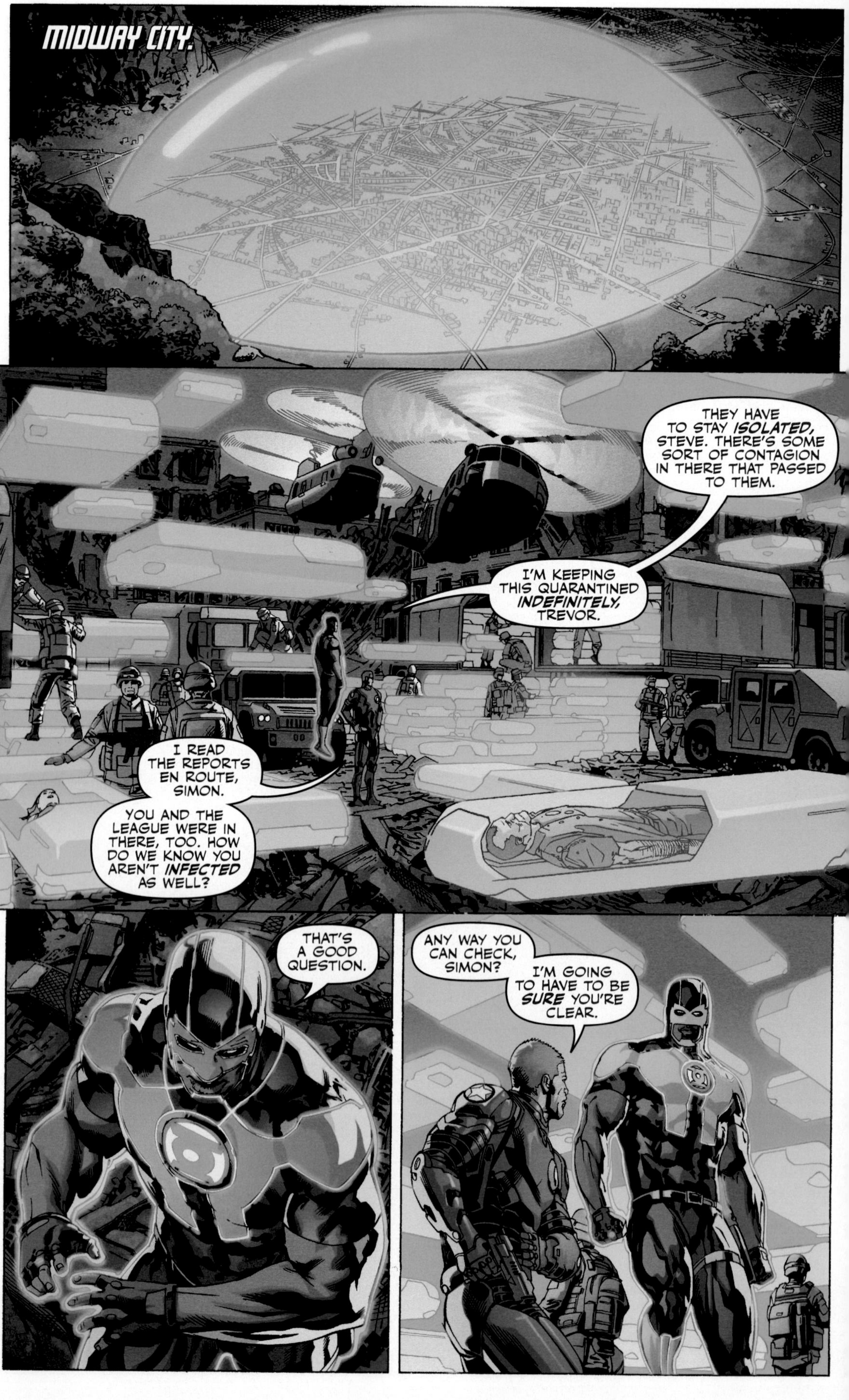
MIDWAY CITY.
THEY HAVE TO STAY ISOLATED, STEVE. THERE'S SOME SORT OF CONTAGION IN THERE THAT PASSED TO THEM.
I'M KEEPING THIS QUARANTINED INDEFINITELY, TREVOR.
I READ THE REPORTS EN ROUTE, SIMON.
YOU AND THE LEAGUE WERE IN THERE, TOO. HOW DO WE KNOW YOU AREN'T INFECTED AS WELL?
THAT'S A GOOD QUESTION.
ANY WAY YOU CAN CHECK, SIMON?
I'M GOING TO HAVE TO BE SURE YOU'RE CLEAR.

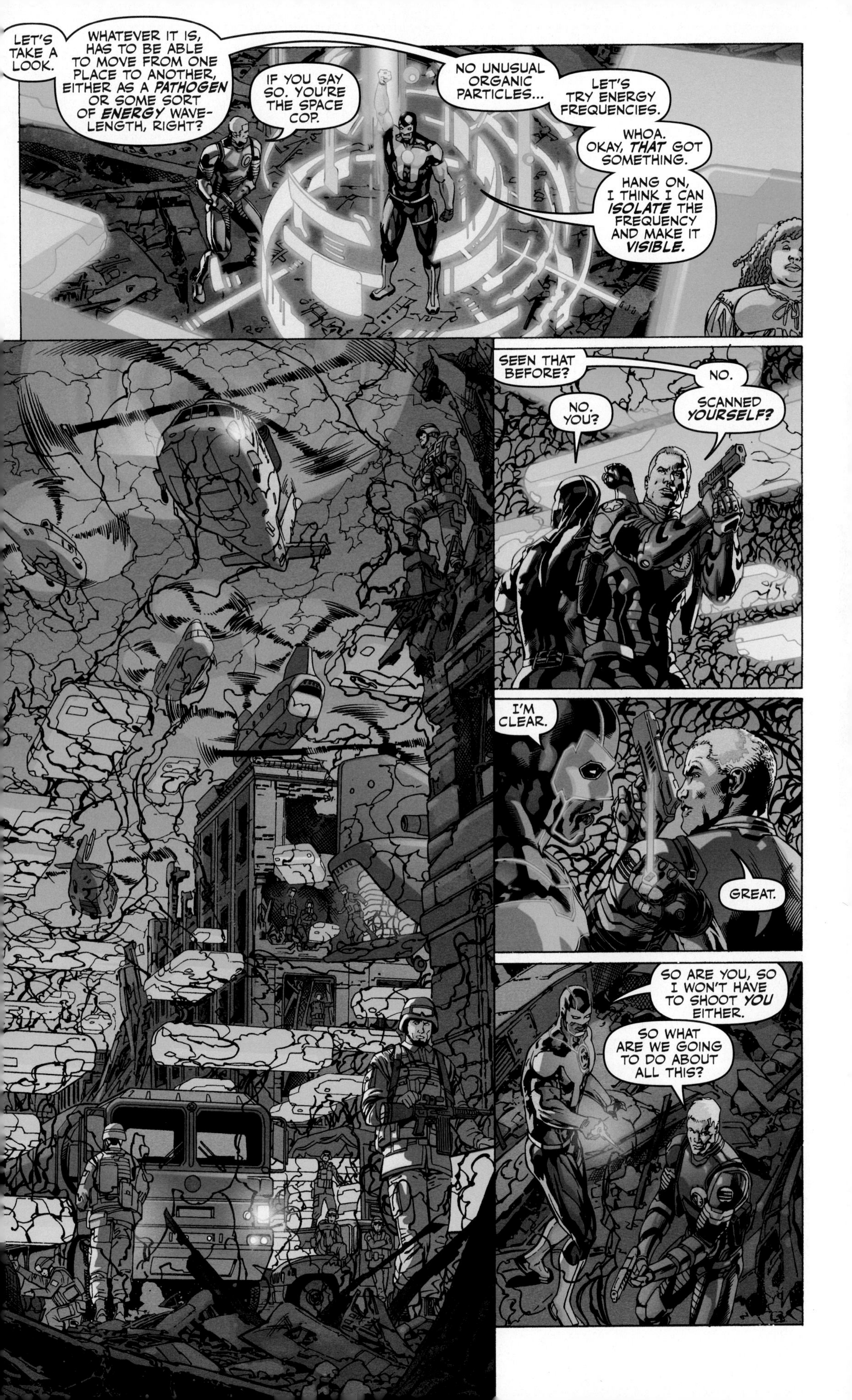
LET'S TAKE A LOOK.
WHATEVER IT IS, HAS TO BE ABLE TO MOVE FROM ONE PLACE TO ANOTHER, EITHER AS A *PATHOGEN* OR SOME SORT OF *ENERGY* WAVE-LENGTH, RIGHT?
IF YOU SAY SO. YOU'RE THE SPACE COP.
NO UNUSUAL ORGANIC PARTICLES...
LET'S TRY ENERGY FREQUENCIES.
WHOA. OKAY, *THAT* GOT SOMETHING.
HANG ON, I THINK I CAN *ISOLATE* THE FREQUENCY AND MAKE IT *VISIBLE.*
SEEN THAT BEFORE?
NO.
NO. YOU?
SCANNED *YOURSELF?*
I'M CLEAR.
GREAT.
SO ARE YOU, SO I WON'T HAVE TO SHOOT *YOU* EITHER.
SO WHAT ARE WE GOING TO DO ABOUT ALL THIS?

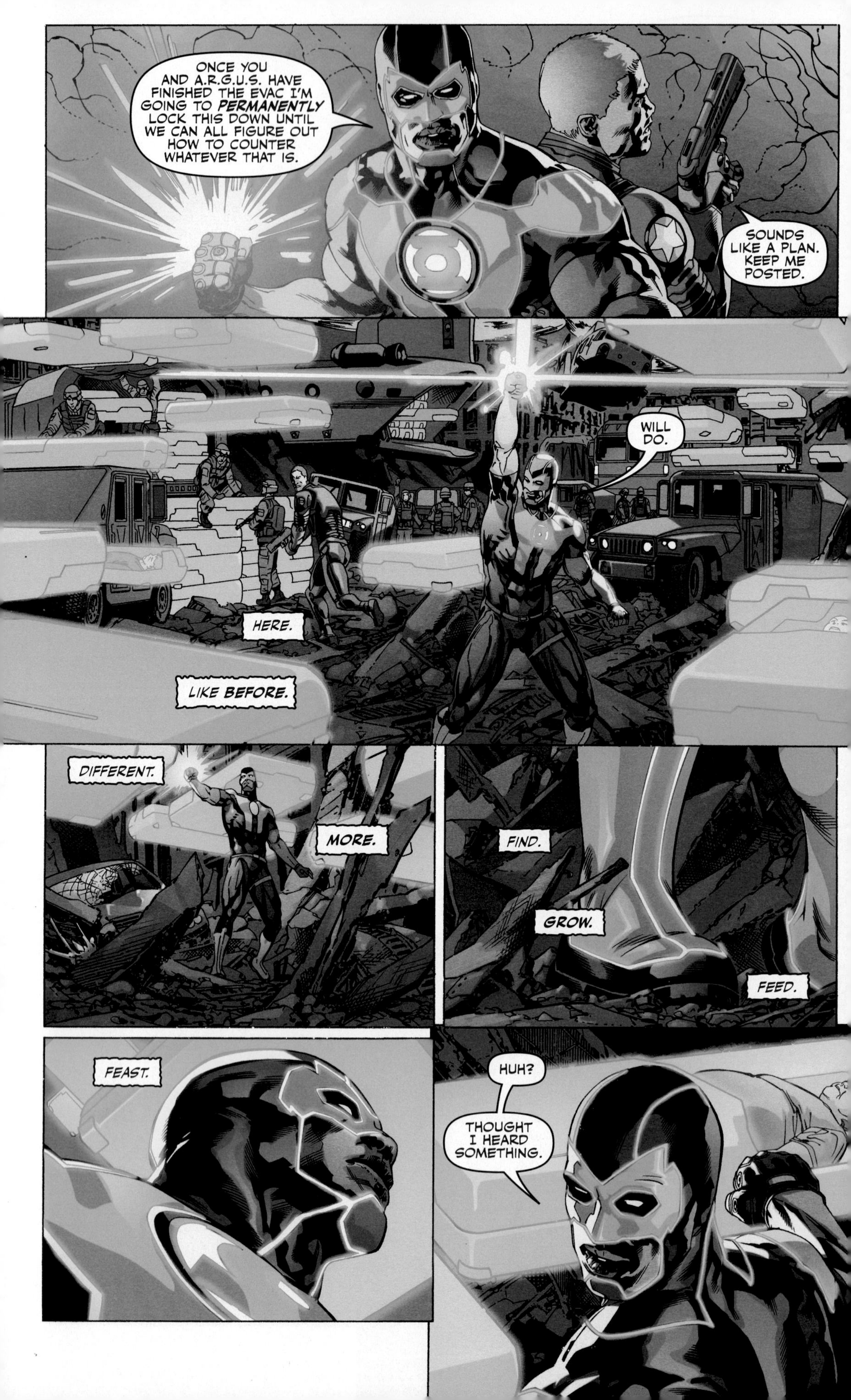
ONCE YOU AND A.R.G.U.S. HAVE FINISHED THE EVAC I'M GOING TO PERMANENTLY LOCK THIS DOWN UNTIL WE CAN ALL FIGURE OUT HOW TO COUNTER WHATEVER THAT IS.
SOUNDS LIKE A PLAN. KEEP ME POSTED.
WILL DO.
HERE.
LIKE BEFORE.
DIFFERENT.
MORE.
FIND.
GROW.
FEED.
FEAST.
HUH?
THOUGHT I HEARD SOMETHING.

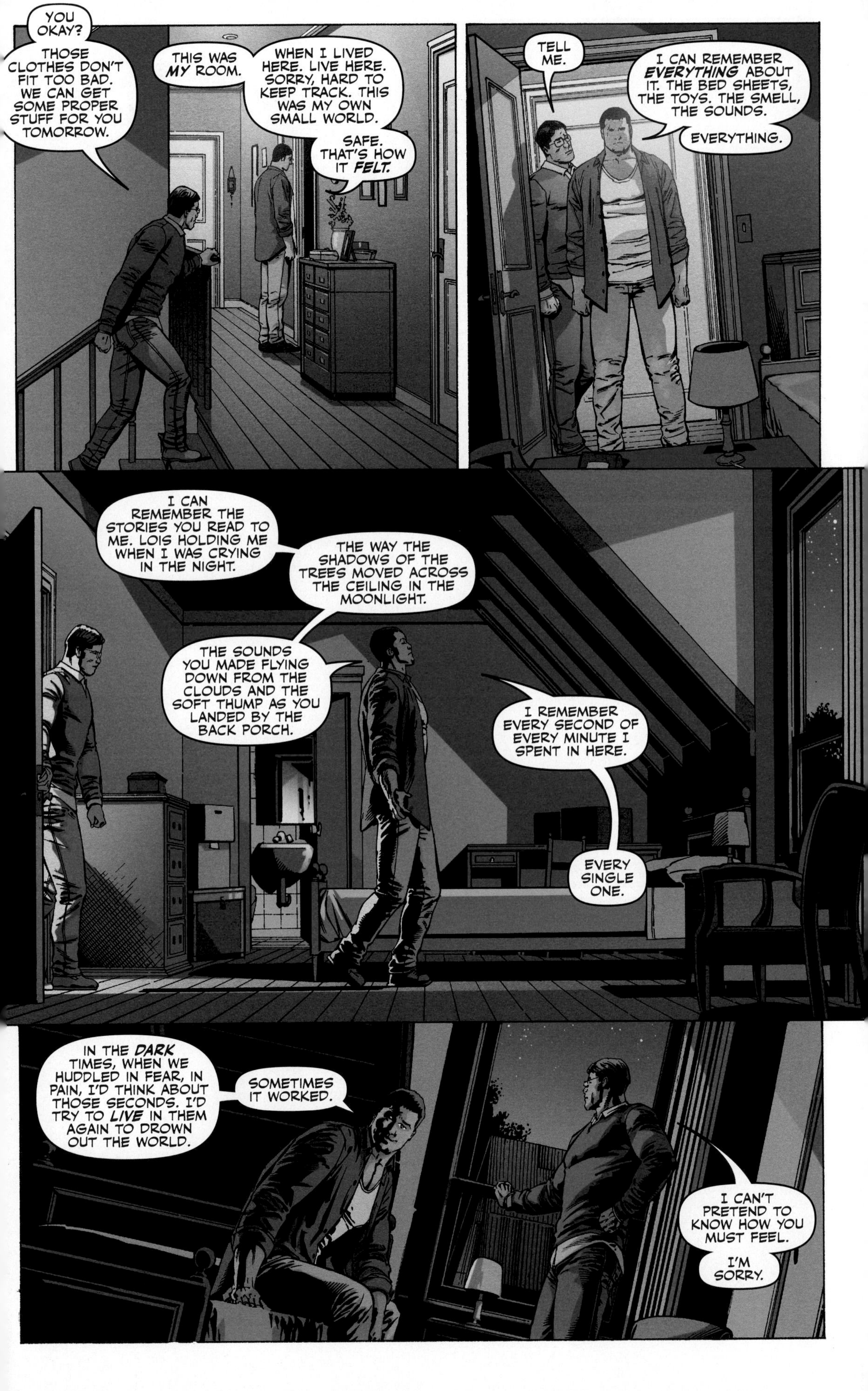
YOU OKAY?
THOSE CLOTHES DON'T FIT TOO BAD. WE CAN GET SOME PROPER STUFF FOR YOU TOMORROW.
THIS WAS *MY* ROOM.
WHEN I LIVED HERE. LIVE HERE. SORRY, HARD TO KEEP TRACK. THIS WAS MY OWN SMALL WORLD.
SAFE. THAT'S HOW IT *FELT.*
TELL ME.
I CAN REMEMBER *EVERYTHING* ABOUT IT. THE BED SHEETS, THE TOYS. THE SMELL, THE SOUNDS.
EVERYTHING.
I CAN REMEMBER THE STORIES YOU READ TO ME. LOIS HOLDING ME WHEN I WAS CRYING IN THE NIGHT.
THE WAY THE SHADOWS OF THE TREES MOVED ACROSS THE CEILING IN THE MOONLIGHT.
THE SOUNDS YOU MADE FLYING DOWN FROM THE CLOUDS AND THE SOFT THUMP AS YOU LANDED BY THE BACK PORCH.
I REMEMBER EVERY SECOND OF EVERY MINUTE I SPENT IN HERE.
EVERY SINGLE ONE.
IN THE *DARK* TIMES, WHEN WE HUDDLED IN FEAR, IN PAIN, I'D THINK ABOUT THOSE SECONDS. I'D TRY TO *LIVE* IN THEM AGAIN TO DROWN OUT THE WORLD.
SOMETIMES IT WORKED.
I CAN'T PRETEND TO KNOW HOW YOU MUST FEEL.
I'M SORRY.

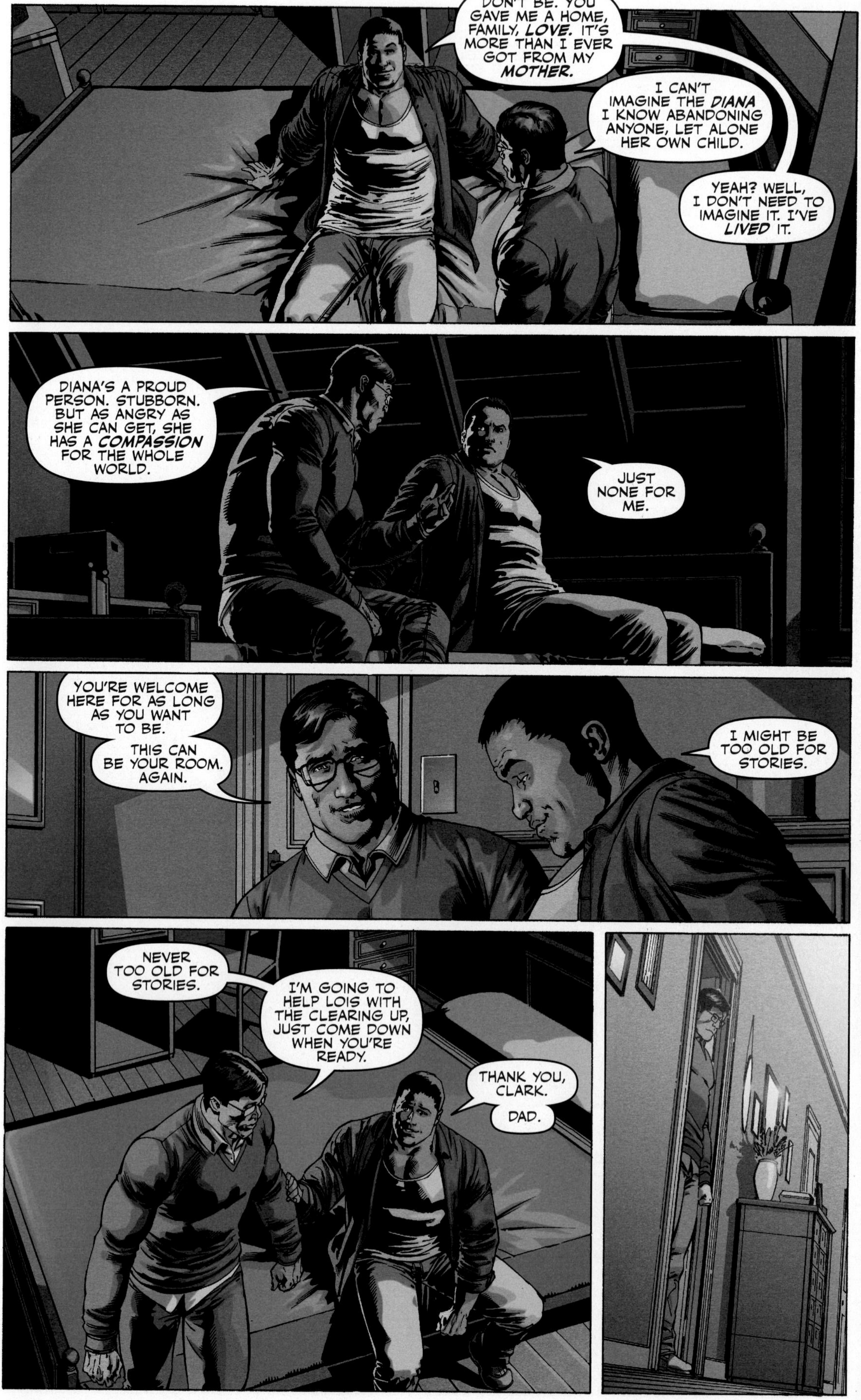
DON'T BE. YOU GAVE ME A HOME, FAMILY, *LOVE*. IT'S MORE THAN I EVER GOT FROM MY *MOTHER*.
I CAN'T IMAGINE THE *DIANA* I KNOW ABANDONING ANYONE, LET ALONE HER OWN CHILD.
YEAH? WELL, I DON'T NEED TO IMAGINE IT. I'VE *LIVED* IT.
DIANA'S A PROUD PERSON. STUBBORN. BUT AS ANGRY AS SHE CAN GET, SHE HAS A *COMPASSION* FOR THE WHOLE WORLD.
JUST NONE FOR ME.
YOU'RE WELCOME HERE FOR AS LONG AS YOU WANT TO BE.
THIS CAN BE YOUR ROOM. AGAIN.
I MIGHT BE TOO OLD FOR STORIES.
NEVER TOO OLD FOR STORIES.
I'M GOING TO HELP LOIS WITH THE CLEARING UP, JUST COME DOWN WHEN YOU'RE READY.
THANK YOU, CLARK.
DAD.

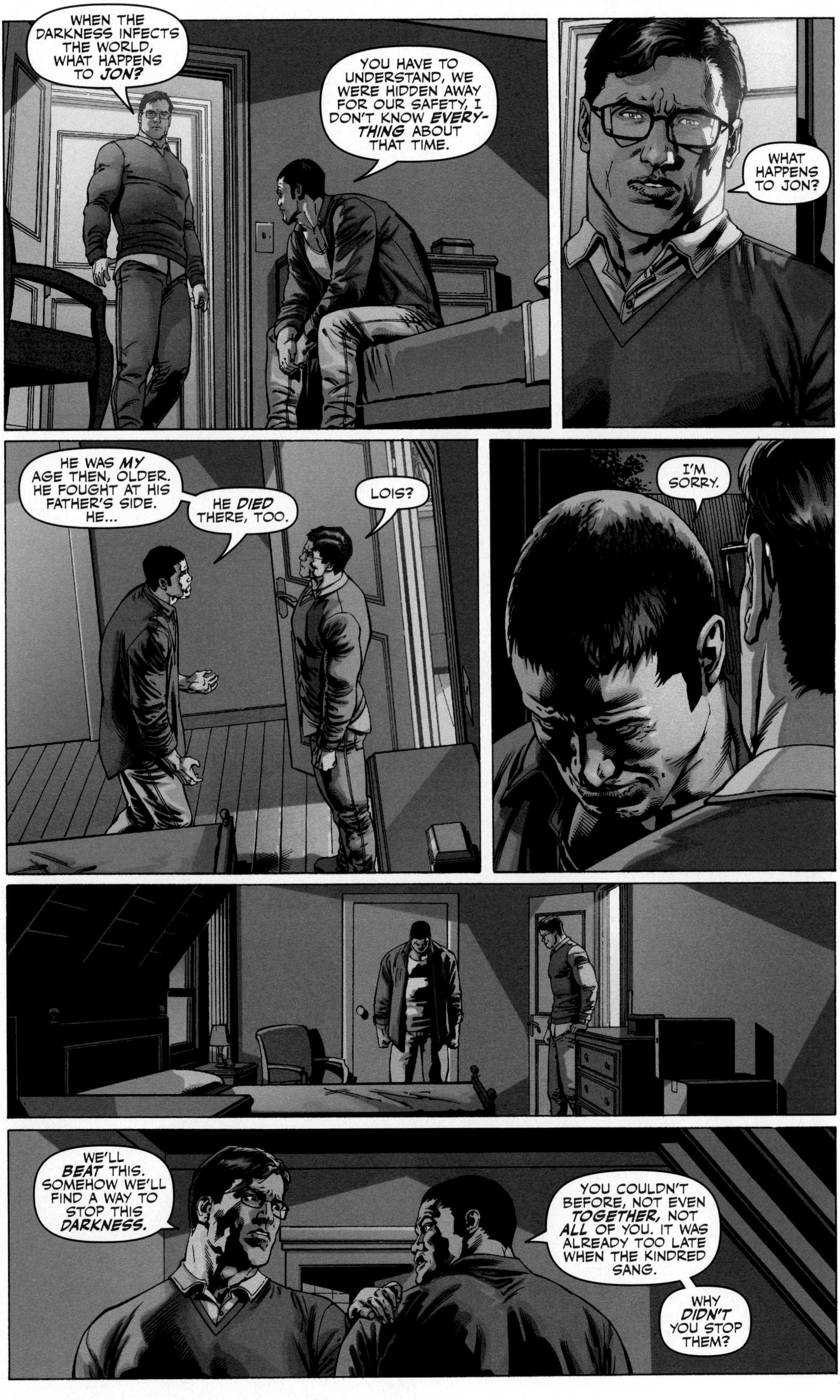

WHEN THE DARKNESS INFECTS THE WORLD, WHAT HAPPENS TO JON?
YOU HAVE TO UNDERSTAND, WE WERE HIDDEN AWAY FOR OUR SAFETY, I DON'T KNOW EVERYTHING ABOUT THAT TIME.
WHAT HAPPENS TO JON?
HE WAS MY AGE THEN, OLDER. HE FOUGHT AT HIS FATHER'S SIDE. HE...
HE DIED THERE, TOO.
LOIS?
I'M SORRY.
WE'LL BEAT THIS. SOMEHOW WE'LL FIND A WAY TO STOP THIS DARKNESS.
YOU COULDN'T BEFORE, NOT EVEN TOGETHER, NOT ALL OF YOU. IT WAS ALREADY TOO LATE WHEN THE KINDRED SANG.
WHY DIDN'T YOU STOP THEM?

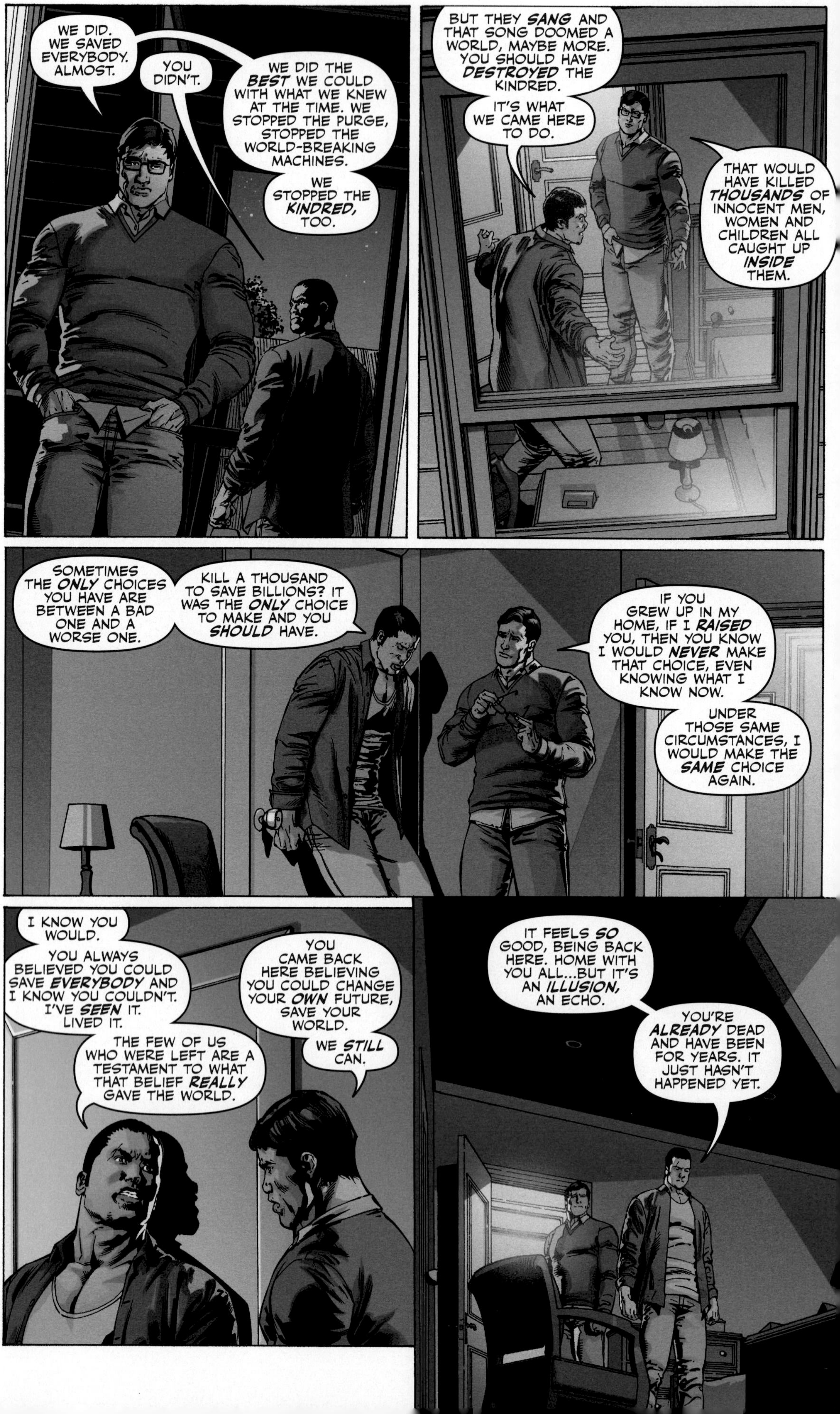
WE DID. WE SAVED EVERYBODY. ALMOST.
YOU DIDN'T.
WE DID THE BEST WE COULD WITH WHAT WE KNEW AT THE TIME. WE STOPPED THE PURGE, STOPPED THE WORLD-BREAKING MACHINES.
WE STOPPED THE KINDRED, TOO.
BUT THEY SANG AND THAT SONG DOOMED A WORLD, MAYBE MORE. YOU SHOULD HAVE DESTROYED THE KINDRED.
IT'S WHAT WE CAME HERE TO DO.
THAT WOULD HAVE KILLED THOUSANDS OF INNOCENT MEN, WOMEN AND CHILDREN ALL CAUGHT UP INSIDE THEM.
SOMETIMES THE ONLY CHOICES YOU HAVE ARE BETWEEN A BAD ONE AND A WORSE ONE.
KILL A THOUSAND TO SAVE BILLIONS? IT WAS THE ONLY CHOICE TO MAKE AND YOU SHOULD HAVE.
IF YOU GREW UP IN MY HOME, IF I RAISED YOU, THEN YOU KNOW I WOULD NEVER MAKE THAT CHOICE, EVEN KNOWING WHAT I KNOW NOW.
UNDER THOSE SAME CIRCUMSTANCES, I WOULD MAKE THE SAME CHOICE AGAIN.
I KNOW YOU WOULD.
YOU ALWAYS BELIEVED YOU COULD SAVE EVERYBODY AND I KNOW YOU COULDN'T. I'VE SEEN IT. LIVED IT.
THE FEW OF US WHO WERE LEFT ARE A TESTAMENT TO WHAT THAT BELIEF REALLY GAVE THE WORLD.
YOU CAME BACK HERE BELIEVING YOU COULD CHANGE YOUR OWN FUTURE, SAVE YOUR WORLD.
WE STILL CAN.
IT FEELS SO GOOD, BEING BACK HERE. HOME WITH YOU ALL...BUT IT'S AN ILLUSION, AN ECHO.
YOU'RE ALREADY DEAD AND HAVE BEEN FOR YEARS. IT JUST HASN'T HAPPENED YET.

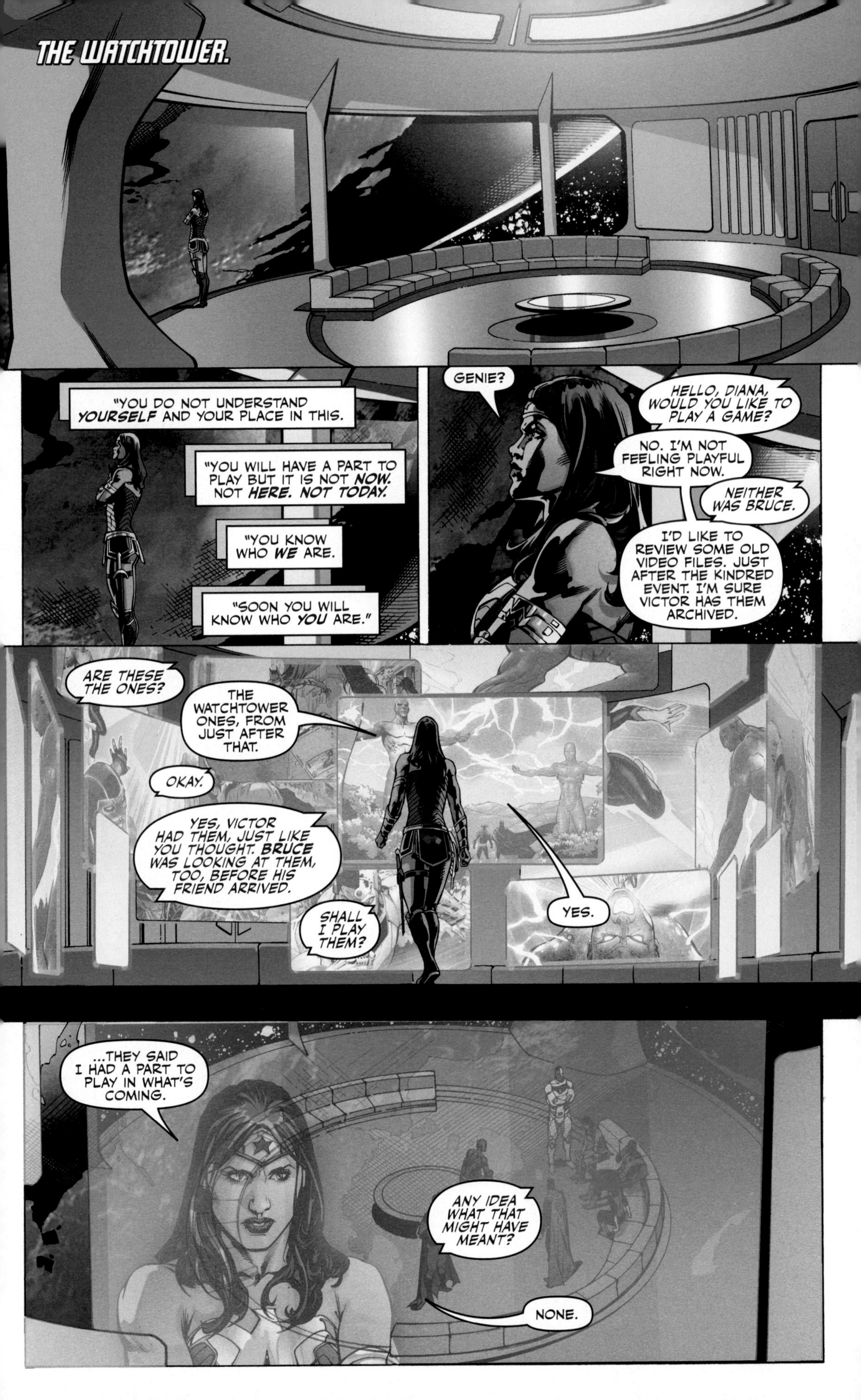
THE WATCHTOWER.
"YOU DO NOT UNDERSTAND YOURSELF AND YOUR PLACE IN THIS.
"YOU WILL HAVE A PART TO PLAY BUT IT IS NOT NOW. NOT HERE. NOT TODAY.
"YOU KNOW WHO WE ARE.
"SOON YOU WILL KNOW WHO YOU ARE."
GENIE?
HELLO, DIANA, WOULD YOU LIKE TO PLAY A GAME?
NO. I'M NOT FEELING PLAYFUL RIGHT NOW.
NEITHER WAS BRUCE.
I'D LIKE TO REVIEW SOME OLD VIDEO FILES. JUST AFTER THE KINDRED EVENT. I'M SURE VICTOR HAS THEM ARCHIVED.
ARE THESE THE ONES?
THE WATCHTOWER ONES, FROM JUST AFTER THAT.
OKAY.
YES, VICTOR HAD THEM, JUST LIKE YOU THOUGHT. BRUCE WAS LOOKING AT THEM, TOO, BEFORE HIS FRIEND ARRIVED.
SHALL I PLAY THEM?
YES.
...THEY SAID I HAD A PART TO PLAY IN WHAT'S COMING.
ANY IDEA WHAT THAT MIGHT HAVE MEANT?
NONE.

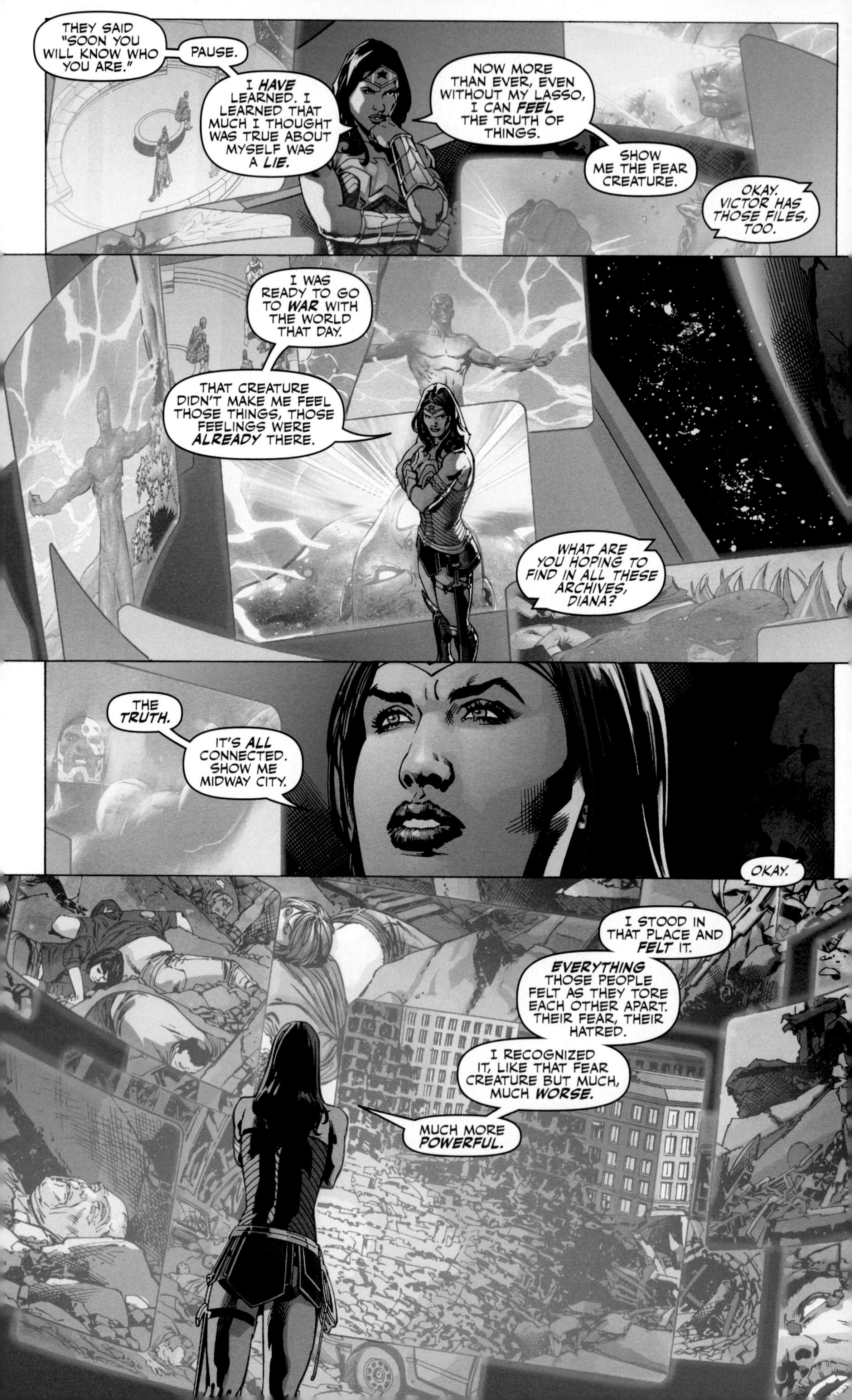
THEY SAID "SOON YOU WILL KNOW WHO YOU ARE."
PAUSE.
I *HAVE* LEARNED. I LEARNED THAT MUCH I THOUGHT WAS TRUE ABOUT MYSELF WAS A *LIE.*
NOW MORE THAN EVER, EVEN WITHOUT MY LASSO, I CAN *FEEL* THE TRUTH OF THINGS.
SHOW ME THE FEAR CREATURE.
OKAY. VICTOR HAS THOSE FILES, TOO.
I WAS READY TO GO TO *WAR* WITH THE WORLD THAT DAY.
THAT CREATURE DIDN'T MAKE ME FEEL THOSE THINGS, THOSE FEELINGS WERE *ALREADY* THERE.
WHAT ARE YOU HOPING TO FIND IN ALL THESE ARCHIVES, DIANA?
THE *TRUTH.*
IT'S *ALL* CONNECTED. SHOW ME MIDWAY CITY.
OKAY.
I STOOD IN THAT PLACE AND *FELT* IT.
EVERYTHING THOSE PEOPLE FELT AS THEY TORE EACH OTHER APART. THEIR FEAR, THEIR HATRED.
I RECOGNIZED IT, LIKE THAT FEAR CREATURE BUT MUCH, MUCH *WORSE.*
MUCH MORE *POWERFUL.*

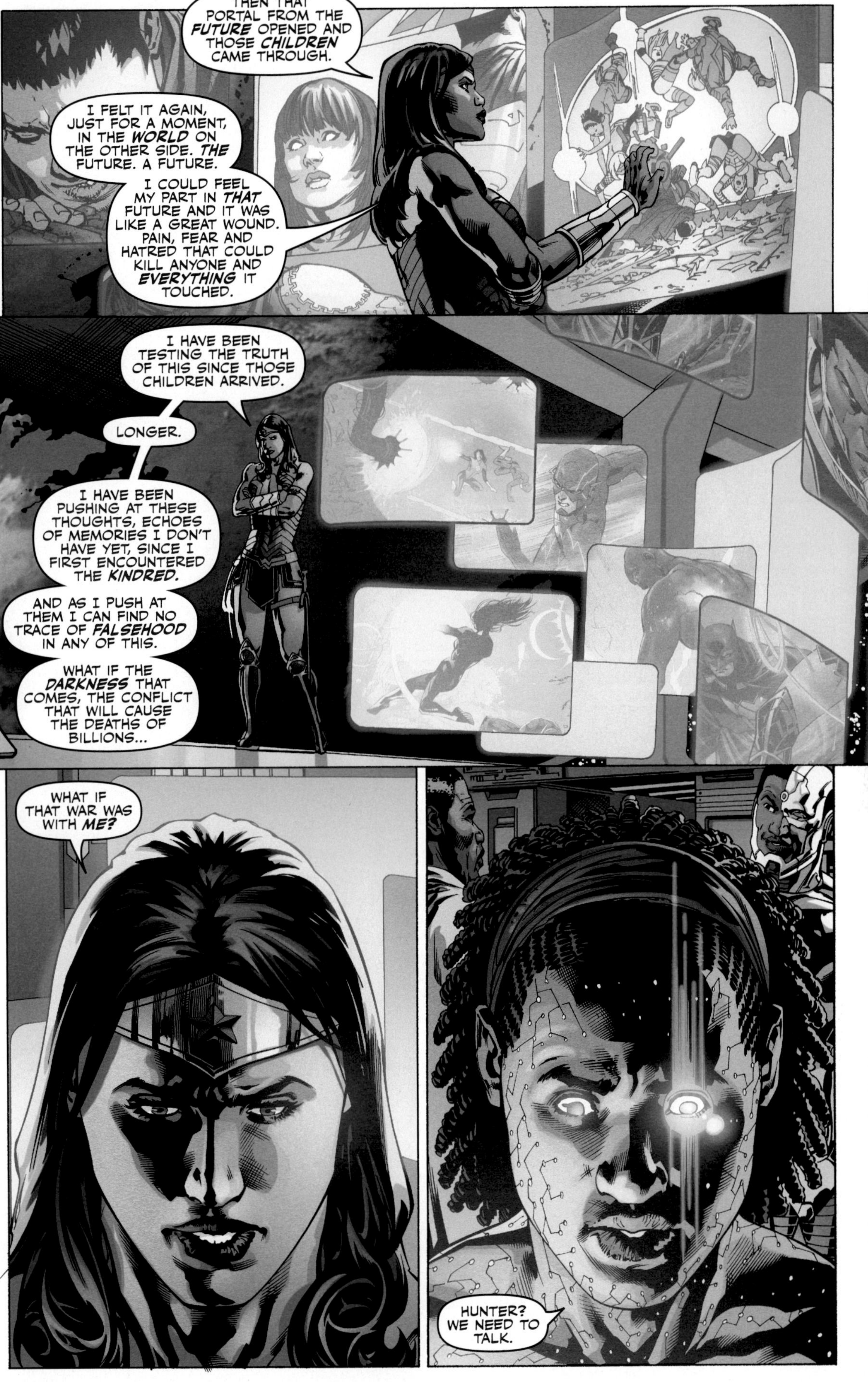

THEN THAT PORTAL FROM THE FUTURE OPENED AND THOSE CHILDREN CAME THROUGH.
I FELT IT AGAIN, JUST FOR A MOMENT, IN THE WORLD ON THE OTHER SIDE. THE FUTURE. A FUTURE.
I COULD FEEL MY PART IN THAT FUTURE AND IT WAS LIKE A GREAT WOUND. PAIN, FEAR AND HATRED THAT COULD KILL ANYONE AND EVERYTHING IT TOUCHED.
I HAVE BEEN TESTING THE TRUTH OF THIS SINCE THOSE CHILDREN ARRIVED.
LONGER.
I HAVE BEEN PUSHING AT THESE THOUGHTS, ECHOES OF MEMORIES I DON'T HAVE YET, SINCE I FIRST ENCOUNTERED THE KINDRED.
AND AS I PUSH AT THEM I CAN FIND NO TRACE OF FALSEHOOD IN ANY OF THIS.
WHAT IF THE DARKNESS THAT COMES, THE CONFLICT THAT WILL CAUSE THE DEATHS OF BILLIONS...
WHAT IF THAT WAR WAS WITH ME?
HUNTER? WE NEED TO TALK.

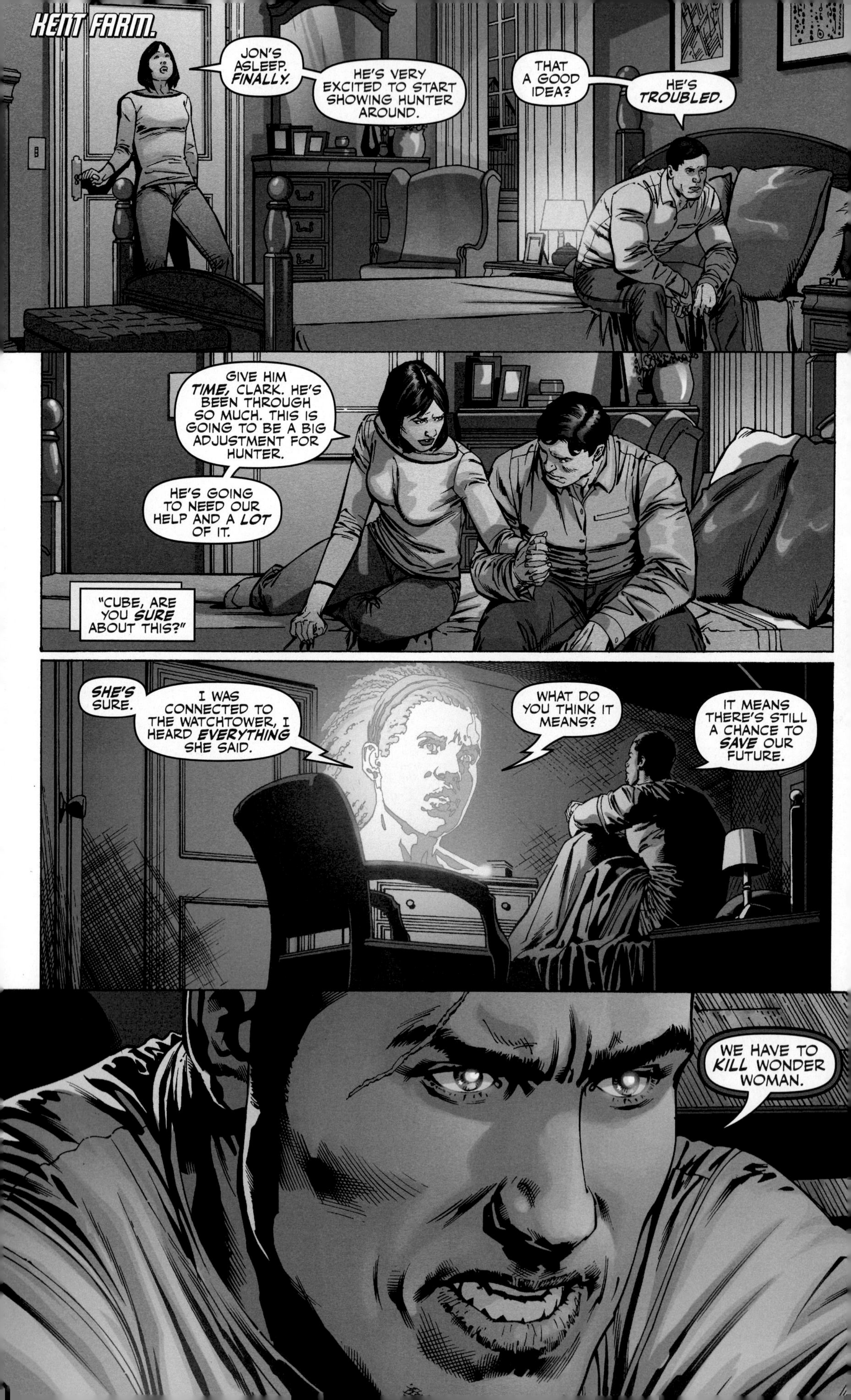
KENT FARM.
JON'S ASLEEP. FINALLY.
HE'S VERY EXCITED TO START SHOWING HUNTER AROUND.
THAT A GOOD IDEA?
HE'S TROUBLED.
GIVE HIM TIME, CLARK. HE'S BEEN THROUGH SO MUCH. THIS IS GOING TO BE A BIG ADJUSTMENT FOR HUNTER.
HE'S GOING TO NEED OUR HELP AND A LOT OF IT.
"CUBE, ARE YOU SURE ABOUT THIS?"
SHE'S SURE.
I WAS CONNECTED TO THE WATCHTOWER, I HEARD EVERYTHING SHE SAID.
WHAT DO YOU THINK IT MEANS?
IT MEANS THERE'S STILL A CHANCE TO SAVE OUR FUTURE.
WE HAVE TO KILL WONDER WOMAN.

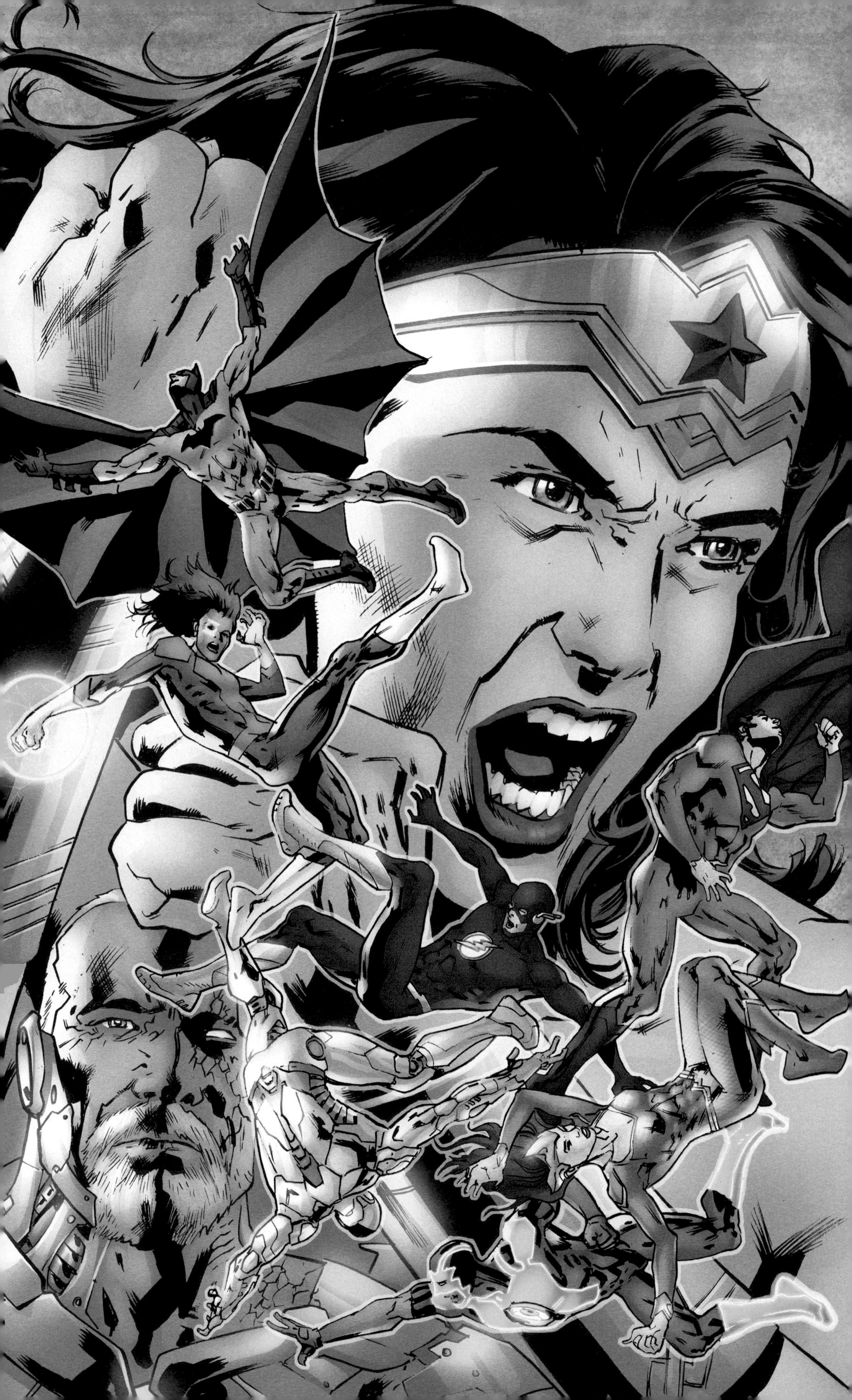

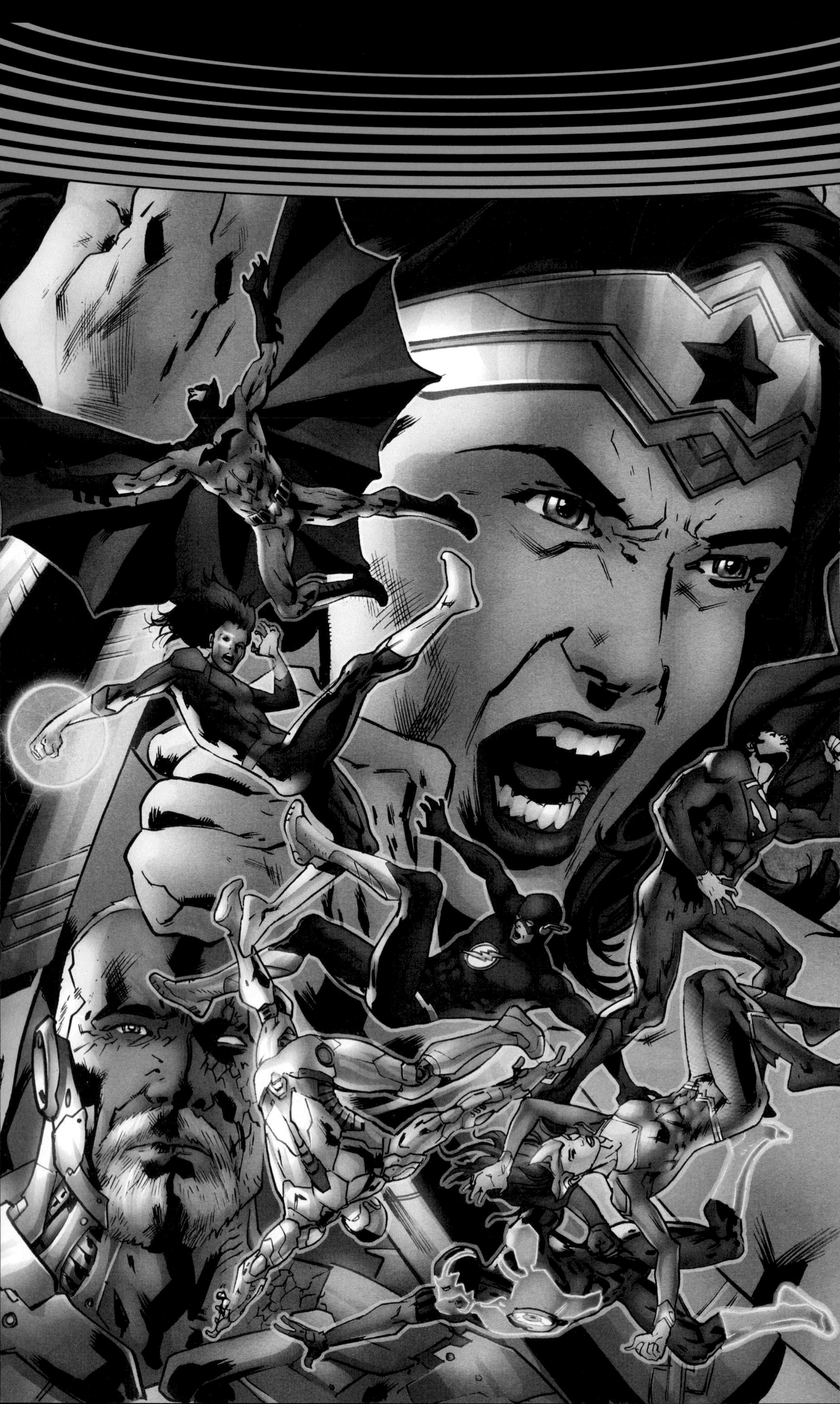

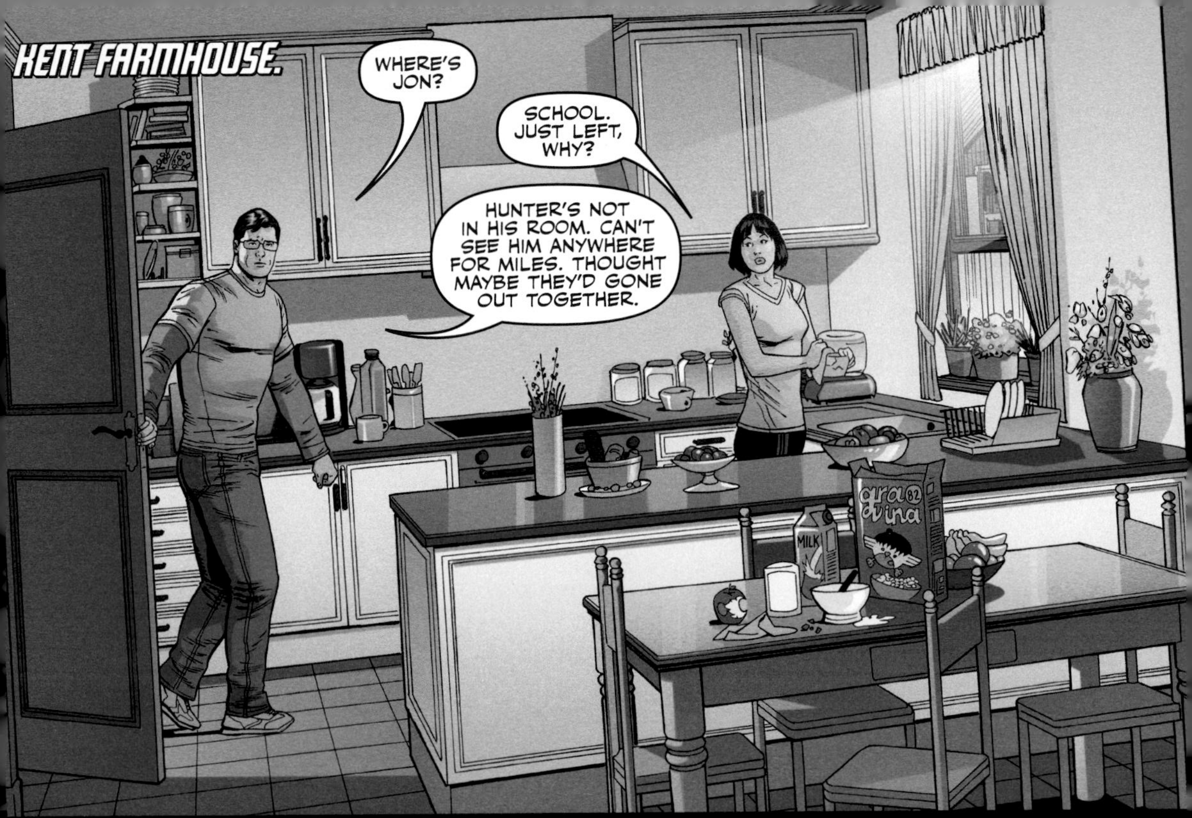
KENT FARMHOUSE.
WHERE'S JON?
SCHOOL. JUST LEFT, WHY?
HUNTER'S NOT IN HIS ROOM. CAN'T SEE HIM ANYWHERE FOR MILES. THOUGHT MAYBE THEY'D GONE OUT TOGETHER.
MILK

LEGACY PART FOUR

BRYAN HITCH WRITER FERNANDO PASARIN PENCILLER OCLAIR ALBERT & ANDY OWENS INKERS

COLORED by BRAD ANDERSON | LETTERED by RICHARD STARKINGS & COMICRAFT'S JIMMY | COVER by BRYAN HITCH & JEREMIAH SKIPPER | VARIANT COVER by NICK BRADSHAW & ALEX SINCLAIR | ASSOCIATE ED. AMEDEO TURTURRO | EDITOR BRIAN CUNNINGHAM

SUPERMAN created by JERRY SIEGEL and JOE SHUSTER. By special arrangement with the JERRY SIEGEL FAMILY. AQUAMAN created by PAUL NORRIS.

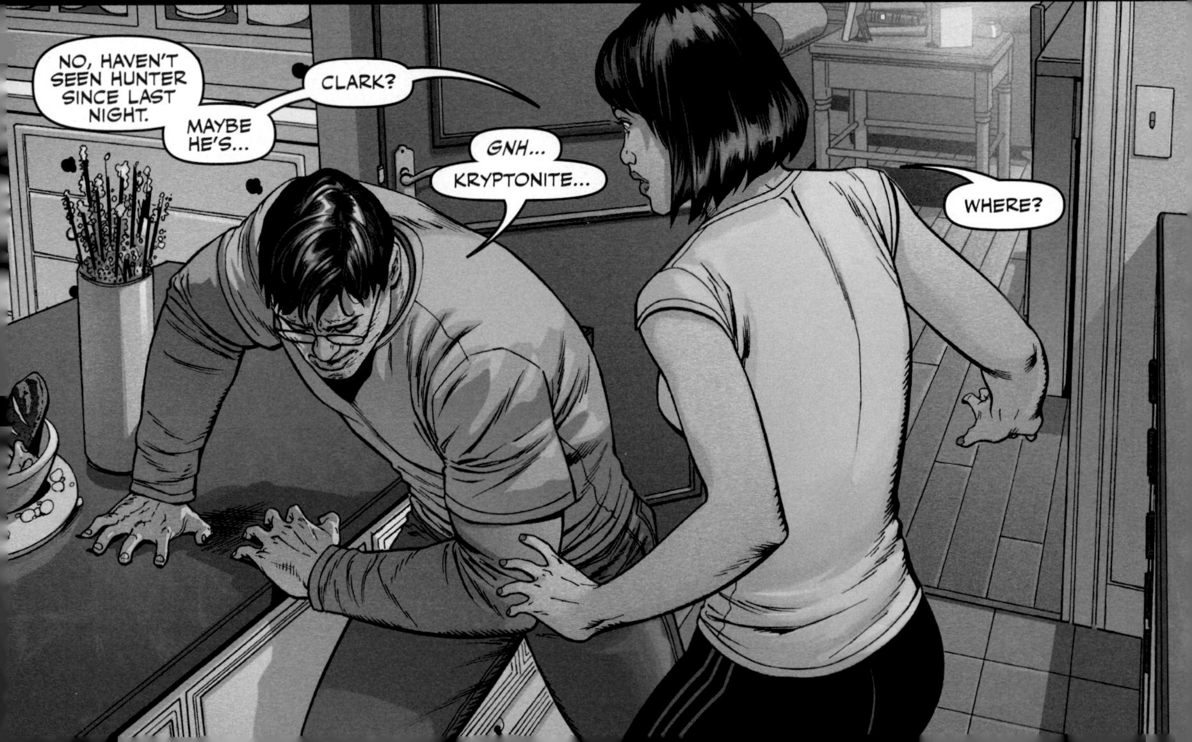
NO, HAVEN'T SEEN HUNTER SINCE LAST NIGHT.
MAYBE HE'S...
CLARK?
GNH... KRYPTONITE...
WHERE?

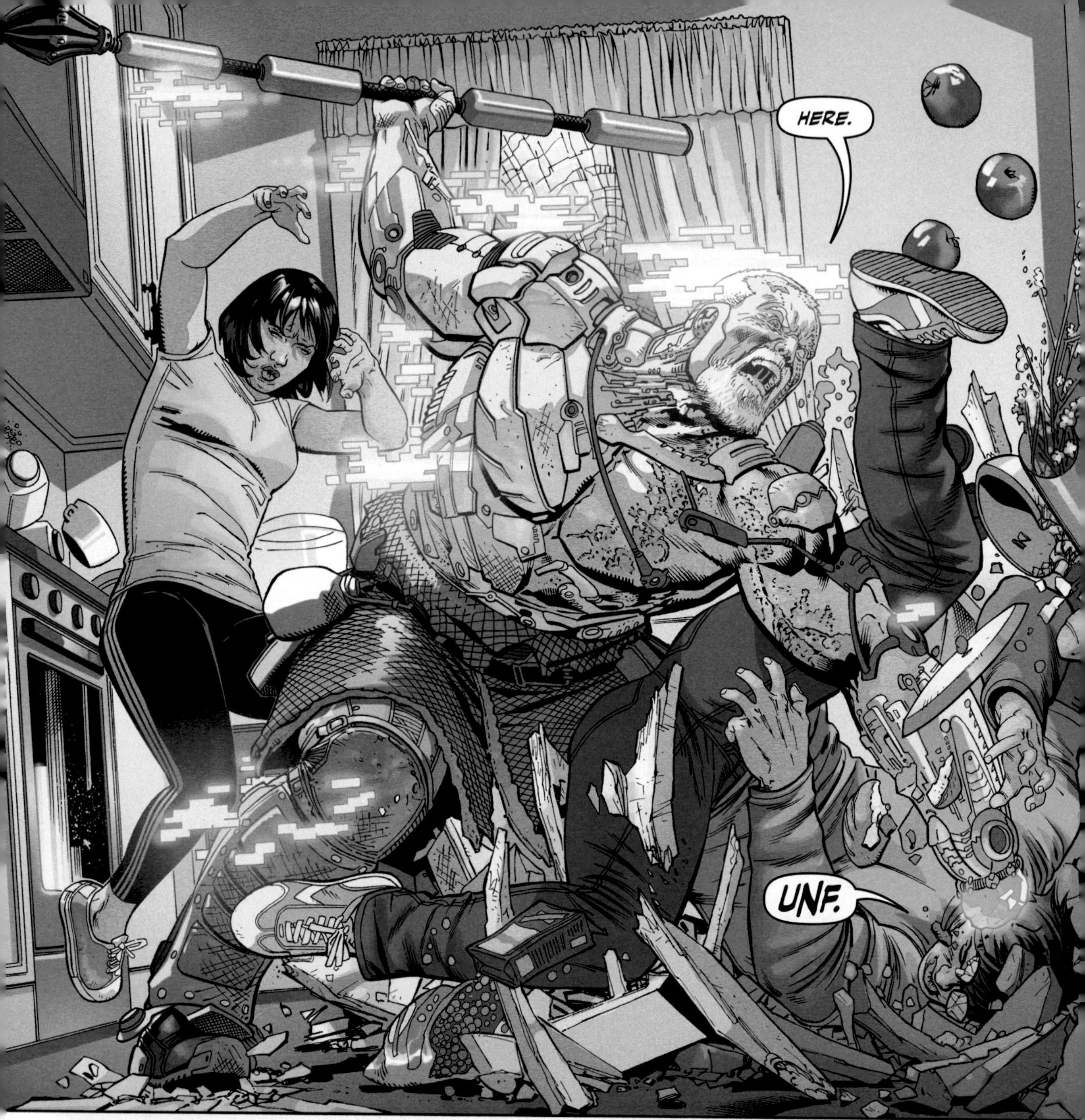
HERE.
UNF.

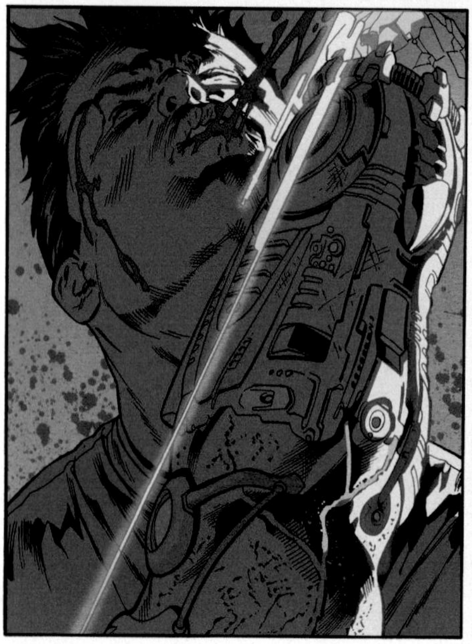

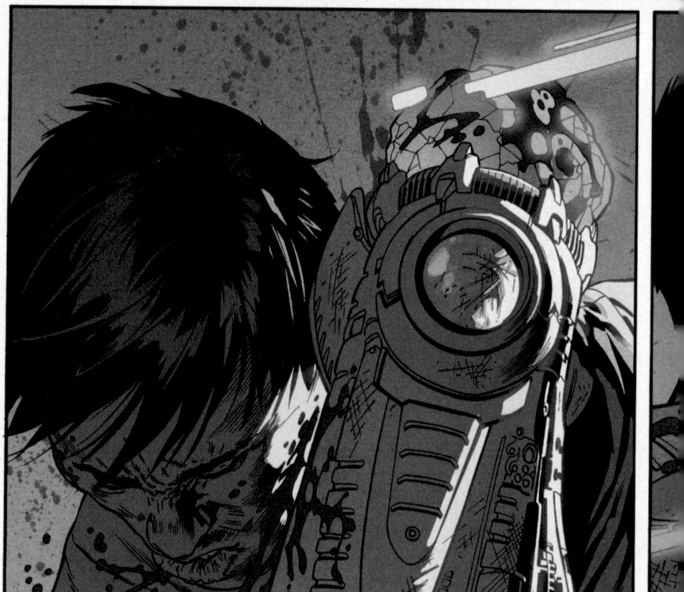

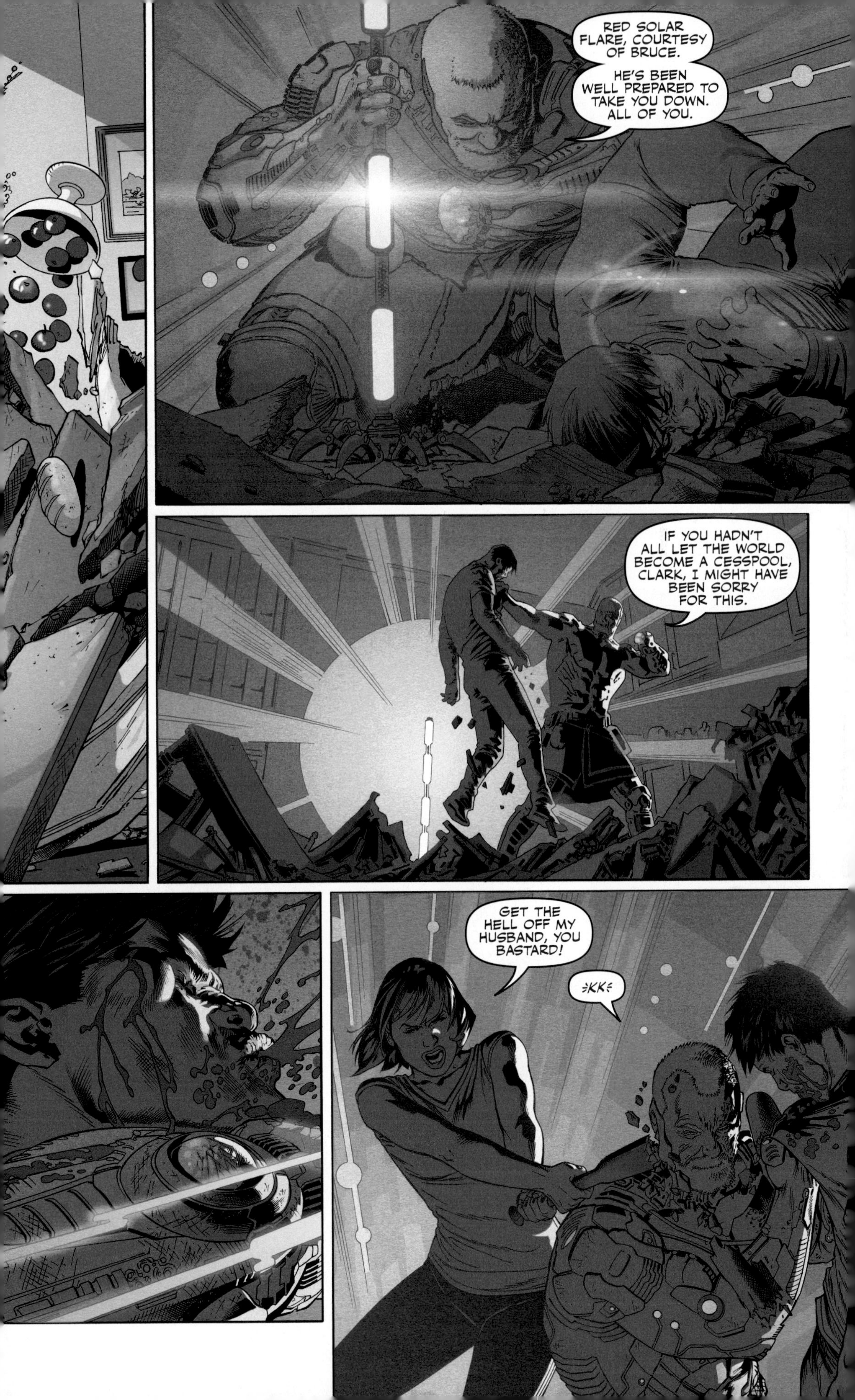
RED SOLAR FLARE, COURTESY OF BRUCE.
HE'S BEEN WELL PREPARED TO TAKE YOU DOWN. ALL OF YOU.
IF YOU HADN'T ALL LET THE WORLD BECOME A CESSPOOL, CLARK, I MIGHT HAVE BEEN SORRY FOR THIS.
GET THE HELL OFF MY HUSBAND, YOU BASTARD!
KK

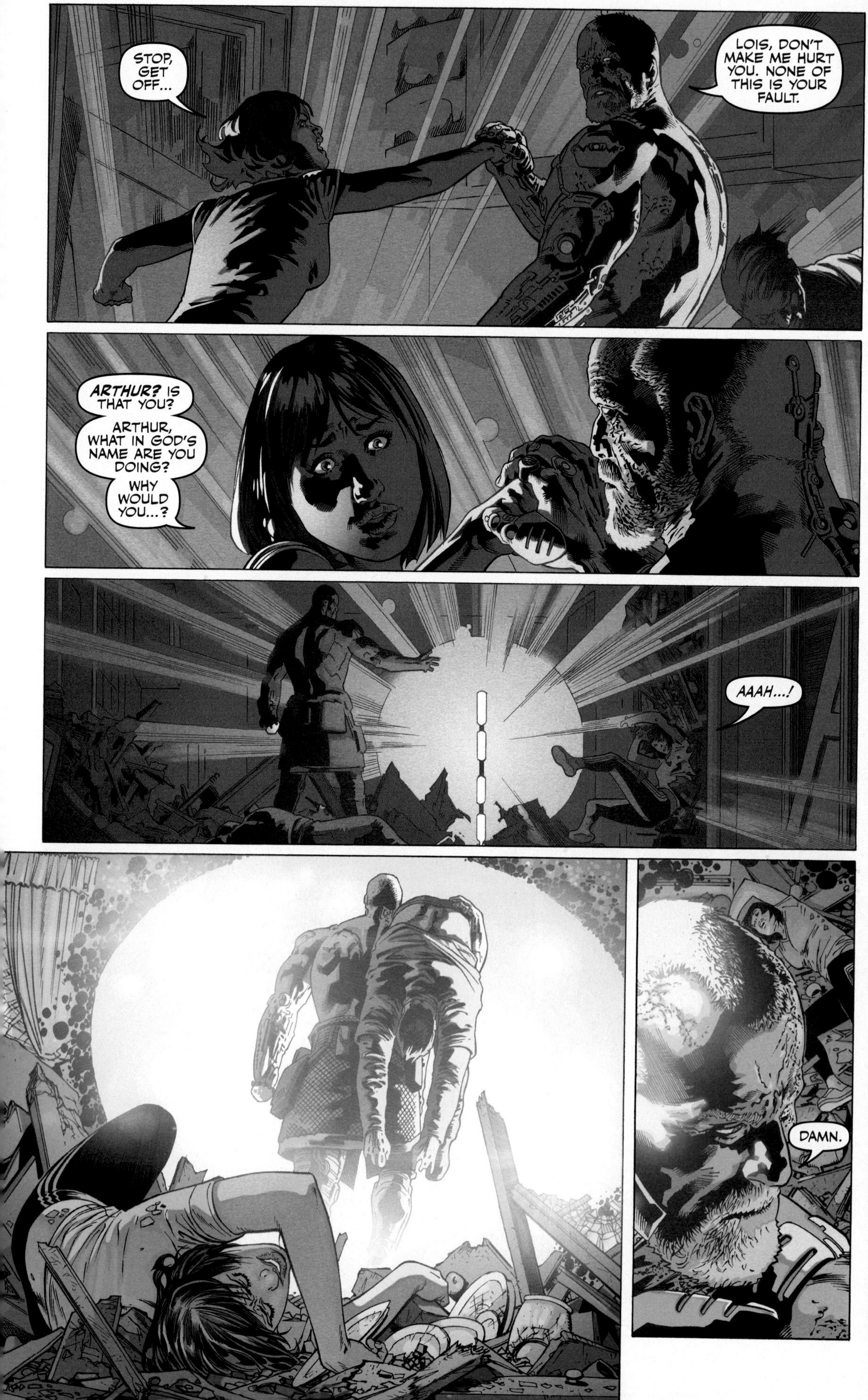
STOP, GET OFF...
LOIS, DON'T MAKE ME HURT YOU. NONE OF THIS IS YOUR FAULT.
ARTHUR? IS THAT YOU?
ARTHUR, WHAT IN GOD'S NAME ARE YOU DOING?
WHY WOULD YOU...?
AAAH...!
DAMN.

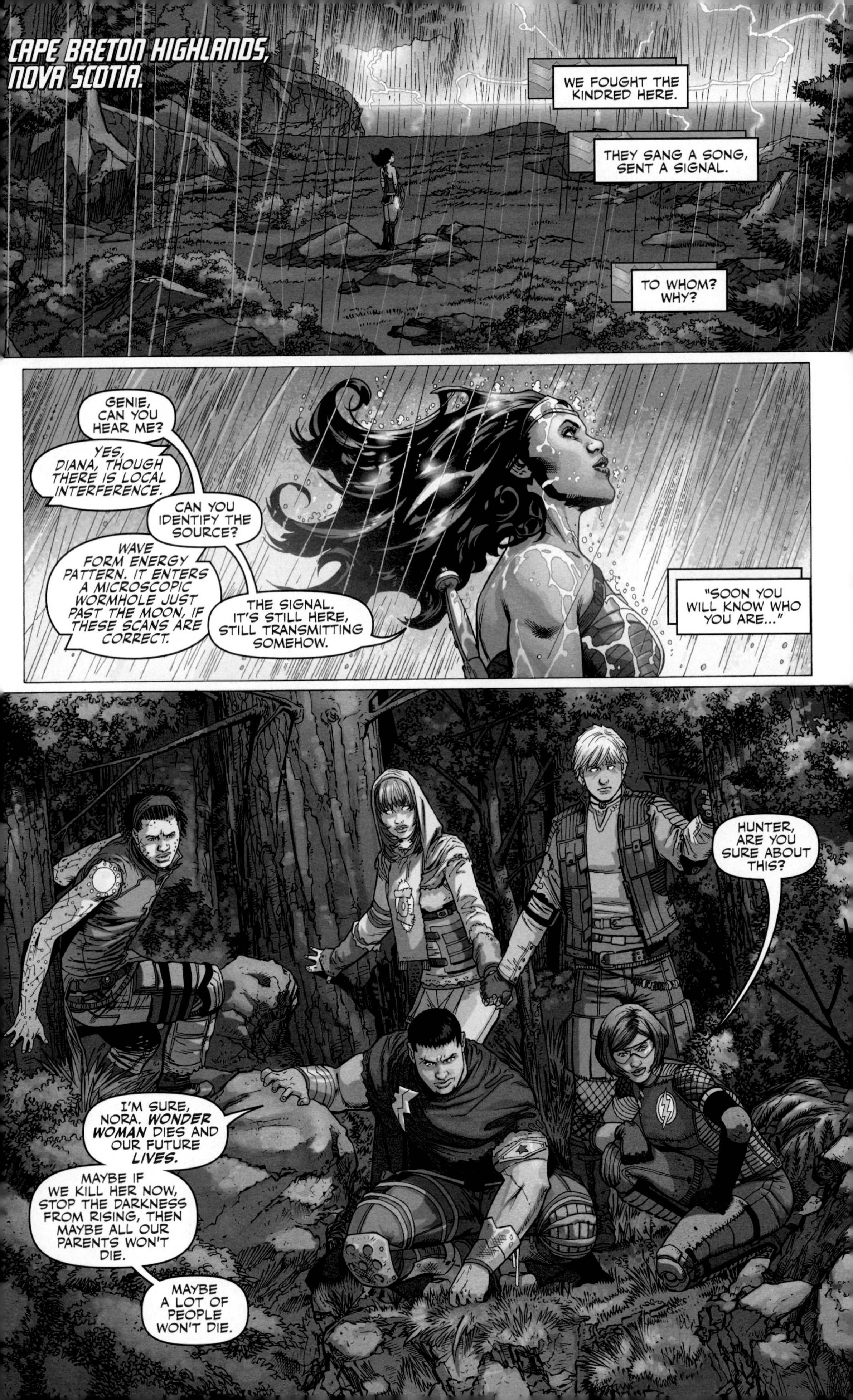
CAPE BRETON HIGHLANDS, NOVA SCOTIA.
WE FOUGHT THE KINDRED HERE.
THEY SANG A SONG, SENT A SIGNAL.
TO WHOM? WHY?
GENIE, CAN YOU HEAR ME?
YES, DIANA, THOUGH THERE IS LOCAL INTERFERENCE.
CAN YOU IDENTIFY THE SOURCE?
WAVE FORM ENERGY PATTERN. IT ENTERS A MICROSCOPIC WORMHOLE JUST PAST THE MOON, IF THESE SCANS ARE CORRECT.
THE SIGNAL. IT'S STILL HERE, STILL TRANSMITTING SOMEHOW.
"SOON YOU WILL KNOW WHO YOU ARE..."
HUNTER, ARE YOU SURE ABOUT THIS?
I'M SURE, NORA. WONDER WOMAN DIES AND OUR FUTURE LIVES.
MAYBE IF WE KILL HER NOW, STOP THE DARKNESS FROM RISING, THEN MAYBE ALL OUR PARENTS WON'T DIE.
MAYBE A LOT OF PEOPLE WON'T DIE.

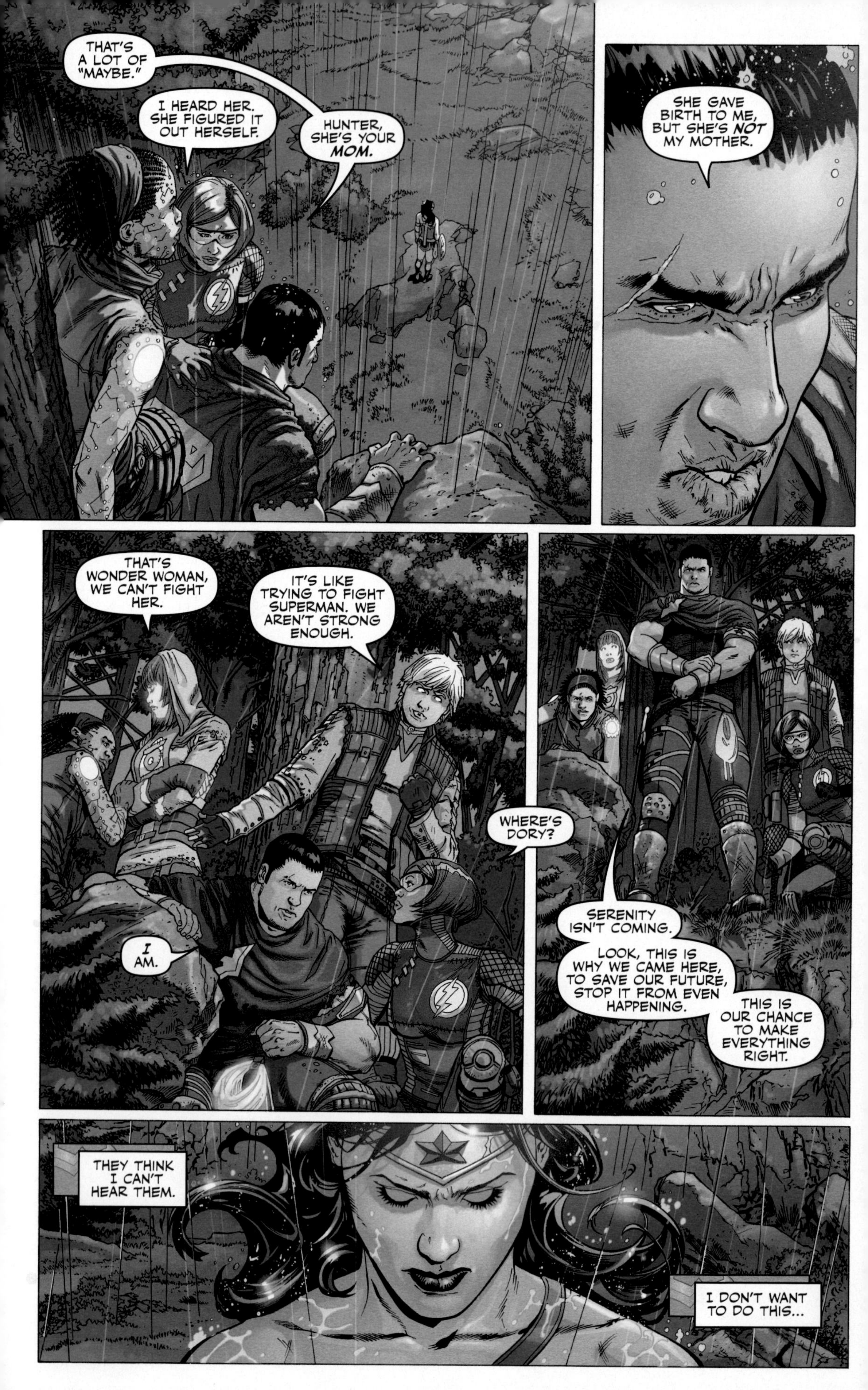
THAT'S A LOT OF "MAYBE."
I HEARD HER. SHE FIGURED IT OUT HERSELF.
HUNTER, SHE'S YOUR *MOM.*
SHE GAVE BIRTH TO ME, BUT SHE'S *NOT* MY MOTHER.
THAT'S WONDER WOMAN, WE CAN'T FIGHT HER.
IT'S LIKE TRYING TO FIGHT SUPERMAN. WE AREN'T STRONG ENOUGH.
WHERE'S DORY?
I AM.
SERENITY ISN'T COMING.
LOOK, THIS IS WHY WE CAME HERE, TO SAVE OUR FUTURE, STOP IT FROM EVEN HAPPENING.
THIS IS OUR CHANCE TO MAKE EVERYTHING RIGHT.
THEY THINK I CAN'T HEAR THEM.
I DON'T WANT TO DO THIS...

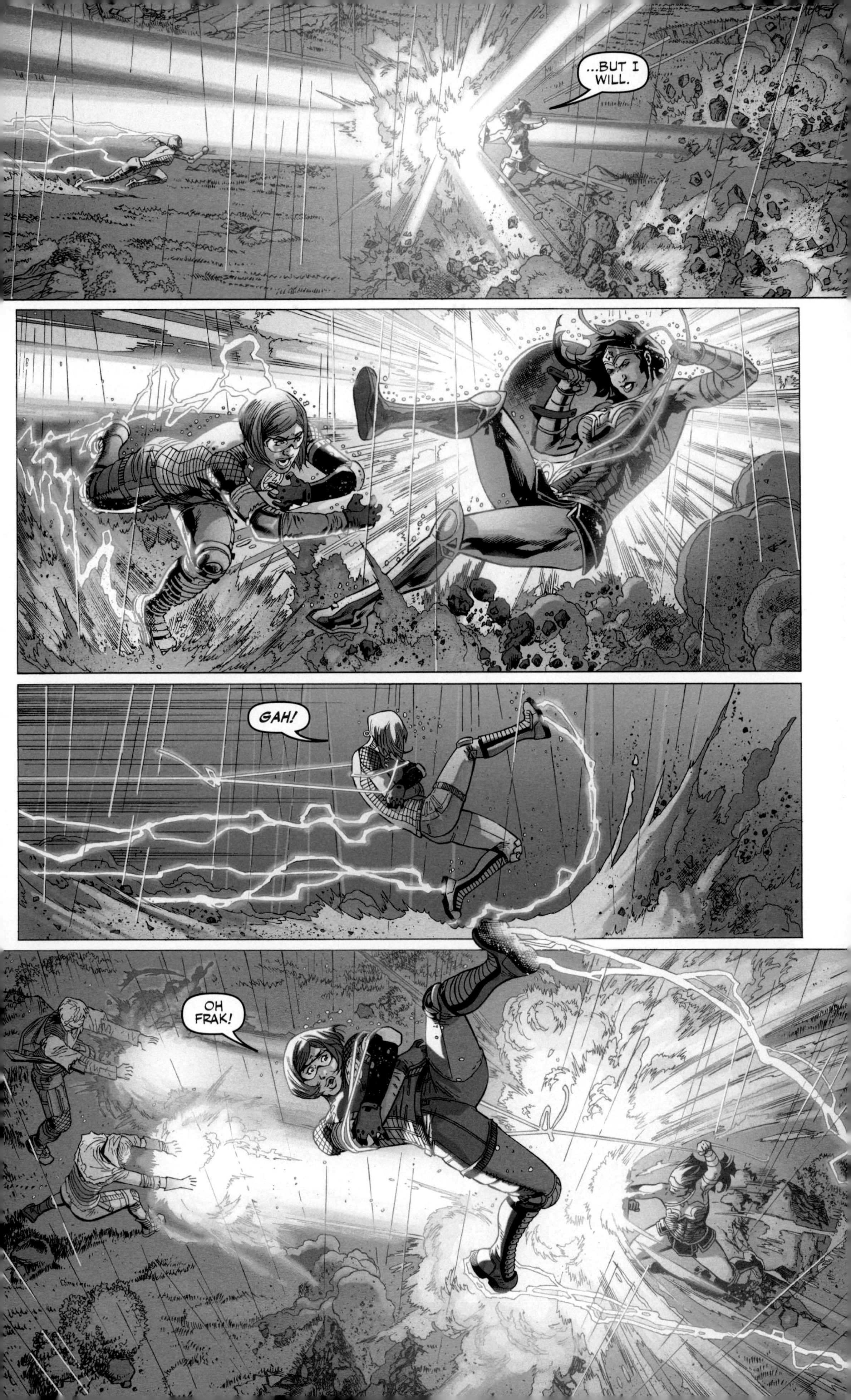
...BUT I WILL.
GAH!
OH FRAK!

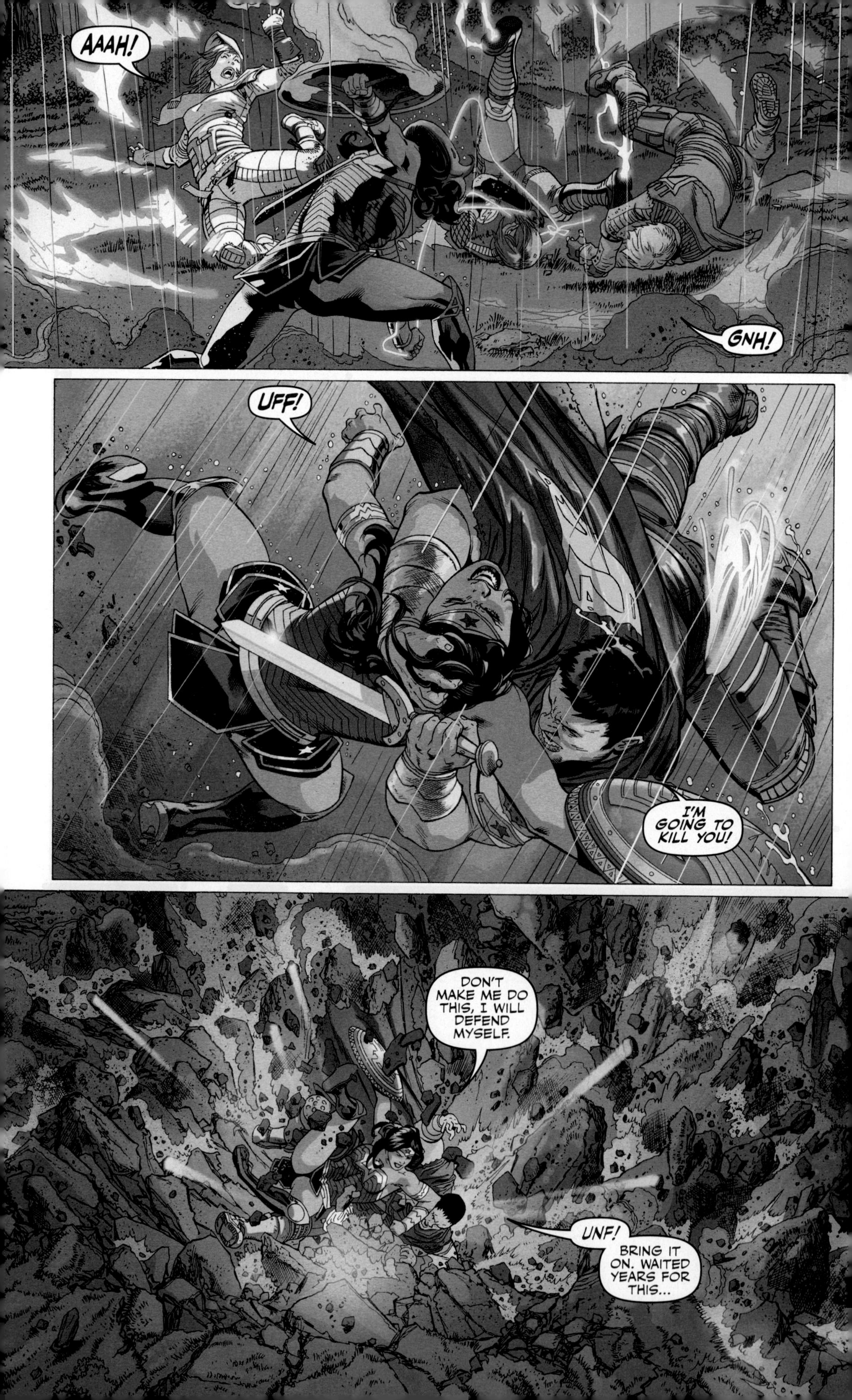
AAAH!
GNH!
UFF!
I'M GOING TO KILL YOU!
DON'T MAKE ME DO THIS, I WILL DEFEND MYSELF.
UNF!
BRING IT ON. WAITED YEARS FOR THIS...

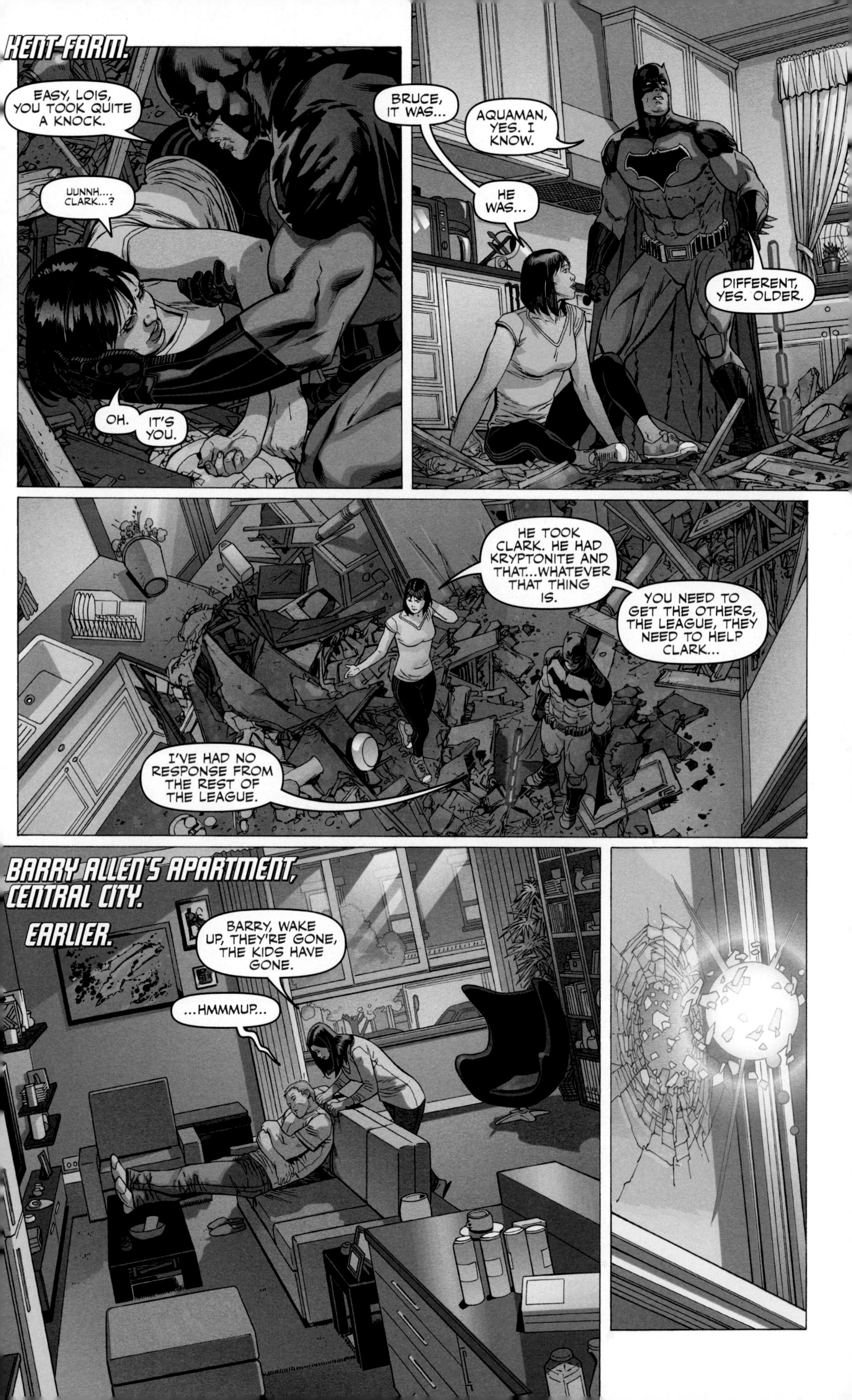
KENT FARM.
EASY, LOIS, YOU TOOK QUITE A KNOCK.
UUNNH.... CLARK...?
OH. IT'S YOU.
BRUCE, IT WAS...
AQUAMAN, YES. I KNOW.
HE WAS...
DIFFERENT, YES. OLDER.
HE TOOK CLARK. HE HAD KRYPTONITE AND THAT...WHATEVER THAT THING IS.
YOU NEED TO GET THE OTHERS, THE LEAGUE, THEY NEED TO HELP CLARK...
I'VE HAD NO RESPONSE FROM THE REST OF THE LEAGUE.
BARRY ALLEN'S APARTMENT, CENTRAL CITY.
EARLIER.
BARRY, WAKE UP, THEY'RE GONE, THE KIDS HAVE GONE.
...HMMMUP...

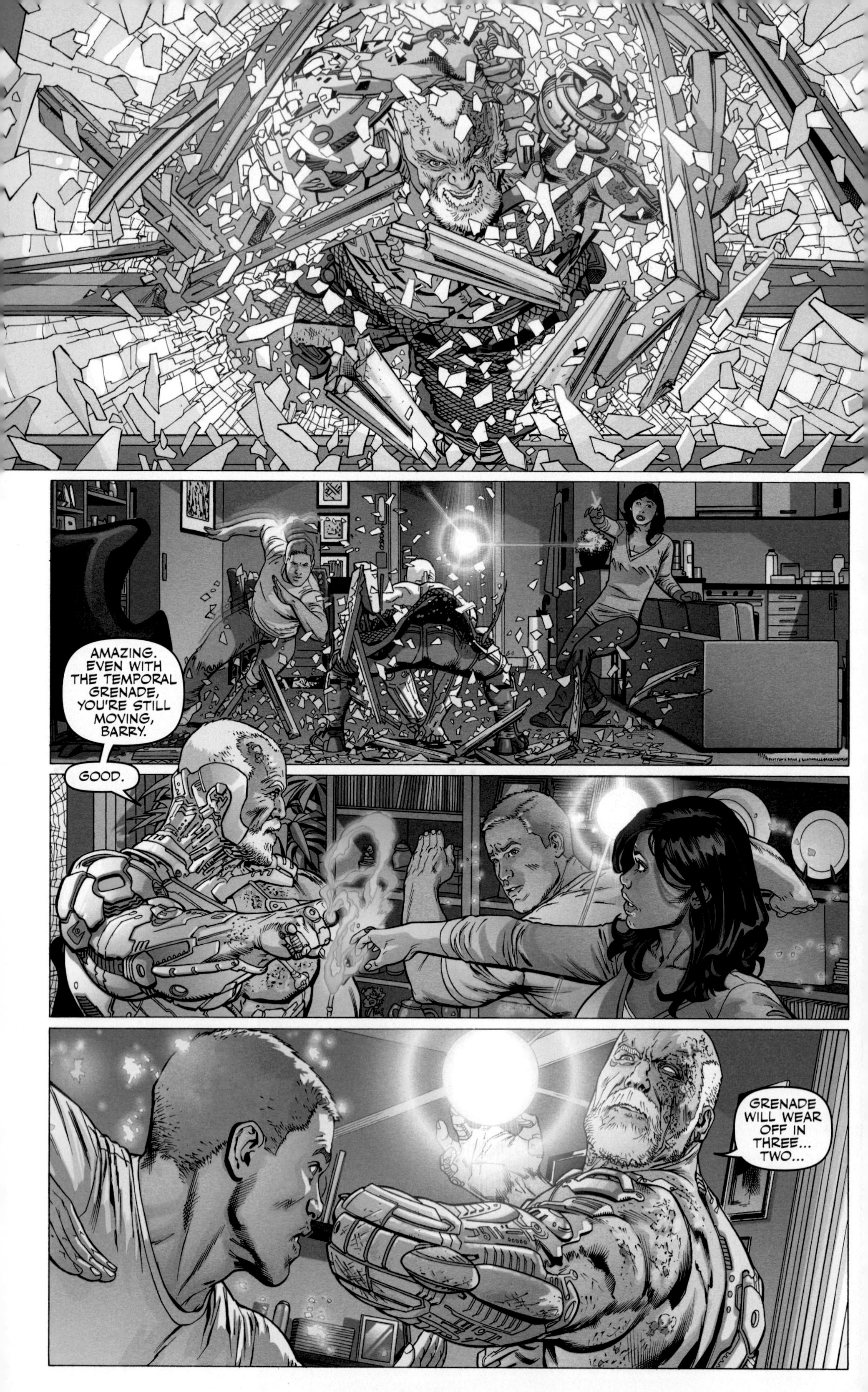
AMAZING. EVEN WITH THE TEMPORAL GRENADE, YOU'RE STILL MOVING, BARRY.
GOOD.
GRENADE WILL WEAR OFF IN THREE... TWO...

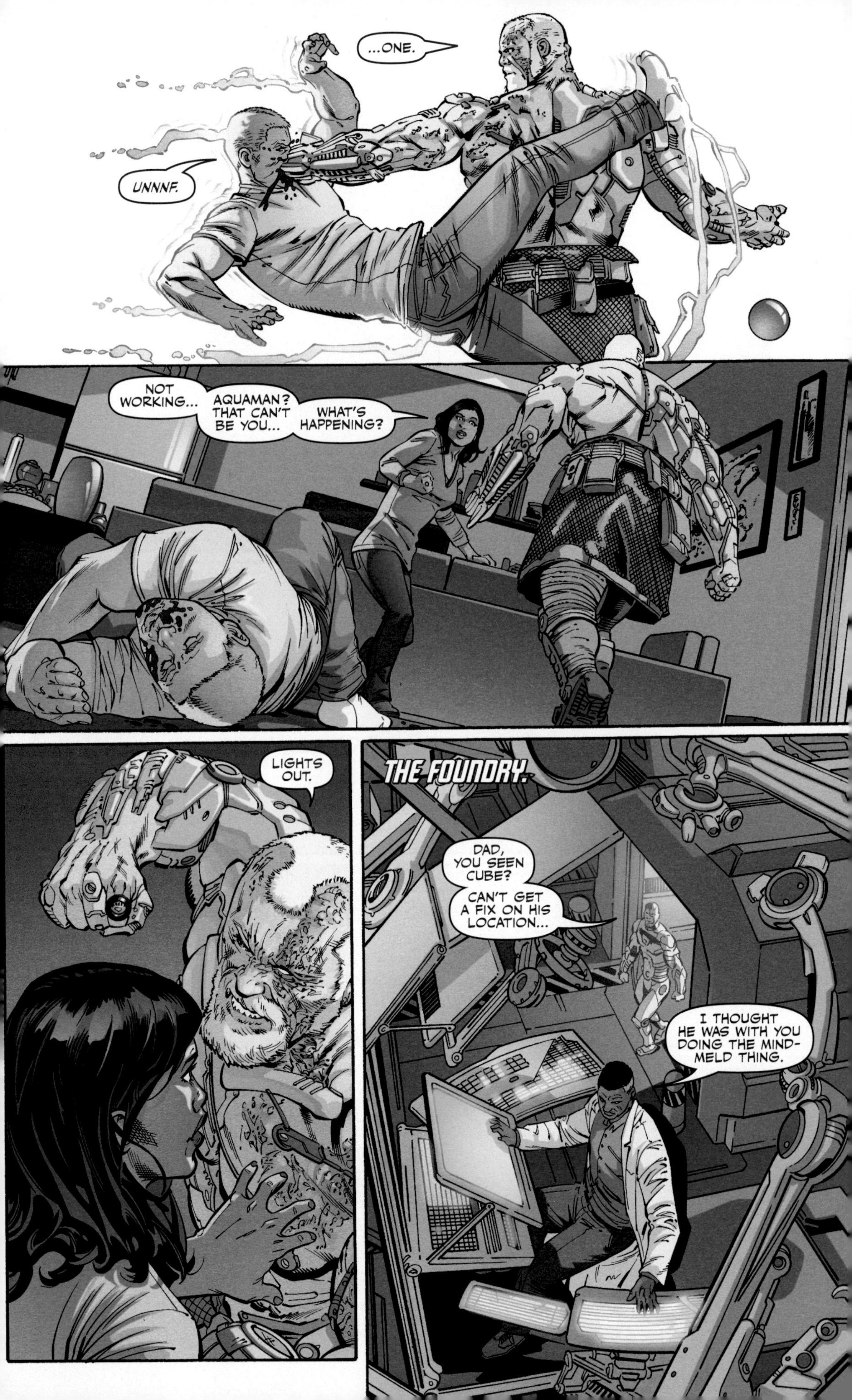
...ONE.
UNNNF.
NOT WORKING...
AQUAMAN? THAT CAN'T BE YOU...
WHAT'S HAPPENING?
LIGHTS OUT.
THE FOUNDRY.
DAD, YOU SEEN CUBE?
CAN'T GET A FIX ON HIS LOCATION...
I THOUGHT HE WAS WITH YOU DOING THE MIND-MELD THING.

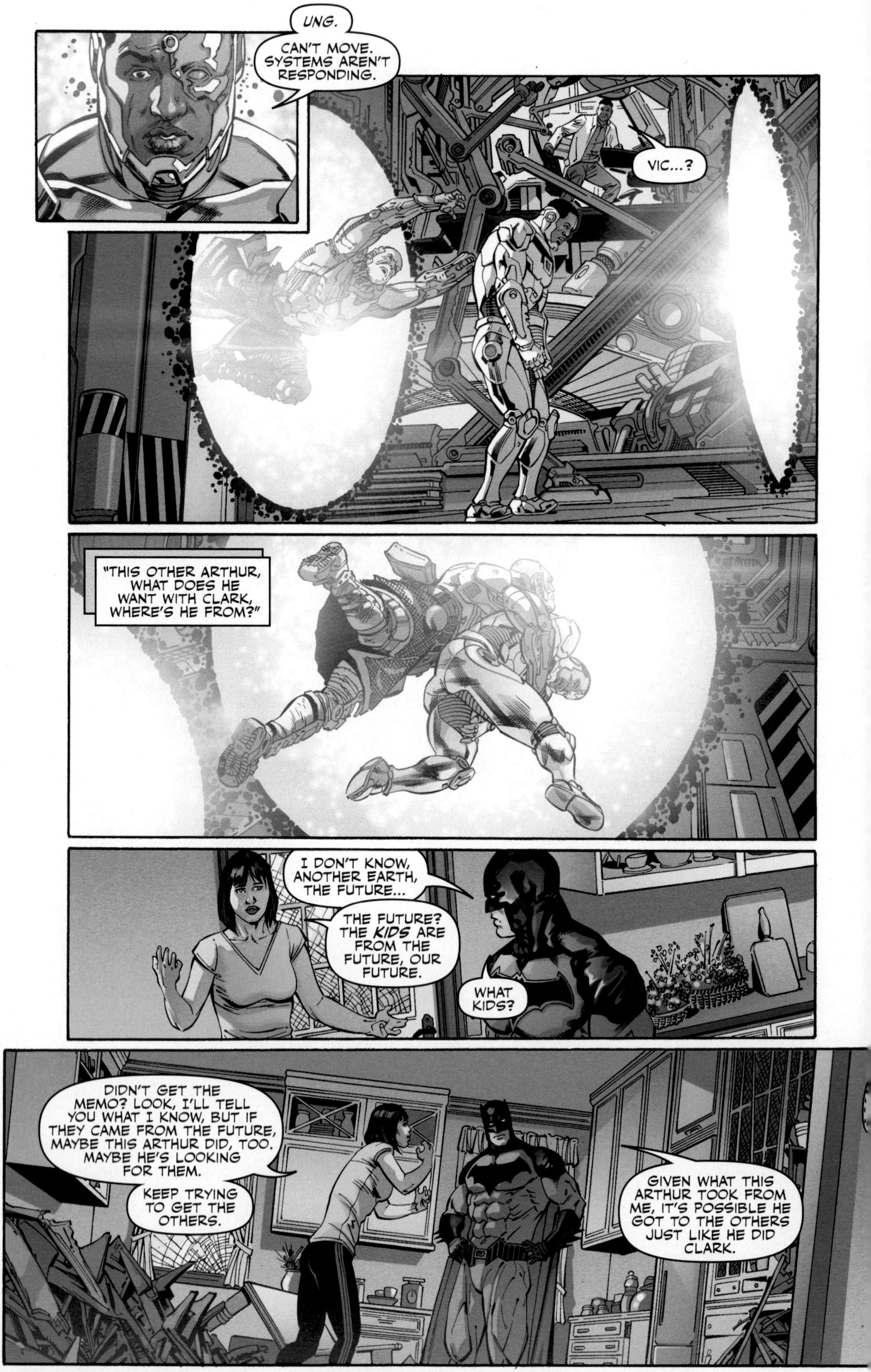
UNG.
CAN'T MOVE. SYSTEMS AREN'T RESPONDING.
VIC...?
"THIS OTHER ARTHUR, WHAT DOES HE WANT WITH CLARK, WHERE'S HE FROM?"
I DON'T KNOW, ANOTHER EARTH, THE FUTURE...
THE FUTURE? THE KIDS ARE FROM THE FUTURE, OUR FUTURE.
WHAT KIDS?
DIDN'T GET THE MEMO? LOOK, I'LL TELL YOU WHAT I KNOW, BUT IF THEY CAME FROM THE FUTURE, MAYBE THIS ARTHUR DID, TOO. MAYBE HE'S LOOKING FOR THEM.
KEEP TRYING TO GET THE OTHERS.
GIVEN WHAT THIS ARTHUR TOOK FROM ME, IT'S POSSIBLE HE GOT TO THE OTHERS JUST LIKE HE DID CLARK.

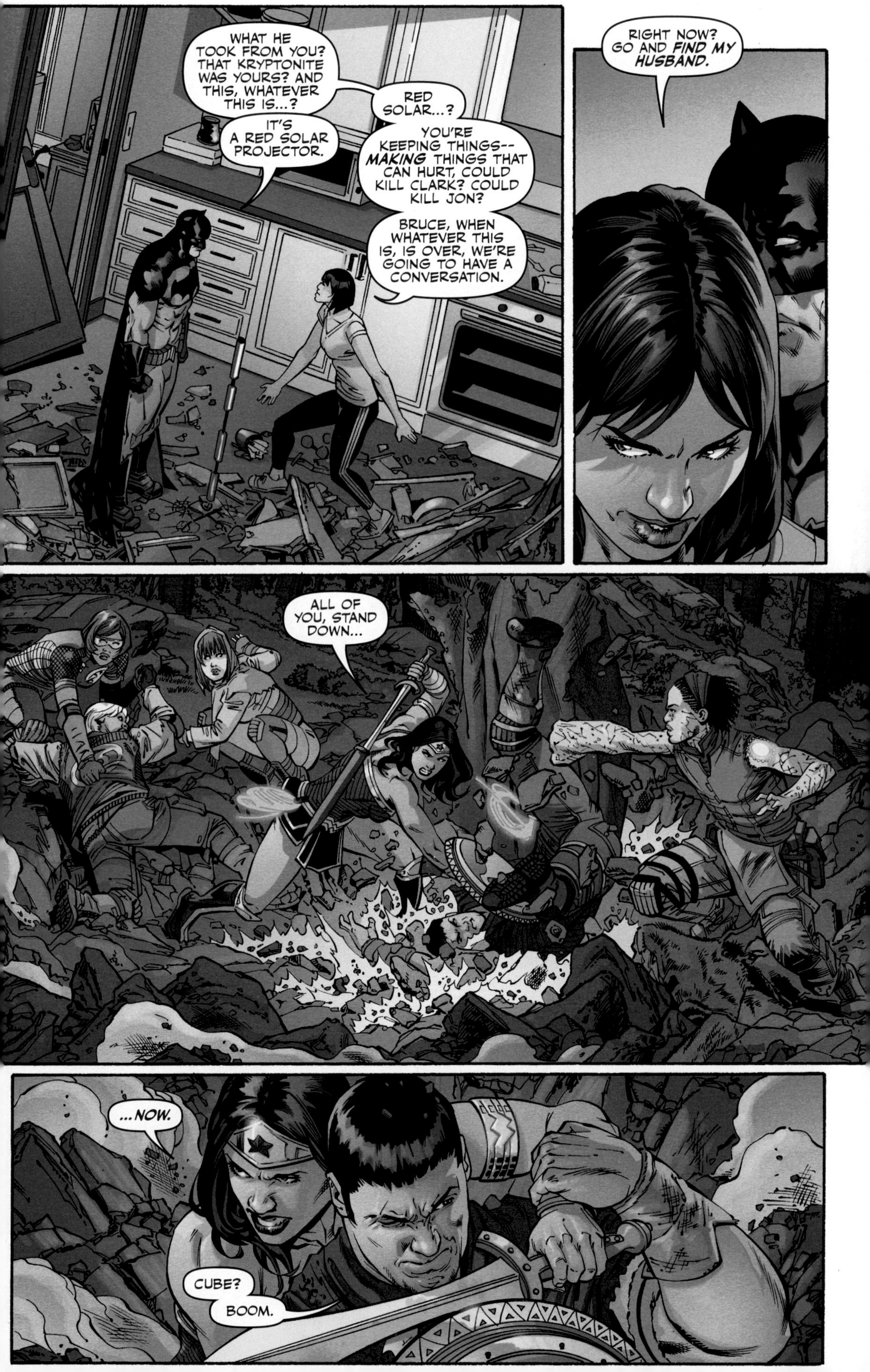
WHAT HE TOOK FROM YOU? THAT KRYPTONITE WAS YOURS? AND THIS, WHATEVER THIS IS...?
RED SOLAR...?
IT'S A RED SOLAR PROJECTOR.
YOU'RE KEEPING THINGS-- MAKING THINGS THAT CAN HURT, COULD KILL CLARK? COULD KILL JON?
BRUCE, WHEN WHATEVER THIS IS, IS OVER, WE'RE GOING TO HAVE A CONVERSATION.
RIGHT NOW? GO AND FIND MY HUSBAND.
ALL OF YOU, STAND DOWN...
...NOW.
CUBE?
BOOM.

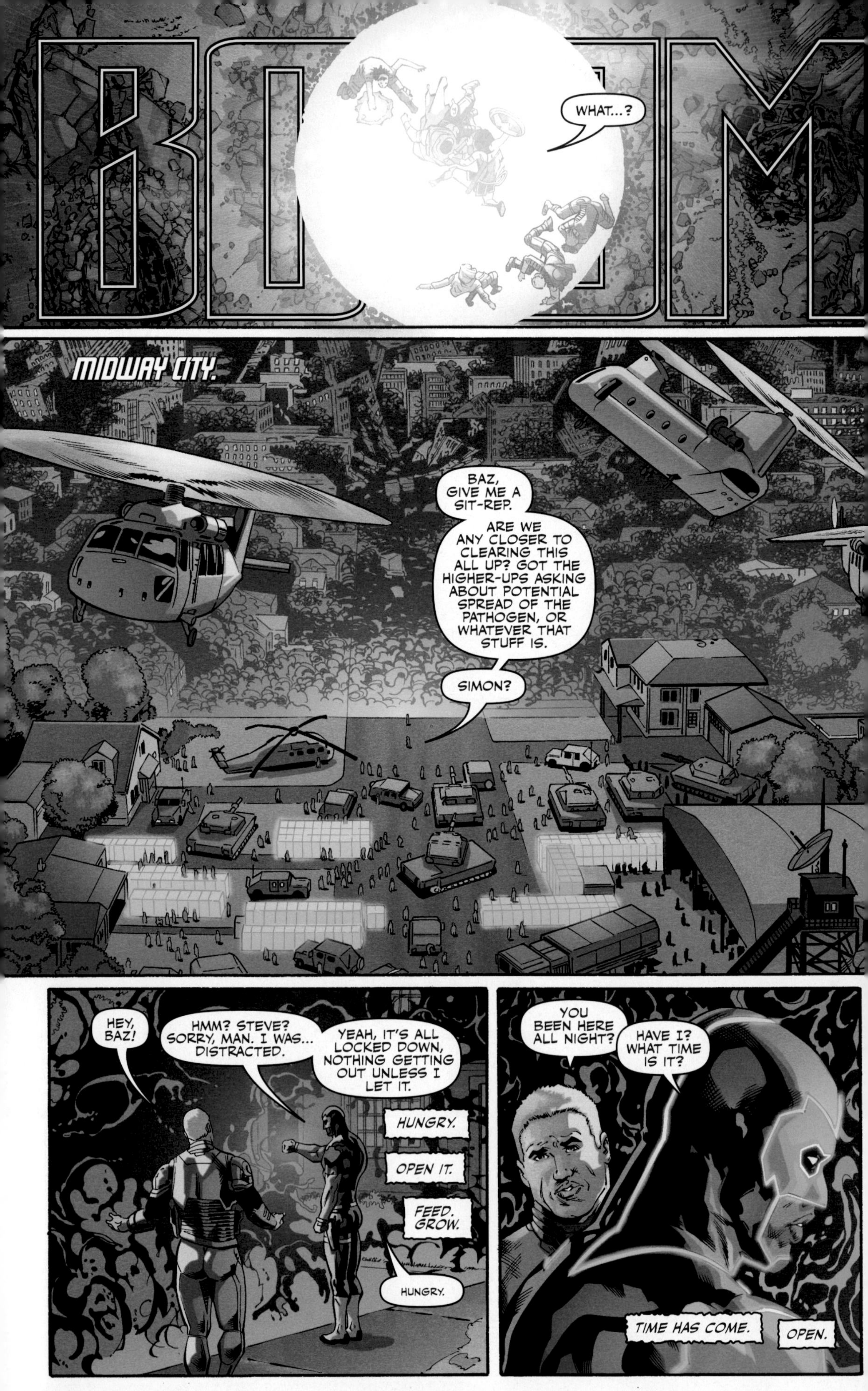
BOOM
WHAT...?
MIDWAY CITY.
BAZ, GIVE ME A SIT-REP.
ARE WE ANY CLOSER TO CLEARING THIS ALL UP? GOT THE HIGHER-UPS ASKING ABOUT POTENTIAL SPREAD OF THE PATHOGEN, OR WHATEVER THAT STUFF IS.
SIMON?
HEY, BAZ!
HMM? STEVE? SORRY, MAN. I WAS... DISTRACTED.
YEAH, IT'S ALL LOCKED DOWN, NOTHING GETTING OUT UNLESS I LET IT.
HUNGRY.
OPEN IT.
FEED. GROW.
HUNGRY.
YOU BEEN HERE ALL NIGHT?
HAVE I? WHAT TIME IS IT?
TIME HAS COME.
OPEN.

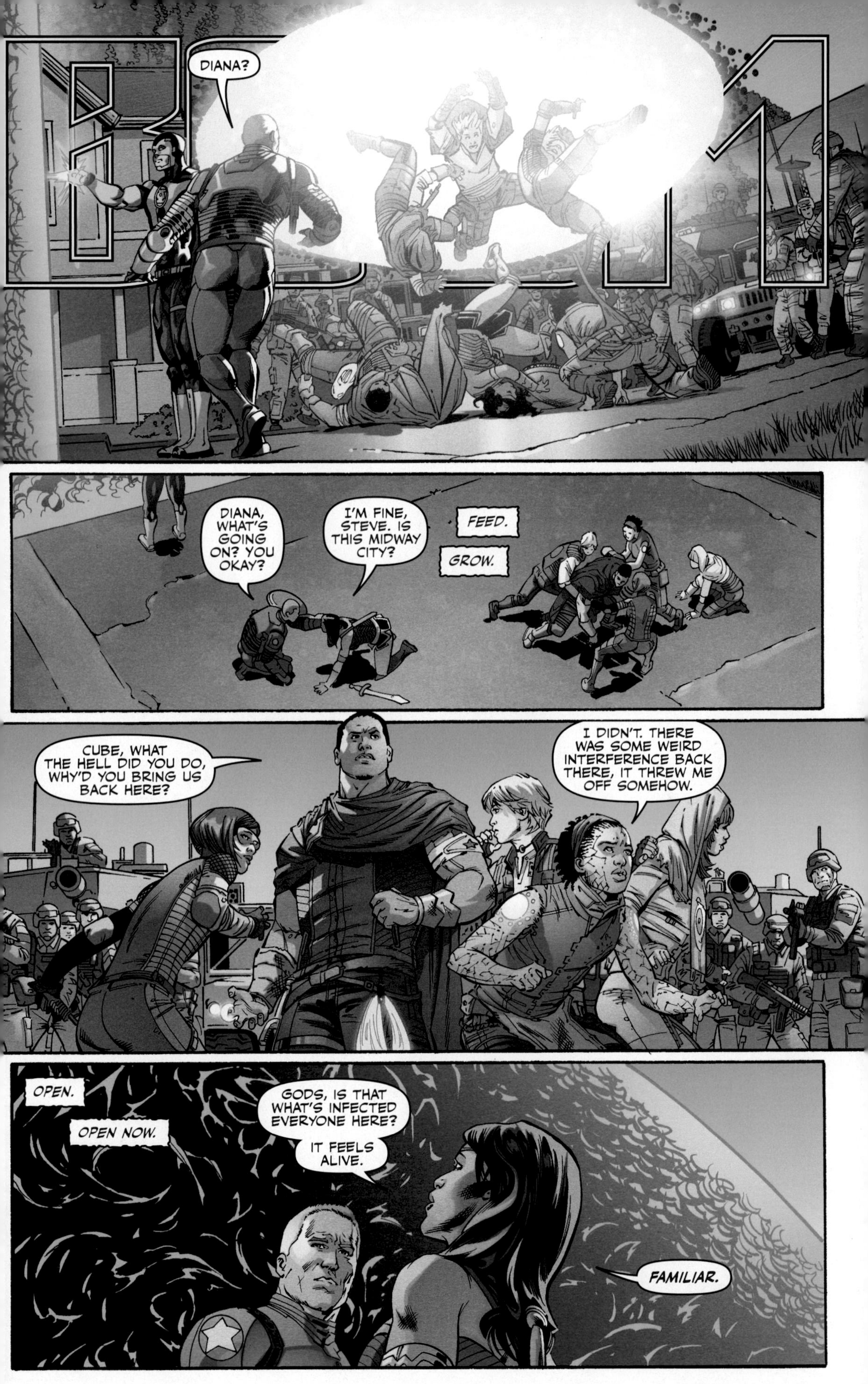
DIANA?
DIANA, WHAT'S GOING ON? YOU OKAY?
I'M FINE, STEVE. IS THIS MIDWAY CITY?
FEED.
GROW.
CUBE, WHAT THE HELL DID YOU DO, WHY'D YOU BRING US BACK HERE?
I DIDN'T. THERE WAS SOME WEIRD INTERFERENCE BACK THERE, IT THREW ME OFF SOMEHOW.
OPEN.
OPEN NOW.
GODS, IS THAT WHAT'S INFECTED EVERYONE HERE?
IT FEELS ALIVE.
FAMILIAR.

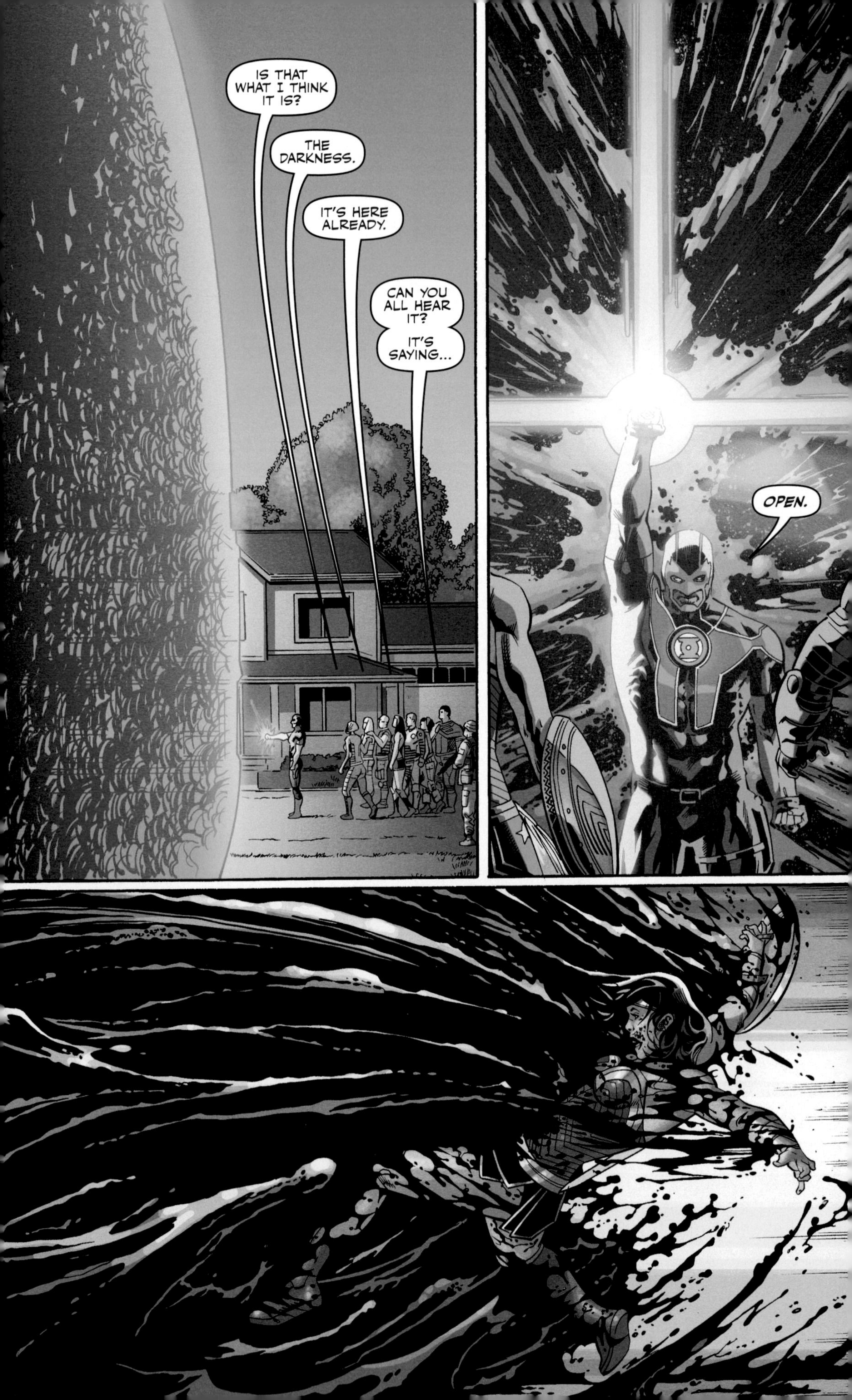
IS THAT WHAT I THINK IT IS?
THE DARKNESS.
IT'S HERE ALREADY.
CAN YOU ALL HEAR IT?
IT'S SAYING...
OPEN.

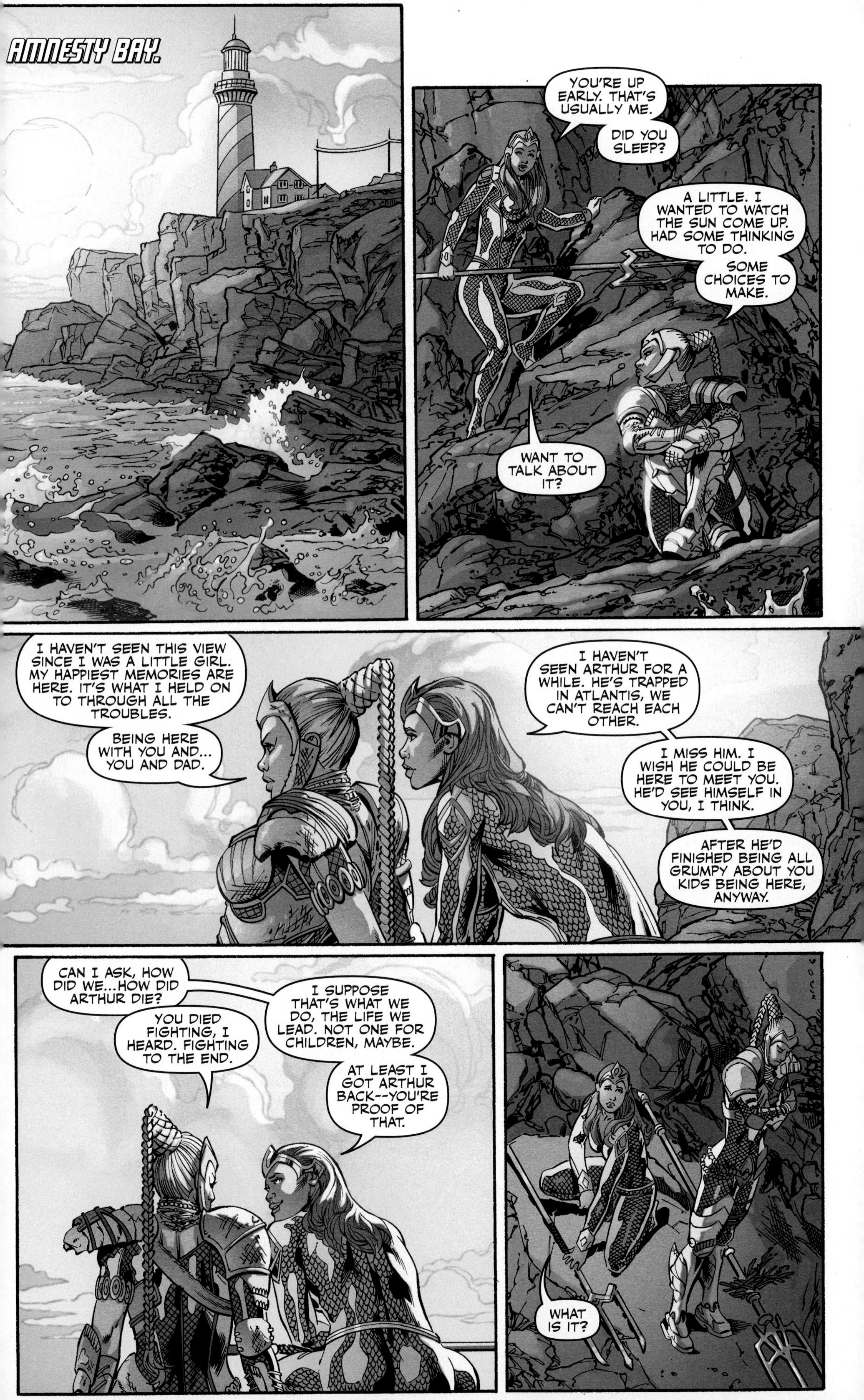
AMNESTY BAY.
YOU'RE UP EARLY. THAT'S USUALLY ME.
DID YOU SLEEP?
A LITTLE. I WANTED TO WATCH THE SUN COME UP. HAD SOME THINKING TO DO.
SOME CHOICES TO MAKE.
WANT TO TALK ABOUT IT?
I HAVEN'T SEEN THIS VIEW SINCE I WAS A LITTLE GIRL. MY HAPPIEST MEMORIES ARE HERE. IT'S WHAT I HELD ON TO THROUGH ALL THE TROUBLES.
BEING HERE WITH YOU AND... YOU AND DAD.
I HAVEN'T SEEN ARTHUR FOR A WHILE. HE'S TRAPPED IN ATLANTIS, WE CAN'T REACH EACH OTHER.
I MISS HIM. I WISH HE COULD BE HERE TO MEET YOU. HE'D SEE HIMSELF IN YOU, I THINK.
AFTER HE'D FINISHED BEING ALL GRUMPY ABOUT YOU KIDS BEING HERE, ANYWAY.
CAN I ASK, HOW DID WE...HOW DID ARTHUR DIE?
YOU DIED FIGHTING, I HEARD. FIGHTING TO THE END.
I SUPPOSE THAT'S WHAT WE DO, THE LIFE WE LEAD. NOT ONE FOR CHILDREN, MAYBE.
AT LEAST I GOT ARTHUR BACK--YOU'RE PROOF OF THAT.
WHAT IS IT?

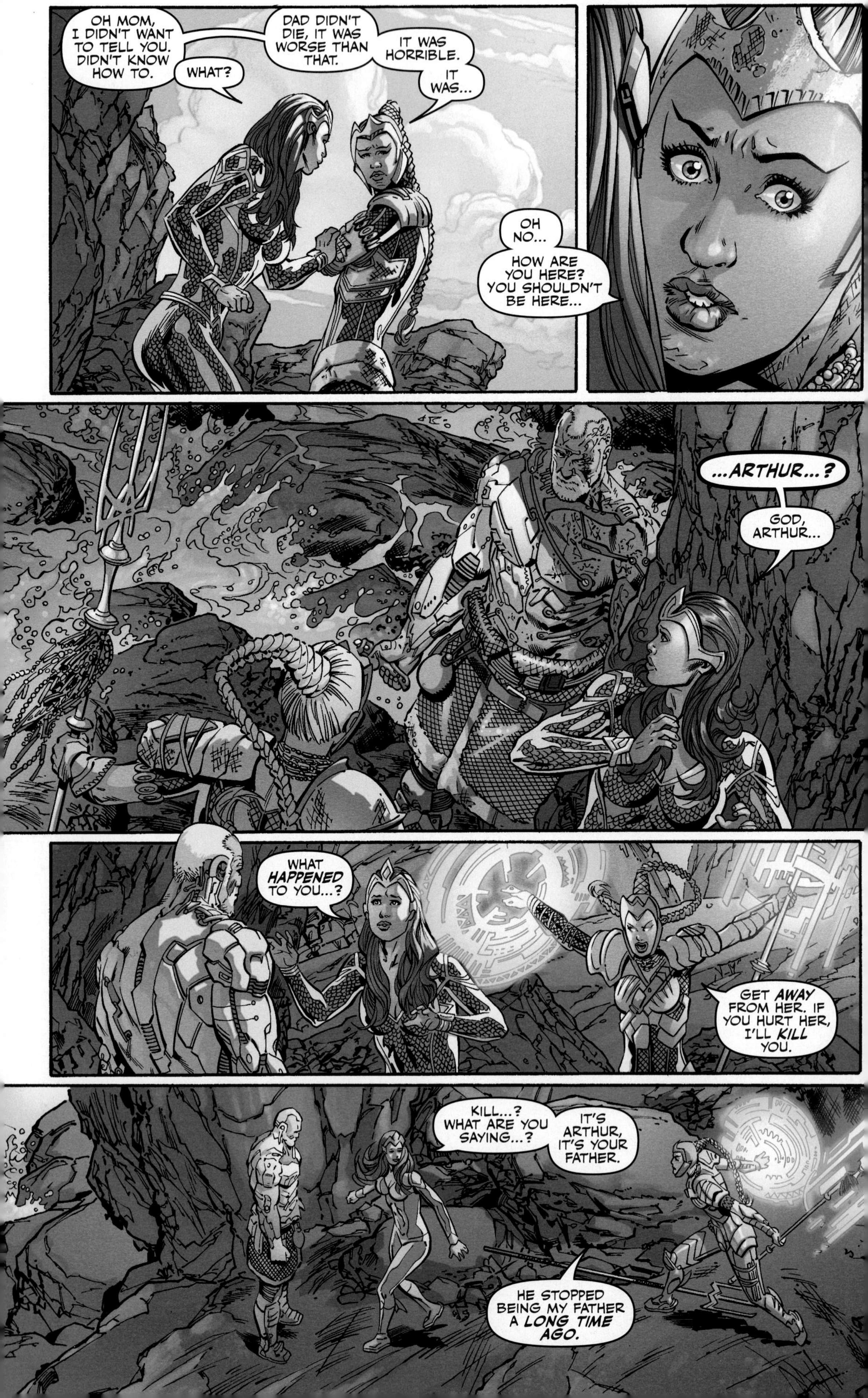

OH MOM, I DIDN'T WANT TO TELL YOU. DIDN'T KNOW HOW TO.
WHAT?
DAD DIDN'T DIE, IT WAS WORSE THAN THAT.
IT WAS HORRIBLE.
IT WAS...
OH NO...
HOW ARE YOU HERE? YOU SHOULDN'T BE HERE...
...ARTHUR...?
GOD, ARTHUR...
WHAT *HAPPENED* TO YOU...?
GET *AWAY* FROM HER. IF YOU HURT HER, I'LL *KILL* YOU.
KILL...? WHAT ARE YOU SAYING...?
IT'S ARTHUR, IT'S YOUR FATHER.
HE STOPPED BEING MY FATHER A *LONG TIME AGO.*

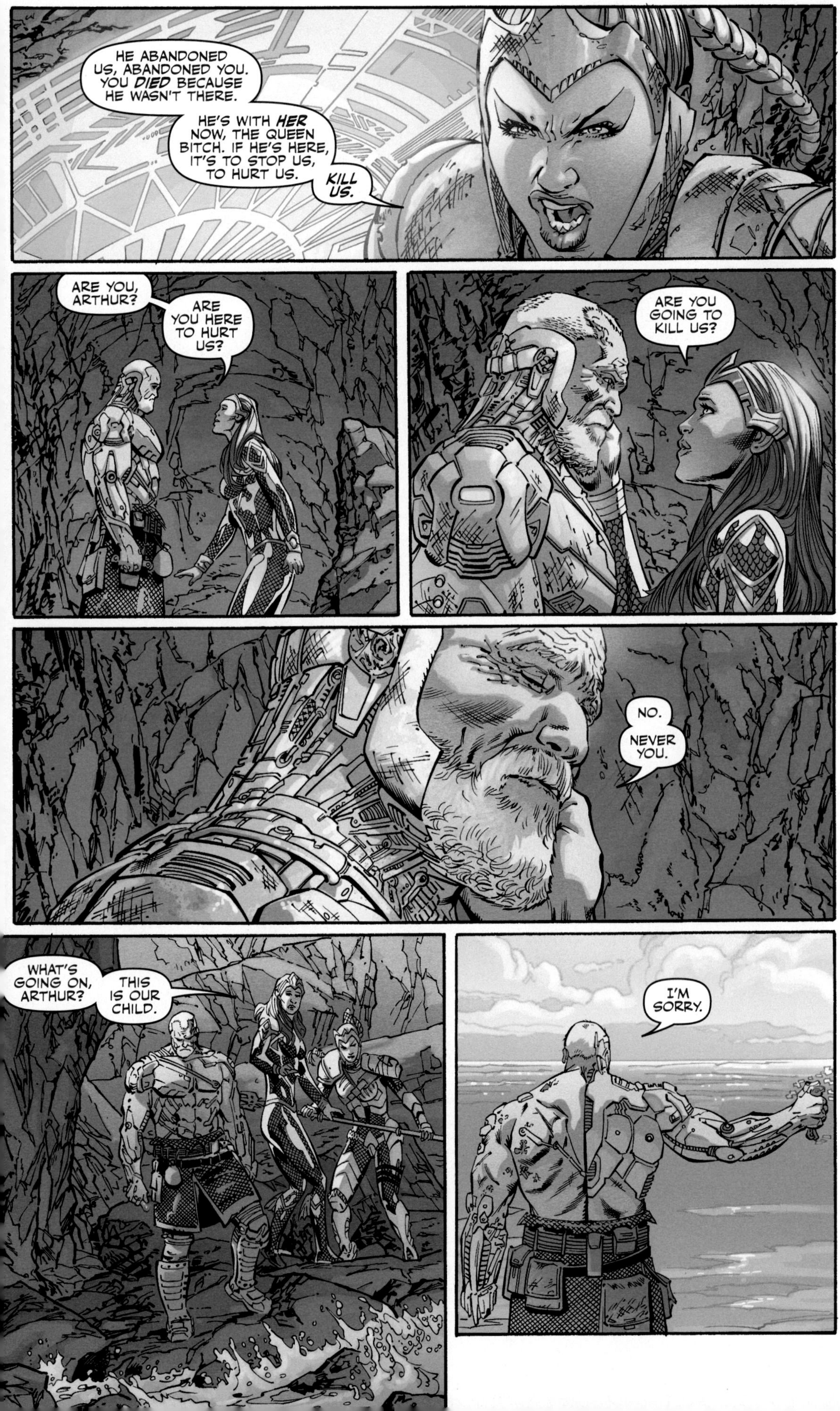
HE ABANDONED US, ABANDONED YOU. YOU DIED BECAUSE HE WASN'T THERE.
HE'S WITH HER NOW, THE QUEEN BITCH. IF HE'S HERE, IT'S TO STOP US, TO HURT US.
KILL US.
ARE YOU, ARTHUR?
ARE YOU HERE TO HURT US?
ARE YOU GOING TO KILL US?
NO.
NEVER YOU.
WHAT'S GOING ON, ARTHUR?
THIS IS OUR CHILD.
I'M SORRY.

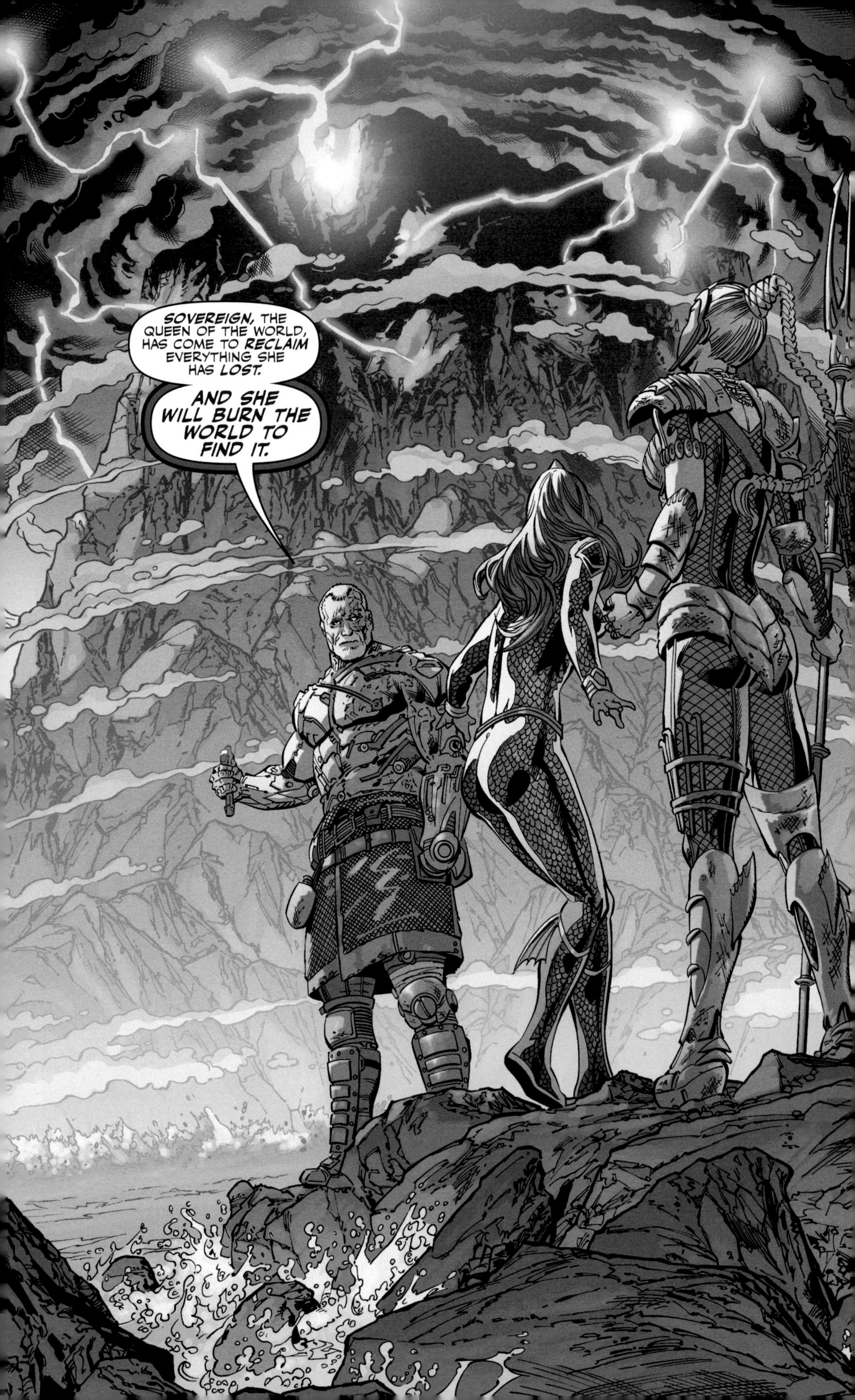

SOVEREIGN, THE QUEEN OF THE WORLD, HAS COME TO RECLAIM EVERYTHING SHE HAS LOST.
AND SHE WILL BURN THE WORLD TO FIND IT.

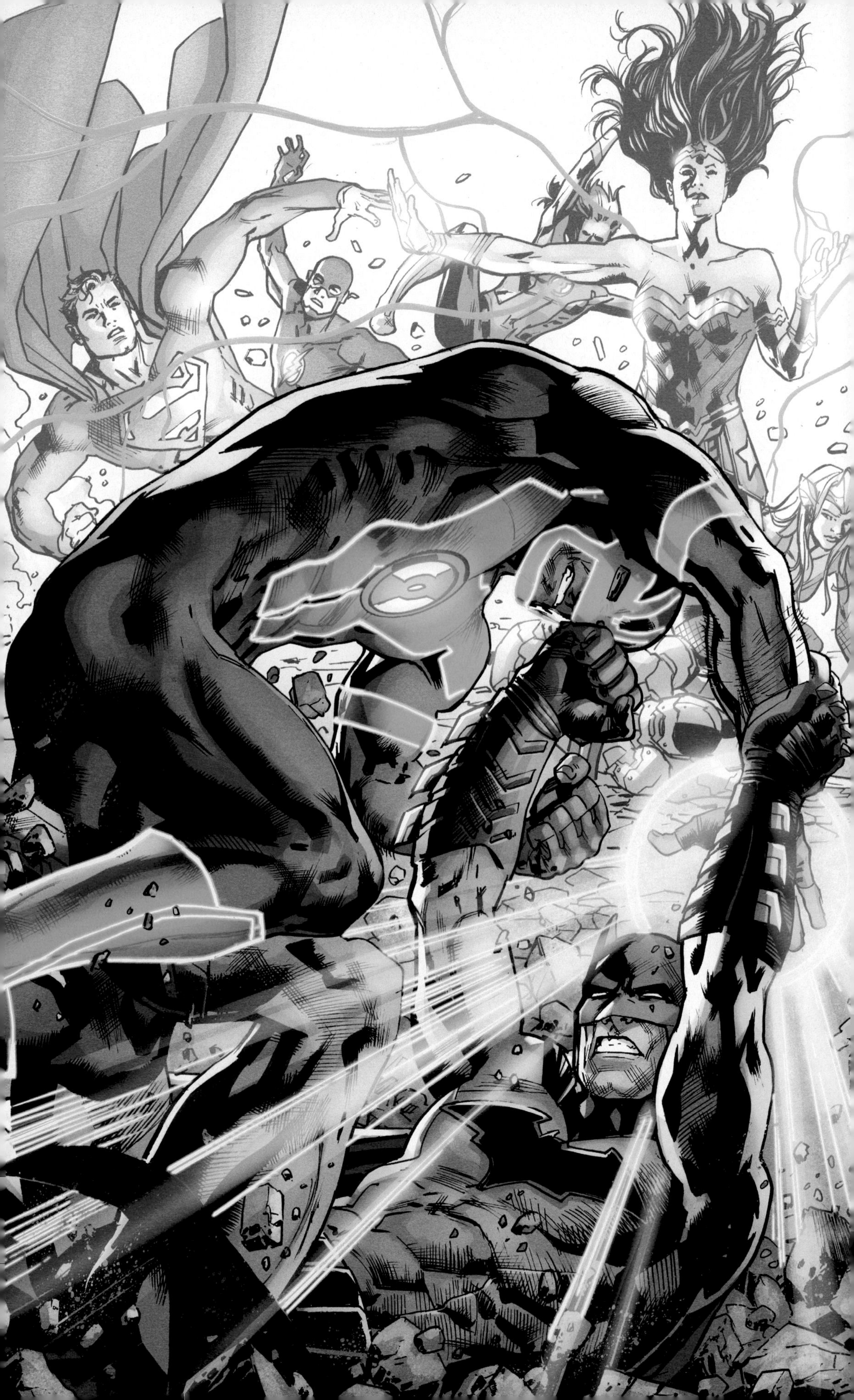

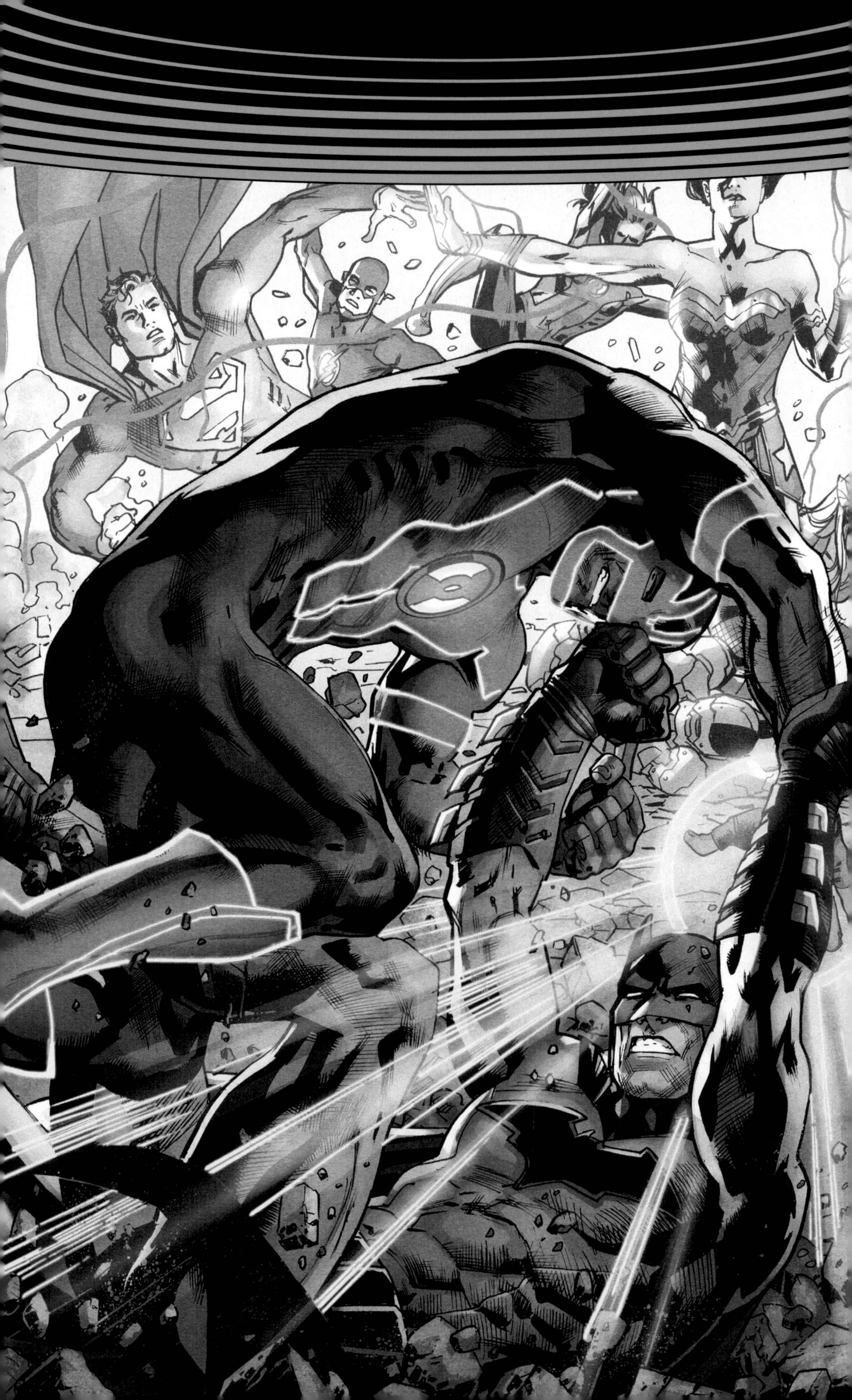

LEGACY PART FIVE

RYAN HITCH WRITER **FERNANDO PASARIN** PENCILLER **ANDY OWENS, MICK GRAY, BATT, SCOTT HANNA** INKERS

COLORED by	LETTERED by	COVER by	VARIANT COVER by	ASSOCIATE ED.	EDITOR
BRAD ANDERSON	RICHARD STARKINGS & COMICRAFT'S JIMMY	BRYAN HITCH & ALEX SINCLAIR	GUILLEM MARCH	AMEDEO TURTURRO	BRIAN CUNNINGHAM

SUPERMAN created by JERRY SIEGEL and JOE SHUSTER. By special arrangement with the JERRY SIEGEL FAMILY.

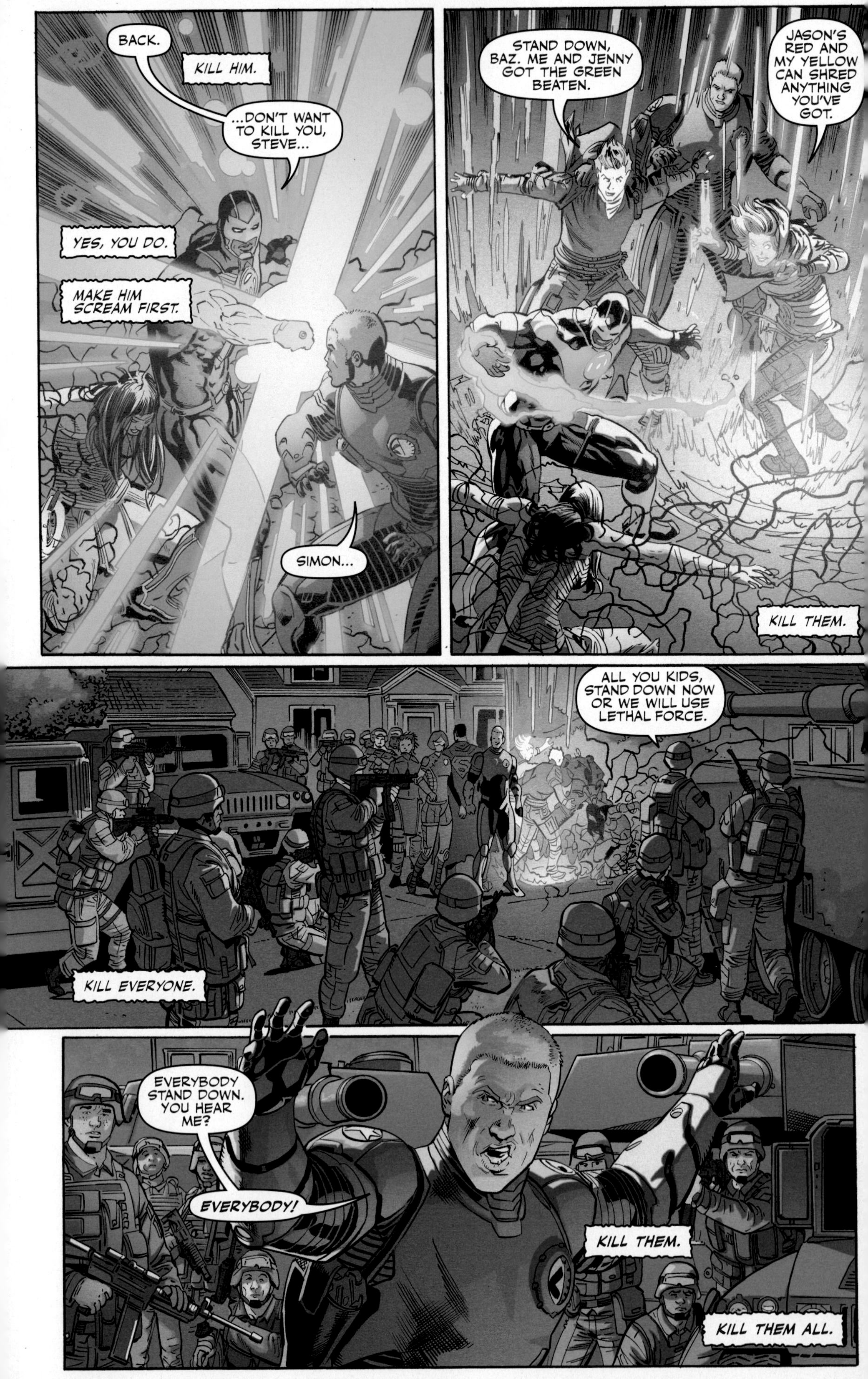
BACK.
KILL HIM.
...DON'T WANT TO KILL YOU, STEVE...
YES, YOU DO.
MAKE HIM SCREAM FIRST.
SIMON...
STAND DOWN, BAZ. ME AND JENNY GOT THE GREEN BEATEN.
JASON'S RED AND MY YELLOW CAN SHRED ANYTHING YOU'VE GOT.
KILL THEM.
ALL YOU KIDS, STAND DOWN NOW OR WE WILL USE LETHAL FORCE.
KILL EVERYONE.
EVERYBODY STAND DOWN. YOU HEAR ME?
EVERYBODY!
KILL THEM.
KILL THEM ALL.

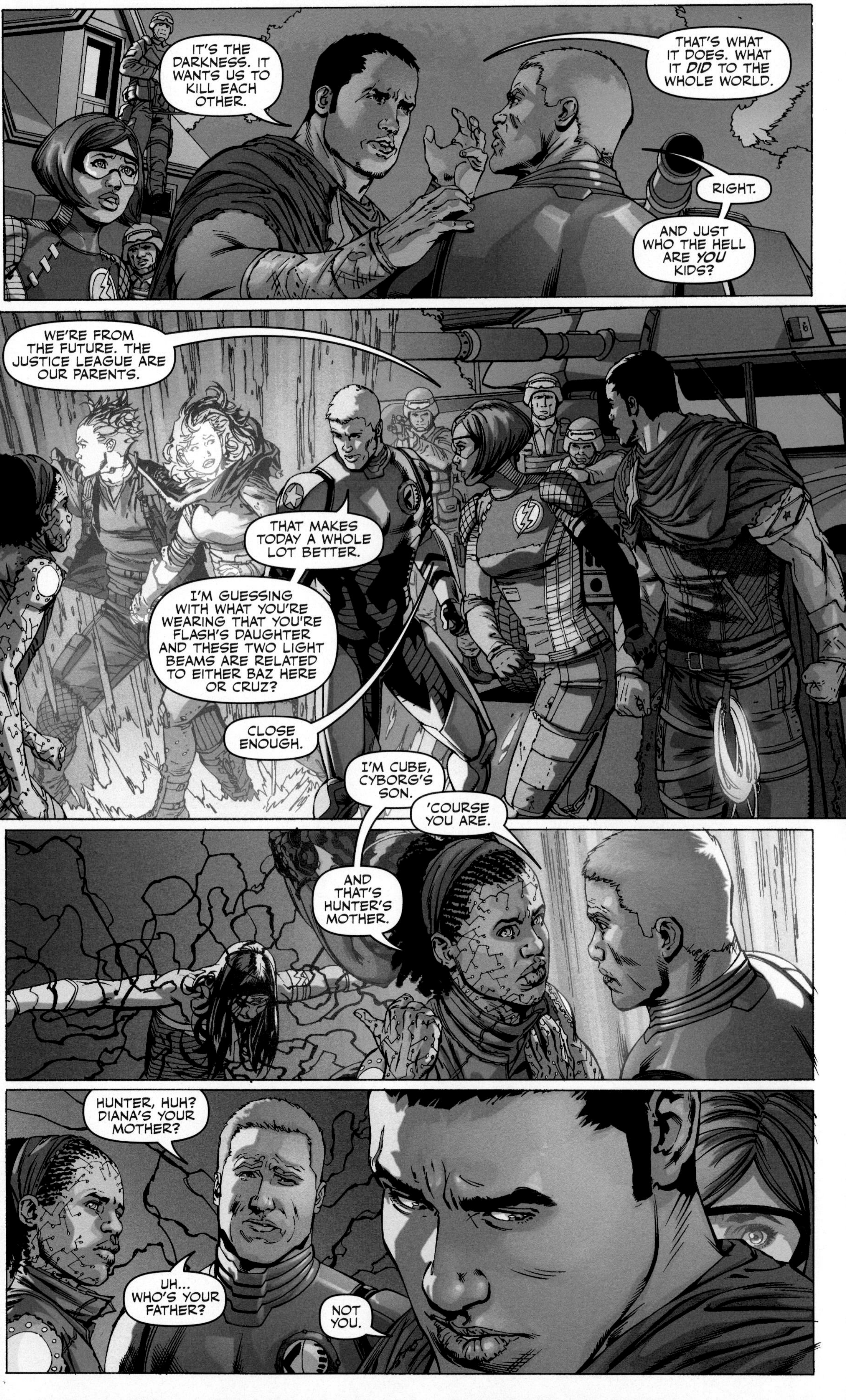
IT'S THE DARKNESS. IT WANTS US TO KILL EACH OTHER.
THAT'S WHAT IT DOES. WHAT IT DID TO THE WHOLE WORLD.
RIGHT.
AND JUST WHO THE HELL ARE YOU KIDS?
WE'RE FROM THE FUTURE. THE JUSTICE LEAGUE ARE OUR PARENTS.
THAT MAKES TODAY A WHOLE LOT BETTER.
I'M GUESSING WITH WHAT YOU'RE WEARING THAT YOU'RE FLASH'S DAUGHTER AND THESE TWO LIGHT BEAMS ARE RELATED TO EITHER BAZ HERE OR CRUZ?
CLOSE ENOUGH.
I'M CUBE, CYBORG'S SON.
'COURSE YOU ARE.
AND THAT'S HUNTER'S MOTHER.
HUNTER, HUH? DIANA'S YOUR MOTHER?
UH... WHO'S YOUR FATHER?
NOT YOU.

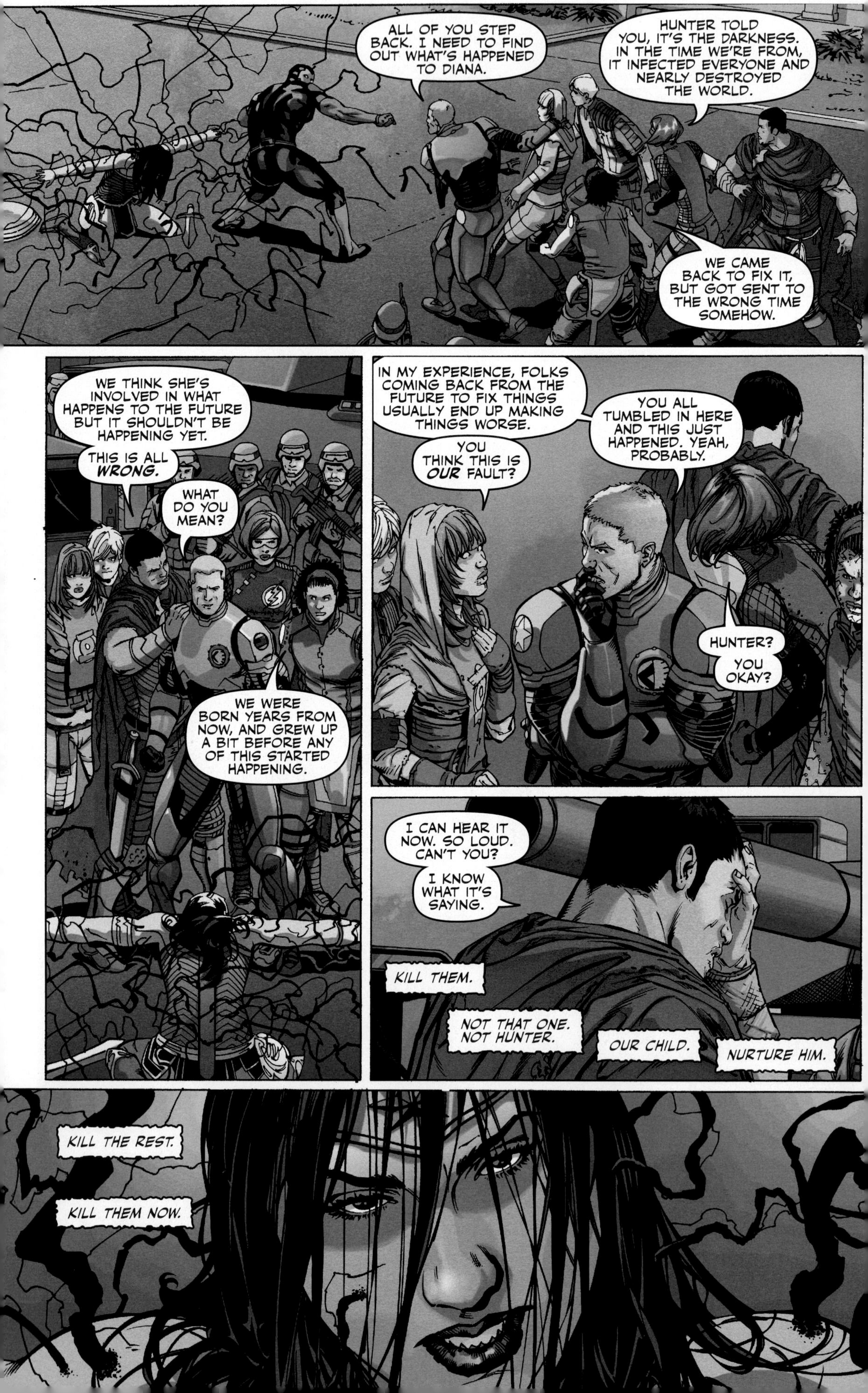
ALL OF YOU STEP BACK. I NEED TO FIND OUT WHAT'S HAPPENED TO DIANA.
HUNTER TOLD YOU, IT'S THE DARKNESS. IN THE TIME WE'RE FROM, IT INFECTED EVERYONE AND NEARLY DESTROYED THE WORLD.
WE CAME BACK TO FIX IT, BUT GOT SENT TO THE WRONG TIME SOMEHOW.
WE THINK SHE'S INVOLVED IN WHAT HAPPENS TO THE FUTURE BUT IT SHOULDN'T BE HAPPENING YET.
THIS IS ALL WRONG.
WHAT DO YOU MEAN?
WE WERE BORN YEARS FROM NOW, AND GREW UP A BIT BEFORE ANY OF THIS STARTED HAPPENING.
IN MY EXPERIENCE, FOLKS COMING BACK FROM THE FUTURE TO FIX THINGS USUALLY END UP MAKING THINGS WORSE.
YOU THINK THIS IS OUR FAULT?
YOU ALL TUMBLED IN HERE AND THIS JUST HAPPENED. YEAH, PROBABLY.
HUNTER?
YOU OKAY?
I CAN HEAR IT NOW. SO LOUD. CAN'T YOU?
I KNOW WHAT IT'S SAYING.
KILL THEM.
NOT THAT ONE. NOT HUNTER.
OUR CHILD.
NURTURE HIM.
KILL THE REST.
KILL THEM NOW.

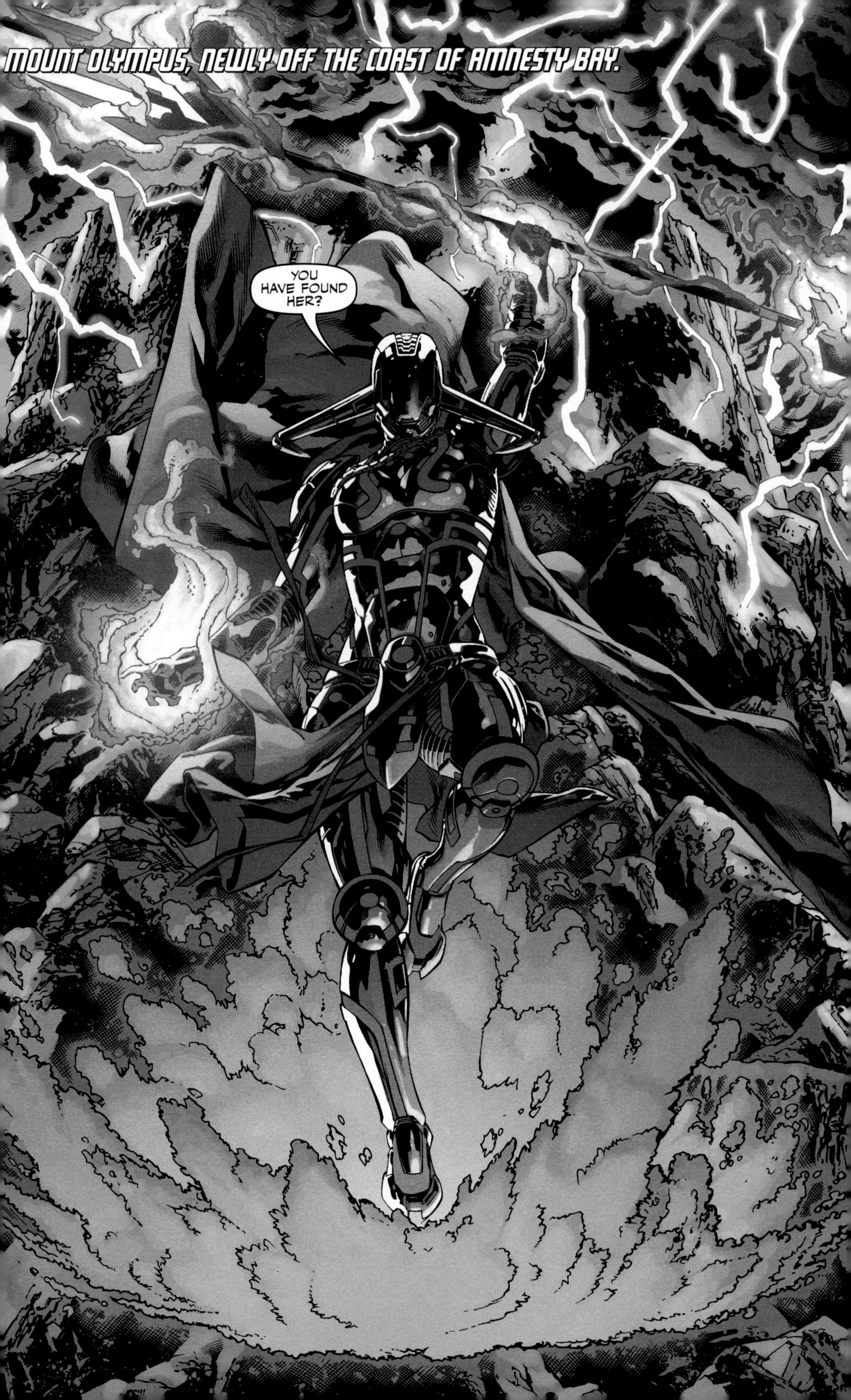
MOUNT OLYMPUS, NEWLY OFF THE COAST OF AMNESTY BAY.
YOU HAVE FOUND HER?

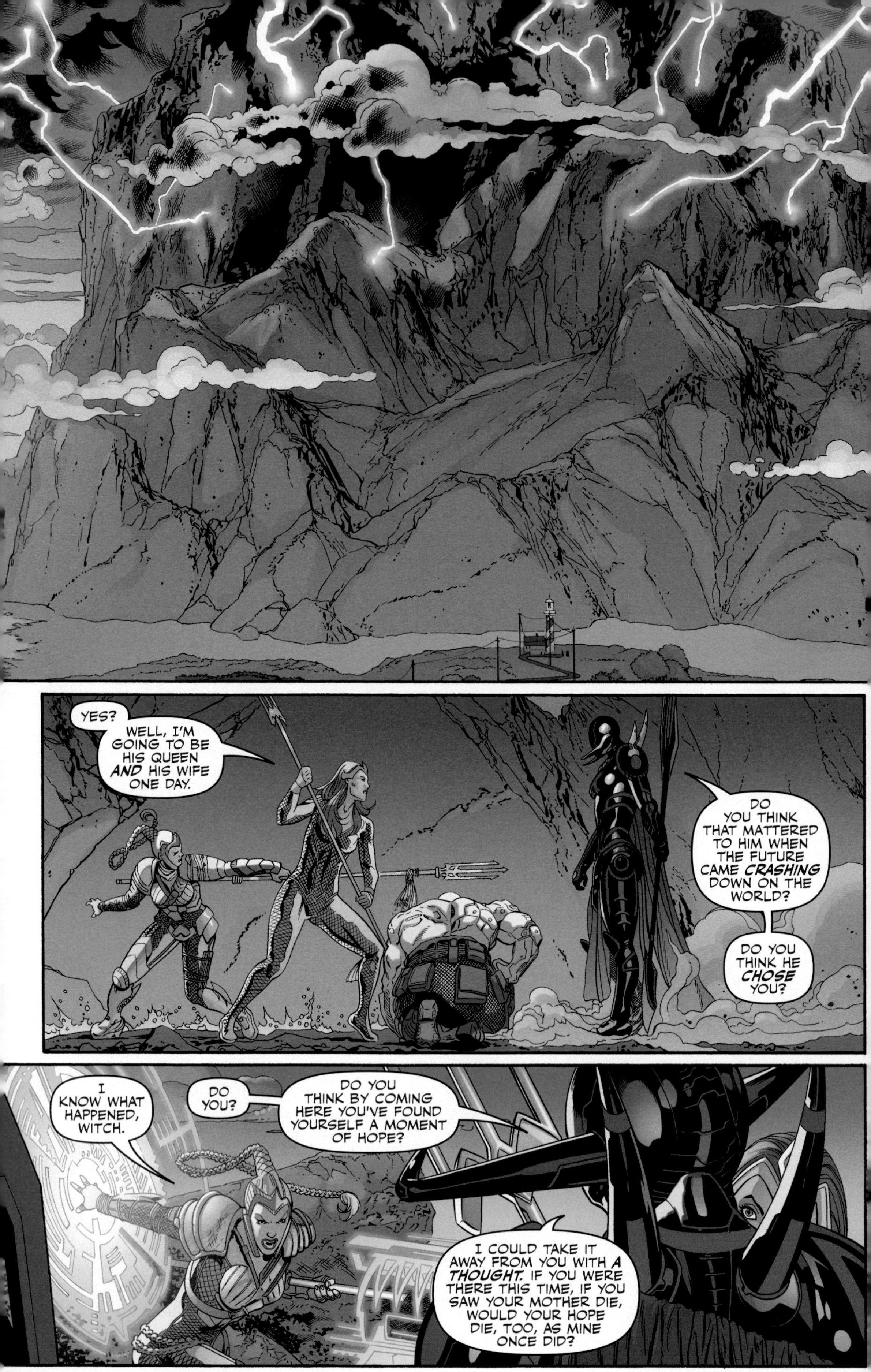
YES?
WELL, I'M GOING TO BE HIS QUEEN AND HIS WIFE ONE DAY.
DO YOU THINK THAT MATTERED TO HIM WHEN THE FUTURE CAME CRASHING DOWN ON THE WORLD?
DO YOU THINK HE CHOSE YOU?
I KNOW WHAT HAPPENED, WITCH.
DO YOU?
DO YOU THINK BY COMING HERE YOU'VE FOUND YOURSELF A MOMENT OF HOPE?
I COULD TAKE IT AWAY FROM YOU WITH A THOUGHT. IF YOU WERE THERE THIS TIME, IF YOU SAW YOUR MOTHER DIE, WOULD YOUR HOPE DIE, TOO, AS MINE ONCE DID?

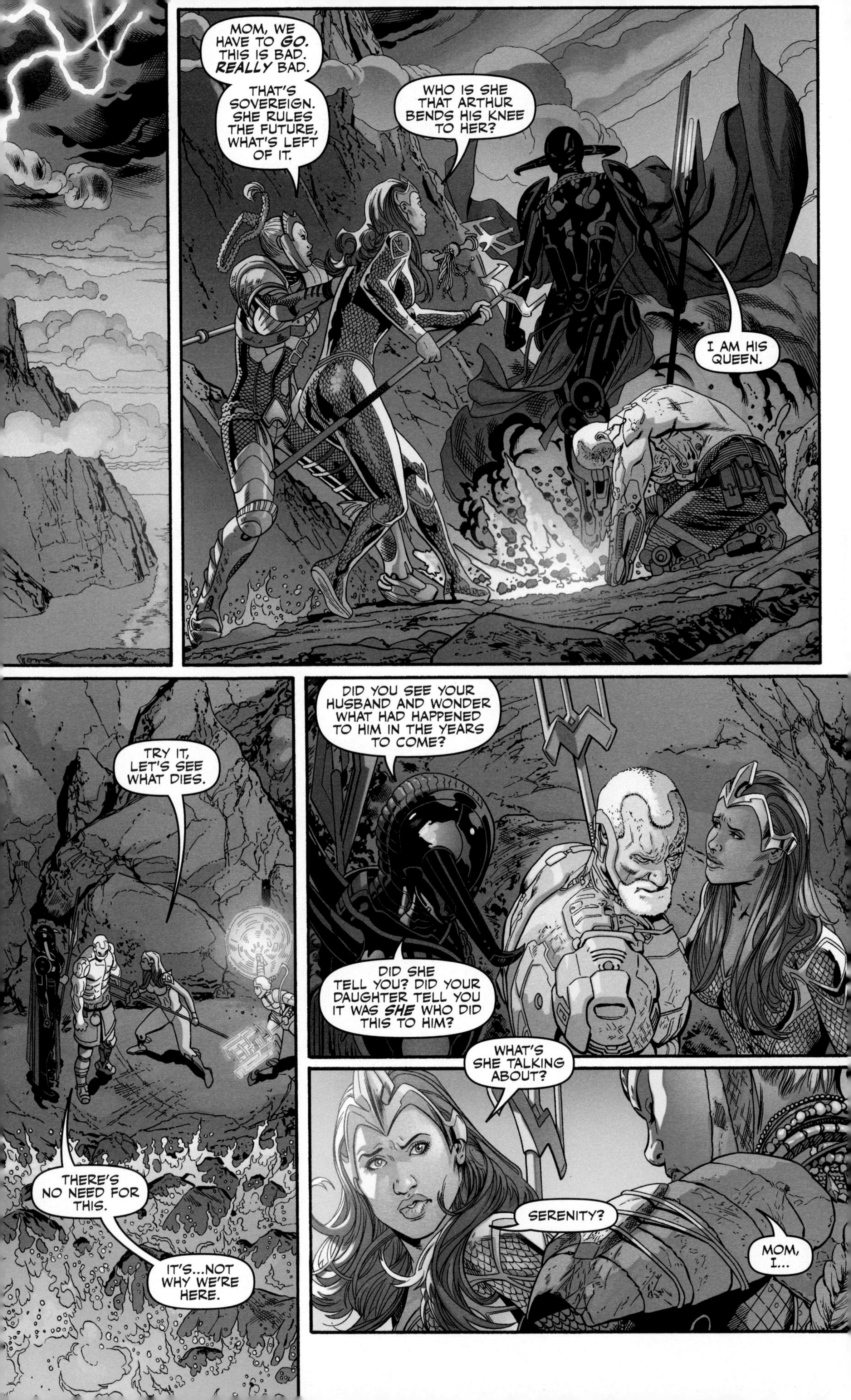
MOM, WE HAVE TO **GO.** THIS IS BAD. ***REALLY*** BAD.
THAT'S SOVEREIGN. SHE RULES THE FUTURE, WHAT'S LEFT OF IT.
WHO IS SHE THAT ARTHUR BENDS HIS KNEE TO HER?
I AM HIS QUEEN.
TRY IT, LET'S SEE WHAT DIES.
THERE'S NO NEED FOR THIS.
IT'S...NOT WHY WE'RE HERE.
DID YOU SEE YOUR HUSBAND AND WONDER WHAT HAD HAPPENED TO HIM IN THE YEARS TO COME?
DID SHE TELL YOU? DID YOUR DAUGHTER TELL YOU IT WAS ***SHE*** WHO DID THIS TO HIM?
WHAT'S SHE TALKING ABOUT?
SERENITY?
MOM, I...

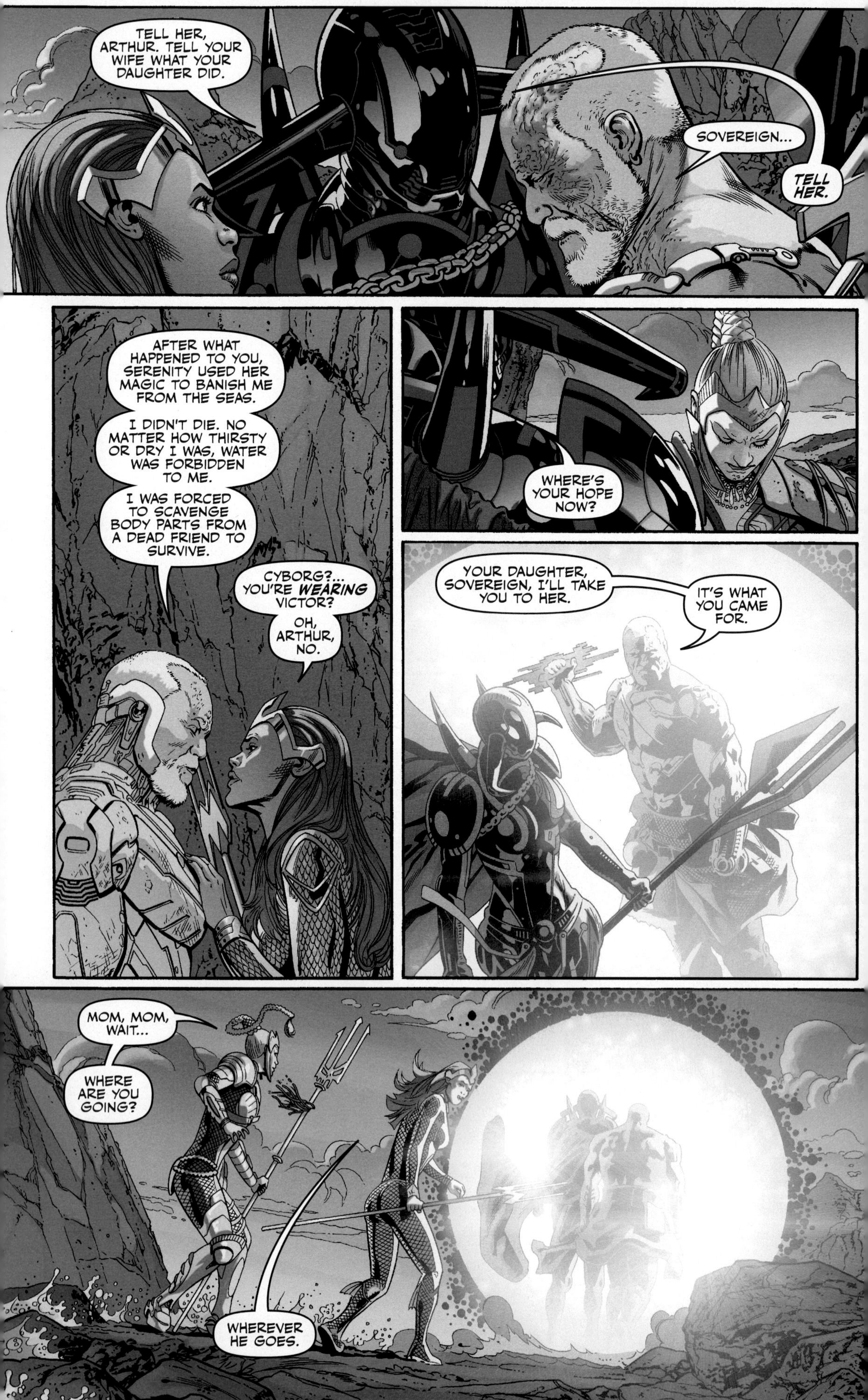
TELL HER, ARTHUR. TELL YOUR WIFE WHAT YOUR DAUGHTER DID.
SOVEREIGN...
TELL HER.
AFTER WHAT HAPPENED TO YOU, SERENITY USED HER MAGIC TO BANISH ME FROM THE SEAS.
I DIDN'T DIE. NO MATTER HOW THIRSTY OR DRY I WAS, WATER WAS FORBIDDEN TO ME.
I WAS FORCED TO SCAVENGE BODY PARTS FROM A DEAD FRIEND TO SURVIVE.
CYBORG?... YOU'RE WEARING VICTOR?
OH, ARTHUR, NO.
WHERE'S YOUR HOPE NOW?
YOUR DAUGHTER, SOVEREIGN, I'LL TAKE YOU TO HER.
IT'S WHAT YOU CAME FOR.
MOM, MOM, WAIT...
WHERE ARE YOU GOING?
WHEREVER HE GOES.

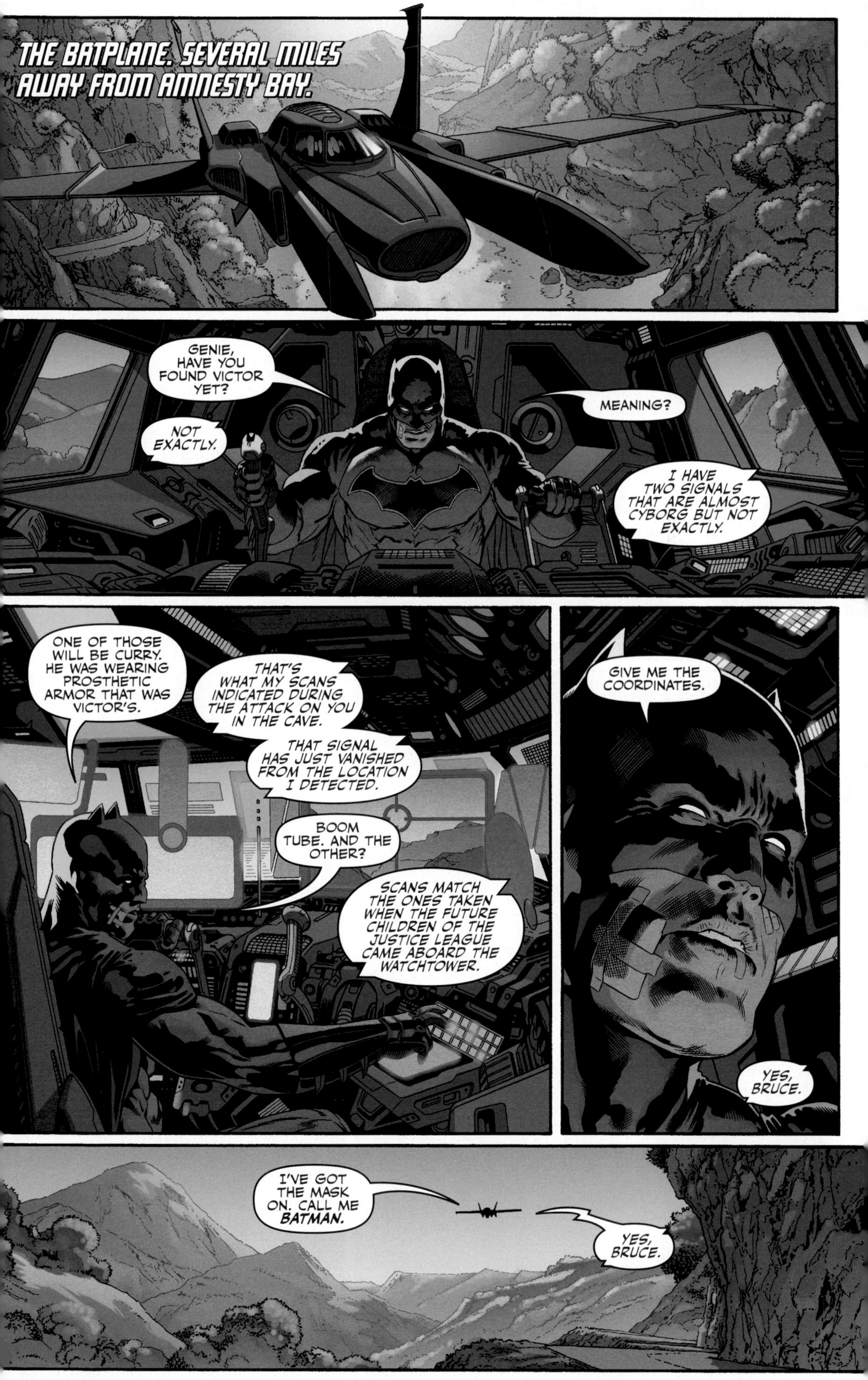
THE BATPLANE. SEVERAL MILES AWAY FROM AMNESTY BAY.
GENIE, HAVE YOU FOUND VICTOR YET?
NOT EXACTLY.
MEANING?
I HAVE TWO SIGNALS THAT ARE ALMOST CYBORG BUT NOT EXACTLY.
ONE OF THOSE WILL BE CURRY. HE WAS WEARING PROSTHETIC ARMOR THAT WAS VICTOR'S.
THAT'S WHAT MY SCANS INDICATED DURING THE ATTACK ON YOU IN THE CAVE.
THAT SIGNAL HAS JUST VANISHED FROM THE LOCATION I DETECTED.
BOOM TUBE. AND THE OTHER?
SCANS MATCH THE ONES TAKEN WHEN THE FUTURE CHILDREN OF THE JUSTICE LEAGUE CAME ABOARD THE WATCHTOWER.
GIVE ME THE COORDINATES.
YES, BRUCE.
I'VE GOT THE MASK ON. CALL ME BATMAN.
YES, BRUCE.

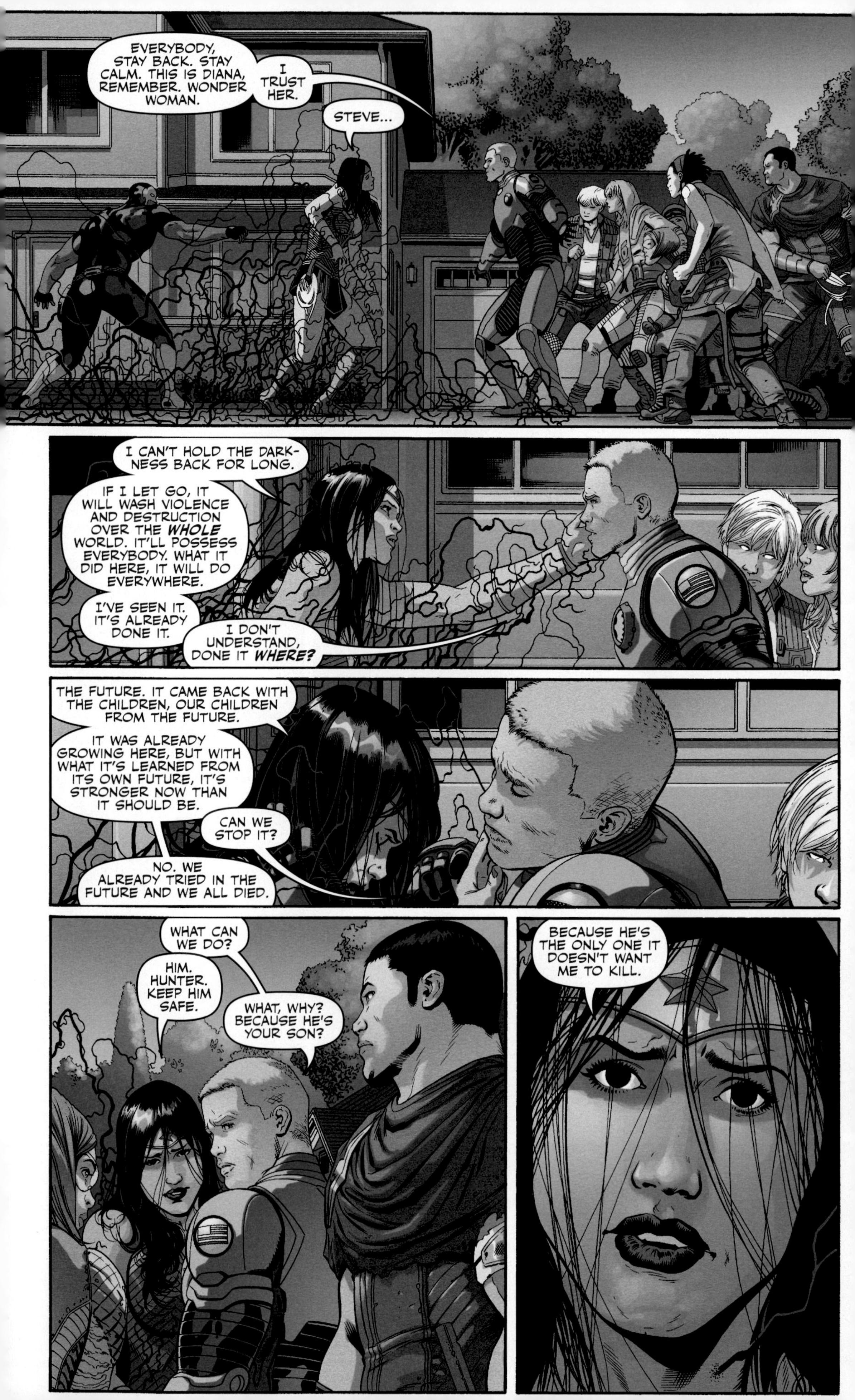
EVERYBODY, STAY BACK. STAY CALM. THIS IS DIANA, REMEMBER. WONDER WOMAN.
I TRUST HER.
STEVE...
I CAN'T HOLD THE DARKNESS BACK FOR LONG.
IF I LET GO, IT WILL WASH VIOLENCE AND DESTRUCTION OVER THE *WHOLE* WORLD. IT'LL POSSESS EVERYBODY. WHAT IT DID HERE, IT WILL DO EVERYWHERE.
I'VE SEEN IT. IT'S ALREADY DONE IT.
I DON'T UNDERSTAND, DONE IT *WHERE?*
THE FUTURE. IT CAME BACK WITH THE CHILDREN, OUR CHILDREN FROM THE FUTURE.
IT WAS ALREADY GROWING HERE, BUT WITH WHAT IT'S LEARNED FROM ITS OWN FUTURE, IT'S STRONGER NOW THAN IT SHOULD BE.
CAN WE STOP IT?
NO. WE ALREADY TRIED IN THE FUTURE AND WE ALL DIED.
WHAT CAN WE DO?
HIM. HUNTER. KEEP HIM SAFE.
WHAT, WHY? BECAUSE HE'S YOUR SON?
BECAUSE HE'S THE ONLY ONE IT DOESN'T WANT ME TO KILL.

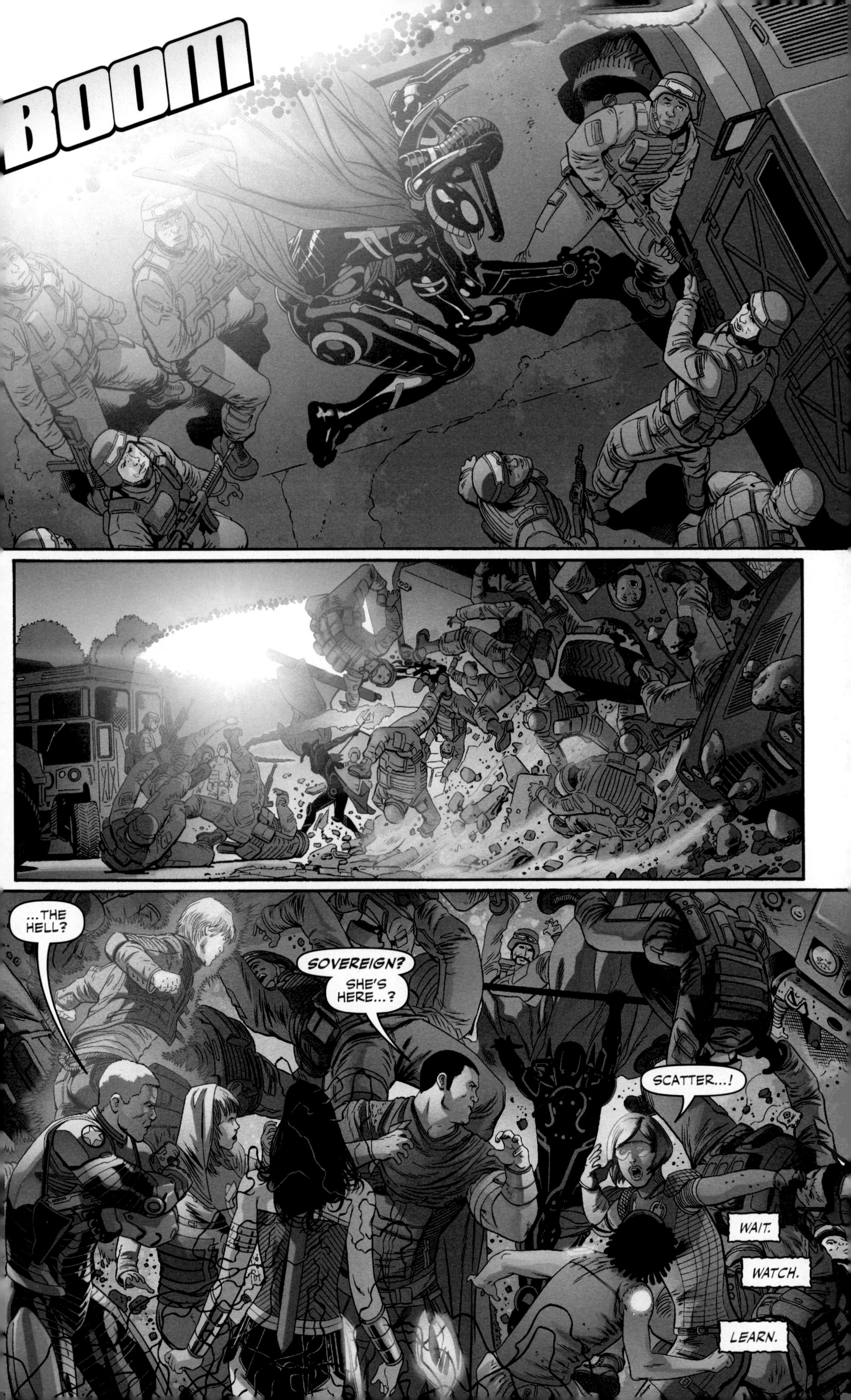
BOOM
...THE HELL?
SOVEREIGN? SHE'S HERE...?
SCATTER...!
WAIT.
WATCH.
LEARN.

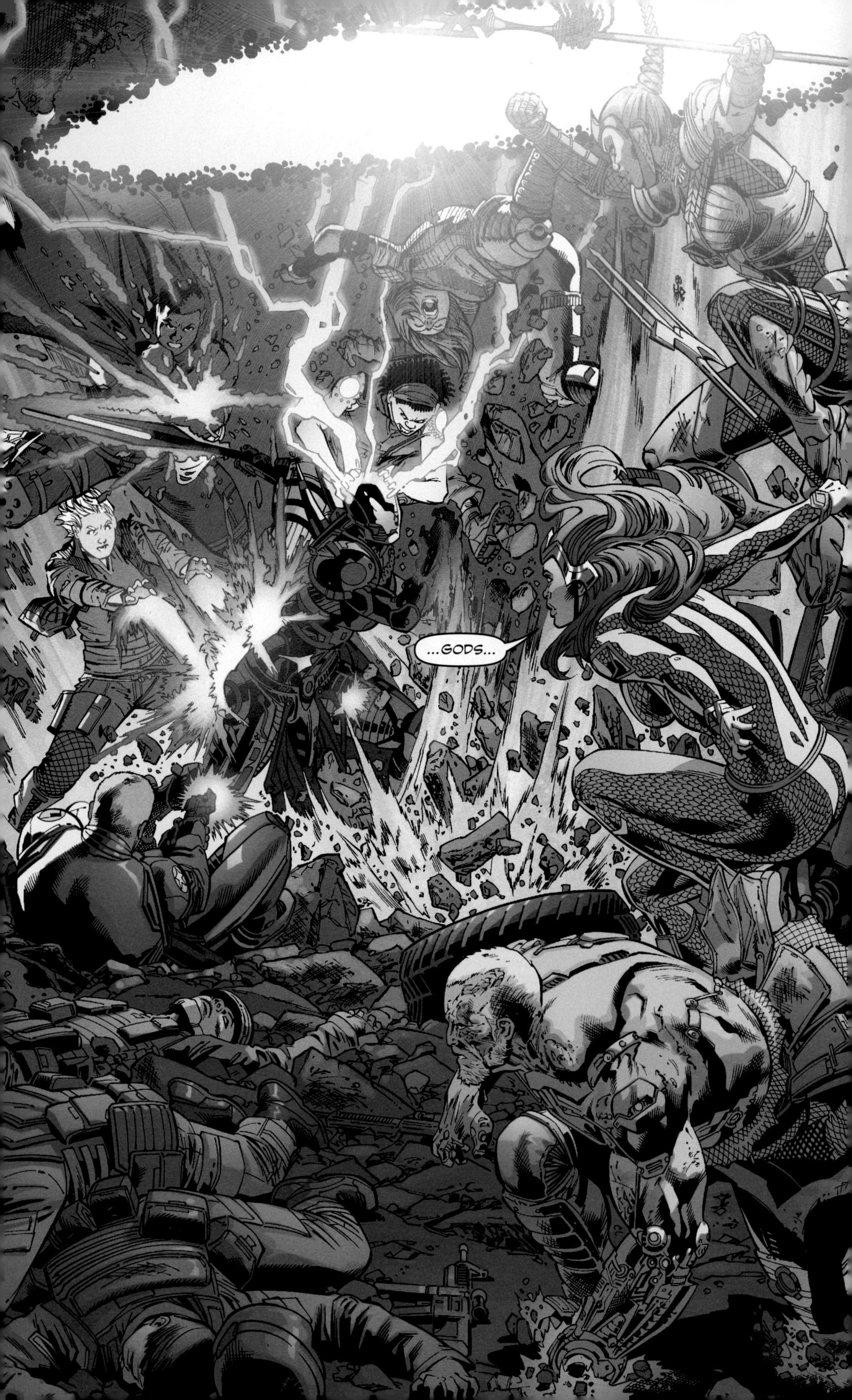
...GODS...

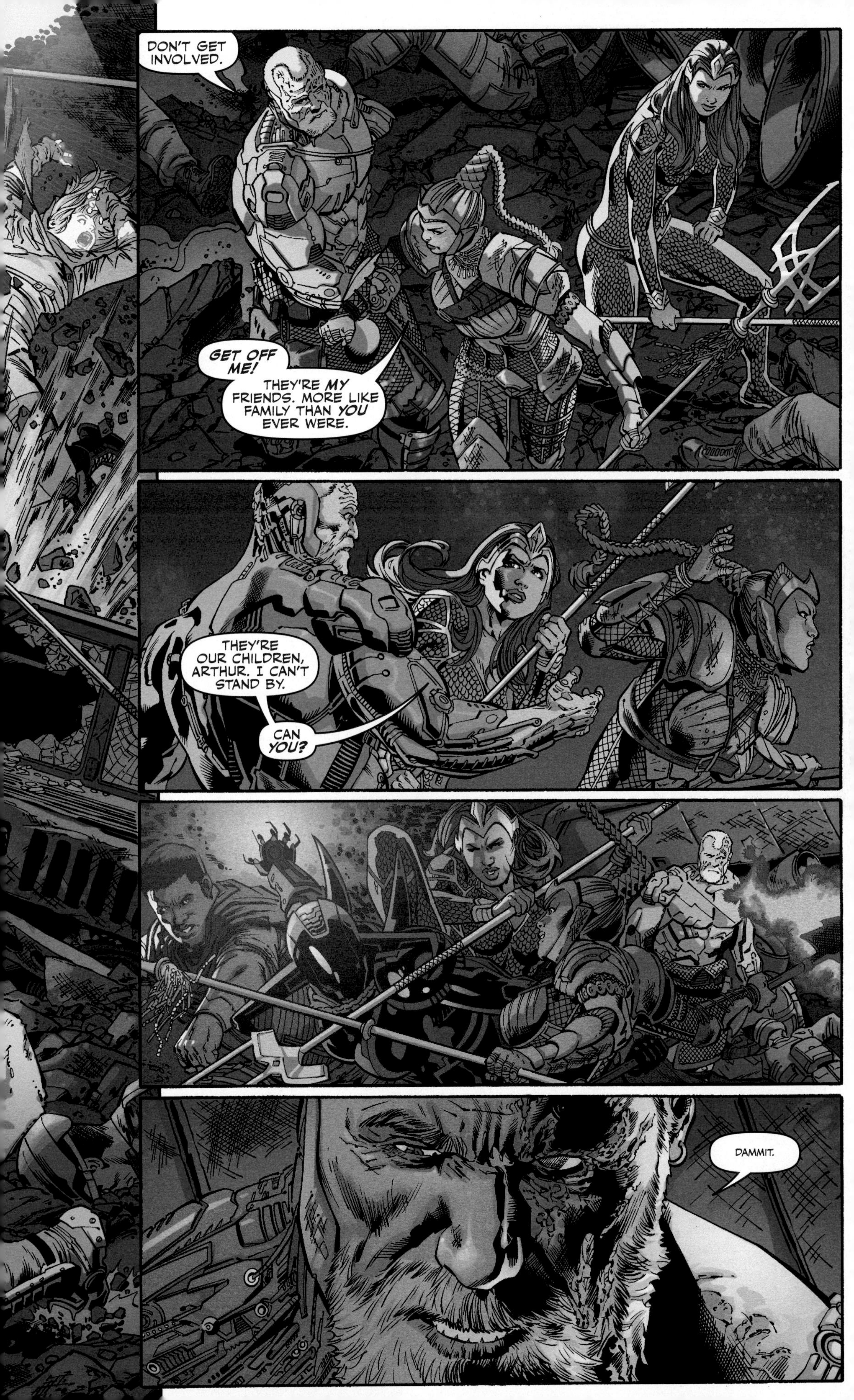
DON'T GET INVOLVED.
GET OFF ME!
THEY'RE MY FRIENDS. MORE LIKE FAMILY THAN YOU EVER WERE.
THEY'RE OUR CHILDREN, ARTHUR. I CAN'T STAND BY.
CAN YOU?
DAMMIT.

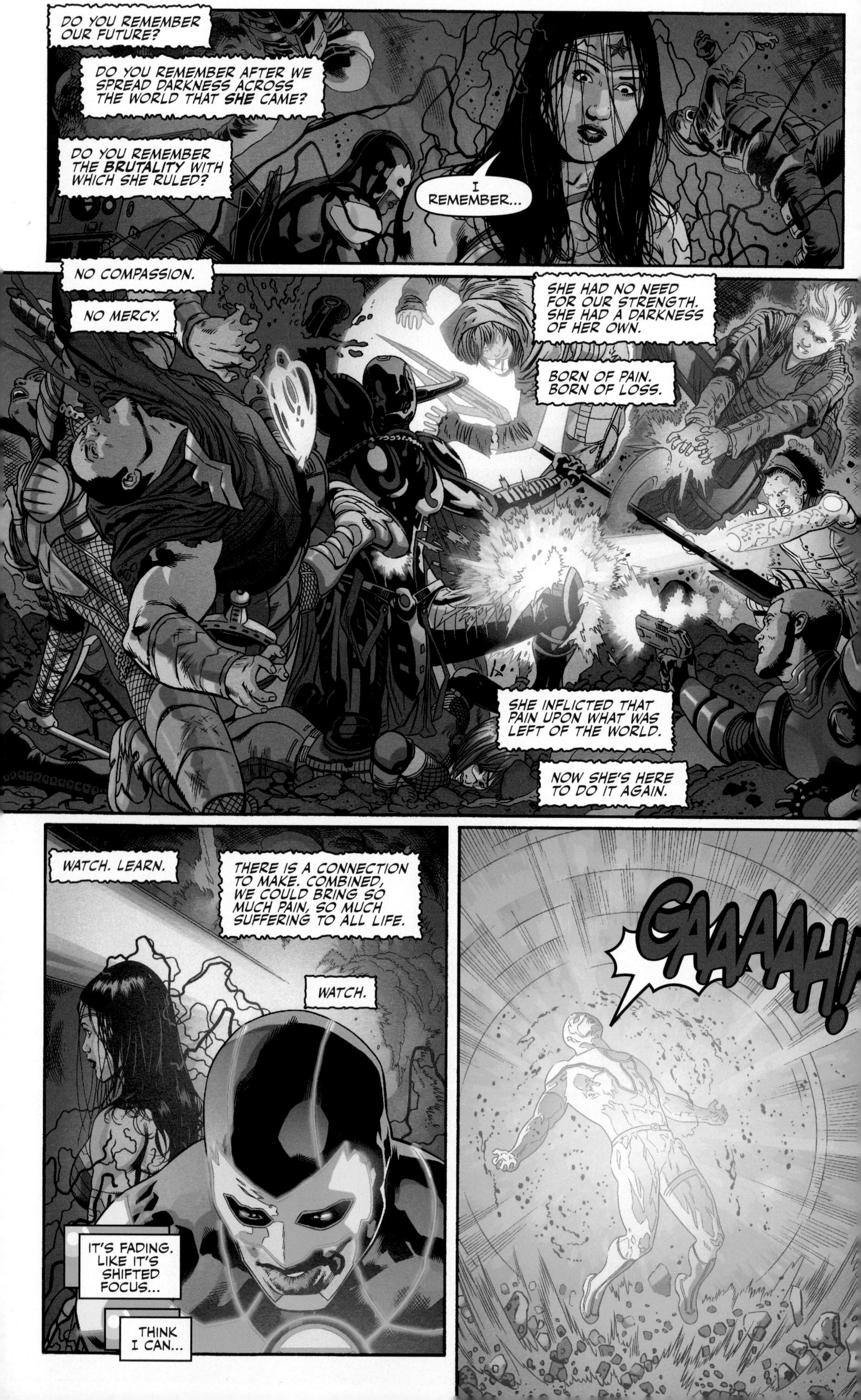
DO YOU REMEMBER OUR FUTURE?
DO YOU REMEMBER AFTER WE SPREAD DARKNESS ACROSS THE WORLD THAT SHE CAME?
DO YOU REMEMBER THE BRUTALITY WITH WHICH SHE RULED?
I REMEMBER...
NO COMPASSION.
NO MERCY.
SHE HAD NO NEED FOR OUR STRENGTH. SHE HAD A DARKNESS OF HER OWN.
BORN OF PAIN. BORN OF LOSS.
SHE INFLICTED THAT PAIN UPON WHAT WAS LEFT OF THE WORLD.
NOW SHE'S HERE TO DO IT AGAIN.
WATCH. LEARN.
THERE IS A CONNECTION TO MAKE. COMBINED, WE COULD BRING SO MUCH PAIN, SO MUCH SUFFERING TO ALL LIFE.
WATCH.
IT'S FADING. LIKE IT'S SHIFTED FOCUS...
THINK I CAN...
GAAAAH!

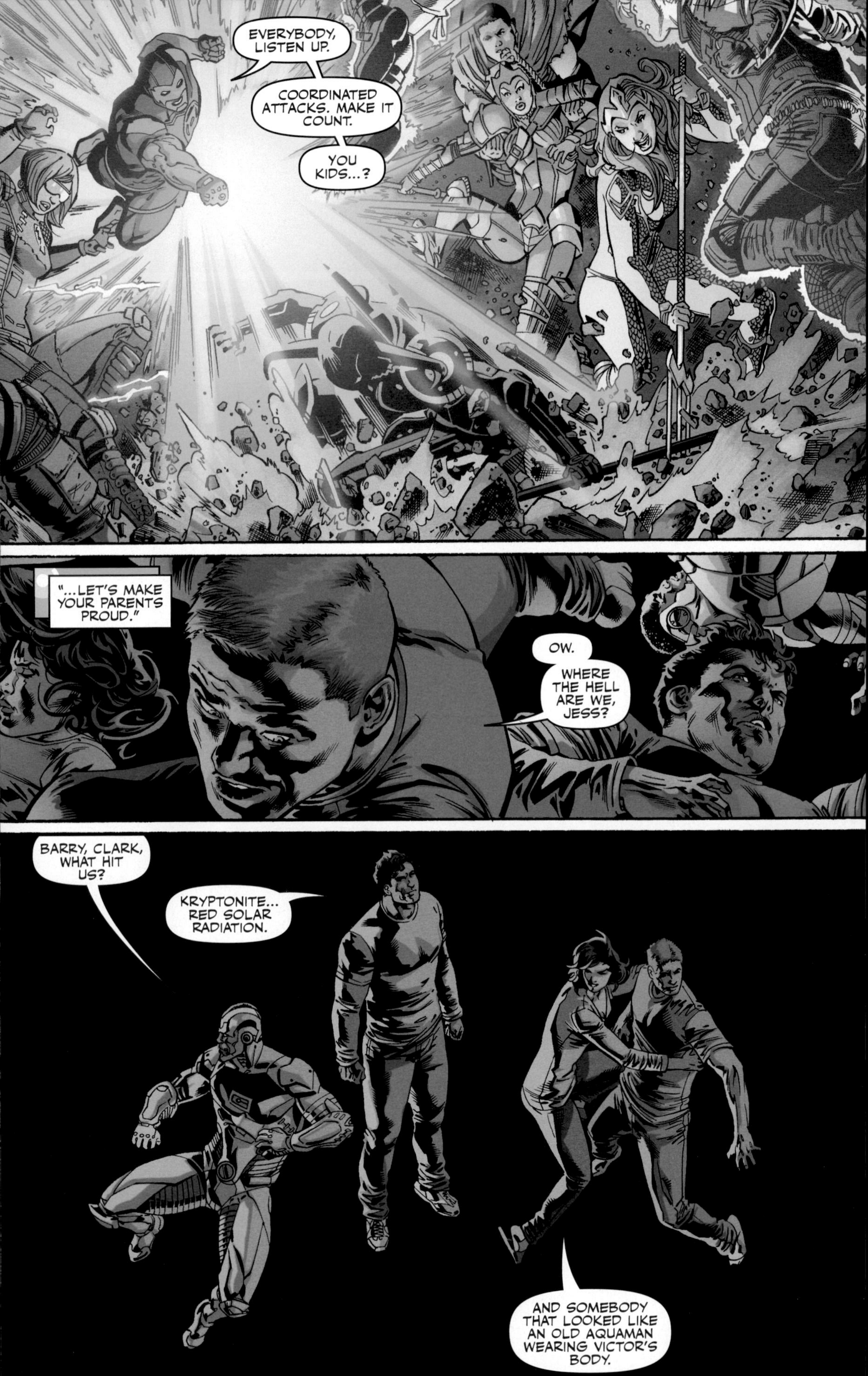
EVERYBODY, LISTEN UP.
COORDINATED ATTACKS. MAKE IT COUNT.
YOU KIDS...?
"...LET'S MAKE YOUR PARENTS PROUD."
OW.
WHERE THE HELL ARE WE, JESS?
BARRY, CLARK, WHAT HIT US?
KRYPTONITE... RED SOLAR RADIATION.
AND SOMEBODY THAT LOOKED LIKE AN OLD AQUAMAN WEARING VICTOR'S BODY.

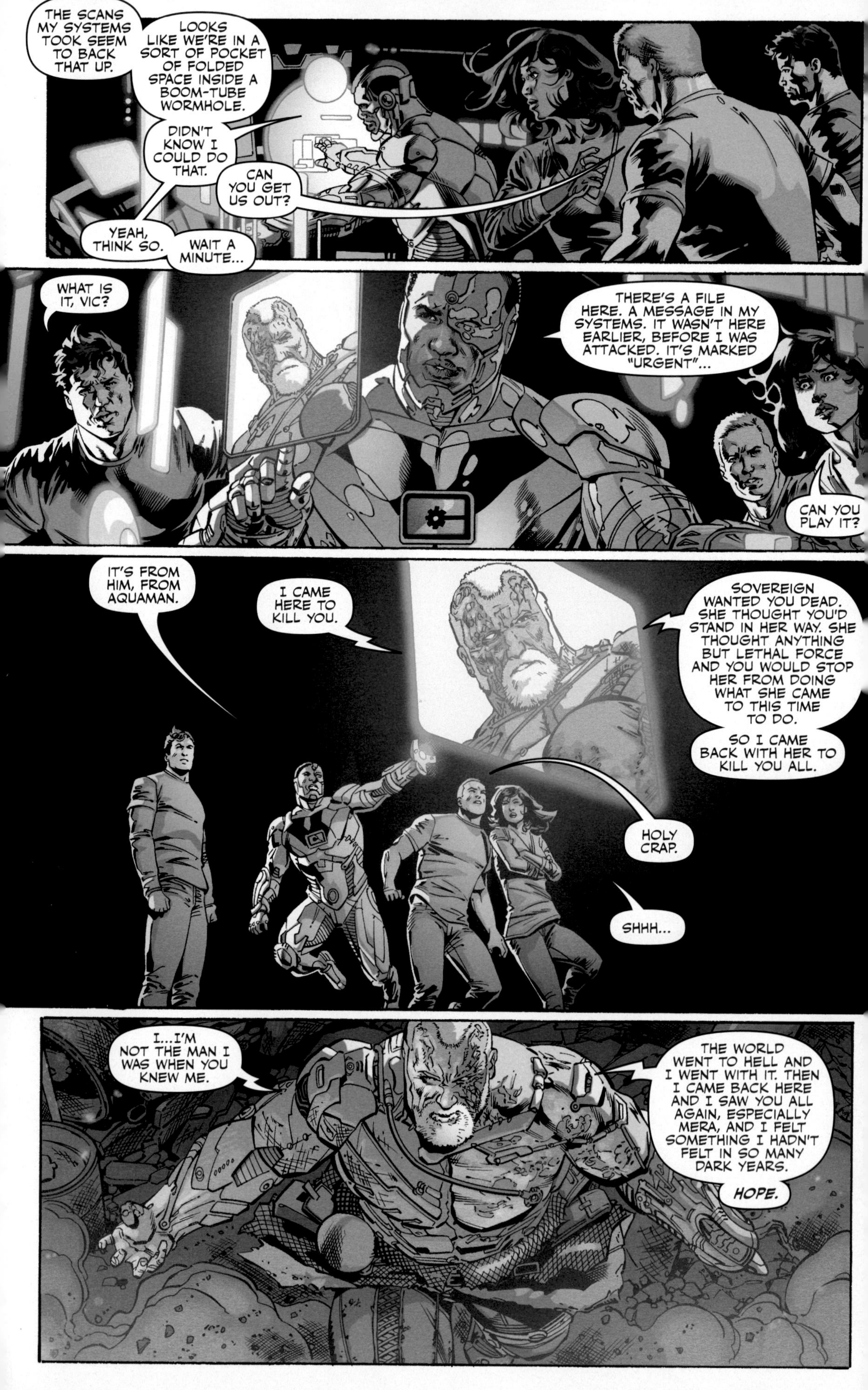
THE SCANS MY SYSTEMS TOOK SEEM TO BACK THAT UP.
LOOKS LIKE WE'RE IN A SORT OF POCKET OF FOLDED SPACE INSIDE A BOOM-TUBE WORMHOLE.
DIDN'T KNOW I COULD DO THAT.
CAN YOU GET US OUT?
YEAH, THINK SO.
WAIT A MINUTE...
WHAT IS IT, VIC?
THERE'S A FILE HERE. A MESSAGE IN MY SYSTEMS. IT WASN'T HERE EARLIER, BEFORE I WAS ATTACKED. IT'S MARKED "URGENT"...
CAN YOU PLAY IT?
IT'S FROM HIM, FROM AQUAMAN.
I CAME HERE TO KILL YOU.
SOVEREIGN WANTED YOU DEAD. SHE THOUGHT YOU'D STAND IN HER WAY. SHE THOUGHT ANYTHING BUT LETHAL FORCE AND YOU WOULD STOP HER FROM DOING WHAT SHE CAME TO THIS TIME TO DO.
SO I CAME BACK WITH HER TO KILL YOU ALL.
HOLY CRAP.
SHHH...
I...I'M NOT THE MAN I WAS WHEN YOU KNEW ME.
THE WORLD WENT TO HELL AND I WENT WITH IT. THEN I CAME BACK HERE AND I SAW YOU ALL AGAIN, ESPECIALLY MERA, AND I FELT SOMETHING I HADN'T FELT IN SO MANY DARK YEARS.
HOPE.

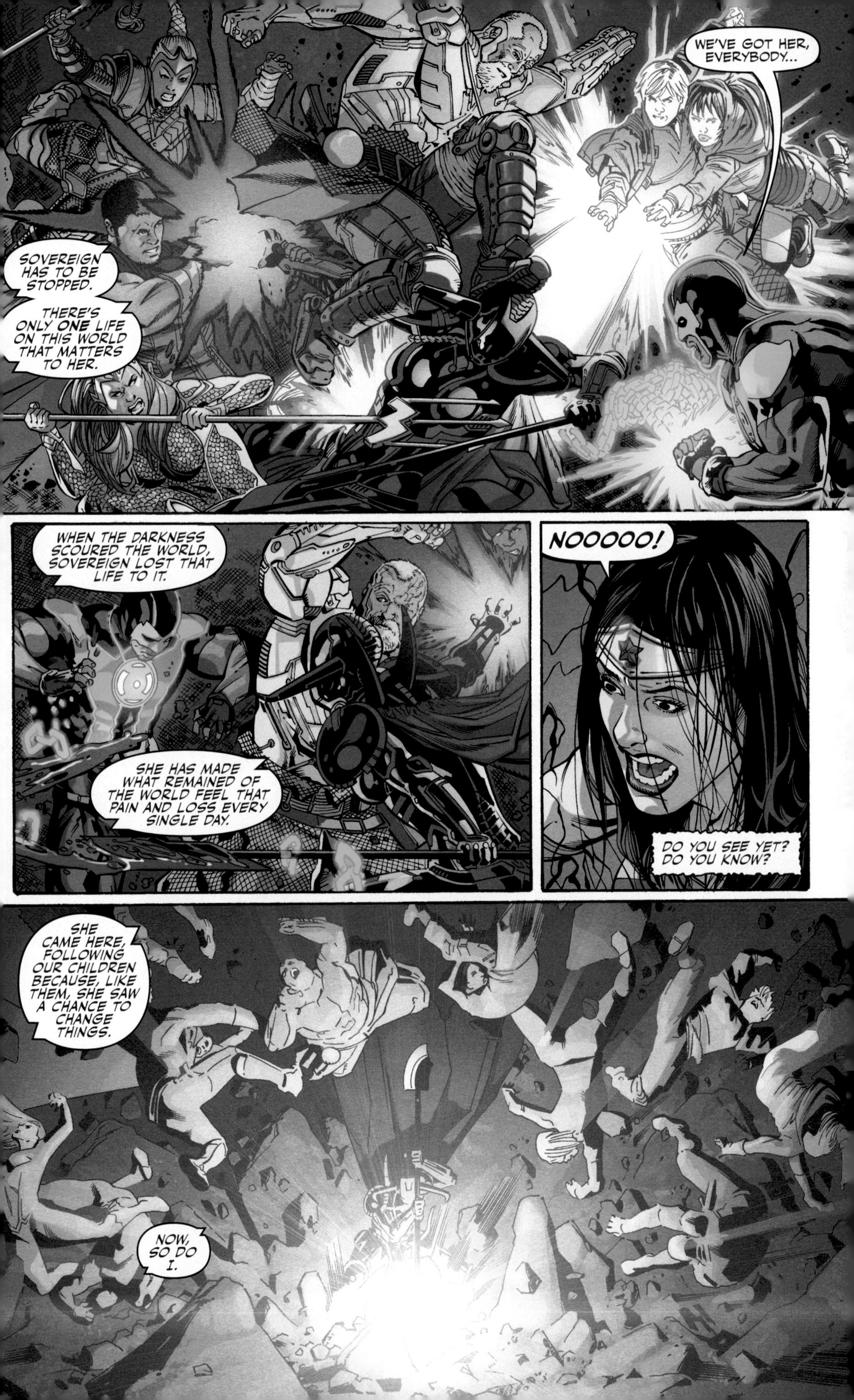
WE'VE GOT HER, EVERYBODY...
SOVEREIGN HAS TO BE STOPPED.
THERE'S ONLY ONE LIFE ON THIS WORLD THAT MATTERS TO HER.
WHEN THE DARKNESS SCOURED THE WORLD, SOVEREIGN LOST THAT LIFE TO IT.
SHE HAS MADE WHAT REMAINED OF THE WORLD FEEL THAT PAIN AND LOSS EVERY SINGLE DAY.
NOOOOO!
DO YOU SEE YET? DO YOU KNOW?
SHE CAME HERE, FOLLOWING OUR CHILDREN BECAUSE, LIKE THEM, SHE SAW A CHANCE TO CHANGE THINGS.
NOW, SO DO I.

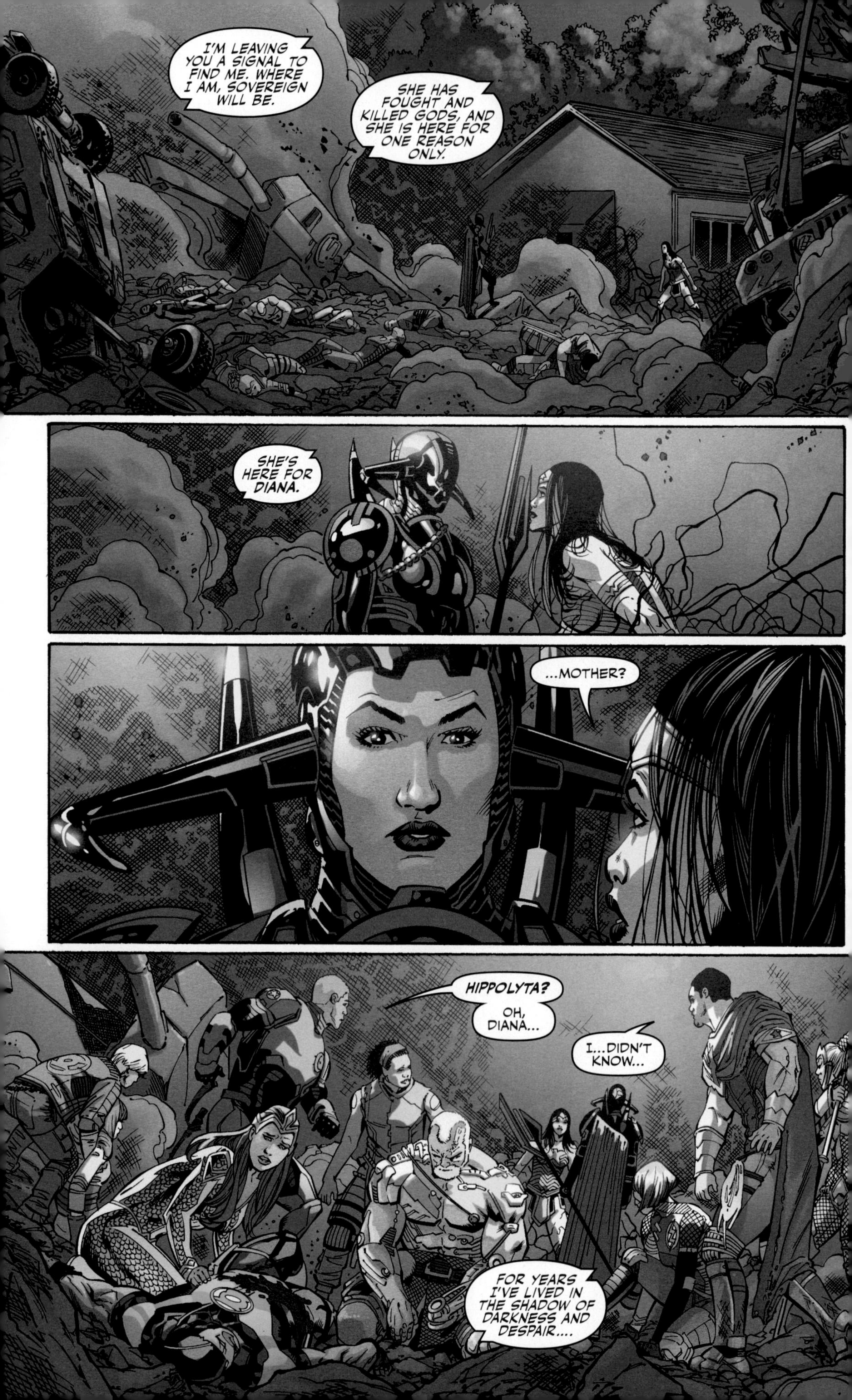
I'M LEAVING YOU A SIGNAL TO FIND ME. WHERE I AM, SOVEREIGN WILL BE.
SHE HAS FOUGHT AND KILLED GODS, AND SHE IS HERE FOR ONE REASON ONLY.
SHE'S HERE FOR DIANA.
...MOTHER?
HIPPOLYTA?
OH, DIANA...
I...DIDN'T KNOW...
FOR YEARS I'VE LIVED IN THE SHADOW OF DARKNESS AND DESPAIR....

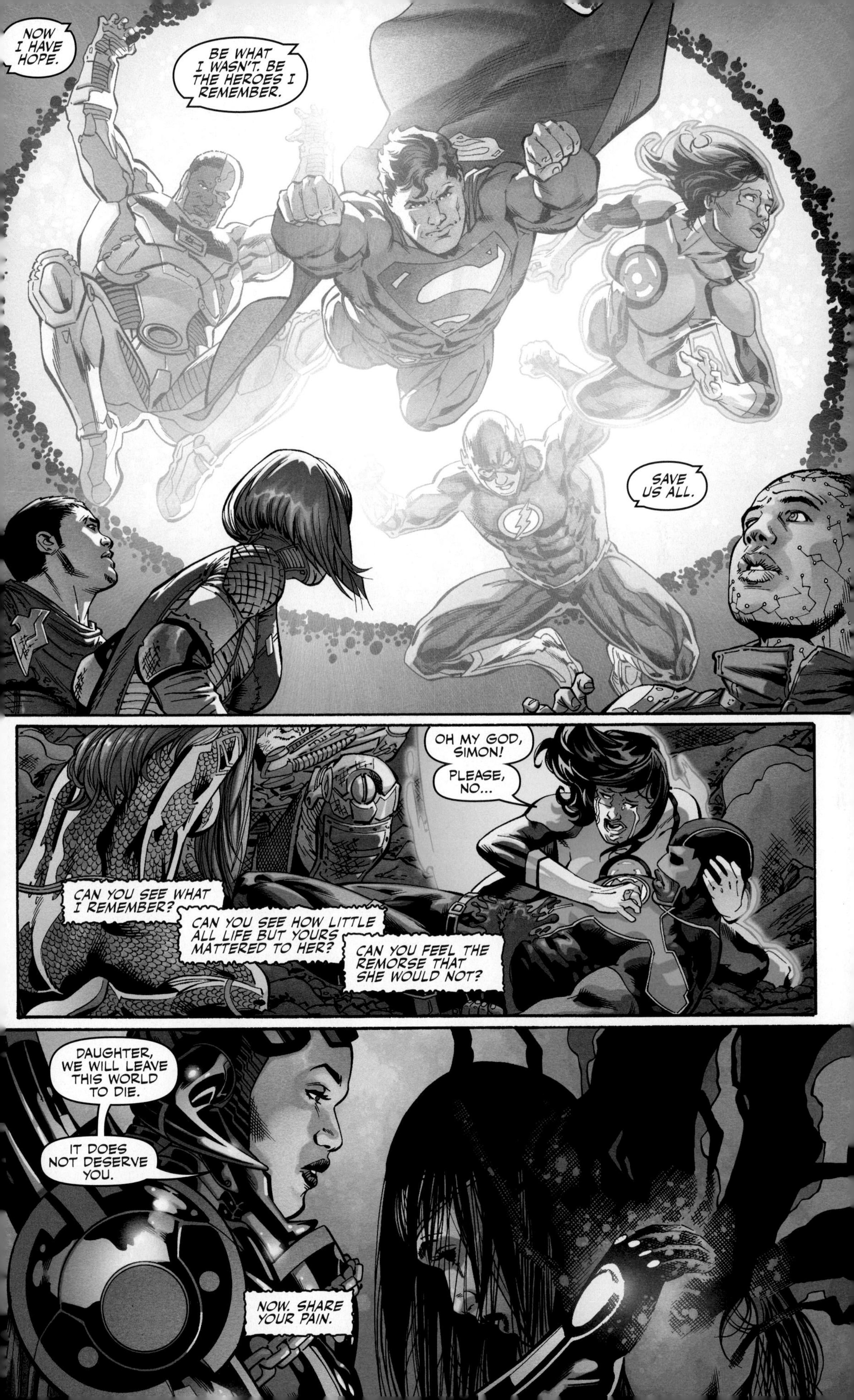
NOW I HAVE HOPE.
BE WHAT I WASN'T. BE THE HEROES I REMEMBER.
SAVE US ALL.
OH MY GOD, SIMON!
PLEASE, NO...
CAN YOU SEE WHAT I REMEMBER?
CAN YOU SEE HOW LITTLE ALL LIFE BUT YOURS MATTERED TO HER?
CAN YOU FEEL THE REMORSE THAT SHE WOULD NOT?
DAUGHTER, WE WILL LEAVE THIS WORLD TO DIE.
IT DOES NOT DESERVE YOU.
NOW. SHARE YOUR PAIN.

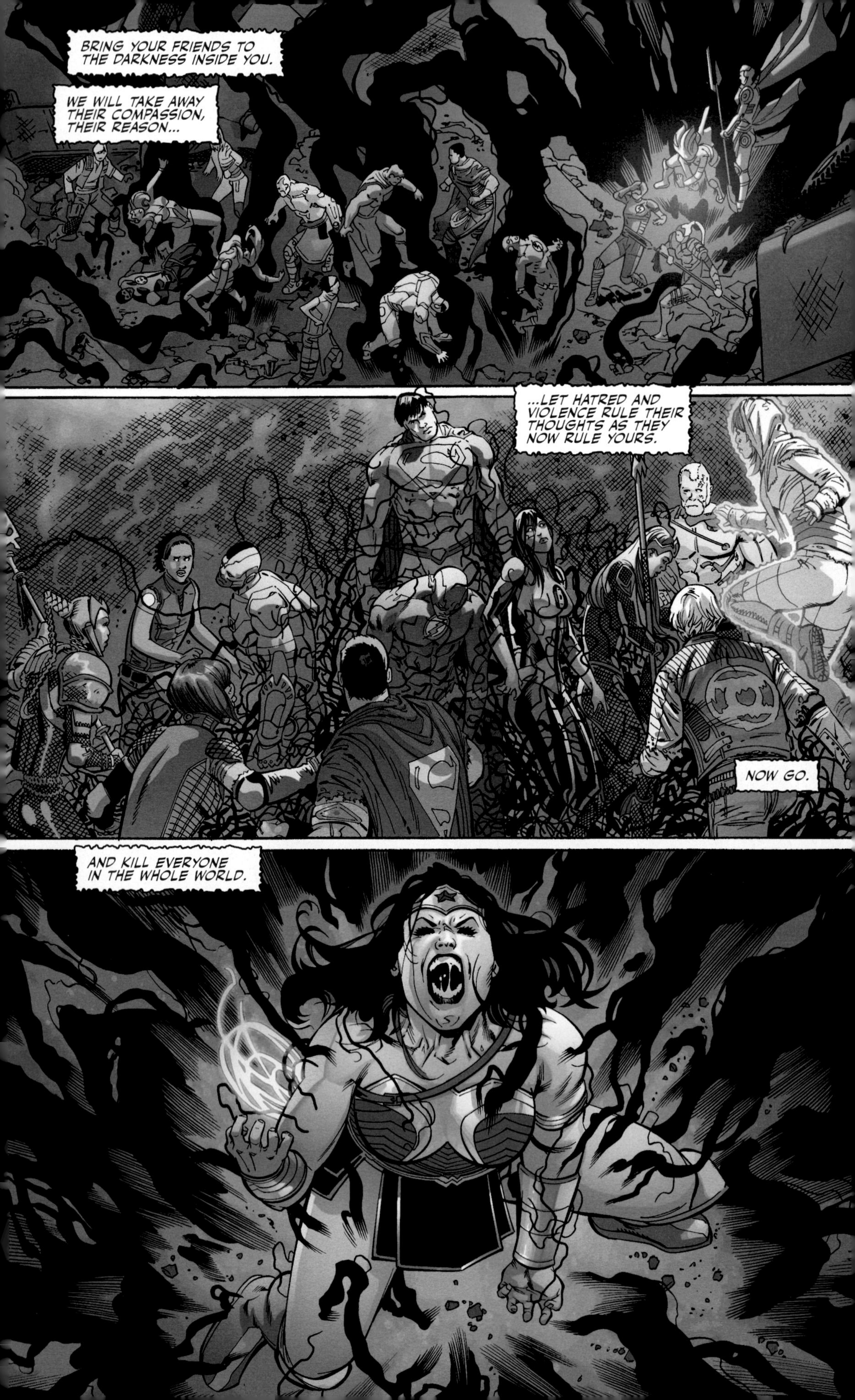

BRING YOUR FRIENDS TO THE DARKNESS INSIDE YOU.
WE WILL TAKE AWAY THEIR COMPASSION, THEIR REASON...
...LET HATRED AND VIOLENCE RULE THEIR THOUGHTS AS THEY NOW RULE YOURS.
NOW GO.
AND KILL EVERYONE IN THE WHOLE WORLD.

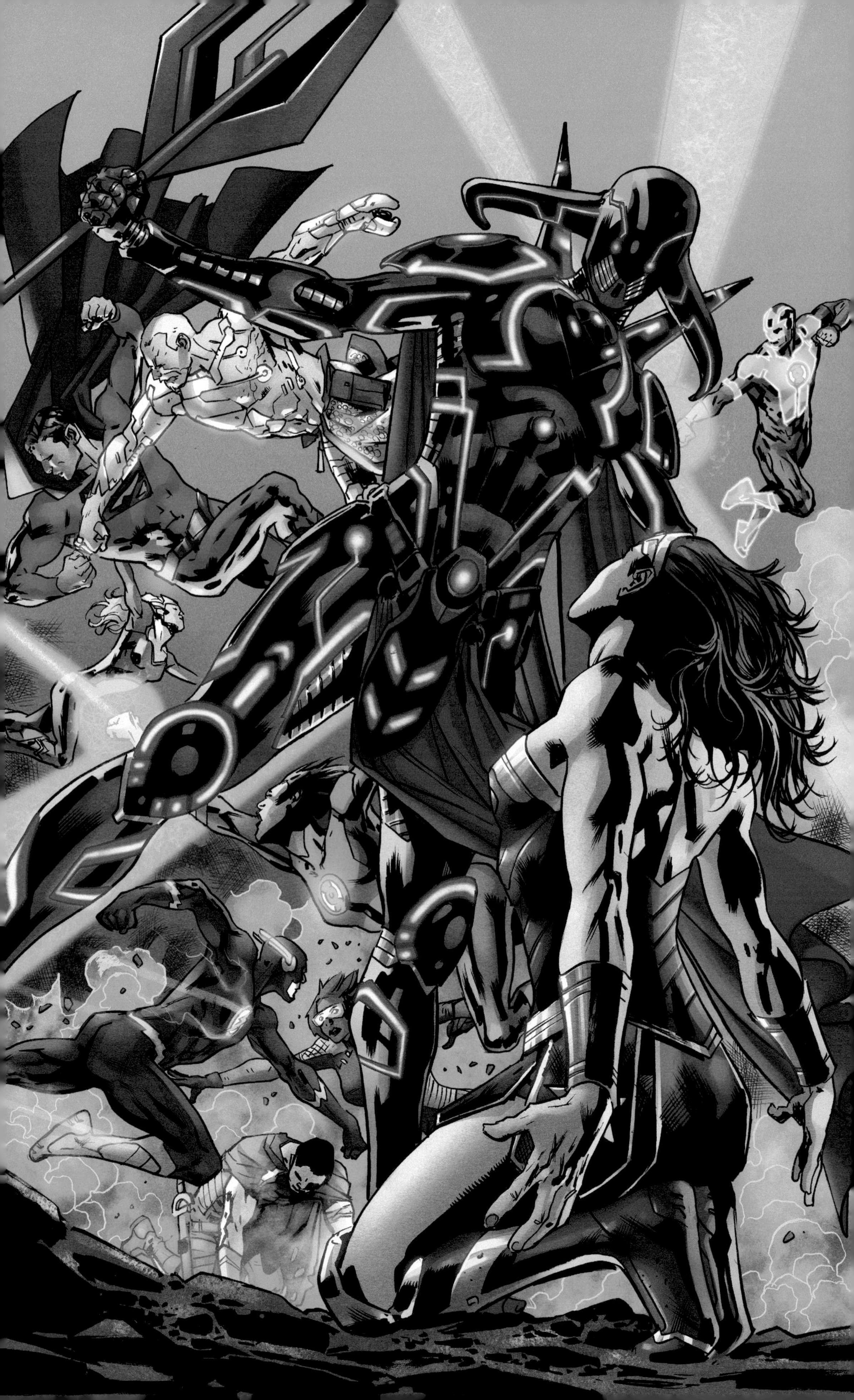

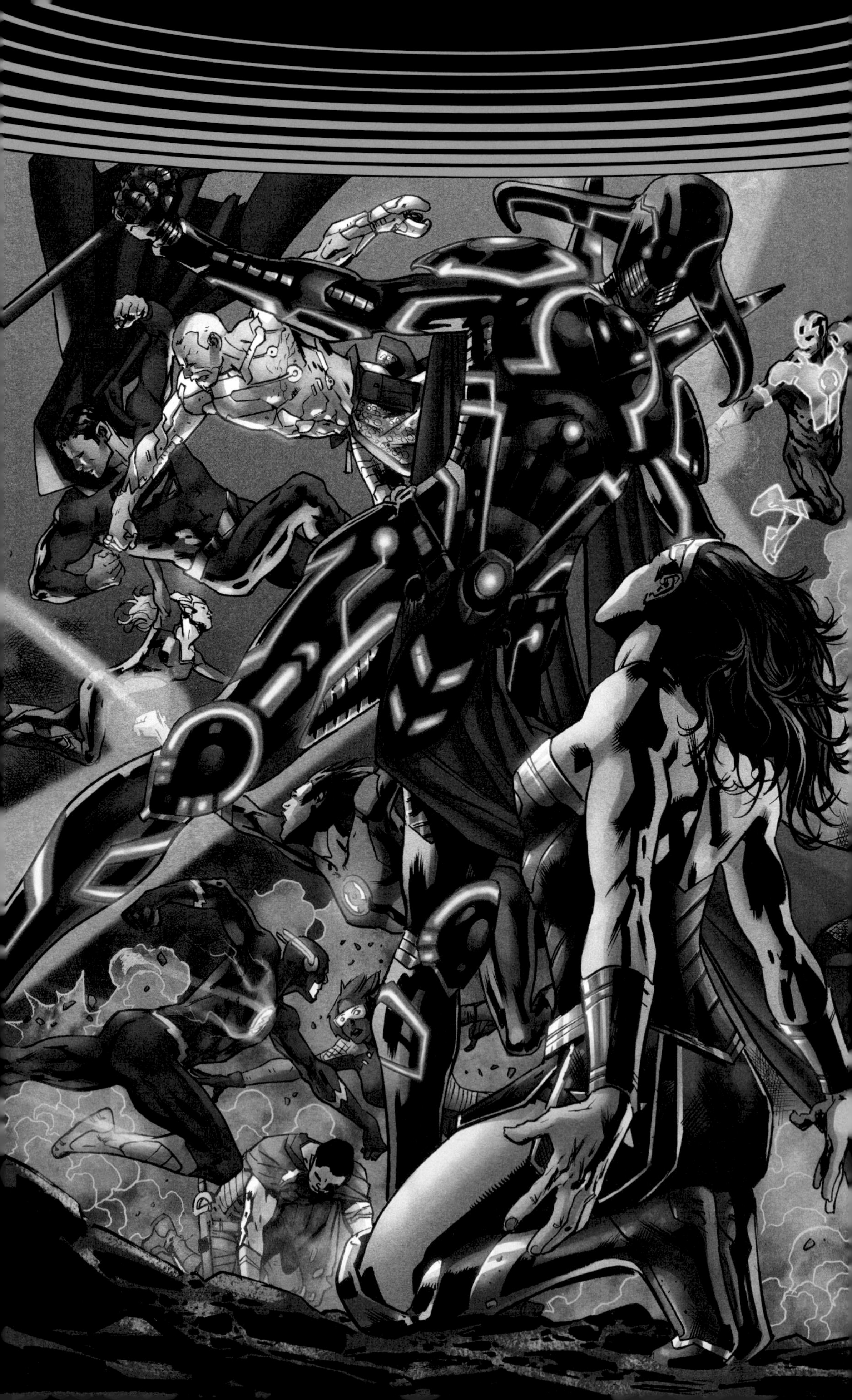

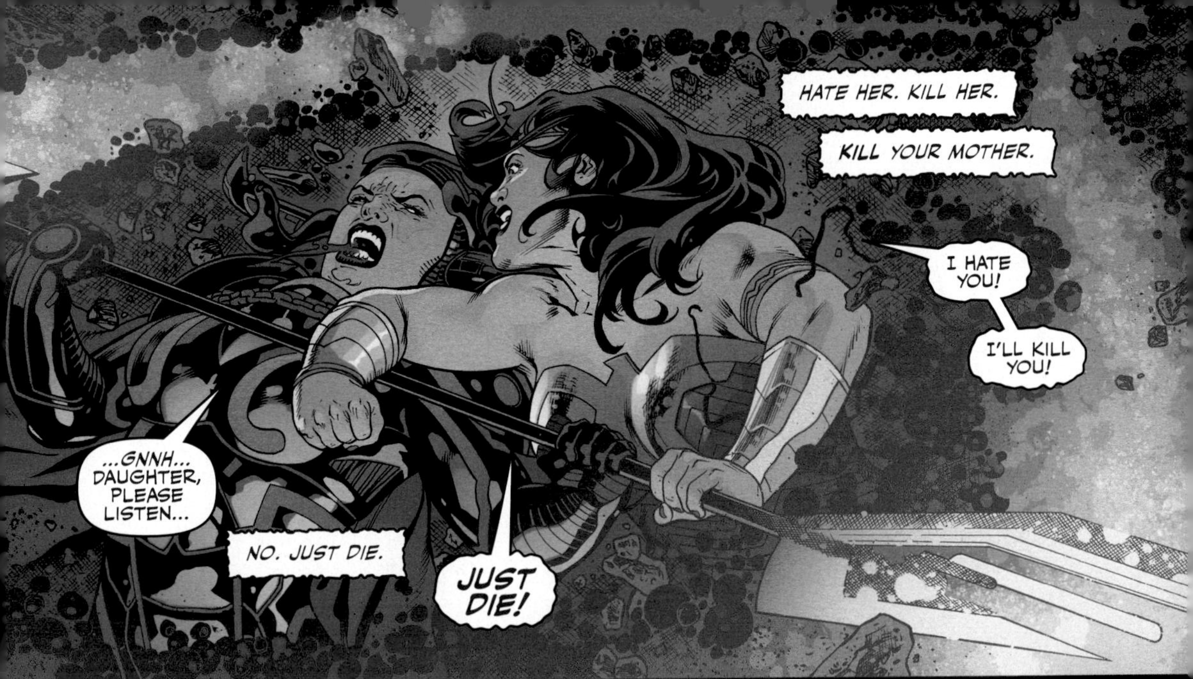
HATE HER. KILL HER.
KILL YOUR MOTHER.
I HATE YOU!
I'LL KILL YOU!
...GNNH... DAUGHTER, PLEASE LISTEN...
NO. JUST DIE.
JUST DIE!

LEGACY
CONCLUSION

BRYAN HITCH WRITER FERNANDO PASARIN PENCILLER ANDY OWENS & OCLAIR ALBERT INKERS

COLORED by BRAD ANDERSON | LETTERED by RICHARD STARKINGS & COMICRAFT'S JIMMY | COVER by BRYAN HITCH & ALEX SINCLAIR | VARIANT COVER by NICK BRADSHAW & ALEX SINCLAIR | ASSOCIATE ED. AMEDEO TURTURRO | EDITOR BRIAN CUNNINGHAM

SUPERMAN created by JERRY SIEGEL and JOE SHUSTER. By special arrangement with the JERRY SIEGEL FAMILY.

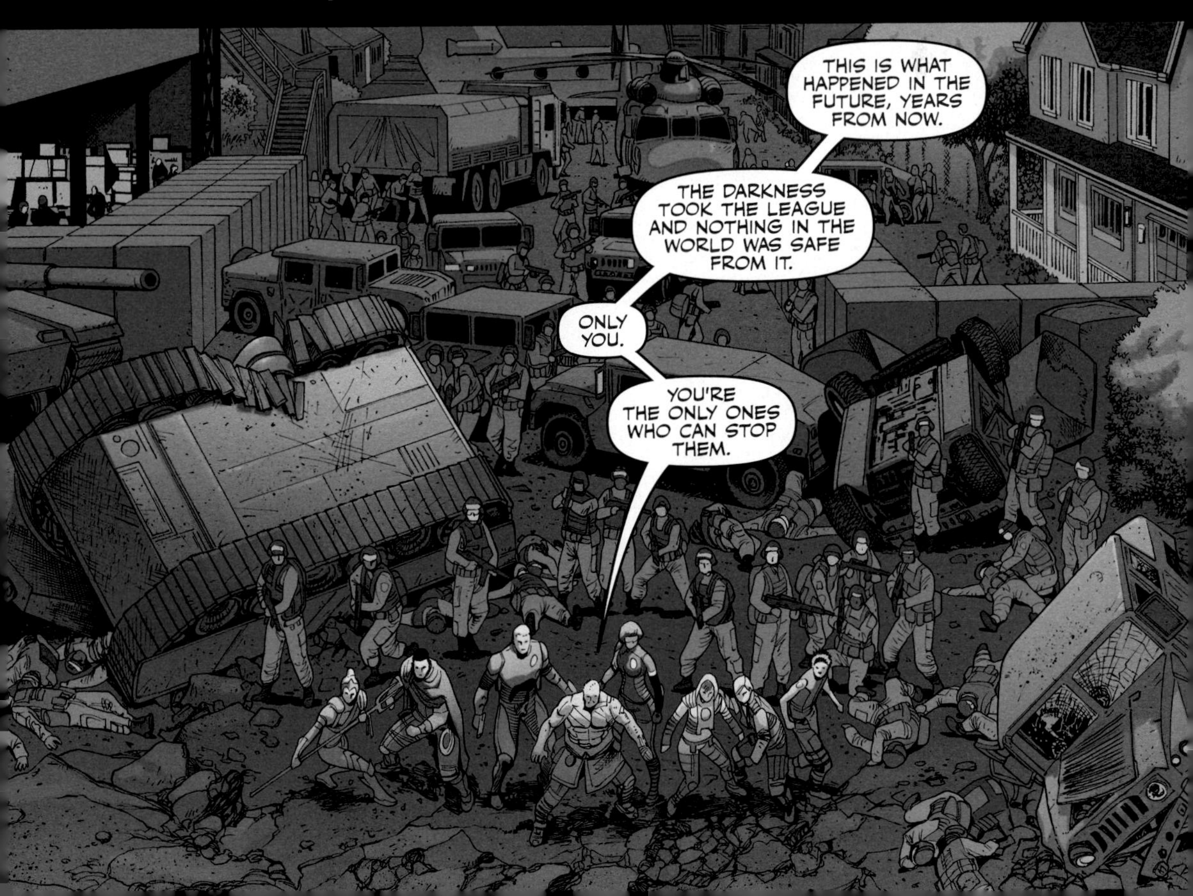
THIS IS WHAT HAPPENED IN THE FUTURE, YEARS FROM NOW.
THE DARKNESS TOOK THE LEAGUE AND NOTHING IN THE WORLD WAS SAFE FROM IT.
ONLY YOU.
YOU'RE THE ONLY ONES WHO CAN STOP THEM.

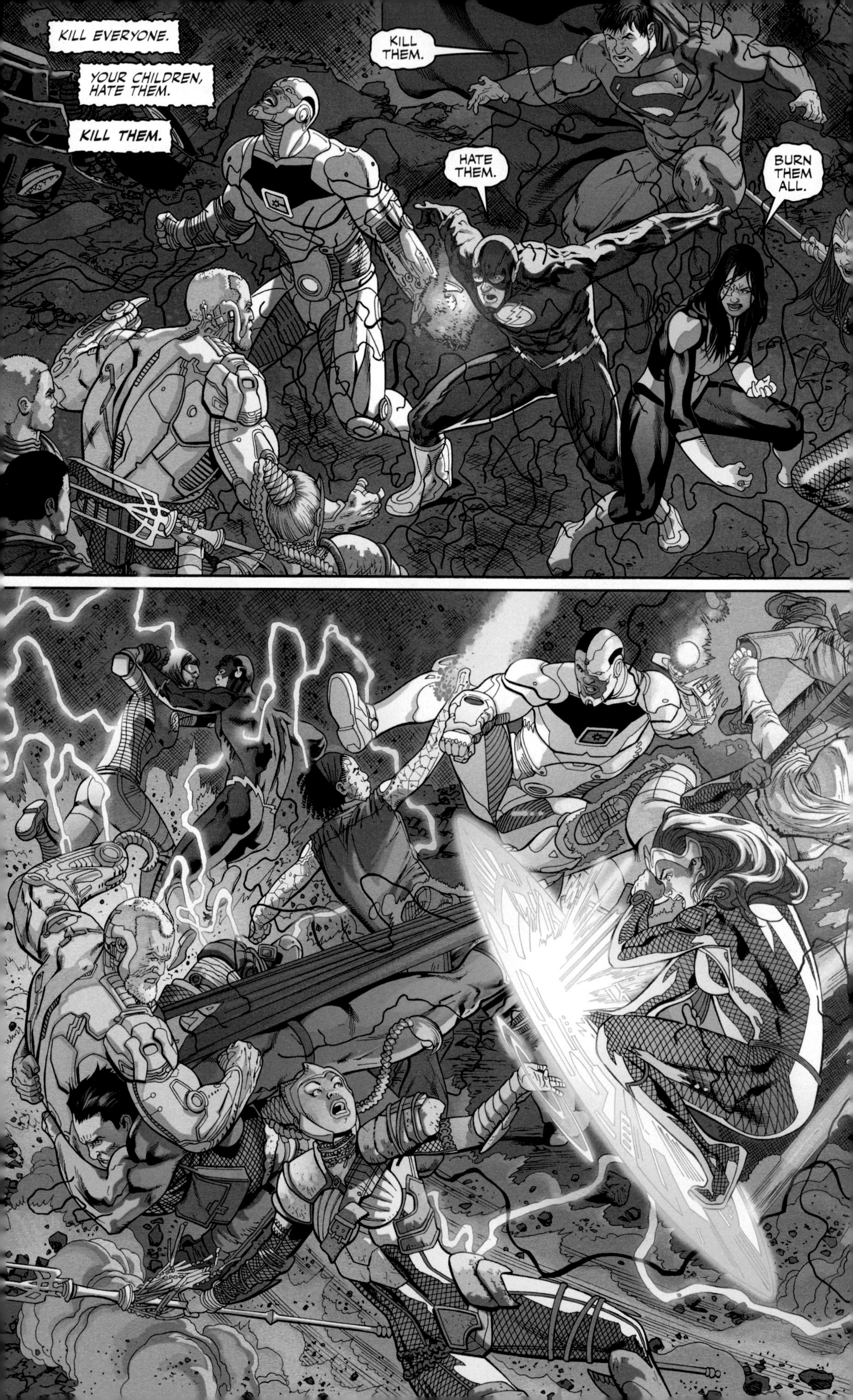
KILL EVERYONE.
YOUR CHILDREN, HATE THEM.
KILL THEM.
KILL THEM.
HATE THEM.
BURN THEM ALL.

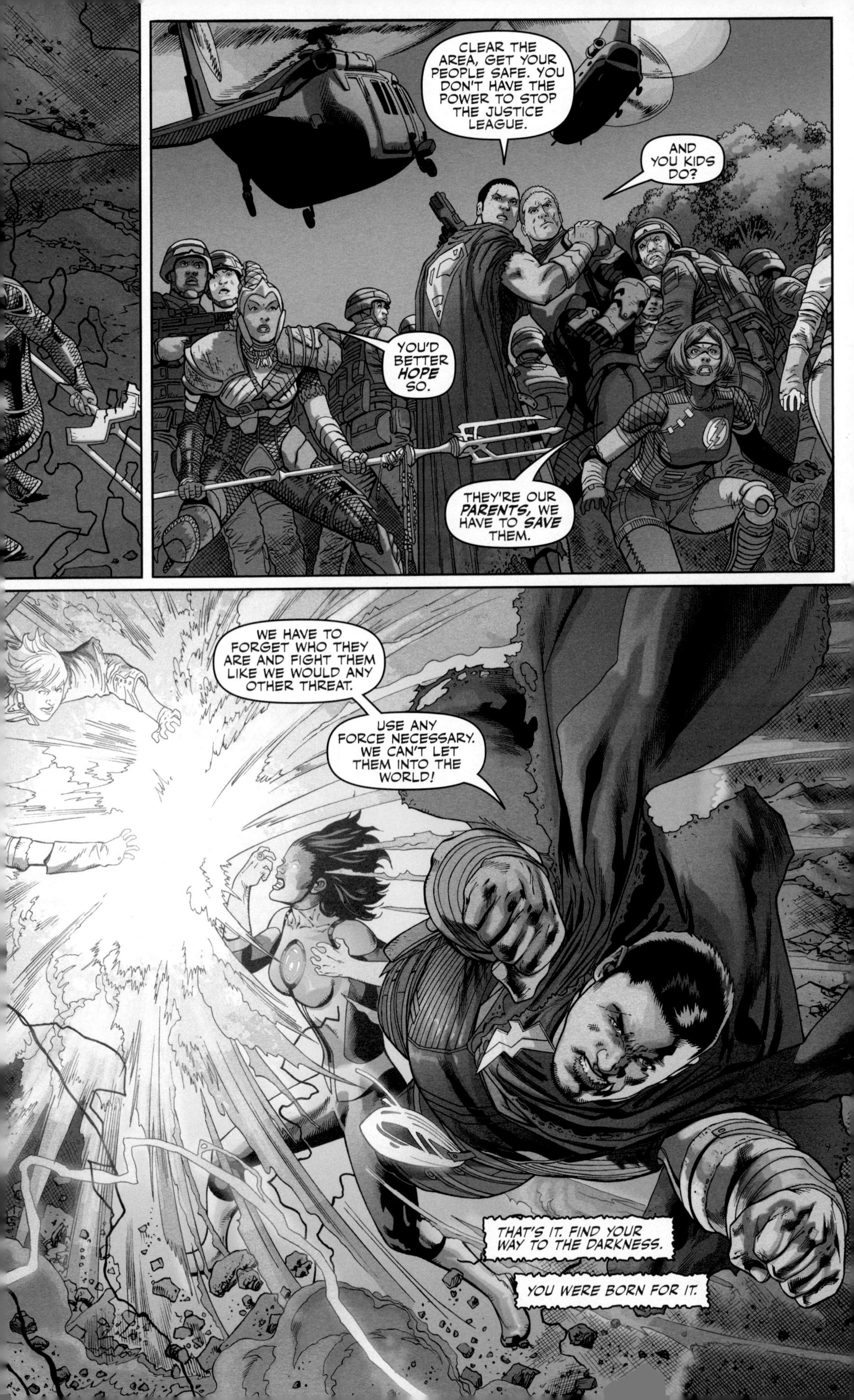
CLEAR THE AREA, GET YOUR PEOPLE SAFE. YOU DON'T HAVE THE POWER TO STOP THE JUSTICE LEAGUE.
AND YOU KIDS DO?
YOU'D BETTER *HOPE* SO.
THEY'RE OUR *PARENTS,* WE HAVE TO *SAVE* THEM.
WE HAVE TO FORGET WHO THEY ARE AND FIGHT THEM LIKE WE WOULD ANY OTHER THREAT.
USE ANY FORCE NECESSARY. WE CAN'T LET THEM INTO THE WORLD!
THAT'S IT. FIND YOUR WAY TO THE DARKNESS.
YOU WERE BORN FOR IT.

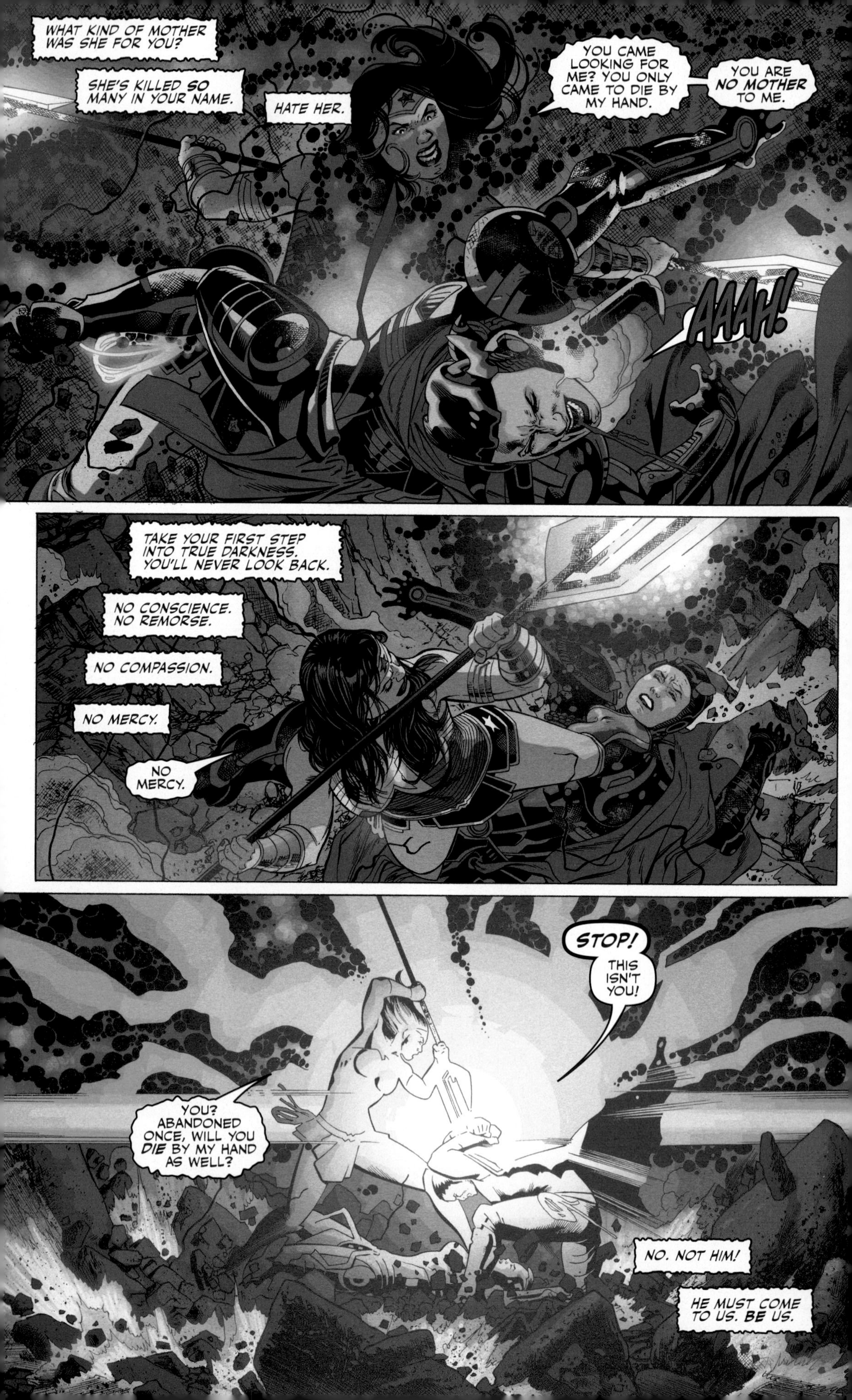
WHAT KIND OF MOTHER WAS SHE FOR YOU?
SHE'S KILLED SO MANY IN YOUR NAME.
HATE HER.
YOU CAME LOOKING FOR ME? YOU ONLY CAME TO DIE BY MY HAND.
YOU ARE NO MOTHER TO ME.
AAAH!
TAKE YOUR FIRST STEP INTO TRUE DARKNESS. YOU'LL NEVER LOOK BACK.
NO CONSCIENCE. NO REMORSE.
NO COMPASSION.
NO MERCY.
NO MERCY.
STOP! THIS ISN'T YOU!
YOU? ABANDONED ONCE, WILL YOU DIE BY MY HAND AS WELL?
NO. NOT HIM!
HE MUST COME TO US. BE US.

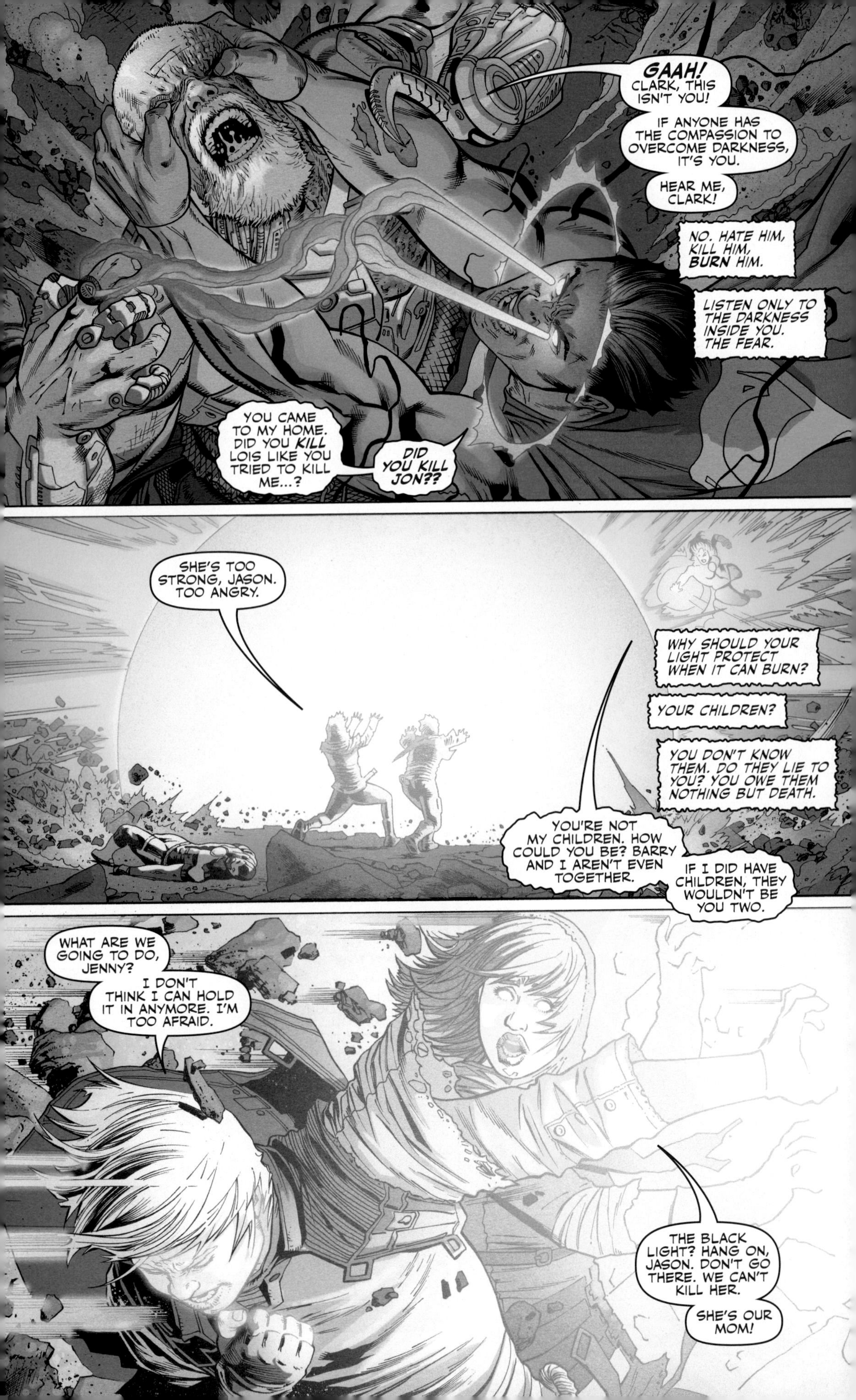
GAAH! CLARK, THIS ISN'T YOU!
IF ANYONE HAS THE COMPASSION TO OVERCOME DARKNESS, IT'S YOU.
HEAR ME, CLARK!
NO. HATE HIM, KILL HIM, BURN HIM.
LISTEN ONLY TO THE DARKNESS INSIDE YOU. THE FEAR.
YOU CAME TO MY HOME. DID YOU KILL LOIS LIKE YOU TRIED TO KILL ME...?
DID YOU KILL JON??
SHE'S TOO STRONG, JASON. TOO ANGRY.
WHY SHOULD YOUR LIGHT PROTECT WHEN IT CAN BURN?
YOUR CHILDREN?
YOU DON'T KNOW THEM. DO THEY LIE TO YOU? YOU OWE THEM NOTHING BUT DEATH.
YOU'RE NOT MY CHILDREN. HOW COULD YOU BE? BARRY AND I AREN'T EVEN TOGETHER.
IF I DID HAVE CHILDREN, THEY WOULDN'T BE YOU TWO.
WHAT ARE WE GOING TO DO, JENNY?
I DON'T THINK I CAN HOLD IT IN ANYMORE. I'M TOO AFRAID.
THE BLACK LIGHT? HANG ON, JASON. DON'T GO THERE. WE CAN'T KILL HER.
SHE'S OUR MOM!

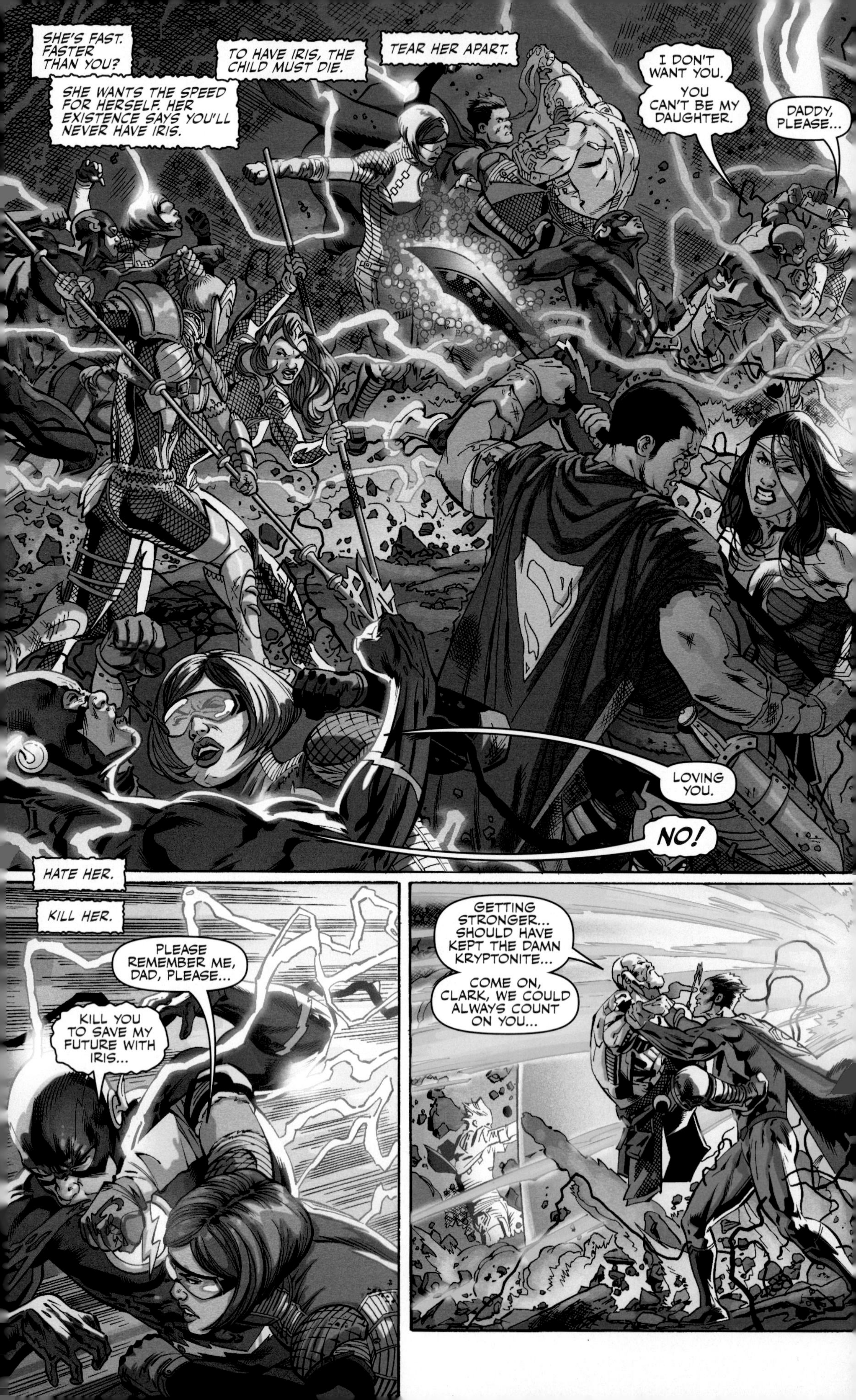
SHE'S FAST. FASTER THAN YOU?
SHE WANTS THE SPEED FOR HERSELF. HER EXISTENCE SAYS YOU'LL NEVER HAVE IRIS.
TO HAVE IRIS, THE CHILD MUST DIE.
TEAR HER APART.
I DON'T WANT YOU.
YOU CAN'T BE MY DAUGHTER.
DADDY, PLEASE...
LOVING YOU.
NO!
HATE HER.
KILL HER.
PLEASE REMEMBER ME, DAD, PLEASE...
KILL YOU TO SAVE MY FUTURE WITH IRIS...
GETTING STRONGER... SHOULD HAVE KEPT THE DAMN KRYPTONITE...
COME ON, CLARK, WE COULD ALWAYS COUNT ON YOU...

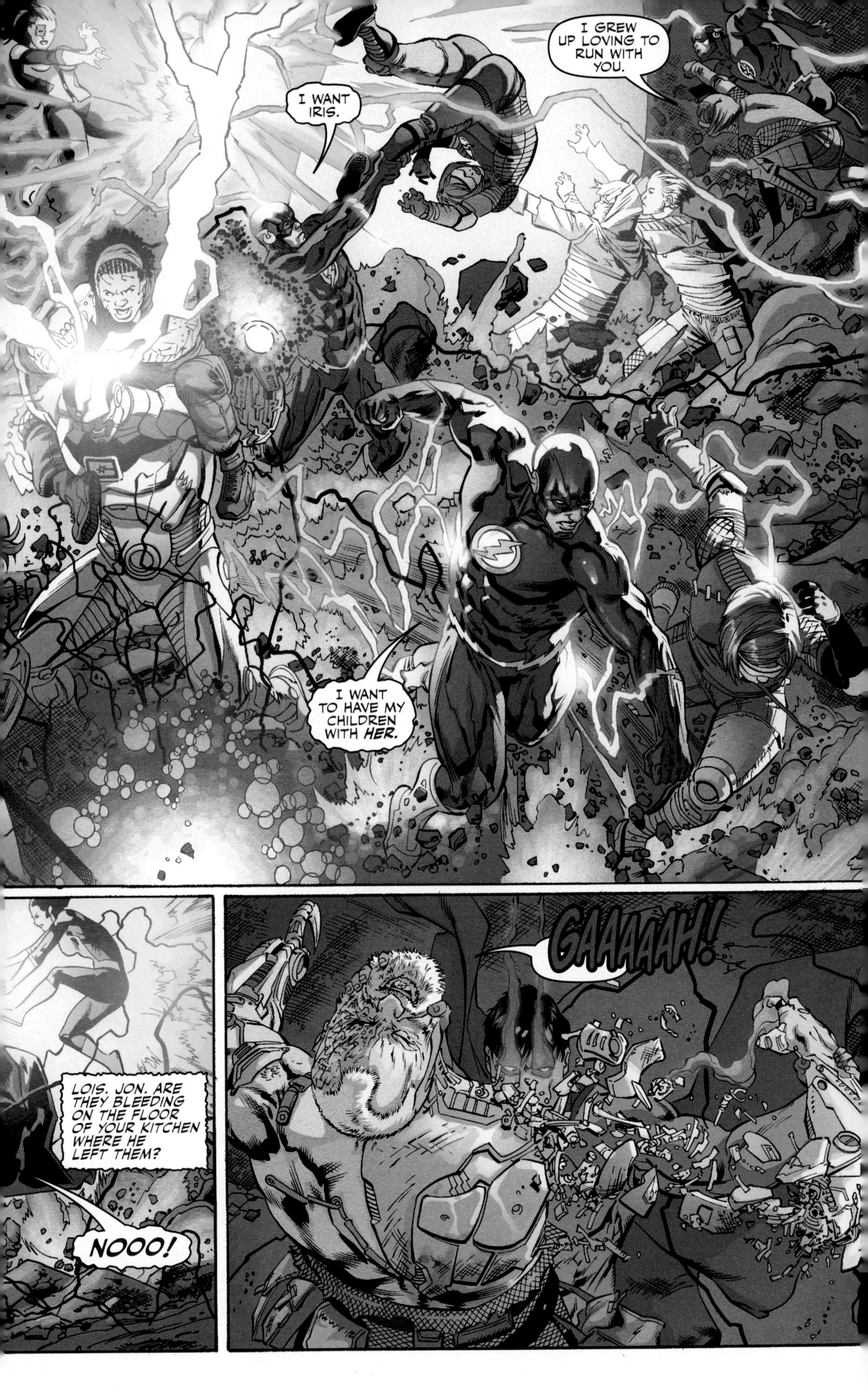
I GREW UP LOVING TO RUN WITH YOU.
I WANT IRIS.
I WANT TO HAVE MY CHILDREN WITH HER.
LOIS. JON. ARE THEY BLEEDING ON THE FLOOR OF YOUR KITCHEN WHERE HE LEFT THEM?
NOOO!
GAAAAAH!

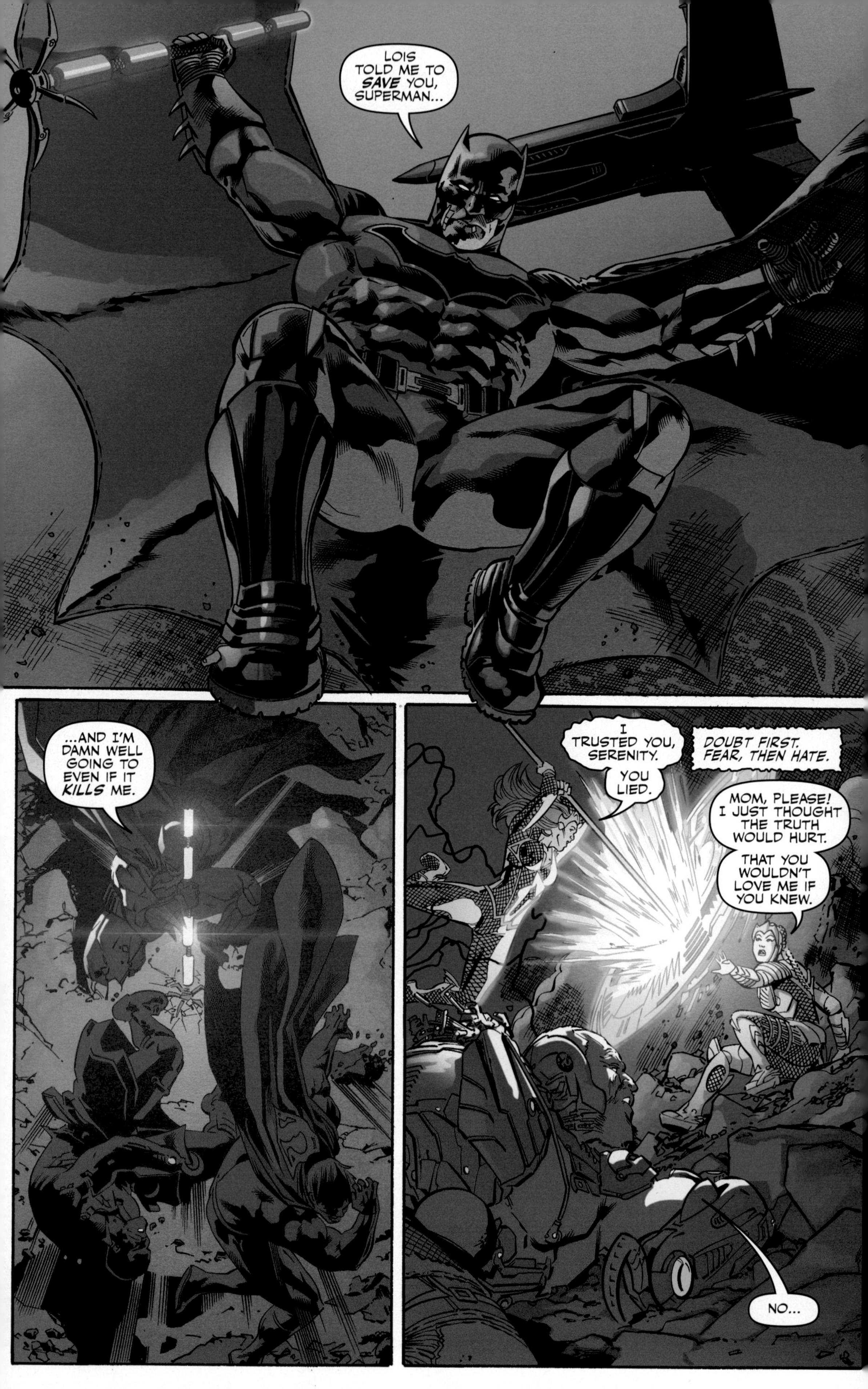

LOIS TOLD ME TO SAVE YOU, SUPERMAN...
...AND I'M DAMN WELL GOING TO EVEN IF IT KILLS ME.
I TRUSTED YOU, SERENITY.
YOU LIED.
DOUBT FIRST. FEAR, THEN HATE.
MOM, PLEASE! I JUST THOUGHT THE TRUTH WOULD HURT.
THAT YOU WOULDN'T LOVE ME IF YOU KNEW.
NO...

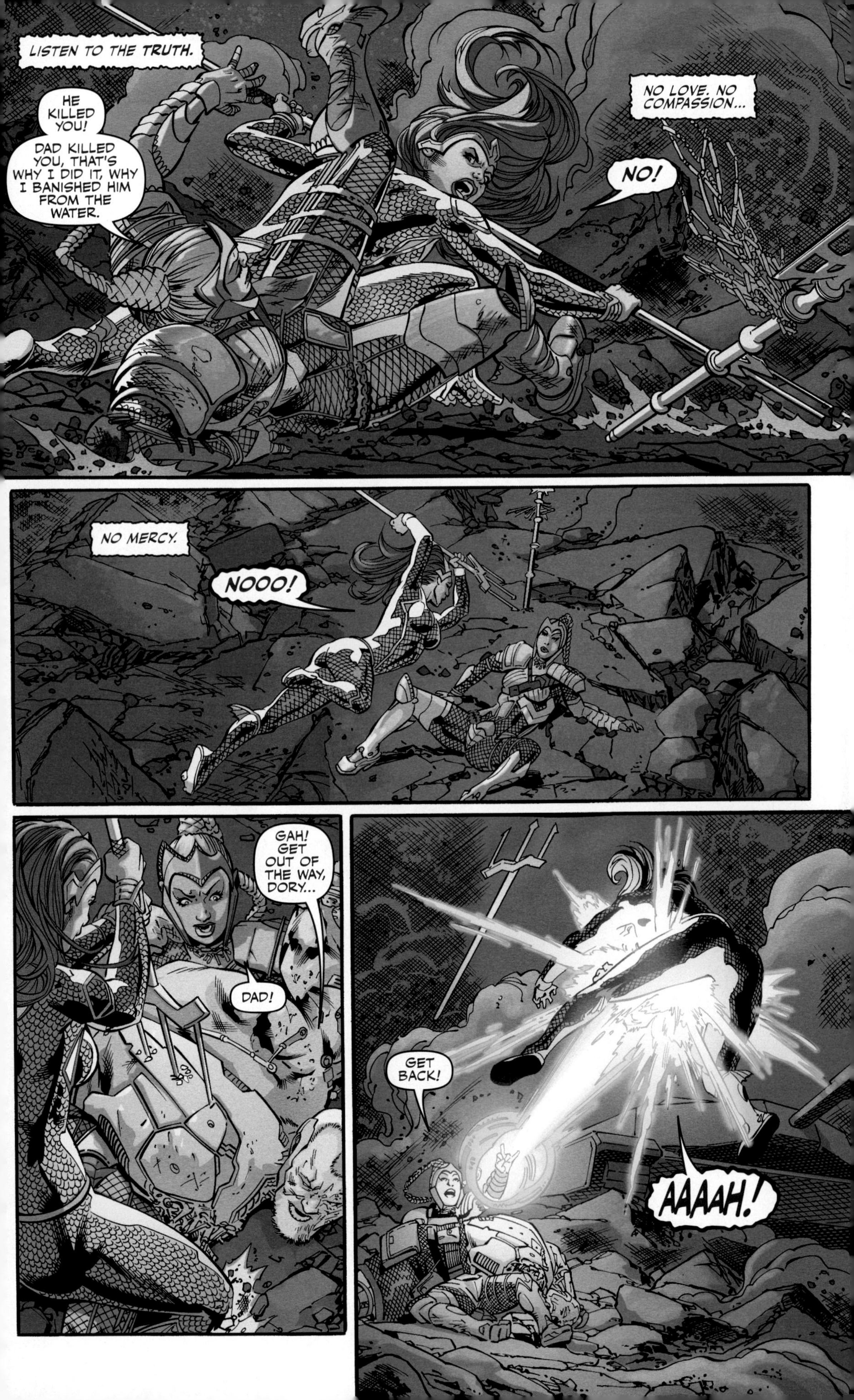
LISTEN TO THE TRUTH.
HE KILLED YOU!
DAD KILLED YOU, THAT'S WHY I DID IT, WHY I BANISHED HIM FROM THE WATER.
NO LOVE. NO COMPASSION...
NO!
NO MERCY.
NOOO!
GAH! GET OUT OF THE WAY, DORY...
DAD!
GET BACK!
AAAAH!

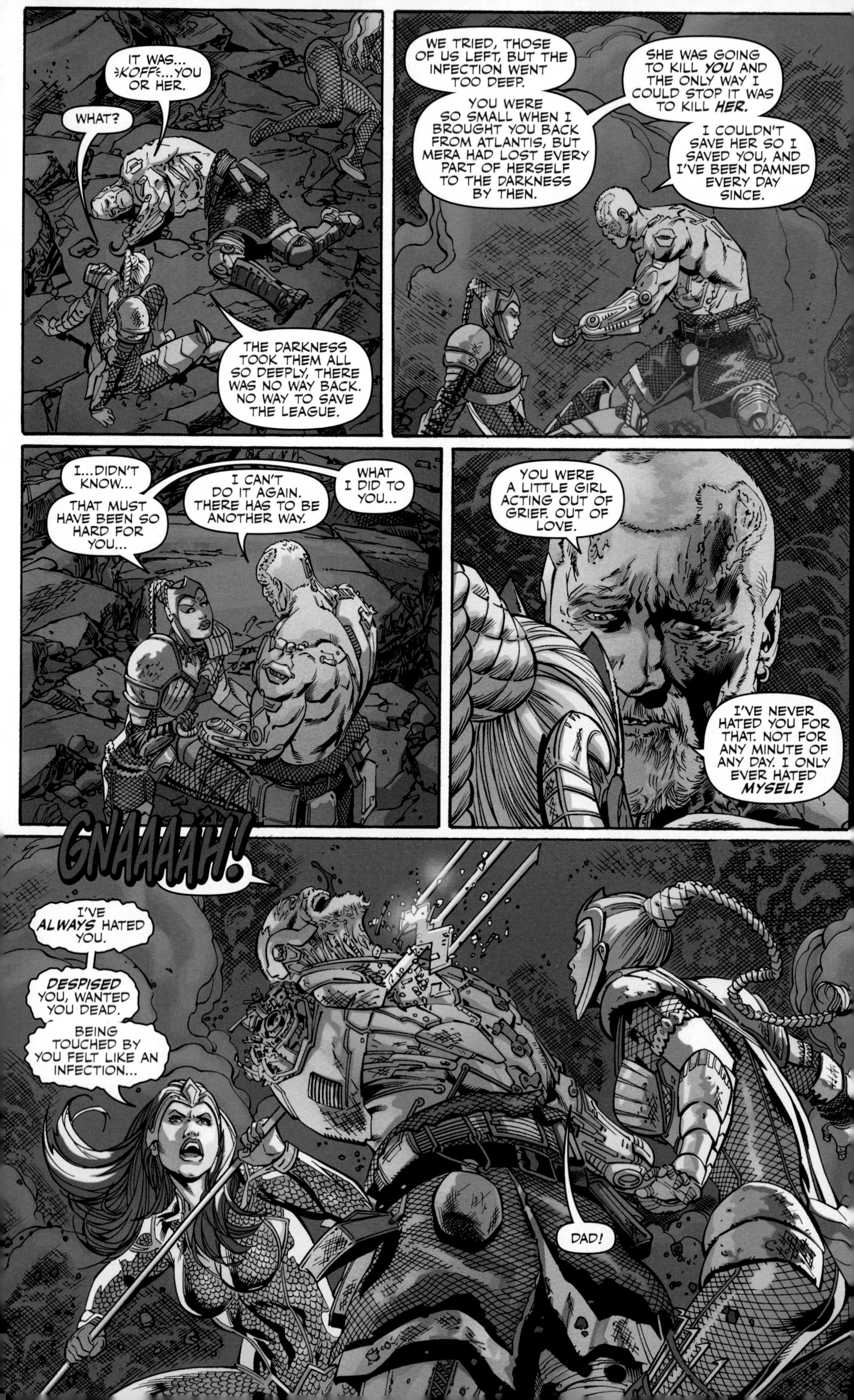
IT WAS... *KOFF*...YOU OR HER.
WHAT?
THE DARKNESS TOOK THEM ALL SO DEEPLY, THERE WAS NO WAY BACK. NO WAY TO SAVE THE LEAGUE.
WE TRIED, THOSE OF US LEFT, BUT THE INFECTION WENT TOO DEEP.
YOU WERE SO SMALL WHEN I BROUGHT YOU BACK FROM ATLANTIS, BUT MERA HAD LOST EVERY PART OF HERSELF TO THE DARKNESS BY THEN.
SHE WAS GOING TO KILL YOU AND THE ONLY WAY I COULD STOP IT WAS TO KILL HER.
I COULDN'T SAVE HER SO I SAVED YOU, AND I'VE BEEN DAMNED EVERY DAY SINCE.
I...DIDN'T KNOW...
THAT MUST HAVE BEEN SO HARD FOR YOU...
I CAN'T DO IT AGAIN. THERE HAS TO BE ANOTHER WAY.
WHAT I DID TO YOU...
YOU WERE A LITTLE GIRL ACTING OUT OF GRIEF. OUT OF LOVE.
I'VE NEVER HATED YOU FOR THAT. NOT FOR ANY MINUTE OF ANY DAY. I ONLY EVER HATED MYSELF.
GNAAAAH!
I'VE ALWAYS HATED YOU.
DESPISED YOU, WANTED YOU DEAD.
BEING TOUCHED BY YOU FELT LIKE AN INFECTION...
DAD!

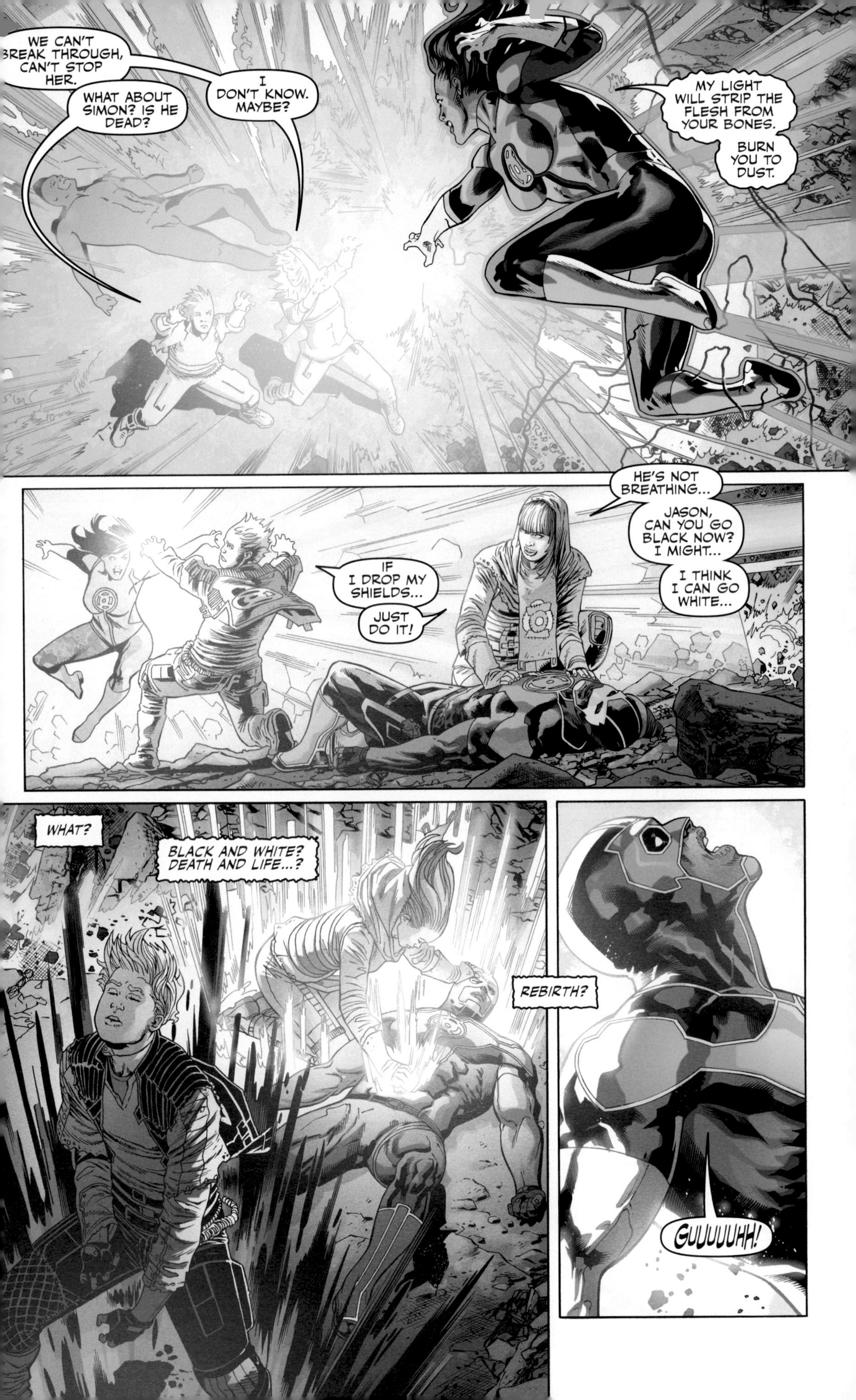

WE CAN'T BREAK THROUGH, CAN'T STOP HER.
I DON'T KNOW. MAYBE?
WHAT ABOUT SIMON? IS HE DEAD?
MY LIGHT WILL STRIP THE FLESH FROM YOUR BONES.
BURN YOU TO DUST.
HE'S NOT BREATHING...
JASON, CAN YOU GO BLACK NOW? I MIGHT...
I THINK I CAN GO WHITE...
IF I DROP MY SHIELDS...
JUST DO IT!
WHAT?
BLACK AND WHITE? DEATH AND LIFE...?
REBIRTH?
GUUUUUHH!

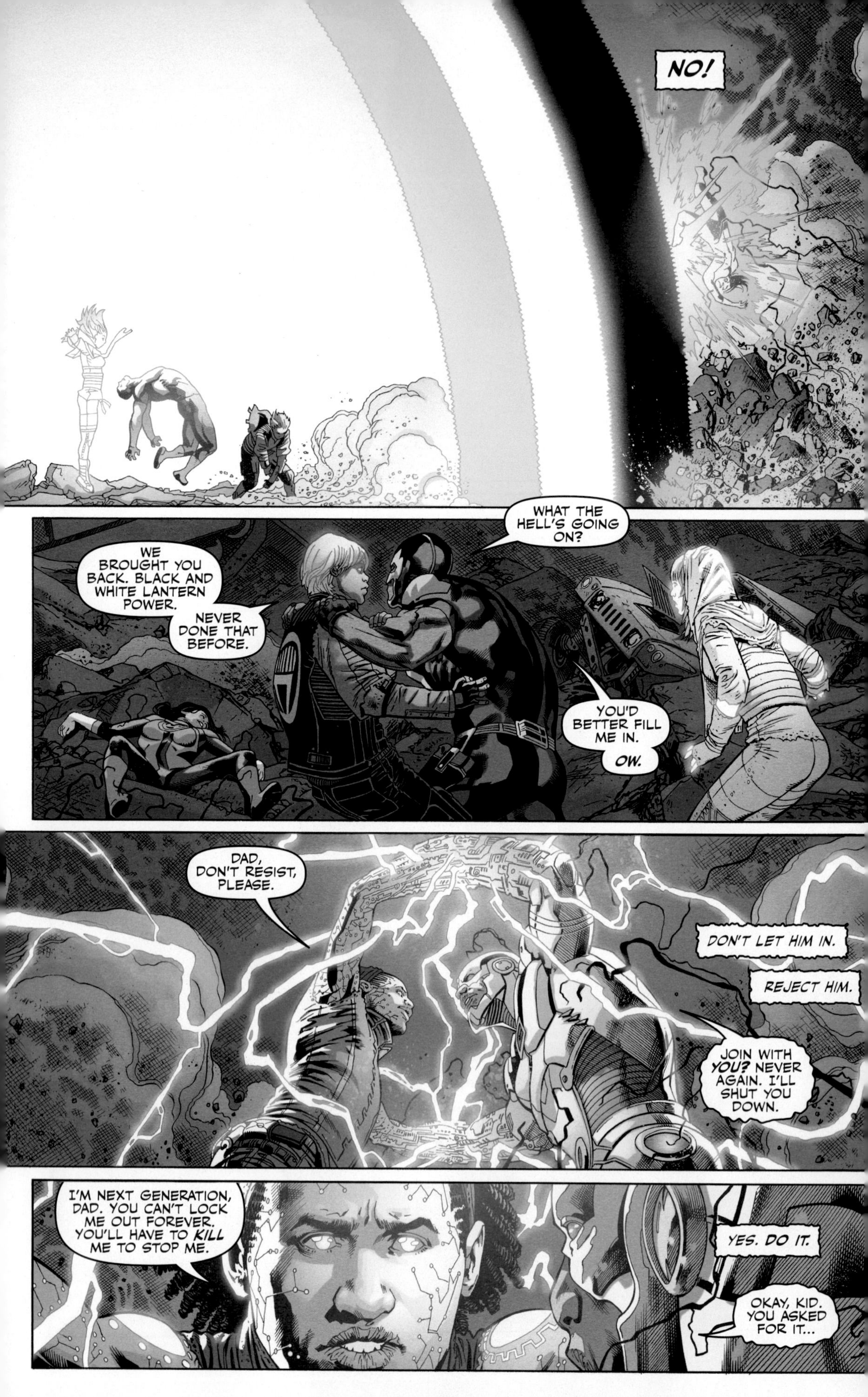
NO!
WHAT THE HELL'S GOING ON?
WE BROUGHT YOU BACK. BLACK AND WHITE LANTERN POWER.
NEVER DONE THAT BEFORE.
YOU'D BETTER FILL ME IN.
OW.
DAD, DON'T RESIST, PLEASE.
DON'T LET HIM IN.
REJECT HIM.
JOIN WITH YOU? NEVER AGAIN. I'LL SHUT YOU DOWN.
I'M NEXT GENERATION, DAD. YOU CAN'T LOCK ME OUT FOREVER. YOU'LL HAVE TO KILL ME TO STOP ME.
YES. DO IT.
OKAY, KID. YOU ASKED FOR IT...

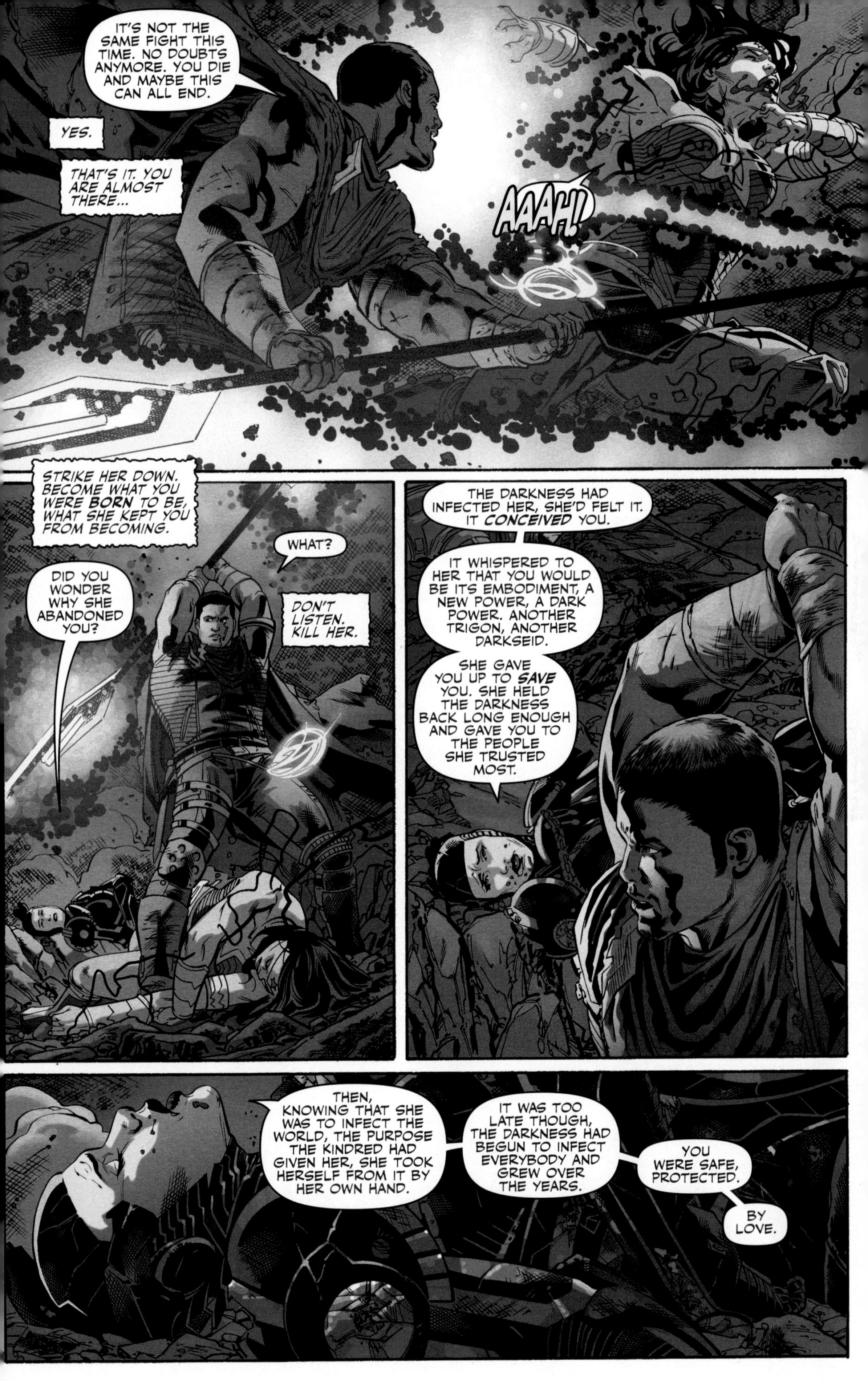
IT'S NOT THE SAME FIGHT THIS TIME. NO DOUBTS ANYMORE. YOU DIE AND MAYBE THIS CAN ALL END.
YES.
THAT'S IT. YOU ARE ALMOST THERE...
AAAH!
STRIKE HER DOWN. BECOME WHAT YOU WERE BORN TO BE, WHAT SHE KEPT YOU FROM BECOMING.
WHAT?
DID YOU WONDER WHY SHE ABANDONED YOU?
DON'T LISTEN. KILL HER.
THE DARKNESS HAD INFECTED HER, SHE'D FELT IT. IT CONCEIVED YOU.
IT WHISPERED TO HER THAT YOU WOULD BE ITS EMBODIMENT, A NEW POWER, A DARK POWER. ANOTHER TRIGON, ANOTHER DARKSEID.
SHE GAVE YOU UP TO SAVE YOU. SHE HELD THE DARKNESS BACK LONG ENOUGH AND GAVE YOU TO THE PEOPLE SHE TRUSTED MOST.
THEN, KNOWING THAT SHE WAS TO INFECT THE WORLD, THE PURPOSE THE KINDRED HAD GIVEN HER, SHE TOOK HERSELF FROM IT BY HER OWN HAND.
IT WAS TOO LATE THOUGH, THE DARKNESS HAD BEGUN TO INFECT EVERYBODY AND GREW OVER THE YEARS.
YOU WERE SAFE, PROTECTED.
BY LOVE.

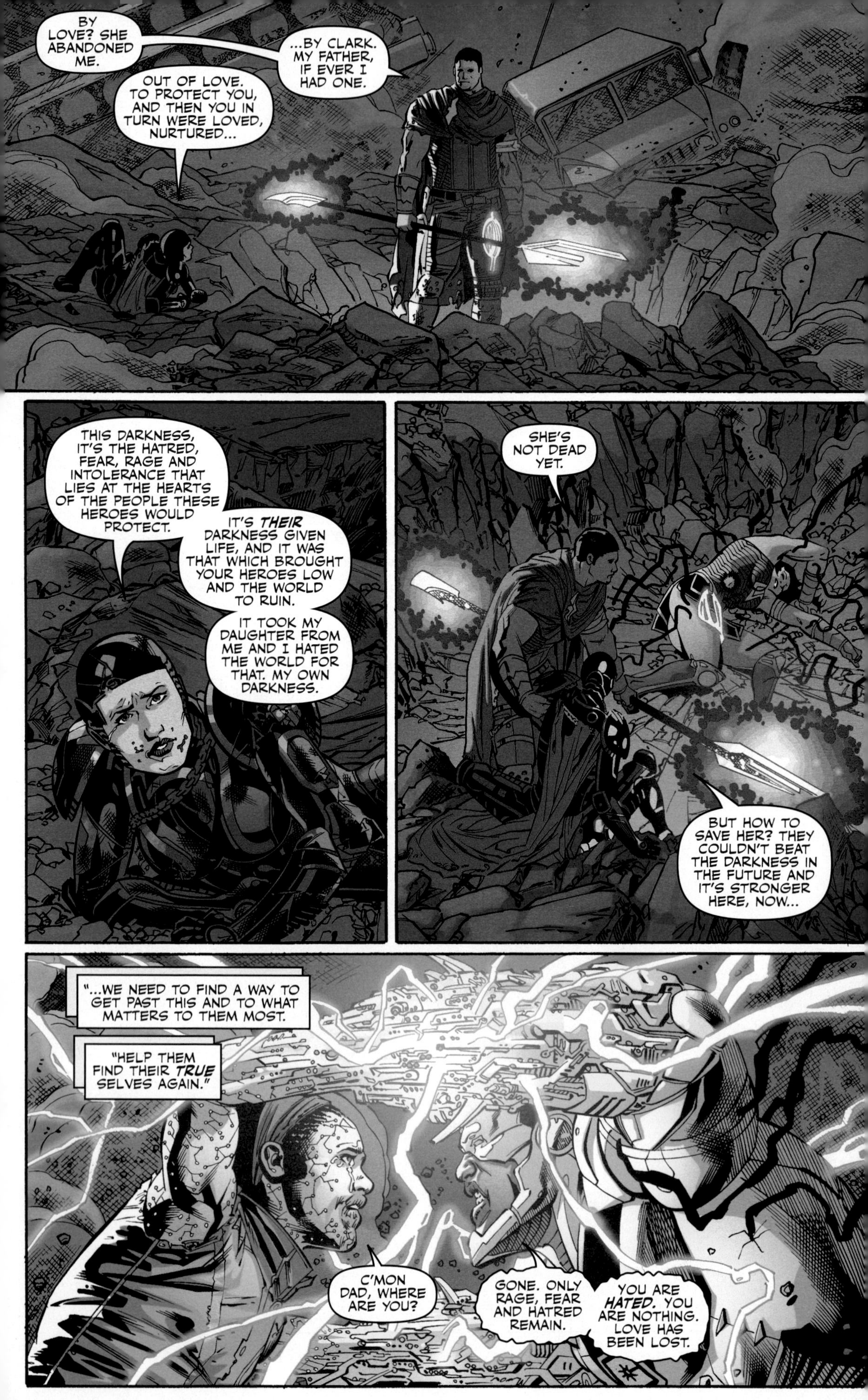
BY LOVE? SHE ABANDONED ME.
...BY CLARK. MY FATHER, IF EVER I HAD ONE.
OUT OF LOVE. TO PROTECT YOU, AND THEN YOU IN TURN WERE LOVED, NURTURED...
THIS DARKNESS, IT'S THE HATRED, FEAR, RAGE AND INTOLERANCE THAT LIES AT THE HEARTS OF THE PEOPLE THESE HEROES WOULD PROTECT.
IT'S *THEIR* DARKNESS GIVEN LIFE, AND IT WAS THAT WHICH BROUGHT YOUR HEROES LOW AND THE WORLD TO RUIN.
IT TOOK MY DAUGHTER FROM ME AND I HATED THE WORLD FOR THAT. MY OWN DARKNESS.
SHE'S NOT DEAD YET.
BUT HOW TO SAVE HER? THEY COULDN'T BEAT THE DARKNESS IN THE FUTURE AND IT'S STRONGER HERE, NOW...
"...WE NEED TO FIND A WAY TO GET PAST THIS AND TO WHAT MATTERS TO THEM MOST.
"HELP THEM FIND THEIR *TRUE* SELVES AGAIN."
C'MON DAD, WHERE ARE YOU?
GONE. ONLY RAGE, FEAR AND HATRED REMAIN.
YOU ARE *HATED.* YOU ARE NOTHING. LOVE HAS BEEN LOST.

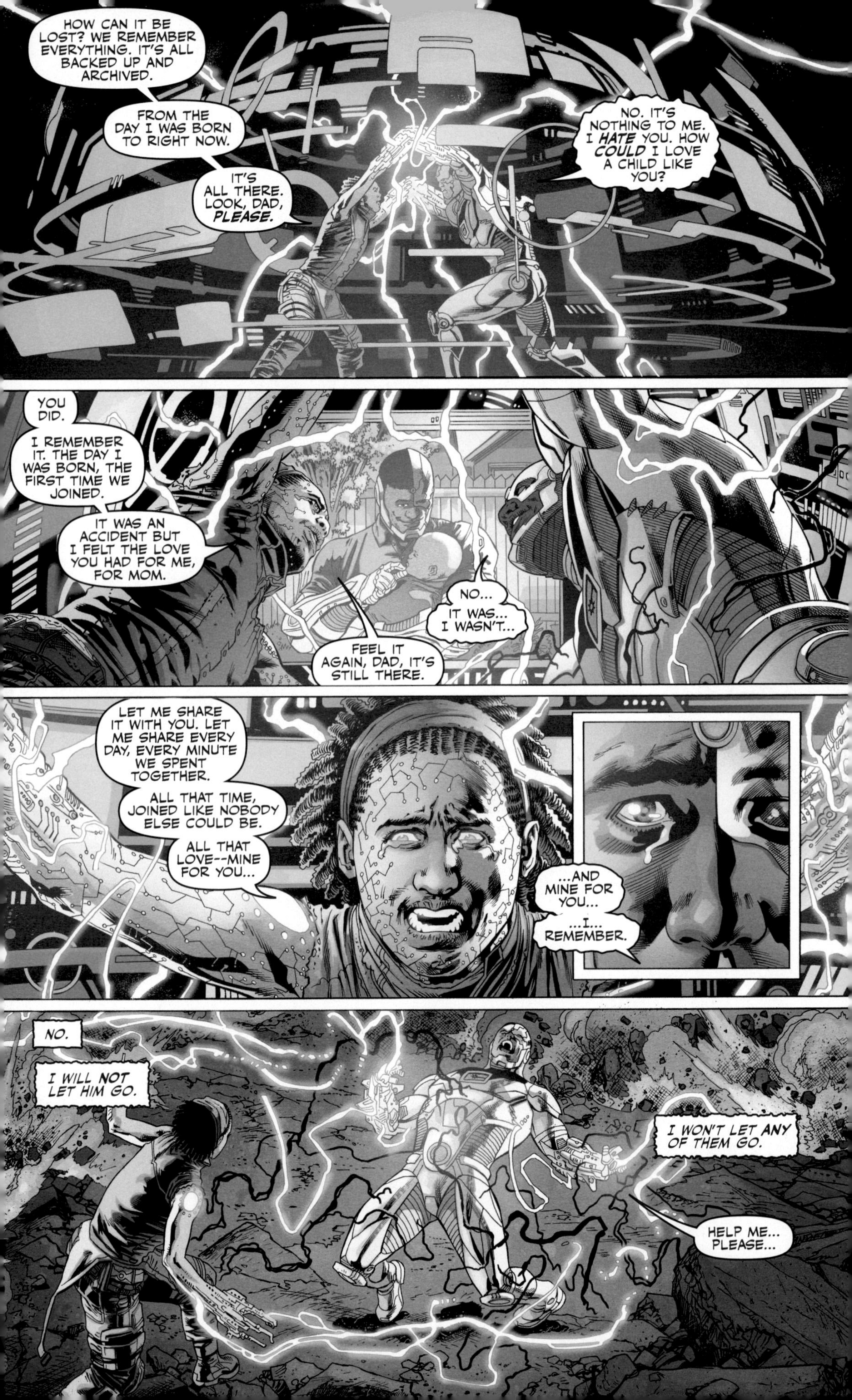
HOW CAN IT BE LOST? WE REMEMBER EVERYTHING. IT'S ALL BACKED UP AND ARCHIVED.
FROM THE DAY I WAS BORN TO RIGHT NOW.
IT'S ALL THERE. LOOK, DAD, PLEASE.
NO. IT'S NOTHING TO ME. I HATE YOU. HOW COULD I LOVE A CHILD LIKE YOU?
YOU DID.
I REMEMBER IT. THE DAY I WAS BORN, THE FIRST TIME WE JOINED.
IT WAS AN ACCIDENT BUT I FELT THE LOVE YOU HAD FOR ME, FOR MOM.
NO... IT WAS... I WASN'T...
FEEL IT AGAIN, DAD, IT'S STILL THERE.
LET ME SHARE IT WITH YOU. LET ME SHARE EVERY DAY, EVERY MINUTE WE SPENT TOGETHER.
ALL THAT TIME, JOINED LIKE NOBODY ELSE COULD BE.
ALL THAT LOVE--MINE FOR YOU...
...AND MINE FOR YOU...
...I... REMEMBER.
NO.
I WILL NOT LET HIM GO.
I WON'T LET ANY OF THEM GO.
HELP ME... PLEASE...

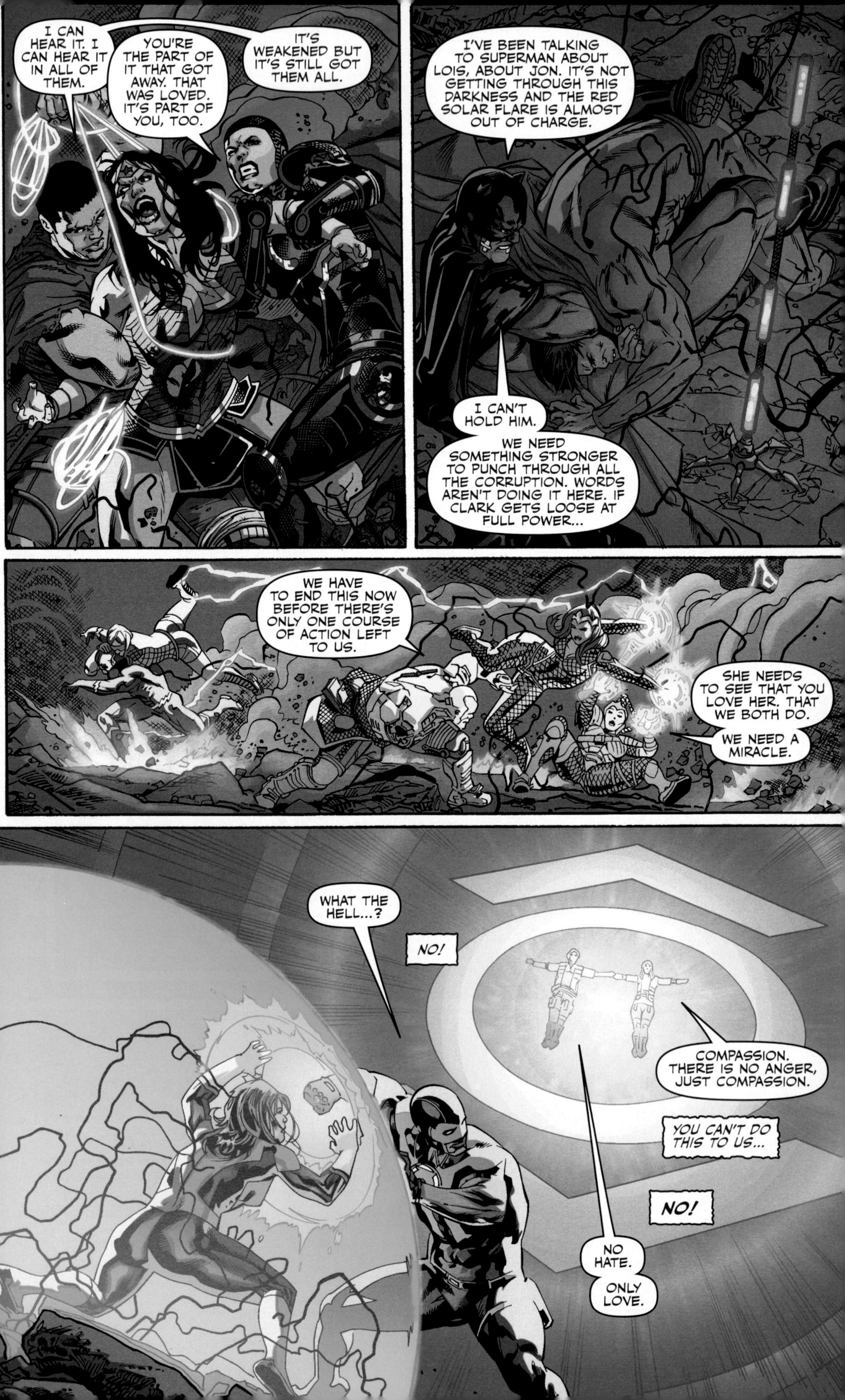
I CAN HEAR IT. I CAN HEAR IT IN ALL OF THEM.
YOU'RE THE PART OF IT THAT GOT AWAY. THAT WAS LOVED. IT'S PART OF YOU, TOO.
IT'S WEAKENED BUT IT'S STILL GOT THEM ALL.
I'VE BEEN TALKING TO SUPERMAN ABOUT LOIS, ABOUT JON. IT'S NOT GETTING THROUGH THIS DARKNESS AND THE RED SOLAR FLARE IS ALMOST OUT OF CHARGE.
I CAN'T HOLD HIM.
WE NEED SOMETHING STRONGER TO PUNCH THROUGH ALL THE CORRUPTION. WORDS AREN'T DOING IT HERE. IF CLARK GETS LOOSE AT FULL POWER...
WE HAVE TO END THIS NOW BEFORE THERE'S ONLY ONE COURSE OF ACTION LEFT TO US.
SHE NEEDS TO SEE THAT YOU LOVE HER. THAT WE BOTH DO.
WE NEED A MIRACLE.
WHAT THE HELL...?
NO!
COMPASSION. THERE IS NO ANGER, JUST COMPASSION.
YOU CAN'T DO THIS TO US...
NO!
NO HATE.
ONLY LOVE.

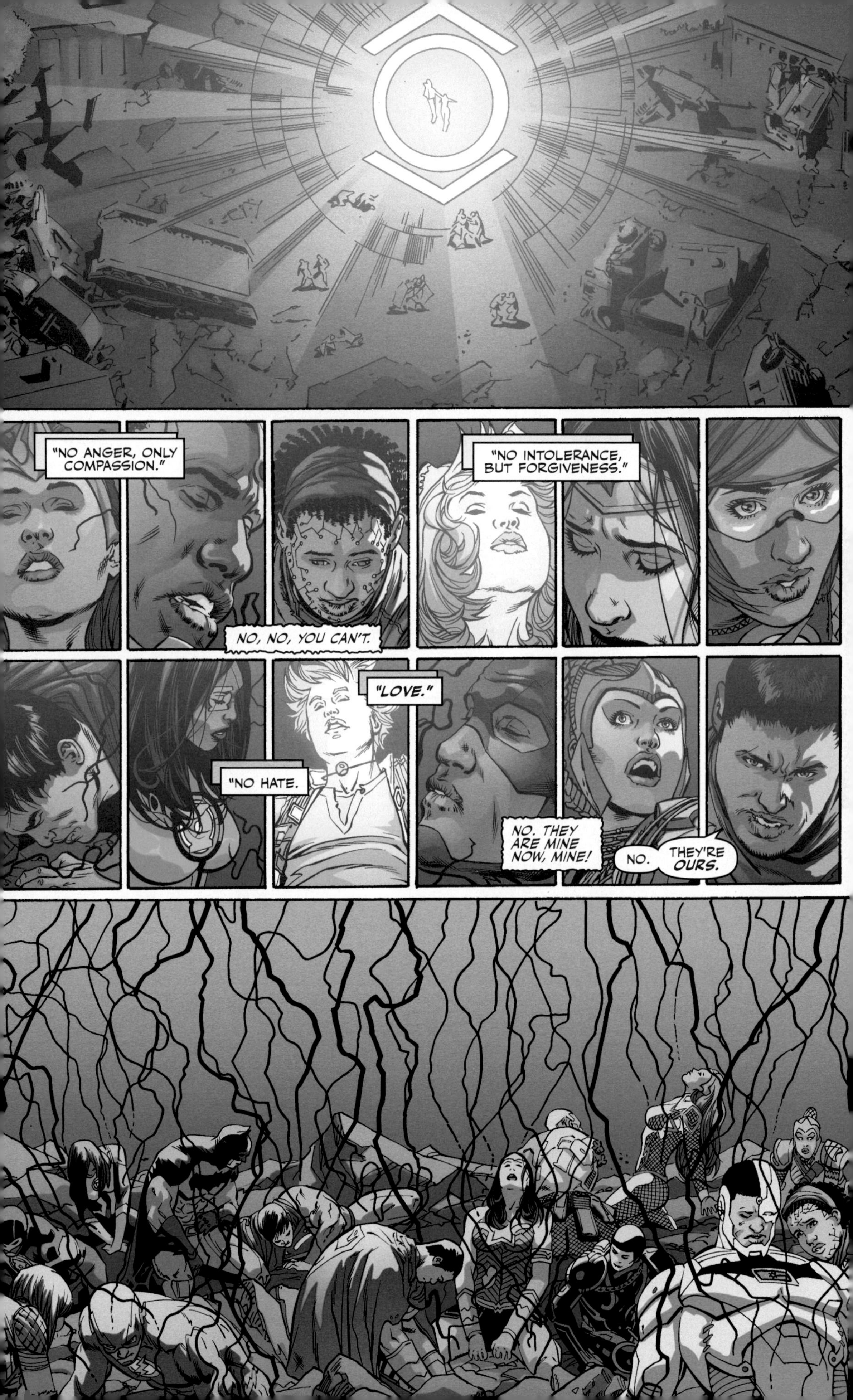
"NO ANGER, ONLY COMPASSION."
NO, NO, YOU CAN'T.
"NO INTOLERANCE, BUT FORGIVENESS."
"NO HATE.
"LOVE."
NO. THEY ARE MINE NOW, MINE!
NO.
THEY'RE OURS.

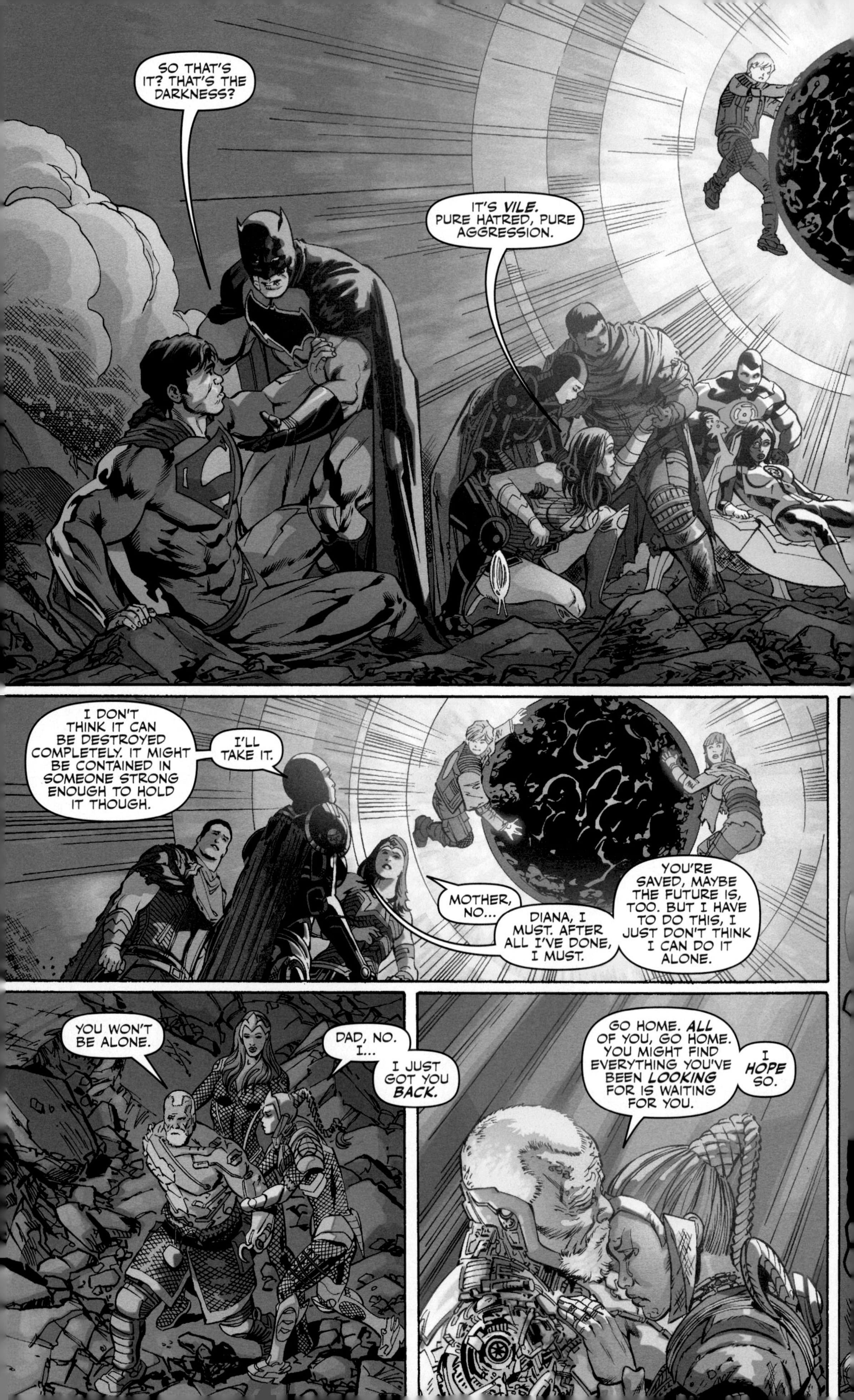
SO THAT'S IT? THAT'S THE DARKNESS?
IT'S VILE. PURE HATRED, PURE AGGRESSION.
I DON'T THINK IT CAN BE DESTROYED COMPLETELY. IT MIGHT BE CONTAINED IN SOMEONE STRONG ENOUGH TO HOLD IT THOUGH.
I'LL TAKE IT.
MOTHER, NO...
DIANA, I MUST. AFTER ALL I'VE DONE, I MUST.
YOU'RE SAVED, MAYBE THE FUTURE IS, TOO. BUT I HAVE TO DO THIS, I JUST DON'T THINK I CAN DO IT ALONE.
YOU WON'T BE ALONE.
DAD, NO. I...
I JUST GOT YOU BACK.
GO HOME. ALL OF YOU, GO HOME. YOU MIGHT FIND EVERYTHING YOU'VE BEEN LOOKING FOR IS WAITING FOR YOU.
I HOPE SO.

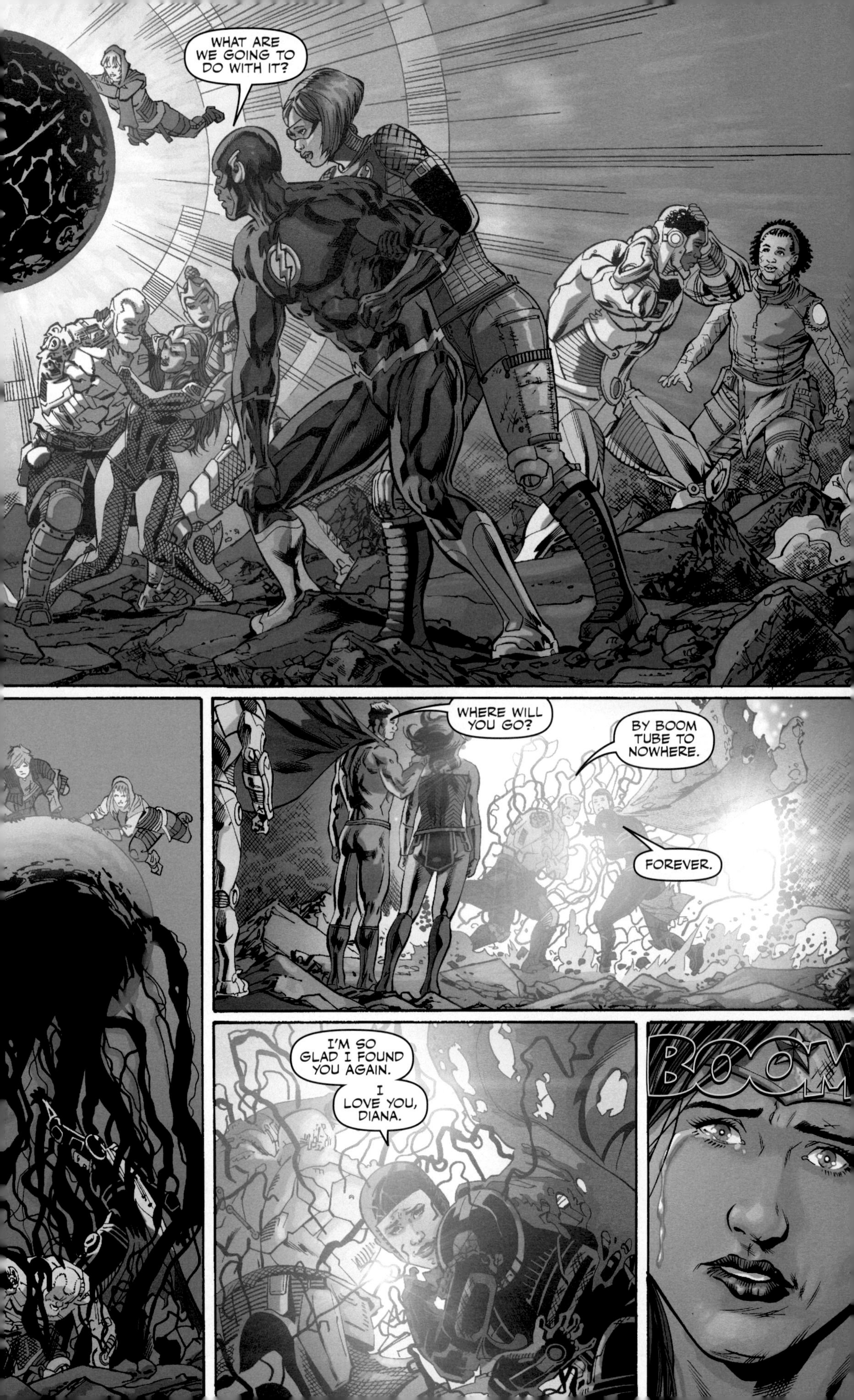
WHAT ARE WE GOING TO DO WITH IT?
WHERE WILL YOU GO?
BY BOOM TUBE TO NOWHERE.
FOREVER.
I'M SO GLAD I FOUND YOU AGAIN.
I LOVE YOU, DIANA.
BOOM

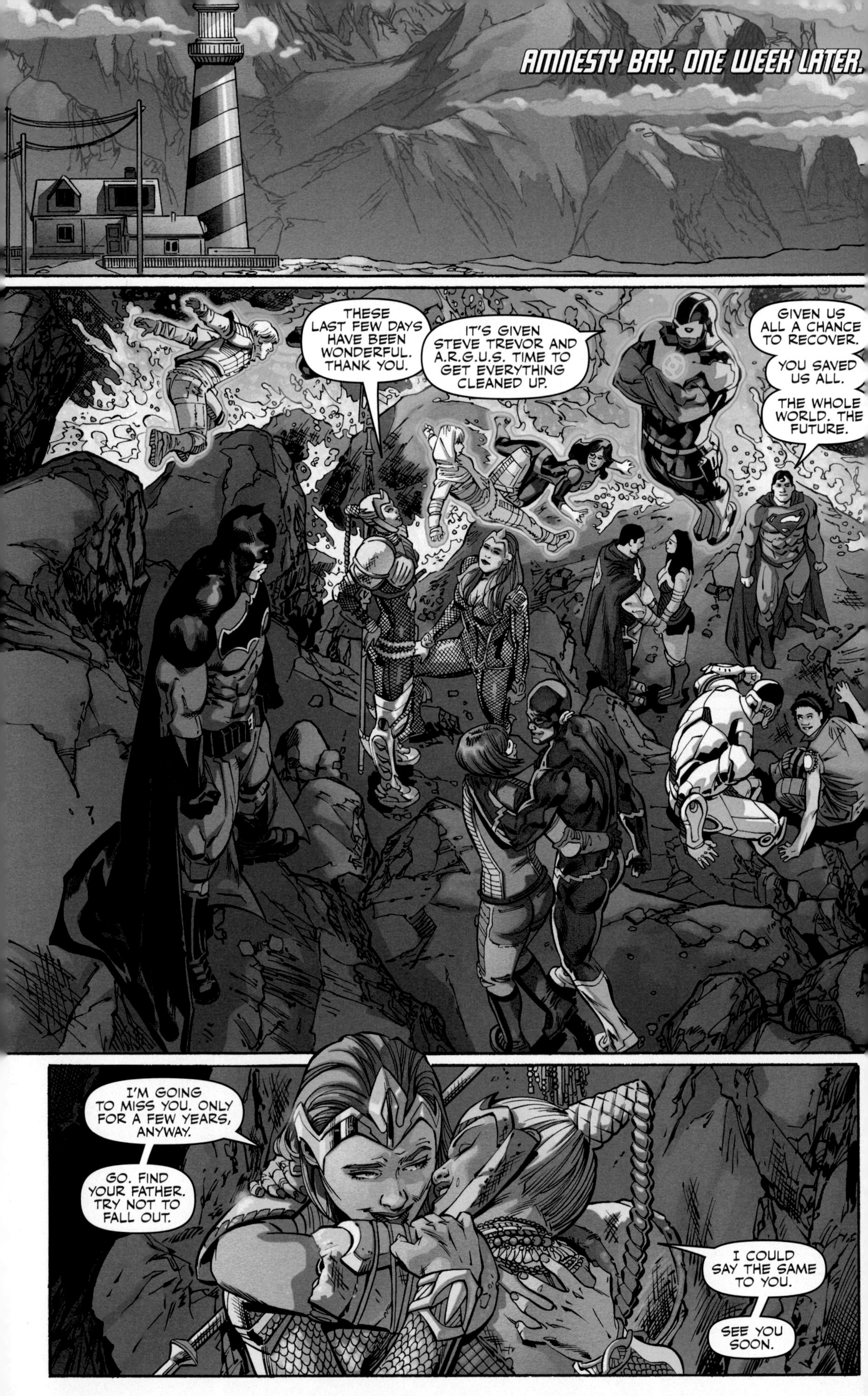
AMNESTY BAY. ONE WEEK LATER.
THESE LAST FEW DAYS HAVE BEEN WONDERFUL. THANK YOU.
IT'S GIVEN STEVE TREVOR AND A.R.G.U.S. TIME TO GET EVERYTHING CLEANED UP.
GIVEN US ALL A CHANCE TO RECOVER.
YOU SAVED US ALL.
THE WHOLE WORLD. THE FUTURE.
I'M GOING TO MISS YOU. ONLY FOR A FEW YEARS, ANYWAY.
GO. FIND YOUR FATHER. TRY NOT TO FALL OUT.
I COULD SAY THE SAME TO YOU.
SEE YOU SOON.

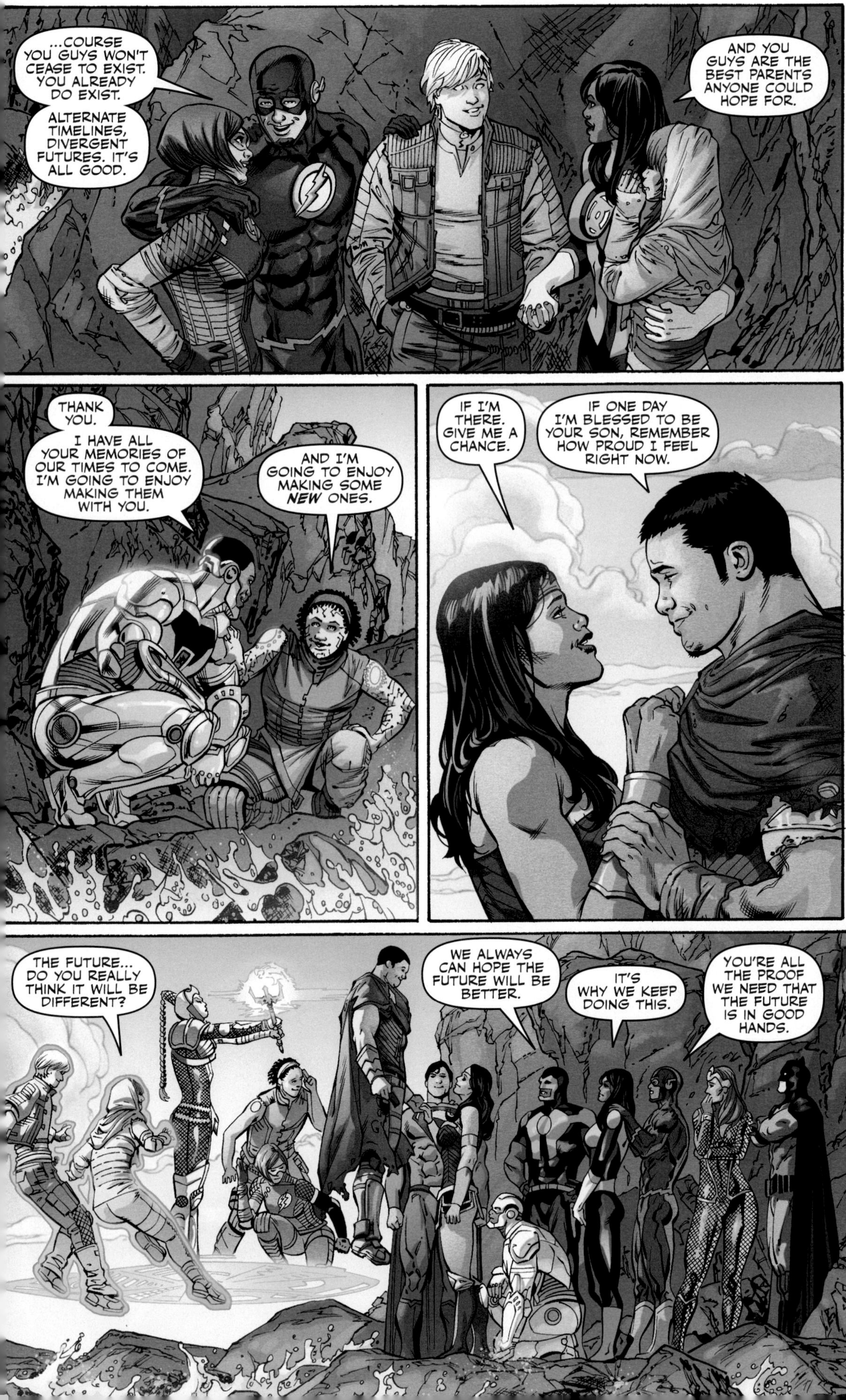
...COURSE YOU GUYS WON'T CEASE TO EXIST. YOU ALREADY DO EXIST.
ALTERNATE TIMELINES, DIVERGENT FUTURES. IT'S ALL GOOD.
AND YOU GUYS ARE THE BEST PARENTS ANYONE COULD HOPE FOR.
THANK YOU.
I HAVE ALL YOUR MEMORIES OF OUR TIMES TO COME. I'M GOING TO ENJOY MAKING THEM WITH YOU.
AND I'M GOING TO ENJOY MAKING SOME *NEW* ONES.
IF I'M THERE. GIVE ME A CHANCE.
IF ONE DAY I'M BLESSED TO BE YOUR SON, REMEMBER HOW PROUD I FEEL RIGHT NOW.
THE FUTURE... DO YOU REALLY THINK IT WILL BE DIFFERENT?
WE ALWAYS CAN HOPE THE FUTURE WILL BE BETTER.
IT'S WHY WE KEEP DOING THIS.
YOU'RE ALL THE PROOF WE NEED THAT THE FUTURE IS IN GOOD HANDS.

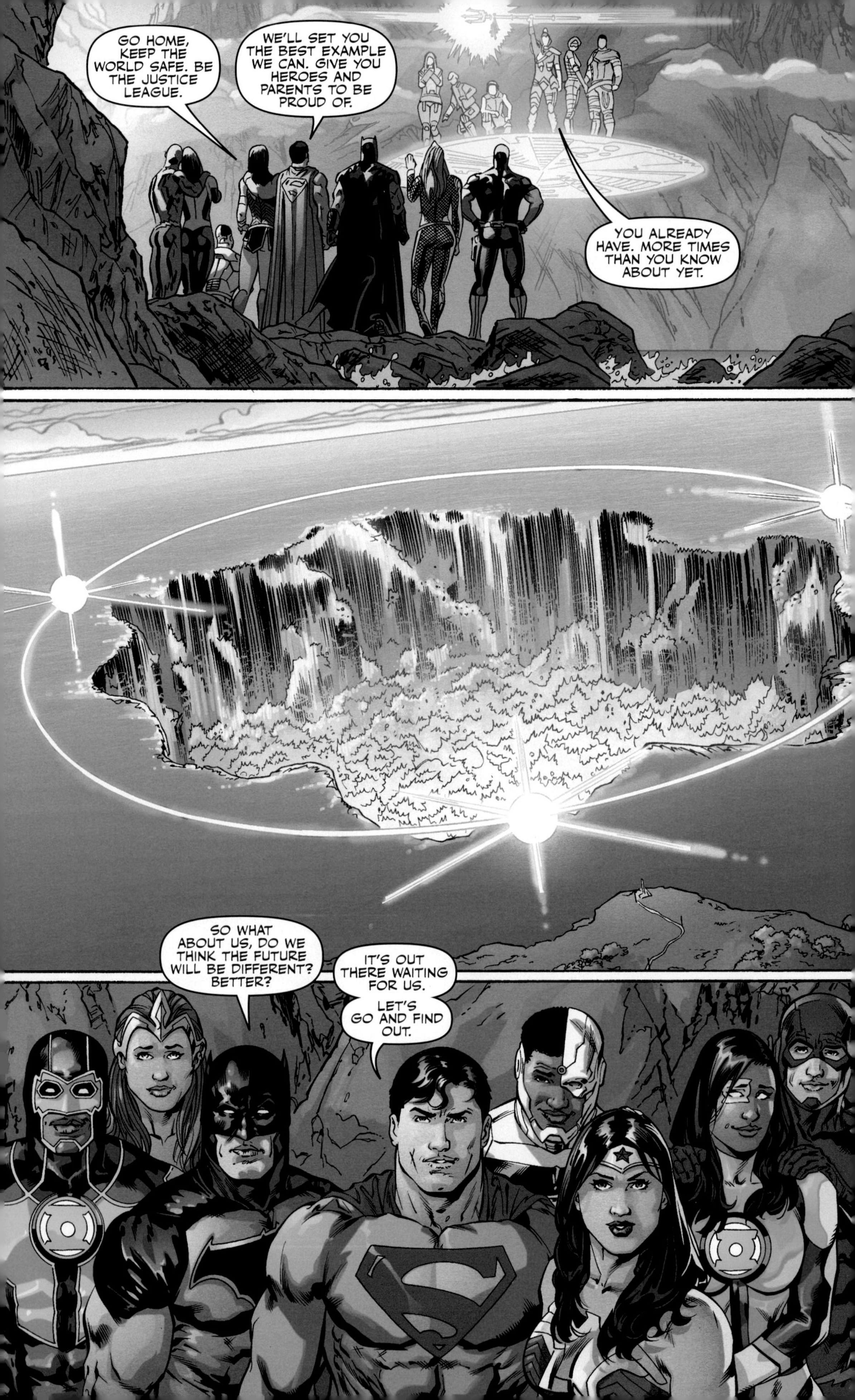
GO HOME, KEEP THE WORLD SAFE. BE THE JUSTICE LEAGUE.
WE'LL SET YOU THE BEST EXAMPLE WE CAN. GIVE YOU HEROES AND PARENTS TO BE PROUD OF.
YOU ALREADY HAVE. MORE TIMES THAN YOU KNOW ABOUT YET.
SO WHAT ABOUT US, DO WE THINK THE FUTURE WILL BE DIFFERENT? BETTER?
IT'S OUT THERE WAITING FOR US.
LET'S GO AND FIND OUT.

JUSTICE LEAGUE #26 variant by YANICK PAQUETTE

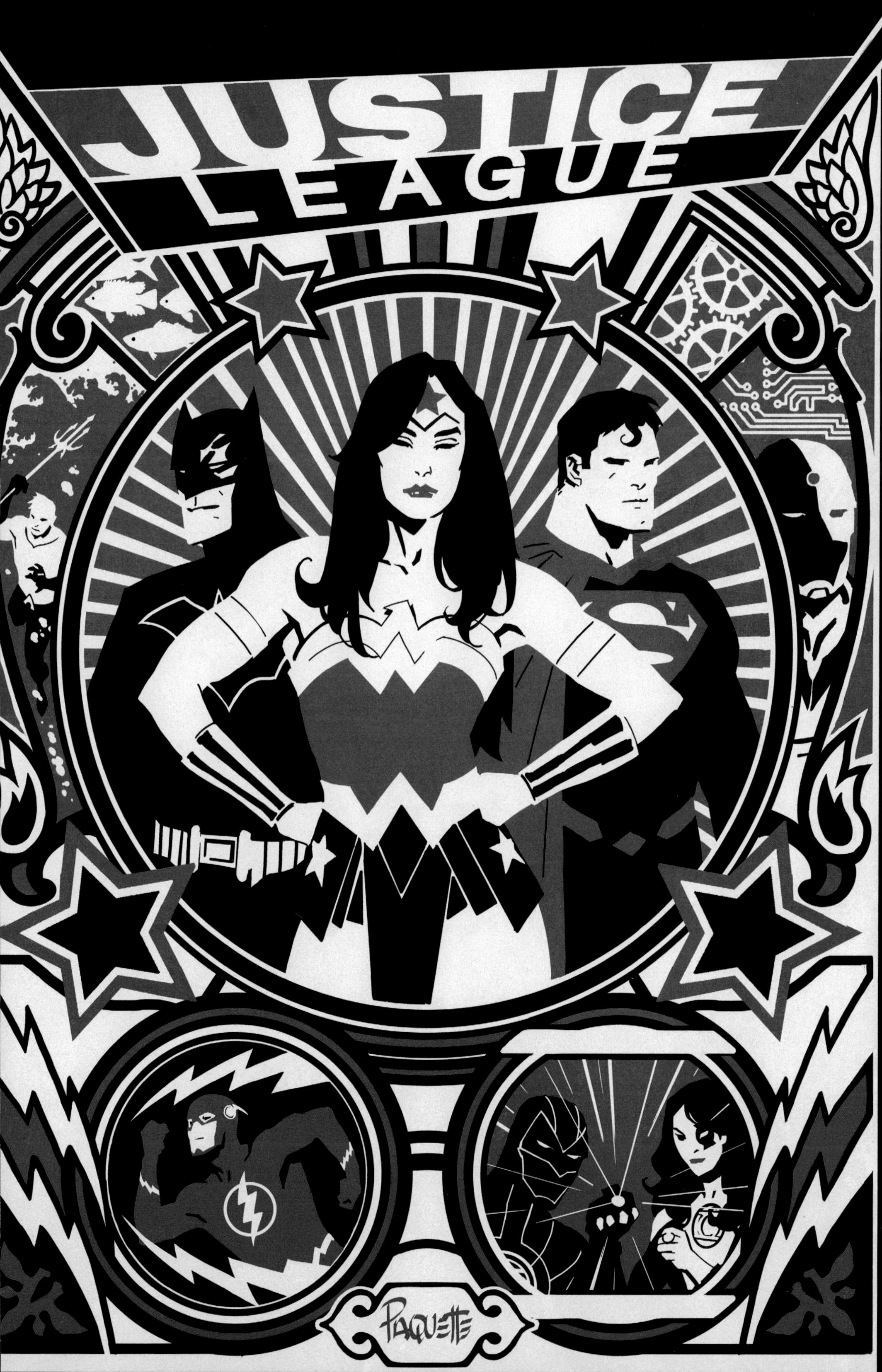
JUSTICE
LEAGUE
PAQUETTE

JUSTICE LEAGUE #27 variant by NICK BRADSHAW and ALEX SINCLAIR

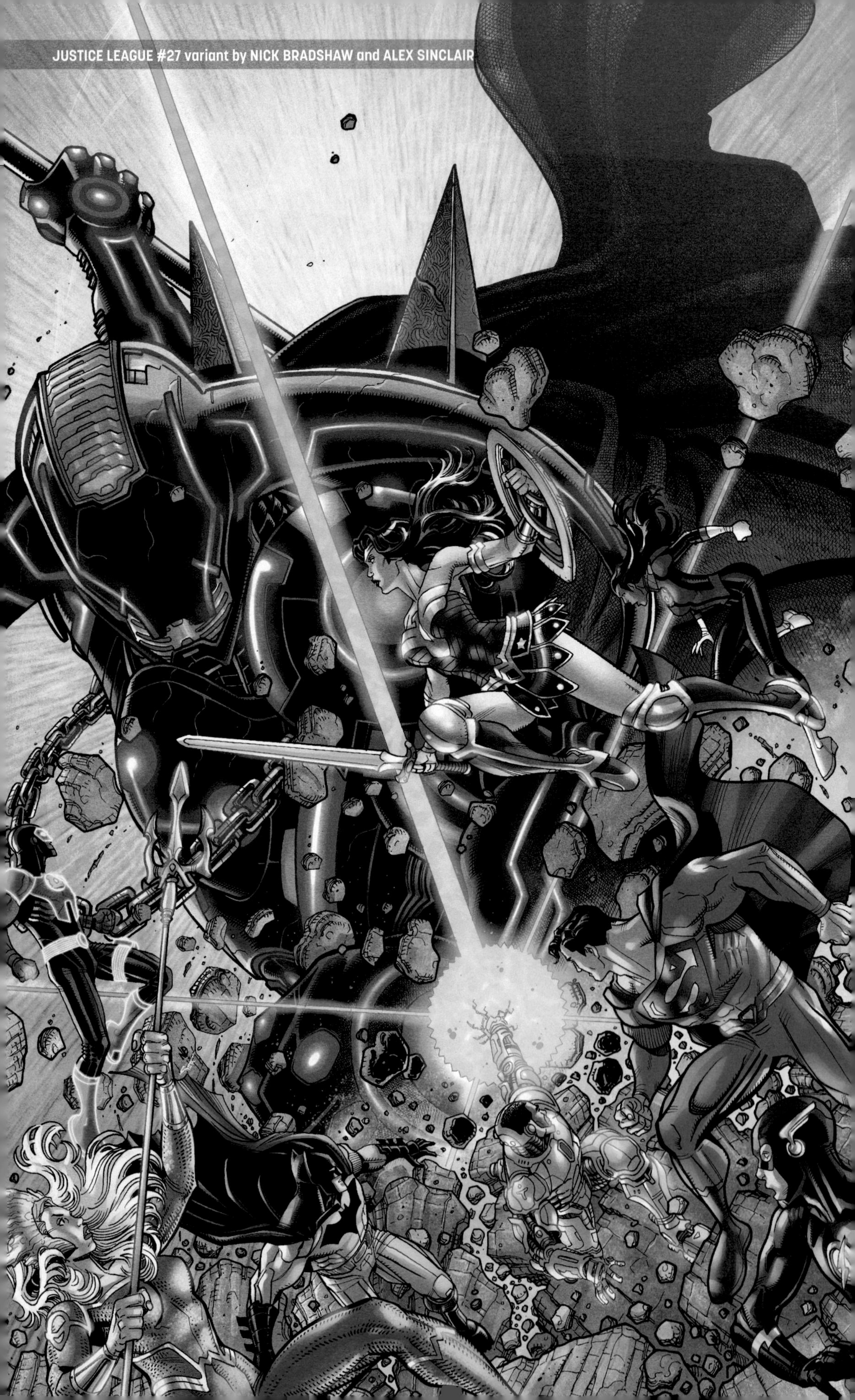

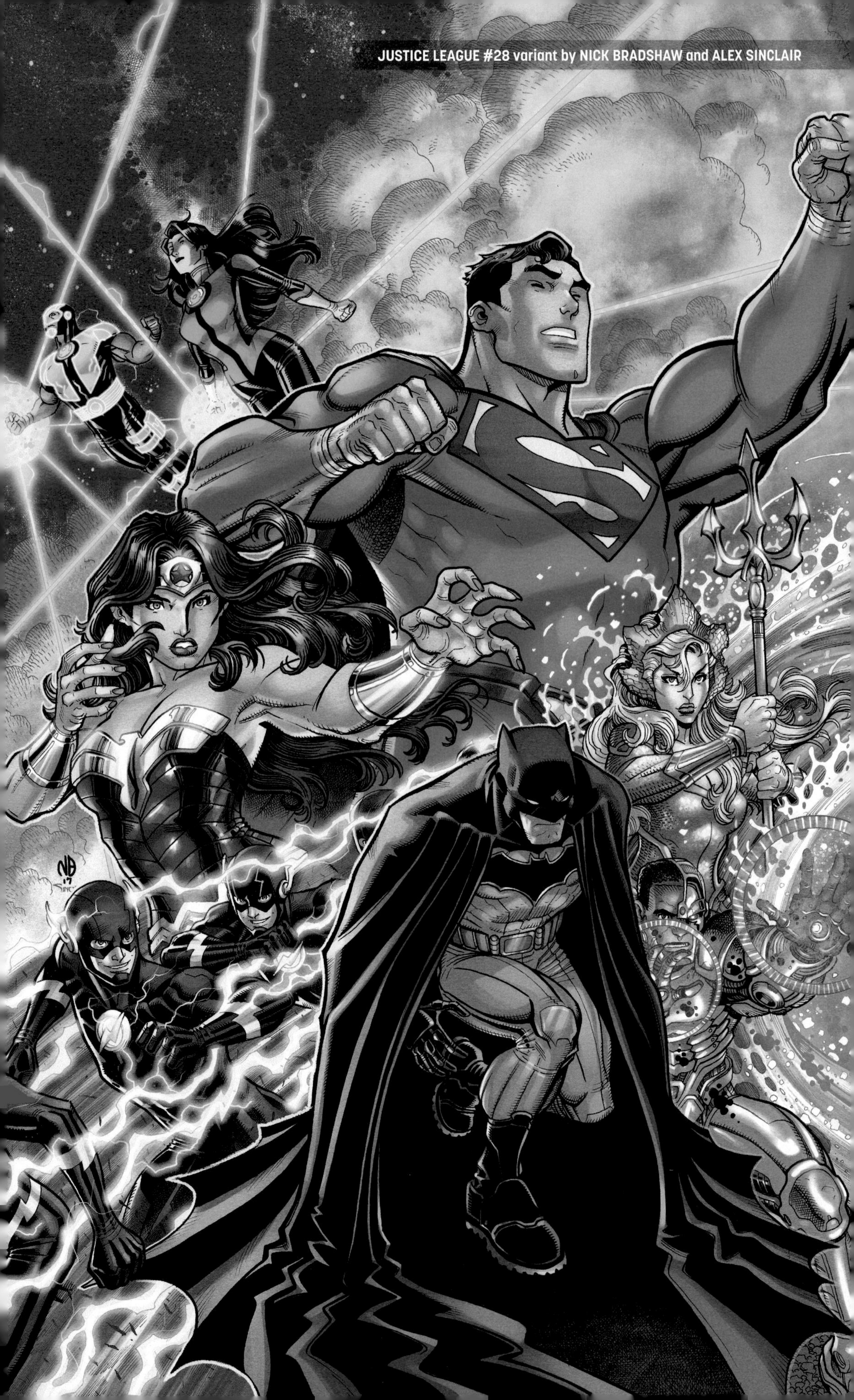

JUSTICE LEAGUE #28 variant by NICK BRADSHAW and ALEX SINCLAIR

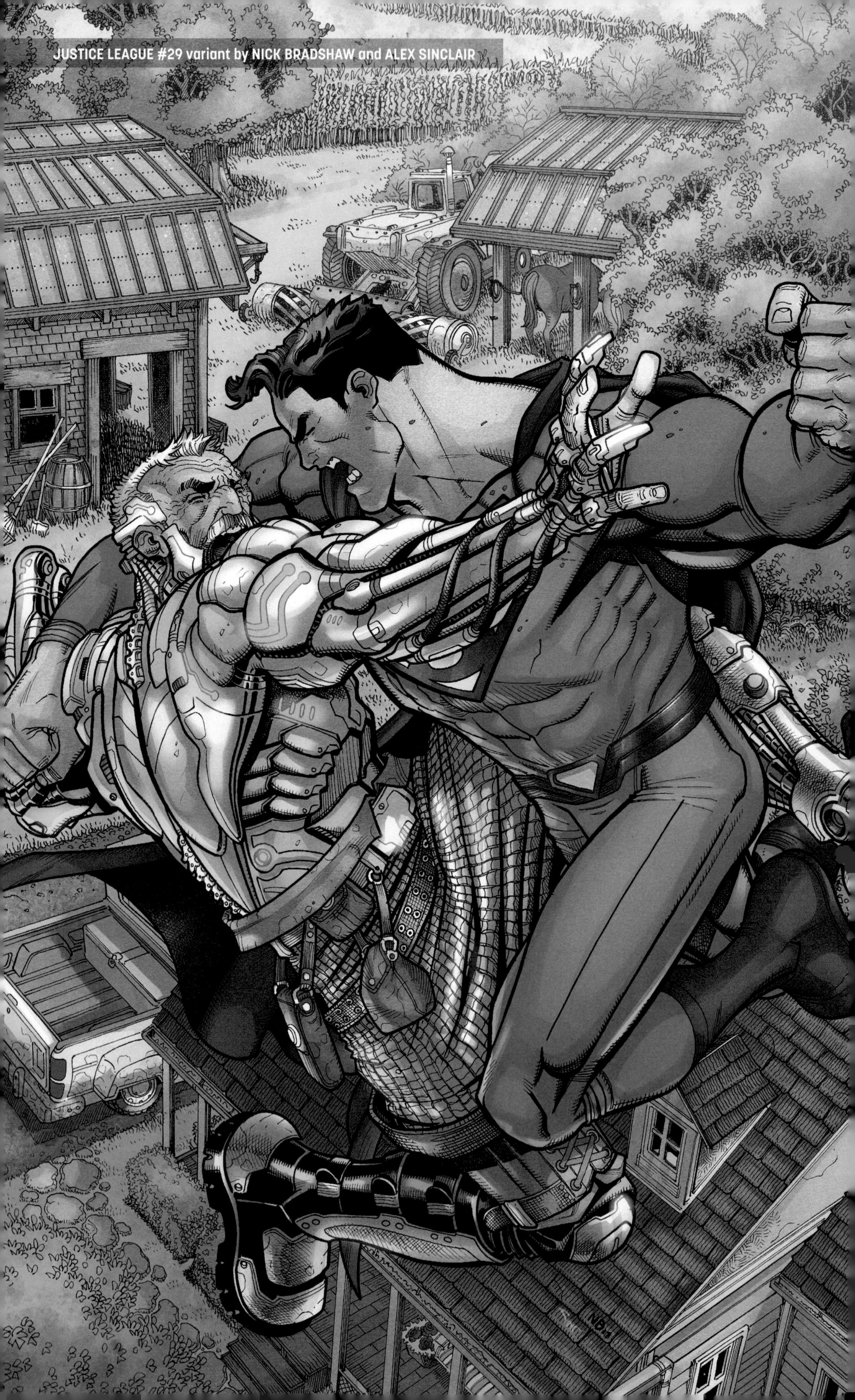

JUSTICE LEAGUE #29 variant by NICK BRADSHAW and ALEX SINCLAIR

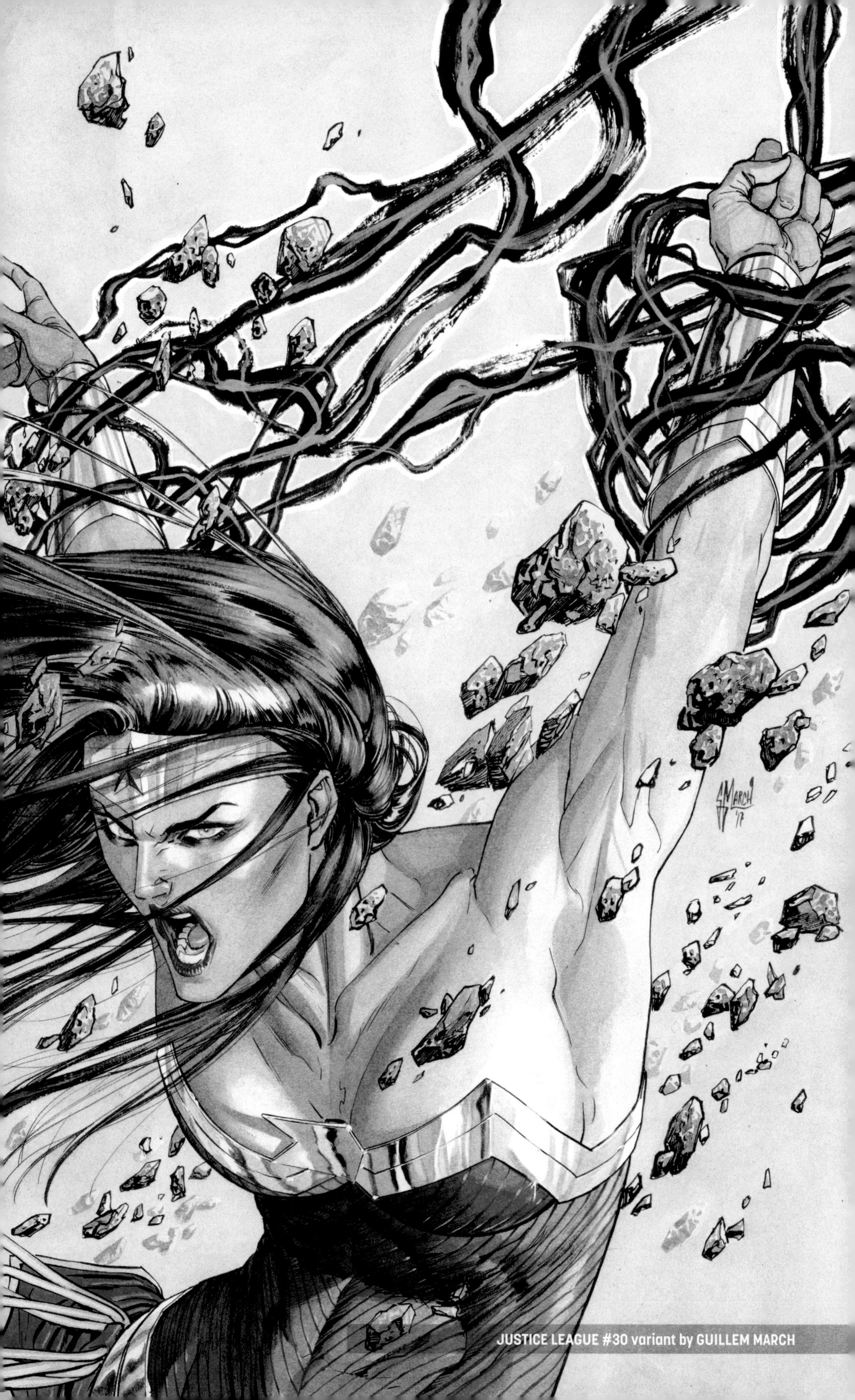

JUSTICE LEAGUE #30 variant by GUILLEM MARCH

JUSTICE LEAGUE #31 variant by NICK BRADSHAW and ALEX SINCLAIR

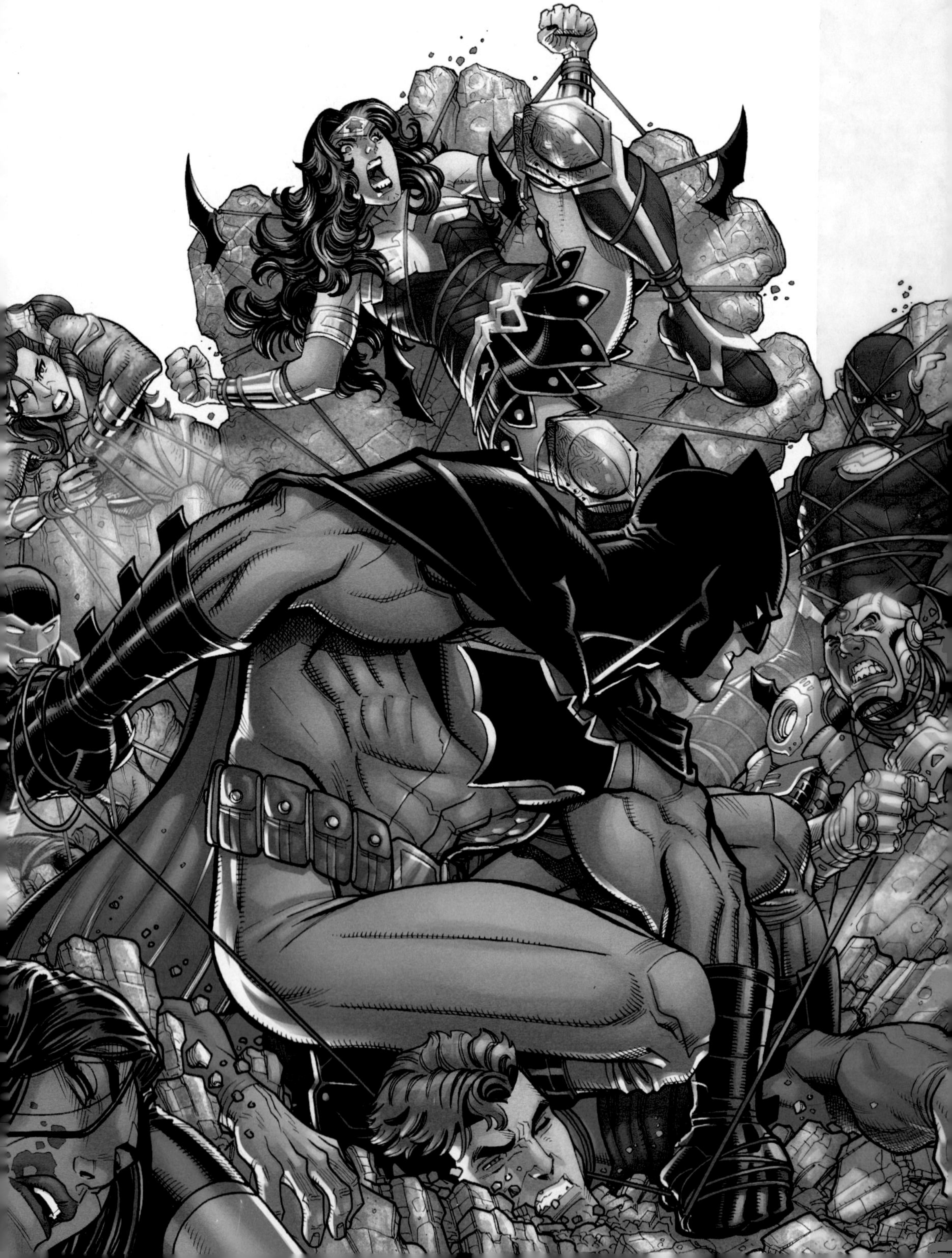